FILM AND LITERATURE:
AN INTRODUCTION AND READER

Timothy Corrigan

Temple University

Prentice
Hall

PRENTICE HALL, UPPER SADDLE RIVER, NEW JERSEY 07458

Library of Congress Cataloging-in-Publication Data

CORRIGAN, TIMOTHY.
    Film and literature: an introduction and reader/Timothy Corrigan.
        p.   cm.
    Includes bibliographical references and index.
    ISBN 0-13-526542-8
    1. Motion pictures and literature.   I. Title.
PN1995.3.C68   1998
791.43'6—dc21   98-31413
                                                              CIP

Editorial Director: Charlyce Jones Owen
Editor in Chief: Leah Jewell
Acquisitions Editor: Carrie Brandon
Editorial Assistant: Gianna Caradonna
Director of Production and Manufacturing: Barbara Kittle
Managing Editor: Bonnie Biller
Project Liaison: Randy Pettit
Production Editor: Kari Callaghan Mazzola
Manufacturing Manager: Nick Sklitsis
Prepress and Manufacturing Buyer: Mary Ann Gloriande
Marketing Manager: Susan Brekka
Electronic Page Makeup and Interior Design: Kari Callaghan Mazzola
    and John P. Mazzola
Director, Image Resource Center: Lori Morris-Nantz
Photo Research Supervisor: Melinda Lee Reo
Image Permission Supervisor: Kay Dellosa
Photo Researcher: Beth Boyd
Cover Designer: Bruce Kenselaar
Cover Photos: Still photos of Gwyneth Paltrow in *Emma* and Alicia Silverstone
    in *Clueless* from Motion Picture & Television Photo Archives

*Grateful acknowledgment is made to the copyright holders on pages 365–366,
which are hereby a continuation of this copyright page.*

This book was set in 10/12 New Century Schoolbook by Big Sky Composition
and was printed and bound by Courier Companies, Inc.
The cover was printed by Phoenix Color Corp.

Printed in the United States of America
10   9
Reprinted with corrections November, 2000.

ISBN 0-13-526542-8

For Cecilia, Graham, and Anna,
my wonderful companions
through so many books and movies

CONTENTS

PREFACE

I wrote and assembled this book because I teach film and literature and know the challenges and rewards in dealing with this combination of subjects. The heart of most courses on film and literature is usually specific movies and different works of literature, and any one course will follow its own focus in selecting individual novels, poems, plays, and movies. Studying and discussing film and literature also involves, however, other crucial materials that enrich any particular work of film or literature and how we understand it. These include materials about film history as part of a larger cultural history, about film forms that clarify and differentiate the connections between film and literature, and about the different approaches used to analyze film and literature throughout the twentieth century. These important materials are what this book aims to provide.

Given the enormous scope of the topic, an introductory text such as this must be fairly modest and very flexible. With those guidelines, I aim here, first, to suggest a range of issues and approaches and, second, to provide tools and signposts that will allow readers to follow their own interests in further exploring certain topics. An introduction can, of course, only go so far, and one of its chief functions is, I believe, to emphasize where introductory discussion ends and where more advanced work begins, to highlight places in the readings that are in fact openings for more thinking and debate. Through the various inserts and questions that punctuate the book, I hope I've accomplished that.

I wish to thank Marcia Ferguson, who read this manuscript at various stages with both encouragement and criticism. Rick Prouty and Annalisa Castaldo helped with the research, and Dana Polan gave me excellent advice early on, the wisdom of which sank in only later. Temple University provided me with a Summer Research Fellowship for the final stages of this work. I also wish to thank the following reviewers for their suggestions: Susan Scrivner, Bemidji State University; Anthony J. Mazzella, William Paterson University; and Jere Real, Lynchburg College. Finally, my undergraduate and graduate students at Temple University demonstrated through their patience and enthusiasm that scholarship and research can be an exciting and integral part of teaching and learning on every level.

Timothy Corrigan

INTRODUCTION

The history of the relationship between film and literature is a history of ambivalence, confrontation, and mutual dependence. From the late nineteenth century to the present, these two ways of seeing and describing the world have at different times despised each other, redeemed each other, learned from each other, and distorted each other's self-proclaimed integrity. In 1859 the French poet Charles Baudelaire had already expressed fear and anger about how photographic images would "corrupt" traditional arts. By 1915 literary spectacles would increasingly become the material for the movies in attempts to distinguish the cinema from its vaudevillian heritage and to offer a new social respectability to a mechanical art (most notably with the 1913 Italian filmed version of the Polish novel *Quo vadis?* and D. W. Griffith's 1916 epic *Intolerance*, which used a visual refrain from the poet Walt Whitman to link the New Testament, two historical tales, and a modern melodrama). With a mixture of regret and pride about the failure to have his novel *The Magic Mountain* adapted for the cinema, Thomas Mann would characterize the position of many respected modern writers in 1932 when he wrote about the film industry, "I despise it myself—but I love it too" (Geduld 131). By 1996, Emma Thompson's mostly faithful *Sense and Sensibility* (1995), a tongue-in-cheek version of *Emma* called *Clueless* (1995), and several other recent adaptations of Jane Austen novels would start a whole new generation reading that nineteenth-century writer.

Today the topic of film and literature seems more lively than ever before, both inside and outside the classroom. The reasons are many: From the cultural questioning of artistic hierarchies and canons to the increased mixing of different media in both literary and film practices, film and literature clash against and invigorate each other in more and more complicated fashions. Once isolated media and literature

1

departments now share materials, students, and methods. Students recognize the intricacies of poetry in the rhetoric of experimental films. Elia Kazan's 1951 film version of Tennessee Williams's *A Streetcar Named Desire* becomes what Maurice Yacowar has called "an invaluable record of a legendary production ... which introduced Method acting to the mass audience" (24). And an understanding of writer Samuel Beckett's work would be incomplete, many would agree, without considering his film and video projects. More today than ever before, adaptations proliferate, novelizations follow rapidly on a movie's success, and debates continue about film as literature and film versus literature. One estimate claims that 30 percent of the movies today derive from novels and that 80 percent of the books classified as best sellers have been adapted to the cinema (Holt). If the connection between the two practices has persisted so adamantly through the years, it seems especially pressing now, at the end of the twentieth century, as an index of why the movies are important, why literature still matters, and what both have to offer a cultural period in which boundaries are continually being redrawn.

One of the consequences of this renewed interest, as well as a consequence of the historical development of film studies over the past thirty years, is that the intersections of film and literature need to be viewed from an unprecedented variety of angles. We increasingly admit and take seriously many different exchanges between literary works and films. Novels, dramatic literature, short stories, poetry, and even the essay have particular counterparts in film form; films influence literary imagery in a myriad of ways; and each of these paths lead to other issues: about the production and reception of movies and literature, about writing and scriptwriting, about reading and viewing. Encompassing this proliferation of practices and directions, four critical frameworks are important to this book.

First, the exchange between film and literature demands, especially now, rigorous historical and cultural distinctions. The connection between French Surrealist poetry and experimental silent film of the late 1920s, for instance, evokes different terms and issues than those used to discuss the Broadway adaptations by Hollywood in the next decade. The more carefully these terms and issues can be situated in terms of their specific historical, national, and cultural contexts, the more accurate a discussion of this literature and these films will be.

Second, the usual cultural hierarchy that places serious literature above supposedly less serious film has been brought usefully into question in recent decades. This is not to say that the movies have as long and as complex a history as literature does but rather to recognize the limited value of assuming commonplaces like "the book is better than the movie." Once there may have been little debate about the fact that a theatrical performance of Shakespeare was far superior to a filmic reproduction. By 1948, Laurence Olivier's *Hamlet* could, however, provoke enormous interest and debate about his controversial filmic interpretation of Shakespeare, and nine years later Akira Kurosawa's *Throne of Blood* had cinema communities lavishing praise on that film as an exceptional recreation of Shakespeare's *Macbeth*. Whether because of its massive social impact, because of the aesthetic development of film art, or because of shifts in cultural literacy, the cinema now demands equal time and attention when we argue the relative value and meaning of movies and literature.

Third, critical perspectives that align and distinguish film and literature are no longer confined to how film is or is not like a language or how expressive film may be of an author or how representative of a reality. When the relationship of literature to the cinema began to expand as a critical topic in the 1930s through the 1950s, much energy was devoted to how fully or how accurately one or the other mirrored the human experience. In the sixties and seventies, the topic shifted its ground to how both were (or were not) like a language that allowed similar formal strategies. Today there are other, if less broad, issues that complement these. The literary art of scriptwriting versus story writing, acting technique as it differs in the theater and on the screen, or the different ways readers and spectators make sense of their experience before a page or screen are just some of the rich and resonant perspectives that are reopening film and literary history in this century.

As a fourth framework for this book, film and literature can now be discussed on the common ground provided by interdisciplinary and cultural studies. Both film and literature can be seen as businesses and industries that participate in technological constraints and advantages. Both enlist or engage dominant figures of gender, race, and class. These expanded cultural perspectives then reverberate back through film and literary history. To what extent, for example, is the demand for "quality films" adapted from older and well-known classic literature a response, at certain times in history, to social and political turbulence? How did Bertolt Brecht's legal battles over the screen adaptation of *The Threepenny Opera* focus acute economic and legal distinctions between film and literature in the early 1930s? Within a larger cultural panorama of cultural studies, apparently unrelated films and texts—such as the gendered territory of American slasher films and Harlequin novels—may have more to say to each other than previously considered.

There are numerous academic agendas that should fit this book, but the primary aim is to serve students, new and old, who wish to begin or to continue reading about and thinking about the relationship between literature and the movies. This subject could be concentrated on any one particular genre—say, the novel and film or Shakespeare and film; and some may wish to approach the topic as three fields, with dramatic literature on a middle ground between written literature and performing arts like film. My aim, however, has been to provide a general foundation for the issues and histories that pervade this topic, and to allow instructors and readers to supplement or refocus their concerns according to their own needs and their particular choices of literary works and films. The specific readings provide, above all else, a historical perspective that, at the same time, addresses different genres and offers different approaches to the question of how the movies and literature interact. While one of my first priorities has been to choose materials that would be accessible to students, there are also essays here that are challenging and demanding. I did this not only because this mix reflects a range of methods and views but because the book hopes to promote a reader's advancing sense of the subject. Vachel Lindsay's writings on film and literature are rich but not overly complex; Alexander Kluge's piece assumes readers will have more experience or more guidance with the questions he raises.

The organization of this book aims, in short, to be at once historical, methodological, and pedagogical, representing a variety of historical periods, cultural practices, and critical methods. Part I attempts to delineate the historical differences and dynamics that have shaped the topic, emphasizing distinctions and heritages that follow the debate through the 1990s. Here I wish to contextualize and highlight those economic, technological, and social issues that add depth and complexity to the specific aesthetic arguments. A reader interested in Cocteau on film or the "angry young" dramatists and filmmakers of England, for instance, will thus have a historical background against which to place their thinking. Throughout this historical narrative, I have introduced short discussions of more focused topics, placing them, when possible, near a relevant historical period. These include the more specific issues and forms permeating the film/literature debates: topics such as novels as films, copyright, authors and auteurism, novelizations, and so forth.

In my experience teaching film and literature, individuals frequently need a basic vocabulary to allow them to discuss and compare cinematic and literary techniques and form. Many of the debates about film and literature can become rather lofty, and it is obviously important that a reader have some basic sense of, for instance, how narrative point of view has been traditionally defined in the two practices, or what mise-en-scène means in the cinema, before (or while) they work through the more complex issues binding film and literature. In Part II there is, therefore, a brief presentation of key critical concepts that film and literature share and that often distinguish their particular practices. Highlighting notions of narrative structure, genres, and formal devices such as camera techniques, figurative languages, and other critical terms and analytic categories, Part II aims to provide individuals with a basic vocabulary for beginning to think about and write about film and works of literature.

Part III is the pedagogical centerpiece of the book, featuring the major statements on the relationship of film and literature that have appeared this century. Such an immensely popular topic has produced, of course, numerous other essays, and many readers will know other essays that might have been included. My goal here, however, is to represent the path of the debates as it has sprung from different cultures, addressed different genres, and taken sometimes very different stances. In this I have also tried to choose texts that might have the most use and flexibility in different classrooms. Instructors and students and general readers should be able to formulate out of this selection an arrangement and direction that responds to more particular concerns. The bibliography at the end of the book describes materials for supplementing the readings in Part III.

What makes these discussions and debates more compelling or topical today than the many other discussions and debates about film or about literature? Why do these issues across film and literature continue to claim our attention? One of the presumptions informing many of these debates is that the interaction of film and literature has special relevance to our culture and times, and the basis for this assumption needs to be examined. One preliminary answer to the question is that film has historically depended on literature for so much of its material. Put simply, movies very often base their scripts on literary texts and traditions. Yet, the complexity, logic, and centrality of the topic goes well beyond this industrial or artistic reliance, I believe, and much of that complexity is what this book intends to open up. Since the end of the nineteenth century, the tension between visuality and literacy has dominated much of Western culture. It has served as a barometer for questions about class, human intelligence, political action, the different statuses of races and genders, and the use and abuse of leisure time. We continue to ask how movies and television affect reading habits of children; we continue to fear or to embrace the power of the image to transcend different languages and speech itself. Twentieth-century history, perhaps more than any other epoch in history, has positioned itself between the "traditional word" and the "technological image," and tracing the directions of this debate through this century as it works through movies, books, and culture dramatizes one of the most pressing motifs of these times.

Works Cited

Geduld, Harry M., ed. *Authors on Film*. Bloomington, IN: Indiana University Press, 1972.

Holt, Patricia. "Turning Best Sellers into Movies." *Publishers Weekly* 22 (October 1979): 36–40.

Yacowar, Maurice. *Tennessee Williams and Film*. New York: Ungar, 1977.

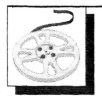

FILM AND LITERATURE IN THE CROSSCURRENTS OF HISTORY

An important first step in studying the relationship between film and literature is to recognize it as a historical pact that has changed through the decades and shifted its terms within different cultures. Dudley Andrew makes a central point when he says that "the study of adaptation is tantamount to the study of the cinema as a whole" (103), and implicit in that claim is that such a study requires large and small distinctions all along the way. Even beginning with the origins of cinema in the late nineteenth century has the disadvantage of a late start since the debates and practices surrounding the connections between words and images extend back through the centuries and around the globe. In this section, historical and cultural landscapes will be sketched to emphasize the evolution of the dominant questions and to highlight some of the social, aesthetic, and technological contexts that have shaped the major points in the debate. The exchanges between film and literature have commonly been addressed in terms of the differences and similarities of their forms of expression and representation—how the image differs from the word or how both practices use narrative conventions. Here, though, we will begin by calling attention to how these textual features change and depend on the cultural and historical conditions and other pressures that surround books and movies. Within these changing contexts, the very meanings of the terms "film" and "literature" change, while their values in relation to each other continually shift as well.

A brief survey of the historical relations of film and literature can only seem incomplete against a history that features so many examples and alternative directions. Histories, certainly concentrated histories such as this one, are always to some extent polemics, and readers should consider this history as a polemic into which individual films can be placed to support or challenge that argument.

THE PREHISTORY
OF FILM AND LITERATURE

It would be impossible to mark and describe here all the different sources, forms, and arguments that anticipate the twentieth-century encounters between film and literature, since the relationship between the word and the image can be traced back to the beginnings of various civilizations. Indeed, many students and scholars of film locate the first connections between film and literature in prehistoric cave drawings, Egyptian hieroglyphics, or the various picture writings of early civilizations, such as Chinese ideograms. In these practices that combine verbal signs and visual images, critics and historians recognize early attempts to record events, tell stories, or evoke spiritual power in a manner that anticipates the combinations of literary forms and technological images used in movies centuries later to present their histories, recount their tales, and generate their own magical charms. From the times of those more ancient civilizations, developments in most Western and non-Western cultures would continue to feature a rich source of materials and debates about the relationship between verbal and visual signs. From illuminated manuscripts and religious iconography to sixteenth-century verbal and visual exercises for memory, from the construction of Renaissance theaters as the visual forum for elaborate dialogue to the storytelling amusements of camera obscuras and other precursors to the camera, the pre-cinematic relationships between seeing and saying would be debated and practiced as central arguments about knowledge, identity, spiritual truth, pleasure, politics, and the meaning of culture.

Publics and Cultures

The historical tale of the relationship between film and literature gained considerable momentum in the late eighteenth and early nineteenth centuries when the recognizable precedents in the debate began to appear. One of these precedents was a social and cultural anxiety about the proliferation of writings, spectacles, and entertainments attracting lower- and middle-class audiences. By the late eighteenth century, the industrial revolution was underway, and the technological implications of this revolution were seen throughout the visual and literary arts. Developments in the printing industry and its mechanics revolutionized many societies, for instance, through the introduction of the iron press in 1798 and later of the steam press. With these inventions, both books and prints proliferated through mass production, and these new technological powers to produce and disseminate words and images paralleled, and in some ways helped to prepare, corresponding social revolutions that were ushering in an expanding middle class of readers, spectators, and cultural consumers.

Throughout this period, from roughly 1750–1825, Western cultures grew increasingly fascinated by visual images and spectacles that drew on but transformed the traditional pictorial arts, as well as by the similarities and differences in images and words as separate means of communication. On the one hand, this promoted immense scientific and cultural development of new mechanisms for reproducing images, theatrical spectacles, and optical toys. These included new methods for mass producing prints in books (welcomed by artists such as William Hogarth, who developed methods for telling satirical tales through a series of engravings), popular illusory dioramas and panoramas that appeared somewhere between legitimate dramatic theater and carnivalesque sideshow (in the 1790s Étienne Gaspard Robertson's *Phantasmagoria* attracted crowds with fantastic specters of Rousseau, Marat, and other celebrities of revolutionary France), and innumerable scientific oddities (such as the kaleidoscope invented by Sir David Brewster in 1814) that anticipated the discovery of photographic methods and instruments between 1826 and 1839. On the other hand, these various cultural and scientific inventions and amusements, not surprisingly, stirred continual debates among literary men and women about the two media and the place of literature in a culture that, even in the early nineteenth century, seemed to be coming more and more under the spell of fascinating images rather than the discriminating power of crafted words.

Although he does not single out the showdown between literature and the technologies of the image, Raymond Williams rightly suggests that what is at stake in these debates in the early nineteenth century (and beyond) is the formation and defense of some notion of "culture," a term that, since then, has figured in many arguments about film and literature. The poet William Wordsworth, defender of the literary tradition in the early nineteenth century, rails against what he sees as the blunt lack of discrimination in this growing image culture (Wordsworth calling on a literary "people" to distinguish itself from the easily amused "public"). His contemporary William Blake, however, envisions a new public and takes advantage of experimental methods for reproducing printed images, setting them as a complex counterpoint to the poetry that faced those images (in his celebrated lyrics such as *Songs of Innocence and Experience* or his epic *Jerusalem*). This particular period in Western history is an especially rich prelude to the cultural, aesthetic, and political issues that would appear full-blown by the end of the nineteenth century. Writers, artists, scientists, philosophers, and entrepreneurs raised questions early that remain unresolved, often in the context of the relationship of literary culture and a new culture of images, about high culture versus popular culture, active reading versus passive fascination, individual sense versus mob sensibility, creative expression versus mechanical reproduction, words versus images as pedagogical tools, and realistic pictures of history versus literary descriptions.

Nineteenth-Century Realism and Melodrama

By the second quarter of the nineteenth century, the encounter between literature and this new image-culture would become as much about realism as about the cultural terrain mapped by these two ways of presenting the world. Although foreshadowed by earlier movements toward more realism (in the characters, settings, and events of literature from Shakespeare through the eighteenth century), the scientific developments in photography in the 1830s mark a major shift in the discussions of painting, literature, theater, and other arts. From then till now, questions about the amount and accuracy of realistic fact and figure dominate much of the debate about connections and differences between new technological modes of representation and the more traditional forms of art and literature. From the novels of Sir Walter Scott at the beginning of this century through the naturalistic narratives of Émile Zola at the other end, an aesthetic of realism parallels and competes with the evolution of photography and early experiments with moving images such as Eadweard Muybridge's famous studies of animal motion in the 1870s. Indeed, much of the literature of the period seems to aim specifically at integrating the detailed objectivity of the photograph into the movement of narrative. In the novels of Flaubert and George Eliot, readers find shocking close-ups or precise panoramas of local scenes; in Nathaniel Hawthorne's *The House of Seven Gables* (1850), the work of a central character, Holgrave, as a daguerrotypist (or early photographer) turns the plot climactically. Even the historical snapshots of Renaissance artists and aristocrats found in Robert

Browning's poetry develop their perspectives through the minute historical, geographical, and physical details associated with the new realism of photography.

At the center of the separate practices of film and literature, new blends and composite works appear: Magic lanterns project scenes of Walter Scott novels and other literary narratives, and serial novels become a compelling blend of the photographic and the narrative through the support of lithographic images or, after 1880, even halftone photoengravings. Often these stories would first appear in the commercial format of newspapers, magazines, and other periodicals that functioned as the commercial forebears of the mass media that would later describe the movie business. One of the most innovative literatures that appears during the second half of this century is appropriately a similar hybrid: The photo-essay that arrives late in this century (Jacob Riis's *How the Other Half Lives*, for example) combines news, personal reflection, and social commentary with the power of illustrative photographs. Its creative blend of the photographic and the literary would continue to evolve through the twentieth century in various kinds of photo-essays (from W. Eugene Smith to Cindy Sherman) and documentary novels (from John Dos Passos to the New Journalism of Norman Mailer in the 1960s). As A. Nicholas Vardac has pointed out in his book *Stage to Screen*, however, the theater is clearly the center stage for these crosscurrents between an established literary tradition and the beginnings of cinematic realism:

> The times rather than the men controlled the ultimate arrival of the motion picture, for at just the point beyond which stage realism would have broken down and in many instances did, the cinema came to meet the need for a greater pictorial realism. By coming at the very peak of the nineteenth century cycle of realism, it upset normal expectations in theatre itself.... Naturally, in these early years, the film and the stage were hardly differentiated from one another; the cinema frequently borrowed from the theatre, while the theatre, in an attempt to counter the new attraction, in its turn borrowed from the film.... The result was that the two styles which defined the nineteenth-century theatre, realism and romanticism, and which most probably would have seen alteration in the early years of the twentieth century, were given a new lease on life. (xxvi)

Especially as the nineteenth century proceeds, the divisions between the established traditions of literature and the technological precursors to the film are never neatly and clearly marked off, and it is more accurate to see both the practices and arguments as moving back and forth in a series of responses and assertions, most prominently about realism. Certainly, some positions were highly oppositional. In

MATERIAL DIFFERENCES IN FILM AND LITERATURE

Despite their similarities and connections, film and literature use materially different ways to describe the world or to express a point of view. Literature usually employs printed words, and often requires a longer reading time than the way we access stories through images on a screen, which are usually presented in a 90- or 100-minute format. Dramatic literature likewise distinguishes itself from film performance, most clearly through the difference of an actual physical performance versus a performance recorded on celluloid or videotape. Like novels and short stories, much poetry is written for a printed page, but many poets prefer their works to be read or performed before a live audience, thus associating their poetry with performative arts like theater.

The tools of each trade can also be quite different and, as basic as they are, they are often a good starting point for considering the different forms. Literature organizes words through sentences, stanzas, chapters, and so forth. Plays use acts and scenes whose breaks are, in most cases, clearly evident. Film may borrow some of these structures but usually works to make any scenic shifts invisible and often seamless.

Many questions and issues surround the distinction between the way individuals watch a performance of a movie and the way they read literature or view a performance of a play at the theater. These include delineating the intellectual activities that distinguish watching images and listening to recorded words from reading words on a page, as well as other psychological, social, and economic dimensions to these experiences. In this regard, television is a related but very different way of adapting literature since the size of a television image and the conditions in which we watch it (at home usually) differ considerably from those of a movie screening.

Although these basic material differences might seem obvious and are rarely considered in comparing different forms of film and literature, keeping them in mind may be the best starting point in an examination of what film and literature finally have or do not have in common. A person may read Charles Dickens's long novel *Nicholas Nickleby* in private over the course of several months, controlling her pace and reflections along the way; she may view the 100-minute version of the 1947 film in the semidarkness of a small movie theater, following rather than controlling the pace of the story; or she may attend, on two different days at a Broadway theater, the 8½-hour production by the Royal Shakespeare Company, her attention divided among the crowd around her, the sets, and the characters. In each of these cases, different meanings of the works may originate in the extremely different conditions and shapes of the specific literary or filmic form, and the value we assign each version should take into account the material possibilities available in each medium.

Recommended Readings   A. Nicholas Vardac's *Stage to Screen* and John Fell's *Film before Griffith*.

1859, the French poet Charles Baudelaire's disdain is typical of the suspicion of many in the literary and artistic community of the "unworthy tricks" of photography: "If photography is allowed to supplement art in some of its functions, it will soon have supplanted or corrupted it altogether" (19, 20). Versions of this position underlie much of the poetic practice in the second half of this century, where the sometimes extreme emphasis placed on private experience or dreamlike, imaginative states—in poetic movements such as those of the Pre-Raphaelites (the poetry of D. G. and Christina Rossetti, for instance) or the Symbolists (the French poetry of Stéphane Mallarmé and Arthur Rimbaud)—become clear moves away from the powerful realism of photography. Similarly, while the revolutionary realist theater of Henrik Ibsen and other nineteenth-century dramatists can usefully be discussed in the context of the incisive and realistic eye of the camera, many of the most notable theatrical achievements of this time are either a reaction to the onslaught of a technological realism or a reinvention of drama in the light of this new realism. Beginning with the so-called "closet drama" of romantic theater and continuing through highly symbolic versions of this practice in the theater of August Strindberg, Maurice Maeterlink, and William Butler Yeats, this other kind of drama works primarily in the invisible regions of the mind and the emotions rather than in the visible centers of society and nature.

In many cases, this tension between the realism of public life and art and the emotional escapisms of private life and art describes less separate spheres dividing individual practices than contested fields within many single works. From one direction there are the forces of society, historical determinism, and realism; from the other, the forces of individualism, personal desire, and imagination. One of the most significant productions of the collision is melodrama, that nineteenth-century form of emotional need and suspense that pits personal desire and dreams against the restrictions of social realism.

Melodramatic plots and situations become a dominant chord in much of the respected literatures of the age (from the poetry of Lord Byron and Goethe to the novels of Charlotte Bronte and Thomas Hardy), but they appear in their most transparent forms in the popular entertainments that were outlining the beginnings of a cultural place for cinema. Following the trends of the first part of the century, lower- and middle-class cultures develop popular institutions and forms, such as music halls, pantomime fantasies, and lavish dramatic spectacles built around special effects. In these institutions and entertainments, melodramatic feelings and desires are often played out against massive backgrounds and tableaux of history and nature. These kinds of melodramatic entertainments would, according to Peter Brooks, transform classical theater into a "mute text," "a visual summary of the emotional situation" (47); as it engaged that other dominant literary concern, realism, melodrama would become one of the prominent linchpins uniting nineteenth-century literature and the forms, audiences, and institutions of the cinema.

Works Cited

Andrew, Dudley. *Concepts in Film Theory*. New York: Oxford University Press, 1984.

Baudelaire, Charles. "The Salon of 1846: On the Heroism of Modern Life." In *Modern Art and Modernism: A Critical Anthology*. Ed. Francis Frascina and Charles Harrison. New York: Harper & Row, 1975.

Brooks, Peter. *The Melodramatic Imagination: Balzac, Henry James, Melodrama, and the Mode of Excess*. New Haven, CT: Yale University Press, 1976.

Vardac, A. Nicholas. *Stage to Screen: Theatrical Method from Garrick to Griffith*. Cambridge, MA: Harvard University Press, 1949.

2

FILMING LITERATURE

FROM PRECLASSICAL FILM AND LITERATURE
TO CLASSICAL FORM, 1895–1925

A common scheme for distinguishing the two major trends at the origins of film history (from 1895 to 1913) is to oppose the films of the Lumière brothers to those of George Méliès, the first associated with documentary realism and the second with fantasy. While this is no doubt too simplistic a summary of the many different strategies taking part in the birth of the cinema, it does highlight two of the main tendencies that early film practice inherits from the confluence of literature and the image cultures of the nineteenth century. The Lumières made short films intended to document various activities and realities in a way that emphasizes the scientific powers of film to investigate the actuality of events. Méliès exploits the theatrical magic of the movies in developing film as an entertainment and imaginative play. The Lumière shorts (like *Arrival of a Train at a Station* [1895]) usually last no more than a few minutes and work as moving snapshots of the world, while George Méliès's dramas (like *A Trip to the Moon* [1902]) create illusions staged theatrically before a stationary camera. Both kinds of early cinema participate in what Tom Gunning has dubbed "a cinema of attraction," a cinema that, like the mass entertainments that precede them, relies less on the form or matter than on sheer novelty and excitement—in this case on the pleasure of seeing a moving spectacle and, possibly, a literary text come to life.

The Attraction of the Literary

For students of film and literature, there are three important dimensions to film practice in these early years: (1) film practice and its connection with literature follow social and aesthetic directions and developments established in the nineteenth century, especially the

Méliès's *The Magic Lantern* (1903) is one of the early silent movies that assimilated the traditions of theatrical illusion into the new art of cinema. This film in fact looks back to optical toys like the magic lantern, forerunners of the cinema that often entertained nineteenth-century audiences with scenes from plays or novels. (*Archive Photos*)

demands for realism and a class-oriented fascination with spectacle; (2) early cinema tends to find its formal literary precedents in the staged perspectives of the theater and less in narrative traditions; and (3) even at this early stage, film turns to literary materials of all kinds for subject matter. The first of these has already been signaled in our discussion of the cultural tensions evolving through the nineteenth century, and it acquires even more weight in the United States at the turn of the century when large immigrant audiences discovered in their neighborhood nickelodeons (storefront movie theaters) fascinating images and entertainments that seemed to transcend all their linguistic differences, promising, for some proponents of the early cinema, to fulfill the dream of a universal language or "esperanto" in the immediately comprehensible realism of the movies. The second point, the theatricality of early films, derives from many influences, including the realism and melodrama of nineteenth-century staged performances, the historical dominance of popular theater traditions such as music halls and vaudeville performances, and, perhaps most important, the necessarily stationary position of the camera that could most easily recreate the perspective of a spectator in a center seat before the stage. The third point calls attention to the immediate appearance of literary subjects in film history, since documentary events could entertain only to a limited degree. Along with topical historical and sporting events, literary figures and topics were a natural choice for preclassical cinema. These literary films were sometimes as much about the performance of a famous player as about the subject (as with the 1896 film of the actor Joseph Jefferson performing *Rip Van Winkle*), but filmmakers were also quick to use the cultural and popular currency of well-known literary tales, such as the filming of staged versions of *Cinderella* (1900), *Robinson Crusoe* (1902), *Gulliver's Travels* (1902), *Uncle Tom's Cabin* (1903), and *The Damnation of Faust* (1904). Besides the condensation of these literary classics as costume spectacles, early movies also turned to less canonized literary sources: bourgeois melodramas or so-called middle-class fiction, dramas and tales from folklore, and many different kinds of vaudevillian traditions.

The literary attraction in these early adaptations, staged often as "action-tableaux" but eventually as narratives, is in many ways pragmatic. As the demand for movies increased exponentially and audiences grew more sophisticated about what they wanted to see on film, literature provided an abundance of ready-made materials that could be transposed to film. Looking for an image, a scene, a concept, or a story, a filmmaker could turn to a literary work to represent on film. That the audiences might sometimes be familiar with the literary precedent could also work to the filmmaker's advantage since part of the interest in the film would be seeing words brought to life, and this piqued interest would dovetail, of course, with the expanding financial possibilities the cinema contained as a growing form of mass entertainment.

At the same time, this tendency to use literature for early movies was more than just pragmatic. It also became a way of negotiating a new, respectable cultural position for movies and their audiences. Perceived in these first years of development as a curiosity and amusement geared toward lower-class audiences, film could, by adapting classics and popular literary figures and types, position itself closer and closer to art and respectable cultural practices and thus add other classes of audiences to its patrons. One of the most significant examples of this move toward respectability on the coattails of theater was the *film d'art* movement. Started by the French Société Film d'Art in 1908, this project made films featuring celebrated performances and performers from the Comédie Française, such as Sarah Bernhardt in *La Dame aux Camelias* (1912). The success of these productions inspired a spate of imitations using theatrical actors and sets, most notably in the

THEATER AND FILM

Once the cinema progressed (early in the twentieth century) beyond the peepshow amusement of kinetoscopes and other optical toys for private viewing, theater and dramatic literature became the primary models that movie makers turned to in the early years of the cinema, for several reasons: (1) Both theater and movies were public and commercial spectacles addressing audiences rather than individuals; (2) early audiences for movies had been socially and culturally prepared by the theatrical traditions of music halls and other popular shows; (3) because of the lack of camera mobility, the best way to film a story was to place the stationary camera before the characters and action and so duplicate the position of a viewer before a stage; and (4) the production materials for theater, specifically sets and actors, became readily available materials for developing the entertainment potential of movies.

Theater and film have, of course, many other structures, materials, and formulas in common. Drama's fundamental roots in *conflict* continue in classical cinema, as both drama and film foreground confrontations between individuals and other individuals and between individuals and societies. Nineteenth-century theater and its paradigm of a "well-made play" provided film with one of the most durable formulas for structuring film action as it organized theatrical action according to exposition, complication, crisis, climax, and resolution. These remain standard developmental structures in much theater and film today.

Theatrical sets, actors, and costumes are fundamental elements of both theater and film, yet the physical presence and concreteness of these features in the theater become transformed in a film image. Acting style, for example, can take advantage of camera close-ups and other positionings; sets and settings in the cinema naturally gravitate more toward realistic locations; and the possibilities for constructing space and time are significantly different in the two media.

Although theater remains a regular source throughout film's relationship with literature in this century, movies often changed the nature of their relationship with dramatic literature. Since Vachel Lindsay's "Thirty Differences Between the Photoplays and the Stage" and other early writings, observers and practitioners of cinema quickly began to urge film to distinguish itself from its theatrical parentage, and the history of filmmaking and film criticism has vacillated between a rejection of theatrical models and creative encounters with them. In the first quarter of this century, the ascension of film's powerful realism is one factor in moving the cinema away from the theater, while, by the 1930s, cinema's power to entertain brought theater spectacles and musicals back into the movies in full force. In recent years, dramatic literature has been used in a myriad of ways, sometimes to take advantage of traditional dramatic values of character and dialogue (drawing actors and filmmakers like Sir John Gielgud and Kenneth Branagh), sometimes to foreground a theatrical artificiality (of space, sets, or costumes) that subverts film's realism.

THEATER AND FILM (CONT.)

More and more, the exchange between theater and film has moved in both directions. Since the 1920s, F. T. Marinetti, Tom Stoppard, Sam Shepard, Richard Foreman and other playwrights have ingenuously incorporated film metaphors and techniques as part of their stage plays, and television drama, which creates original dramatic material for television, has become a subgenre in its own right.

Recommended Readings   Allardyce Nicoll's *Film and Theater*, André Bazin's *What Is Cinema?*, and Roger Manvell's *Theater and Film*.

United States by Adolph Zukor and his Famous Players Film Corporation. One of the important side effects of the widespread success of these movies and their famous players was the birth of a star system that dictated higher prices for the movies and stories centered on a highly visible and recognizable character.

D. W. Griffith and the Birth of Classical Cinema from Literature

For most historians of cinema, classical film develops its main shape and elements in the first quarter of the twentieth century, predominantly through the work of D. W. Griffith around 1913. There are certainly other influential moviemakers who worked alongside Griffith in these efforts, and one of the most important is Giovanni Pastrone, whose grand epic *Cabiria* (1913–1914) features intertitles written by Gabriele D'Annunzio, one of the most celebrated Italian writers of the late nineteenth and early twentieth centuries. Yet most historians credit Griffith with implementing and popularizing the aesthetic and technological changes that move the cinema from its preclassical to classical stage, in an effort, as Griffith put it, "to place pictures on par with the spoken word as a medium of expression appealing to thinking people" (Schickel 275–276).

Many of these moves toward classical cinema are rooted in the nineteenth-century literary prototypes that Griffith adapted directly as subjects for his films or indirectly as formal figures, character types, or references. Often overlooked in this context, serial novels (such as the *Perils of Pauline*) supplied the short episodic tales that fit the one-reel screenings of preclassical cinema and that, through the course of several screenings, could develop a longer tale. As with other filmmakers,

ADAPTATION

A daptation is the most common practice in the exchange between literature and film, describing the transposition of a novel, play, or other literary source to film. Although this term can sometimes suggest a derivative or less creative practice, it is useful to keep in mind that even the most original works of movies and literature might be considered "adaptations" of materials drawn from one source or another. Not only are famous literary works, like the plays of Shakespeare or James Joyce's *Ulysses*, drawn from historical documents or earlier literary sources but, in the broadest sense, even the most seemingly original work develops or "adapts" information or material from conversations, newspapers, dreams, or historical events.

In most discussions of adaptation, a key term is fidelity, a notion that asks to what extent an adaptation is true to or faithful to the original text. Common discussions about fidelity and adaptation presume five questions in determining how faithful the film adaptation is: (1) To what extent are the details of the settings and plot accurately retained or recreated? (2) To what extent do the nuance and complexity of the characters survive the adaptation? (3) To what extent are the themes and ideas of the source communicated in the adaptation? (4) To what extent has a different historical or cultural context altered the original? (5) To what extent has the change in the material or mode of communication (a printed page, a stage, 35 mm film) changed the meaning of the work for a reader or viewer? Pragmatically, these questions are answered in the way an adaptation might emphasize, for instance, action over dialogue or in how much of the plot is kept intact and where it is altered.

Other ways to approach adaptation are to replace notions of fidelity with terms that allow for more creative exchanges between the original text and its adaptation. In Dudley Andrew's essay in this volume, he proposes three kinds of adaptive tactics: borrowing, intersecting, and transforming. Others have suggested adaptation involving other processes: as a matter of generation and regeneration from one work to another, or as an exchange in which the adaptation's relation to the original text can be described as transposition, commentary, or analogy.

It is also important to consider how the literature adapted and the audience's implied awareness of the original work shapes an understanding of a film adaptation. Well-known works of classical literature (*Hamlet* or *Moby Dick*) may assume a viewer's familiarity with the original, and the adaptation may address its audience's awareness or recognition of that prior work through changes or omissions. Conversely, many movie adaptations work with a minor or relatively unknown piece of literature, and essentially treat it as an invisible dimension of its film, which most audiences neither know nor need to know. These and other issues about an audience's expectations should be considered with any adaptation.

One of the wittiest and most intelligent commentaries on film adaptation is Jean-Luc Godard's film *Contempt* (1963). The story is of a scriptwriter attempt-

---

ADAPTATION (CONT.)

ing to negotiate a movie deal with an American producer (played by Jack Palance). Mainly interested in commercial success, the producer hopes to adapt Homer's *Odyssey* with the help of German director Fritz Lang. *Contempt* addresses the numerous cultural, linguistic, and commercial conflicts and compromises involved in the process, but, more than just presenting these issues, Godard, typically, makes them part of the complex images and structures of *Contempt* itself, which is an adaptation of a novel of Alberto Moravia.

Recommended Readings   Jean Mitry's "Remarks on the Problem of Cinematic Adaptation" and Dudley Andrew's "Adaptation" (in *Concepts in Film Theory*).

---

melodramatic theater is another source for Griffith's films, but equally important is poetry, as evidenced in the refrain from Walt Whitman's *Leaves of Grass* that punctuates *Intolerance* in 1916, or in his adaptation of Alfred Lord Tennyson's Victorian poem *Enoch Arden* in 1911. *Enoch Arden*, in fact, figures as a marker of the crucial transition from the preclassical cinema of short one-reel movies (approximately ten to fifteen minutes long) to the longer narratives of classical cinema. After making a one-reel version of the poem *After Many Years* (1908), Griffith made a more faithful, longer adaptation as the two-reeler *Enoch Arden*. Although Biograph, the producer, tried to distribute the film as two distinct parts (believing audiences would not sit still for the long version), the full version proved a success that would alter the direction of the cinema and its relationship with literature.

More than just an idiosyncratic episode in Griffith's career, this incident, marking the evolution of the cinema from one-reel shorts that ran for ten or fifteen minutes to longer narratives of ninety to one hundred minutes, came from the desire to tell stories. This desire, in turn, would draw filmmakers to different sorts of literary models and practices. During the first fifteen years of the twentieth century, a program of short films would stress their variety and their spectacular images, and both the length and the need to differentiate one film from another suggested a specific literary model for the movies: the short stories found in magazines like *The Saturday Evening Post* (with whom they also competed for those stories and their audiences). When movie culture moved to larger nickelodeons and began to expand the kind and size of its audiences, the longer, feature length of the movies began to accommodate the more substantial size of novels and dramatic litera-

D. W. Griffith's *Intolerance* (1916) stands out in film history not only for its massive theatrical sets (here of ancient Babylon), but also for its complex narrative structure, which weaves together four different stories. Griffith links these stories metaphorically with an image and intertitle that freely appropriate a line from Walt Whitman's *Leaves of Grass*: "Out of the cradle endlessly rocking." (*American Stock/Archive Photos*)

ture, thus allowing movies to compete or align with these putatively more respected forms of cultural entertainment. This literary tradition of longer narrative fiction, specifically the novels of Charles Dickens, is what the Russian filmmaker Sergei Eisenstein, in "Dickens, Griffith and the Film Today," describes as the source of Griffith's landmark experiments with classical narrative form and editing techniques such as cross-cutting.

Although always in touch with his theatrical background (he was a stage actor before becoming a filmmaker), Griffith became one of the first filmmakers to recognize, through his explorations of longer narrative literature, the power of freeing the image from its theatrical position as a stationary point of view, watching action as if it took place on a stage. Through the use of different camera angles and distances from the action, as well as editing techniques such as irises and fades, Griffith introduced into movies a version of the unconstrained visual and temporal movement and rhetoric found in and derived from the novel and other forms of narrative fiction. Like the novels and short stories on which so many of these films were based, this allowed for a spatial opening up of movies (moving the action quickly from one locale to a different one) and the coexistence of several temporal registers (whereby actions could take place simultaneously or flashback suddenly to another moment), all within a linear chronology associated with the nineteenth-century novel.

No wonder then that so many of Griffith's films and those of other early directors turned increasingly to narrative fiction for materials that would respond to film's developing technical prowess: Griffith's own inflammatory *Birth of a Nation* (1915) was adapted from Thomas E. Dixon's *The Clansman*, and the silent movies throughout the period from 1915–1925, such as Maurice Tourneur and Clarence Brown's 1920 *The Last of the Mohicans*, consistently used popular and classical fiction for their storylines. Along with the narrative and technical mobility to imitate the spatial and temporal activity found in novels, the movies also became the ideal place to recreate that narrative objectivity that had become the crucial foundation for the nineteenth-century novel. As an interesting parallel, the emphasis at this point in film history on a realistic point of view contrasted sharply with the narrative experiments found in many novels written about this time. While filmmakers like Griffith were perfecting a classical style associated with the historical objectivity of the nineteenth-century novel, writers like James Joyce, Virginia Woolf, and other novelists were experimenting with perspectives aimed to subvert notions of narrative objectivity. Indeed, in some cases, these literary experiments may have been conscious reactions to film's popular realism.

Along with these narrative developments that linked the early cinema to nineteenth-century literature, models for movie characters naturally followed the models of novelistic characters. Unlike stock characters found in plays and unlike epic characters defined by physical actions, film characters like the characters of nineteenth-century novels gradually developed a psychological depth of fears and longings that served to motivate the action of a film. The star system that began to appear around 1910 was indeed partially related to this evolution, for when the individuality that focused and drove nineteenth-century narratives moved to the center of a film narrative, the actors who inhabited those characters soon became the most prominent attraction at the movies. Readers learned to empathize with literary characters like Dickens's Little Nell, but real people and personalities perform movie characters, and one consequence is perhaps a more potent form of sympathy and identification with faces and personalities, a sympathy on which a star system is built. Here, at this juncture at the beginnings of classical cinema, the forces of literary narrative and its psychology of character met

COPYRIGHT, LITERATURE, AND THE MOVIES

Copyright is the legal right granted to an author, playwright, publisher, or distributor to exclusive publication, sale, or distribution of a work of art or literature. From the first years of commercial cinema, the legalities of copyright have played a part in the choice of which literary works to adapt and the liberties taken with those works.

The 1907 version of *Ben-Hur* initiated the first copyright lawsuit in film history by Harper & Row, publisher of Lew Wallace's 1880 novel *Ben-Hur: A Tale of the Christ*. The movie adaptation had followed an extremely successful theatrical tour of the novel as a play. That year was, significantly, the year that the demand for films began to exceed the material available for production. Only after 1911—the year the Supreme Court upheld the *Ben-Hur* suit—were films legally obligated to credit their literary sources, and one of the repercussions of the subsequent copyright pressure on the movie industry was an increased interest in published literature for which copyright ownership could be legally verified and released.

Money and profit are doubtless two of the main issues involved in copyright laws and negotiations, but copyright disputes also foreground historical and aesthetic questions of authorship and creative integrity. In 1926, as Hollywood began buying the screen rights to Broadway plays, the newly formed Dramatist Guild initiated the Minimum Basic Agreement that addressed some of the main questions surrounding movie rights to plays; by subjecting rights to competitive bids that would be divided between the theater producer and the dramatist, it aimed to protect American theater from being cannibalized by Hollywood. In the early 1930s, one of the most famous and definitive cases over copyright was a showdown between German playwright Bertolt Brecht and German filmmaker G. W. Pabst over Pabst's adaptation of Brecht and Kurt Weill's *The Threepenny Opera*. In *The Threepenny Lawsuit*, Brecht summarizes a position continued to be felt by writers who lose their authority but remain attracted to the power of the movies:

> We have often been told (and the court expressed the same opinion) that when we sold our work to the film industry we gave up all our rights; the buyers even purchased the right to destroy what they had bought; all further claim was covered by the money. These people felt that in agreeing to deal with the film industry we put ourselves in the position of a man who lets his laundry be washed in a dirty gutter and then complains that it has been ruined. Anybody who advises us not to make use of such new apparatus just confirms the apparatus's right to do bad work.... At the same time he deprives us in advance of the apparatus which we need in order to produce, since this way of producing is likely more and more to supersede the present one.... (Brecht 47)

Over the decades, specific instances of copyright litigation have highlighted other concerns, as well as the changing power of Hollywood, other film and television industries, and their alignment with larger conglomerations. Today,

COPYRIGHT, LITERATURE, AND THE MOVIES (CONT.)

the sometimes frenzied bidding for the rights to a novel or play—as happened with the adaptation of Tom Wolfe's novel *The Bonfire of the Vanities* (1990)—can reach exorbitant extremes, and is at least partly responsible for one kind of literature that seems written with a possible movie contract in mind. Related to these issues of high-priced copyrights are promotion strategies that make those high costs part of their advertising strategies: A marketplace bidding for copyrights at higher and higher prices can often lose sight of any inherent literary value. In recent years, the literature that a movie industry buys has also stirred up issues about cultural authority in matters of nationality and history. In late 1997, Steven Spielberg was caught in a copyright battle over his film *Amistad* (1997) and its relation to a copyrighted novel dealing with the same story of a nineteenth-century African-American revolt: Barbara Chase-Riboud sued Spielberg's production company, Dream Works, for $10 million, claiming he violated her copyright by stealing specific scenes and materials from her 1989 novel *Echo of Lions*. Dream Works countered by noting that she took material from a 1953 history, *Black Mutiny*. These kinds of legal wranglings raise questions about perspectives on culture's history and how a work of fiction or film can claim authority over that history.

Recommended Readings John Caughie's *Theories of Authorship* and James Monaco's *American Film Now: The People, the Power, the Money, the Movies*.

the materials of the theater; here famous actors could (or could not) choose to be converted into the famous movie stars who propel film narratives.

Works Cited

Brecht, Bertolt. "The Film, the Novel, and Epic Theatre." In *Brecht on Theatre*. Ed. John Willett. New York: Hill & Wang, 1964, pp. 47–51.

Eisenstein, Sergei. "Dickens, Griffith, and the Film Today." In *The Film Form*. Trans. and ed. Jay Leyda. New York: Harcourt, 1947, pp. 195–255.

Gunning, Tom. "A Cinema of Attraction." *Wide Angle* 8, 3 (1986): 63–70.

Schickel, Richard. *D. W. Griffith: An American Life*. New York: Simon & Schuster, 1984.

3

TESTING AND EXPANDING THE VALUE OF FILM AND LITERATURE, 1915–1940

It is appropriate that, just as classical cinema developed culturally and formally to a state that remains its foundation today, those formulas were brilliantly tested by one of the most controversial and daring adaptations of all time: Erich von Stroheim's filming of Frank Norris's *McTeague*, retitled as *Greed* (1924). Originally completed as a ten-and-one-half-hour silent film, *Greed* attempts to retain all the pessimistic complexity of the novel through elaborate and incisive use of filmic techniques and visual detail: Editing techniques that suggest the nuanced themes of greed and determinism, a camera focus that makes ironic connections between characters and their inevitable fates, and almost obsessive framing of narrative details all work to create filmic equivalents for the linguistics of the novel. The film culminates in a stunningly long sequence in Death Valley, giving the film's relentless temporal motifs physical contours that may even surpass the novel. In these attempts to push film's literary and artistic powers to new extremes, however, *Greed* became one of the first of many cases in which the commercial necessities of the film industry stepped in to restrain the literary and artistic visions of the filmmaker. When the studio, Metro-Goldwyn-Mayer, became justifiably concerned about marketing a movie of such an exorbitant length, the film was taken from von Stroheim and cut to two-and-one-half hours. Throughout this period of film history, the growing literary aspirations of many other movies would be tested by the commercial and formal differences of the cinema.

For the most part, literary men and women in the first two decades of the twentieth century avoided or often attacked the movie business. By the 1920s, however, notable shifts of sentiment and practice began to appear as the literary world started to recognize (1) the claims of film as a poetic and narrative art with aesthetic and social

Erich von Stroheim's *Greed* (1924) tested the limits of adaptation when it painstaking-ly recreated Frank Norris's *McTeague* as a ten-and-one-half-hour silent epic. Beside its inordinate length, images in *Greed* are sometimes densely packed with the detailed information and metaphoric suggestions taken from the linguistic layers of the novel. Here the numerous directions of the characters' glances dramatize social positions, atti-tudes, and tensions at the wedding of McTeague and Trina. (*Photofest*)

powers particularly attuned to modern life, and (2) the possibility of using the themes and forms of the movies as part of their literary work. In line with these observations and intimations, the 1920s and 1930s represent one of the most active periods of creative exchange, rather than dependence, between film and literature, one in which film begins to assert its aesthetic claims for creative powers equal to literature. Two kinds of historical activities connecting film and literature during the 1920s and 1930s need to be signaled here: The first relates to the various imagistic movements of modernism and the avant-garde and their indirect relation to a new realism of social reform; the second out-lines the massive impact of the coming of sound on literary adaptations. Through these and other trends, film and literature interact to test and develop their value to society: Film begins to assume new cultural and artistic value, while literature must reevaluate its own abilities to reflect and engage social change.

Modern Images and Social Imperatives

Before and after *Greed*, there has been a great deal of successful and unsuccessful experimentation with the relationship between film and literature, most notably with how film could assimilate or potentially surpass traditional literature in its efforts to create new perspectives and ideas. This is, in part, an aesthetic project that overlaps with various avant-garde practices; frequently the movies borrow from literature to demonstrate how film could not only accommodate poems, novels, and theater but could transform those literary materials into truly modernist works of art. Following some developing precepts of modernism, the technological art of film seemed especially able to organize fragmentary images (as edited "shots") according to the variety of linear and nonlinear patterns explored by the "less modern" modernisms of traditional literature and art.

This modernist interface between film and literature produced movies from a variety of countries and in numerous aesthetic shapes, commercial and noncommercial, narrative and non-narrative, poetic and theatrical. German Expressionist cinema and its most famous product *The Cabinet of Dr. Caligari* (1919)—a film scripted by the artist Carl Mayer and the Czech poet Hans Janowitz—are perhaps the best known and anticipatory examples of this movement toward art and poetry in the cinema: Like some of the most inventive literature and paintings of this period, *Caligari* specifically questions realist notions of time and place before the power of dreams and desires. As part of the same movement but with roots in the earlier *film d'art* movement, theater director Max Reinhardt translated drama onto film through remarkably inventive mise-en-scènes orchestrating lighting, crowds, and set designs (still recognizable in his American-made *A Midsummer Night's Dream* of 1935). Similarly, F. W. Murnau's filmed versions of *Tartuffe* (1925) and his 1922 *Nosferatu* (loosely adapted from Bram Stoker's 1897 *Dracula*) would use film idioms and techniques to retell those stories with an imagistic force that visually actualized shifts in human identity that the literature may only be able to describe; in *Nosferatu* he employed the special effects of the film image to present the horrifying figure of a body there but not there, alive but dead.

With many of these efforts, aesthetic experiments with film and literature are also political and social reevaluations of the relationship between art and culture. In Italy, the Futurist movement of Tommaso Marinetti and others would influence both the avant-garde cinema and the experimental theater movements of the twenties and early thirties by freely trading on the supposed revolutionary powers of technology and technological perspectives to suggest the new velocities and energies of modern society. In Russia, Vsevolod Meyerhold experimented throughout the 1920s with radical theatrical techniques transposed from the cinema, much of this interdisciplinary energy being passed onto filmmaker Sergei Eisenstein, who would envision a renovated social order brought to life by the new theatrics of the cinema. In France, the surrealist overlappings of drama, poetry, and film found in the work of Antoine Artaud and Jean Cocteau reappeared in their films and in the more narrative films of Abel Gance, *J'accuse* (1919), *La Roue* (1922–1923), and his three-screen epic *Napoleon* (1927), the latter demonstrating how modern history could only be apprehended through multiple viewpoints. For all the distinctions and differences in these projects, their creative crossings between various artistic and literary fields demonstrated a deep belief in the way film, at the cultural intersection of art, literature, and technology, might best present the twentieth century that was taking shape. In many cases, these writers, artists, and filmmakers believed that modern society could not be adequately represented by the older forms of literature and the traditional arts. As a technological art with new ways of imagining people and events, film would thus be moved to the forefront of culture where it could absorb literary traditions and transform them. The result would be images and literatures demonstrating the new movements, speeds, industrial powers, unconscious minds, and the expanding social masses of a brave new world.

Not surprisingly then, the direction of the exchange between film and literature often shifts during this period from the adaptation of literature by the movies to the adaptation of film and its techniques by literature. Certain writers, such as Hart Crane (*The Bridge*), Gertrude Stein (*Tender Buttons*), and John Dos Passos (*U.S.A.*), experimented with the metaphors and rhetoric of the cinema to challenge the limitations of literary language, recasting in language, for instance, film's panoramic visual movements, its fragmentary montages of images, or its documentary clarity. If film assimilates literature for both its aesthetic and social value, the literature of this period would often attempt to take advantage of the imagistic energy of film to make the literary more responsive to the visual patterns of the twentieth century.

By the early 1930s those poetic and avant-garde directions met a second powerful direction in film history, that of the social documentary. These two general directions should not be viewed as opposites but as counterpoints, since both sought to challenge cultural assumptions and formulas deemed inadequate to the social and experiential realities of contemporary life. For both the aesthetic experimenters and the social realists the film medium became a tool for redefining the peoples and problems that, from one point of view, conventional literature and other traditional forms of representation excluded. In this sense, the power of modern technology and industry, as manifested in film practice, might supplement or replace those literary forms, and so expand or alter the

POETRY AND FILM

Poets from all cultures and historical periods have responded to the movies. Sometimes this response has taken the shape of a denunciation of the abrasive powers of popular movies as the center of culture. Sometimes films have furnished poets with images or figures that have become symbols or metaphors for a particular idea or problem. Sometimes the cinema describes for poets an entire way of seeing or of constructing vision that works in conjunction with poetic language or that stands out in its difference.

Of the different literary genres that film has drawn on or influenced, poetry has been the most elusive and less common. From the early years of film history, however, there have been notable examples. Griffith adapted Tennyson's poem *Enoch Arden* in 1911. Joseph Moncure March's narrative poems *The Wild Party* (1928) and *The Set-Up* (1928) are other relatively early attempts to put poetry on film and, through the 1920s and early 1930s, the movies demonstrated an especially lively connection with poetry as part of movements such as Dadaism, Futurism, and various schools of Surrealism—all of which recognized the capabilities of film to disrupt and recreate perception that rattled common views and broke through perceptual barriers. Jean Cocteau is one of the most renowned poet-filmmakers, whose films include *The Blood of a Poet* (1930), *Beauty and the Beast* (1946), and *Orpheus* (1950). Added to a screenplay of *Blood of a Poet* is his apocalyptic remark about the regenerative powers of film as part of a literary tradition: "With the cinema, death is killed, literature is killed, poetry is made to live a direct life. Imagine what the cinema of poetry might be" (xii). In the post-World War II years, experimental filmmakers such as Maya Deren and Stan Brakhage found the paradigms for their films in the confrontation with linguistic sense found in twentieth-century poetry, and that tradition has continued to the present in the non-narrative films of Bruce Baillie and Bruce Conner. Even certain narrative films, such as Ingmar Bergman's 1957 *The Seventh Seal*, strike some viewers as more like a poetic allegory than a dramatic story; and Pier Paolo Pasolini argues for the unique powers of film to combine realism and poetry in his 1965 essay "A Cinema of Poetry."

Throughout this century, poets have taken movie matters as subjects or borrowed (sometimes even anticipated) film's imagistic mobility or unique formal structures. For instance, "Imagism" describes a school of poetry active especially in the years 1912–1915; it includes the work of T. E. Hulme, H. D. (Hilda Doolittle), William Carlos Williams, and Ezra Pound (most famously, his poem "In a Station in the Metro"). The main premise of imagism is that the poetry should be, above all else, a visually concrete language stripped of the emotional and intellectual decoration associated with some nineteenth-century poetry. Like some early directors and theoreticians of the cinema, Pound and others saw the Chinese ideogram as a model for this kind of poetry, and poetic imagism might be usefully related to the new aesthetics of photography and film and, in turn, to the more poetic experiments with film form through the 1920s by Man Ray, Marcel Duchamp, Hans Richter, and others.

POETRY AND FILM (CONT.)

What distinguishes poetic films from narrative films, theatrical films, or essay films is an exploration and distillation of the language of the medium in order to incite a viewer's imagination. Like many poems, poetic films aim to intensify or make unfamiliar the formulas of conventional or mainstream movies. With this definition, poetic films would include many experimental films that examine and test the nature of film as a language and medium of expression (such as the films of Brakhage and Michael Snow); it could also include films that border on and participate in the conventions of narrative or storytelling but that emphasize the imaginative or fantastical potential of vision and images (thus making room for the poetry of animation cinema or for the mesmerizing sequences in films such as Werner Herzog's *Heart of Glass* [1976], Glauber Rocha's *Antonio das Mortes* [1969], or Terrence Malick's *Days of Heaven* [1978]).

There are three fundamental ways of discussing film and poetry: (1) how poets were influenced by or how they recreated the structures and figures of the movies in their poetry; (2) how a poetic sensibility or vision is shared by creators of both literature and cinema (and other forms as well) so that one identifies an imaginative or "poetic" quality; and (3) how a film and poem construct metaphors, symbols, and other poetic idioms in different or similar ways.

Recommended Readings   Gabriela Mistral's "The Poet's Attitude toward the Movies," Laurence Goldstein's *The American Poet at the Movies*, Robert Richardson's "The Question of Order and Coherence in Poetry and Film" (in *Literature and Film*), and Philip French and Ken Wlaschin's *The Faber Book of Movie Verse*.

---

older social values associated with literature. From some quarters—the defenders of the cultural sanctuaries of literature, for instance—those traditional values are defended vigorously against the new energies and liberalities of the movies, as many critics during this period condemned what they considered the distorted views disseminated by the movies. For others, however, the values of traditional art and literature remade through the language of film could reveal the possibilities of changing the world for the better. Walter Benjamin's celebrated essay on "The Work of Art in the Age of Mechanical Reproduction" represents, in this historical context, a crucial voice in a lively cross-cultural debate about cinematic realism and its ability to engage its audiences in a new fashion.

The work of many movements and filmmakers should be seen in this context. In Germany there is, besides the aesthetics of expressionism, the "street realism" of Murnau, G. W. Pabst, and others, in which—as in Pabst's *The Love of Jeanne Ney* (1927) or Phil Jutzi's 1931 version of Alfred Döblin's *Berlin Alexanderplatz*—the complex plots of literary nar-

Like a poem, Jean Cocteau's *The Blood of a Poet* (1930) creates a dreamscape of images that resist easy explanation. Statues come to life and rooms lose their gravity. If there is a tale here it is the tale of creativity and imagination being born. (*Photofest*)

ratives would be reduced and intensified through darkly realistic images. In France, one of the most important periods in cinema history, from 1934–1940, has been dubbed "poetic realism," a combination of two of the period's central literary and filmic terms. Film historian George Sadoul defines the poetic realism of French cinema as a combination of poetry and realism developing out of novelist Émile Zola's literary naturalism and the work of several poet/filmmakers, including the avant-garde films of Louis Delluc (*The Woman from Nowhere* [1921]) and the lyrical films of Jean Vigo (*A propos de Nice* [1929] and *Zero for Conduct* [1933]). Two of the most important filmmakers associated with this phase of the film and literature relationship are Jean Renoir and Marcel Carné whose films—such as Renoir's 1934 adaptation of Flaubert's *Madame Bovary*, his 1937 *Grand Illusion*, and Carné's 1938 collaboration with poet-screenwriter Jacques Prévert on *Port of Shadows*—brilliantly develop careful and sometimes elaborate cinematic styles to portray social and historical flashpoints in human and class relations.

Although the world-wide Depression years that defined much of the 1930s promoted escapist fare of nostalgic and sentimental adaptations,

Hollywood was not immune to these demands to produce socially conscious films as part of a new aesthetic. In the United States, the combination of documentary realism and stylistic innovation inspired one of the decade's finest movies and finest literary adaptations of all times: Lewis Milestone's 1930 *All Quiet on the Western Front* (based on Erich Maria Remarque's novel about World War I) began a Hollywood decade that would conclude most famously with the socially stark and disgruntled *The Grapes of Wrath* (1940).

Yet, in the United States the drives toward formal experimentation and social realism would largely be tempered by commercial and political pressures intended to assure certain middle-class values at the movies. This is illustrated most concretely in the 1930–1931 battle over Theodore Dreiser's *An American Tragedy*, a melodramatic but searing critique of modern American society. At the center of this adaptation by Paramount Studios were, besides one of America's greatest novelists, two European directors who embodied the best of the artistic and political potential in film, Sergei Eisenstein and Josef von Sternberg. When Eisenstein submitted a script that Dreiser favored, studio executives

An adaptation of Theodore Dreiser's novel, Josef von Sternberg's *An American Tragedy* (1931) incisively critiques the American social system. The force of the novel, however, became significantly muted by a conservative Hollywood positioned to protect middle-class values. (*Photofest*)

rejected the treatment because it was too political (since Eisenstein carefully followed Dreiser in complicating the hero's guilt and assigning some of it to his social predicament). Over Dreiser's protest, von Sternberg took over the adaptation and made it into a more politically palatable tale of an individual's erotic obsession. Writing for the avant-garde film review *Close Up* (which featured some of the most important literary figures of the time), Harry Potamkin would defend Dreiser's novel and Eisenstein's script by returning to one of the central themes binding film and literature during the period: "The fight for the integrity of this experience [depicted in the novel] is not a personal one, nor even for the rights of authorship. It is a struggle against the debasing of the intellectual and social level of an experience" (186).

Hollywood, Sound, and Literature

As the case of *An American Tragedy* indicates, a very significant, if indirect, force in increased development of literary adaptations is the Production Code or, as it is commonly known, the Hays Code. Established in 1922, the Motion Picture Producers and Distributors Association (MPPDA) aimed to correct the growing image of Hollywood as a den of inequity, scandal, and social subversion, and by the early 1930s the Hays Code had established clear guidelines for the censorship of sexual language and behavior, graphic violence, and other actions that might be deemed immoral or reprehensible. In the 1930s, other groups and codes, such as the 1932–1933 studies by the Payne Fund and the Catholic League of Decency, also attempted to argue guidelines that would prevent movies from becoming too offensive or too far outside the moral mainstream. Of the many effects of these rules and guidelines, one was the growing attraction of literary classics, since literature, even when the subject matter was morally suspect, could often carry a cultural weight sufficient to deflect the censors. In that sense, the Hays Code's encouragement of and the fashion for the cinematic adaptation of literary classics worked as a visible variation on the motif of the 1930s culture attempting to measure and ensure certain social values.

Perhaps even more important to the dialogue between literature and the movies, however, was the coming of sound to the cinema in the late 1920s (usually marked by the phenomenal success of the 1927 *The Jazz Singer*). In her wide-ranging discussion of the theoretical and historical links between film and literature, Marie-Claire Ropars-Wuilleumier has highlighted the critical impact of the introduction of recorded sound on the cinema in the late 1920s. The coming of sound altered and revolutionized many dimensions of film form and film history, but new sound technologies were especially significant in the relationship between film and literature in four far-reaching ways, ways that extended and complicated tendencies already dominating classical cinema: (1) Sound reinforced and expanded the possibilities for realism in the cinema; (2) sound allowed the rapid development of theatrical dialogue within the cinema; (3) the introduction of sound provoked fierce reactions against commercial sound movies since some felt it subverted film's unique artistic potential (and so, ironically watered down its ability to compete aesthetically with literature and other arts) by making the spoken word a major component of film form; and (4) as spoken language enlarged the development of character and character motivation, it expanded narrative or novelistic form as the main structural principle for the movies. In the transition from silent to sound films, from the late 1920s through the early 1930s, these directions for the cinema both confirmed the power of realistic narrative and initiated a reaction against it.

Indeed, the spate of adaptations that appeared in the thirties is one indication of the importance of sound in drawing film and literature closer together. In many ways, the decade of the thirties (and into the forties) represents the golden era of traditional literary adaptations in Hollywood, producing many of the finest examples of literature adapted to classical film form: James Whale's *Frankenstein* (1931), Josef von Sternberg's *Crime and Punishment* (1935), George Cukor's *Dr. Jekyll and Mr. Hyde* (1932) and *Camille* (1936), Rouben Mamoulian's *Becky Sharp* (1935), William Wyler's *Wuthering Heights* (1939), Robert Leonard's *Pride and Prejudice* (1940), and Alfred Hitchcock's *Rebecca* (1940). All of these bear the marks of the technological and stylistic struggles and innovations of the period, upon which literary sources become rich foundations for experimentation and development.

Throughout this period the relationship between the theater world and the film world became especially lively, as elements of the theater once again emerged to counterpoint the forces of narrative realism in the cinema. During this period, theater and film developed particularly strong financial ties as they competed for and exchanged literary materials, as well as personnel, such as director George Cukor, actress Katharine Hepburn, and writer Clifford Odets. The exchange also produced a genre of movies called "backstage musicals" that has continued to the present. Including *On with the Show* (1929), *The Gold Diggers of Broadway* (1929), and *Swingtime* (1936), and later *Singin' in the Rain* (1952), these are movies whose subject matter is the theatrical life behind and in front of the curtain, and they occasionally turn those stories into a commentary on the differences in the two media. In Europe and America, the interplay between theater and film also moved into less commercial ventures, bringing more artistically demanding works from the stage to the screen, such as the 1930 adaptation of Sean O'Casey's

Juno and the Paycock and Paul Robeson's 1933 screen incarnation of Eugene O'Neill's drama *The Emperor Jones.*

Following the swift developments in sound cinema, the surge of dramatic adaptations and novelistic adaptations drew together in a highly creative blend of two regularly contending forces in film history—one emphasizing the external conflictual forces associated with traditional drama and the other exploring character psychology in which internal forces drive a narrative forward. From this creative merger of contending literary forces would appear some of the most accomplished, polished, and successful films in and outside Hollywood, assimilating not only the developing technologies of sound but also, in some cases, the new Technicolor processes of the 1930s. In 1939–1940 Hollywood produced three of the grandest adaptations in the history of cinema, each in its different way fashioning stunning spectacles of human desire and motivation: *The Wizard of Oz* (1939), from L. Frank Baum's 1900 tale; *Gone with the Wind* (1939), based on Margaret Mitchell's 1936 best seller; and *The Grapes of Wrath* (1940), adapted from John Steinbeck's 1939 novel. With

One of the many classic literary adaptations at the end of the 1930s, *The Wizard of Oz* combines Technicolor fantasy and a fundamental narrative quest for home and family. Here the realistic representation of imaginative literary characters illustrates one of the expanding powers of the movies.

THE NOVEL AND FILM

The relationship between the novel (or narrative fiction) and film has always been one of the most dominant and persistent. The origins of the novel extend back through Miguel de Cervantes's seventeenth-century *Don Quixote*, but for many its most notable achievements occurred in the nineteenth century, when a growing middle class of readers was also witnessing the scientific and technological birth of a new realism, a detailed realism that photography and cinema would also promote. Although theatrical structures seemed originally most suited to the stationary camera of early cinema, the development of editing techniques and camera movements pointed the cinema more and more toward the mobile points of view found in the novel and especially in those nineteenth-century prototypes.

Since the turn of the century, most films have used some sort of narrative storyline, making novels (and short stories) attractive to filmmakers. Movies have turned toward a variety of novels—from classics to popular or "pulp" fiction, from eighteenth-century novels to bestsellers that may have appeared only one year earlier. (These choices about the kind of novel and the historical period it comes from are always potentially meaningful in discussing any transposition of a novel into film.) Representing several centuries of literary materials, novels provide fully developed characters and stories that can be easily adapted. If drama offers film models for conflict and spectacle, narrative fiction provides film with materials and models for two primary features of the cinema: (1) *plots* that develop through a *character psychology* that drives the action according to a temporal pattern of (frequently) cause and effect; and (2) a mobile variety of *narrative points of view* that organize those events from one or more perspectives. Thus, in *Gone with the Wind*, the film takes advantage of the novel's chronological depiction of historical and personal change, points of view alternating between spectacles of the Civil War and the individual perspectives of characters like Rhett, the driving desires of Scarlett, and a logic of triumph over the many obstacles and tragedies that confront the characters.

Unlike short stories, novels usually require significant cutting and shrinkage if they are to be recreated in the shorter temporal format of a movie. Thus choices of what to include or omit can be either artistically significant or a matter of economics. If films bring more realism to novels, those films struggle before the novel's *selective* power of descriptive detail (whereby a description is always a meaningful choice of what to describe), the wide variety of numerous points of view available, and the full elaboration of a character's consciousness found in novels. Many novelistic techniques, such as a stream of consciousness style that moves fluidly through a central character's conscious and unconscious perceptions, are extremely difficult to recreate in a film or are considered unpopular with audiences.

Novels respond to the movies in turn. The "Hollywood novel" (e.g., Nathaniel West's *Day of the Locust*) and the "ciné-roman" in France attempt to recreate flat imagistic points of view analogous to the camera eye. In practices of "novelization," successful films are turned into novels that retell the story of the film.

Recommended Readings   George Bluestone's *Novels into Films* and Colin MacCabe's "Realism and the Cinema" (in *Tracking the Signifier*).

all their differences, these films mark, for many, the culmination of the classical film as the most modern of classical literatures.

Despite the remarkable number and quality of film adaptations of literature in the 1930s, at the end of the decade there were signs of strain and unease. Appearing in 1939 alongside that remarkable collection of movies (which also included *Stagecoach* and *Mr. Smith Goes to Washington*), Nathaniel West's 1939 novel *The Day of the Locust*, for instance, is one of the most justly celebrated intersections of literature and the movies. Employing a pictorial style that describes life as if lived across different shots and scenes, the novel sets the desperation of an alienated artist against the numbing frustrations and hysterias produced by the mass media and popular culture of Hollywood. West's novel paints an extremely bleak picture of what movie culture—or at least Hollywood—has to offer individuals struggling to retain their individuality and meaningful social relations. At a moment when narrative and dramatic histories were growing and spreading rapidly into the myths of the screen, West's novel sounds a note of suspicion and warning about the nature and truth of that cinematic literature, a warning that anticipates the next decade.

Works Cited

Cocteau, Jean. *Cocteau on the Film*. New York: Dover, 1972.

Jacobs, Lewis, ed. *The Compound Cinema: The Film Writings of Harry Alan Potamkin*. New York: The Teacher's College Press, 1977.

Ropars-Wuilleumier, Marie-Claire. *De la littérature au cinéma: genèse d'une écriture*. Paris: Armand Colin, 1970.

4

Pens, Pulp, and the Crisis
of the Word, 1940–1960

That the events of World War II altered the perspectives of literature, the cinema, and the relationship between the two is a fundamental fact of this period. For many, the events preceding and informing World War II (as it grew out of the 1914–1918 World War I) represent the violent twists and disruptions of an Enlightenment vision that sees human civilization always progressing through intellectual, technological, and cultural advancements. In a sense, all sides in that global conflict participate, through their increasing technological and industrial resources, in superhuman aspirations: to conquer nature and space, to know more than ever before, to create ideal societies, to make imaginative myths real. The ghastly results of that vision, however, rapidly reveal themselves in the unthinkably inhuman products of those visions: Auschwitz and other Nazi concentration camps and the nuclear victims of Hiroshima and Nagasaki are only the most infamous testimonies to the reversal of a progressive direction in cultural and human history.

Precisely because both had been the vehicles for cultural identities and their myths throughout the twentieth century, film and literature could not help but be affected by this global trauma, a trauma that visibly rattled their confidence in the humanizing truth each claimed to purvey. If during the 1920s and 1930s literature assimilated film as the new vehicle for social change and modern visions, during the 1940s and into the 1950s the failures and inadequacies of that redemption became abundantly clear. Out of these concerns there are two dominant trends that surfaced through the next two decades: (1) The cinema explored and in some cases "deauthorized" the monumental powers of the cultural myths and histories, found often in literary classics and embodied in the figure of the writer and his or her authority; (2) in the cultural rubble left over by the war, claims for personal expression in film, modeled after the individual creativity of writing, attempted to reclaim or to "reauthorize" film as a more personal and human instrument.

Film Exploring Literature

The years of World War II in Europe (1939–1945) continue to produce some of the most accomplished, often literary, epics in film history, featuring such classical movies as *Stagecoach* and *Gone with the Wind* in 1939, *Citizen Kane* in 1941, and Marcel Carné's *Children of Paradise* in 1945. Like many films of this era, these examples sometimes have less a direct relation with a literary source than with the larger cultural place of literary visions. Thus, even though Ford's *Stagecoach* derives directly from an Ernest Haycox story and less directly from Guy de Maupassant's "Boule de suif," it appears an almost archetypal homage to the literary western as an American cultural myth. Cinematic paeans like this are, moreover, only one of many possible ways to represent these stories and myths, which might also be retrieved by the movies as a kind of nostalgia or as an object of criticism. Following these and other strategies, movies throughout this period tend to retrieve a literary or cultural past to measure, sharply or vaguely, the distance between those past cultures and the troubled world of the 1940s. One thematic thread that runs through much of this work is appropriately the struggle to define and understand the history of individuals and nations, and the intersection of film and literature during this period often replays this issue of cultural history and its relation to personal and public memory.

From this angle, Orson Welles's *Citizen Kane* functions as almost an allegory for the relationship between film and literature during this period. Leaving his rocketing stage and radio career to come to Hollywood to make an adaptation of Joseph Conrad's *Heart of Darkness*, Welles makes instead *Citizen Kane*, a film that still bears the oblique marks of that original idea in its story of an obsessive individual whose greed and ideals ultimately alienate him from the world he hoped to remake in his image. The narrative complexities of Conrad's novel also leave their traces on Welles's movie as both construct convoluted narratives in which the search through words and images never finally reveals the truth. Indeed, that Conrad's novel suggests that its demonic hero, Kurtz, is the product of the history of European culture provides a charged link with Welles's cultural icon Kane, who hobnobs proudly with Hitler and other political forces on the brink of World War II and who proudly identifies himself as first and foremost an American.

Two other important films that use cultural masterpieces and memories to address the trauma of history are Marcel Carné's 1945 *Children of Paradise* and Laurence Olivier's *Henry V* (1945). The first tells the story

One of the most celebrated adaptations of a Shakespearean play, Laurence Olivier's *Henry V* (1945) faithfully recreates the stage of Shakespeare's Globe Theatre, only to shift its perspective to the Technicolor realism of the movies. In this way the movie both acknowledges its past and draws attention to the historical distance between the sixteenth and twentieth centuries. (*Archive Photos*)

of the theatrical world of nineteenth-century Paris when the culture of classical theater and the popular boulevard entertainments of mimes and other street performers interact. Its elaborate narrative and complex theatrical mise-en-scènes move in two directions: Most prominently, the film creates a homage to the artistic brilliance of an older period of cultural and social change, yet, concomitantly, its shadowy and wistful perspective on those former times serves to ironize that lost world, making the human vivacity of that former historical moment seem, from the perspective of the 1940s, an illusory dream. With Olivier's film, too, much of the appreciative analysis that has surrounded it seems fully justified, not simply for its inventive stylistic and structural engagements with Shakespeare's play, but also in how those formal features index critical historical shifts in the relationship between film and literature. As the film moves between the staged world of Shakespeare's Elizabethan theater and the cinematic open spaces of Henry's Technicolored forces leaving for France, the film becomes as much about historical distance as about continuities. Although the patriotic fever of the original play pervades this remake completely, the Technicolor orchestrations of its ancient war makes its classic vision an inspiring memory of tropes and gestures, whose distance from the horrors of modern times means that they can only be *performed* in a highly self-conscious way.

In the United States, notable contributors to these reflections on classical forms, literatures, and their value during these times are the immigrant filmmakers, technicians, and actors. Spurred on by the Parufamet agreement of 1926 (a three-way agreement between the American studios, Paramount and MGM, and the German studio UFA), the movement of immigrant artists and movie craftsmen continues through the 1930s and begins to impact Hollywood throughout the thirties and forties. This influx of Europeans such as von Stroheim, Fritz Lang, Max Ophuls, Billy Wilder, Douglas Sirk, and others brings with it a deep commitment to art and poetic cinema; when movies begin to question the forms and assumptions of their cultural heritage in the 1940s, these directors and their films often contribute significantly to the shift toward other relationships for film and literature. Those relationships extend the questioning of history and its instabilities beyond the classical paradigms that thrived on adaptations of literary classics.

Some of the most important films following these alternative literary perspectives in the movies are the detective films and other dark and violent movies associated with the *film noirs* movement. In part a product of the style imported from German Expressionism, these movies—from *The Maltese Falcon* (1941) to *Double Indemnity* (1944), *The Big Sleep* (1946), and *Touch of Evil* (1958)—are characterized by plots of dark passions and crime in which the law can no longer be trusted and a visual style that emphasizes shadows and spatial confusion. More important in the relationship of film and literature, these films of the forties and early fifties turn toward popular (usually detective) fiction and often swerve from the clear linearity and chronologies of classical literature and cinema to foreground multiple plot lines and narrative gaps in the action. Often constructed around a first-person literary narrative recreated through a voice-over film narration, this popular fiction, sometimes dubbed "hard-boiled fiction" or "pulp fiction," concentrates on socially isolated and morally marginal characters in a threatening and shifting world.

There can be little doubt that these new literary inspirations indirectly mirror the larger historical and social disturbances beginning in the 1930s and climaxing in World War II. They likewise reconfirm, first, a move away from classical literature and its association with certain cultural traditions and hierarchies, and, second, a willingness to explore, in search of new realisms, more experimental narrative patterns and characters outside the literary mainstream, specifically through the work of the detective fiction of writers such as Dashiell Hammett, James Cain, and Raymond Chandler. Indeed, one suggestive moment in this shift between critically canonized literatures and minor literatures is the tale of adaptation of *To Have and Have Not* (1944), produced when director Howard Hawks dared Ernest Hemingway to let him have what Hawks considered the writer's worst novel to transform into a successful film. With the screenwriting help of another great American novelist, William Faulkner, this "bad" work of literature became one of the finest examples of a cinema inspired by the rough edges of troubled fiction. Throughout the United States, minor literature and unpolished stories increasingly became the source for some of the most trenchant films of the next decade, including numerous Hitchcock movies of the 1950s and the 1955 films *Night of the Hunter*, produced from a minor Davis Grubb novel, and *Rebel without a Cause*, from the short story "The Blind Run."

That film noir and other innovative kinds of movies throughout this period attracted some of the most important writers of twentieth-century fiction—William Faulkner, Bertolt Brecht, Graham Greene (whose novels were often adapted for the screen), and many others—adds to the paradoxes and contradictions that describe the rapport between the two arts during the forties and fifties. Serious theatrical and literary writers (including journalists) from the thirties through the forties began to gravitate to a film industry that was formerly viewed with deep suspicion; at the same time films and screenplays begin to break away from the dominance of literary culture and to innovate by creatively adapting the much less intimidating forms of popular literature. It is no wonder that scriptwriting during this period drew so many celebrated writers to experiment in a new idiom.

Finally, two cataclysmic industrial and political events added to the turbulence surrounding writers, literature, and movies as the 1940s turned into the 1950s. The first was the 1948 Paramount Decision in which the courts ruled that the main studios (Paramount, Warner Brothers, Loew's [MGM], Twentieth Century-Fox, RKO, Universal, Columbia, and United Artists) violated antitrust laws by monopolizing the film business (through control of theater chains, block-booking, and other means of keeping out independent production and distribution practices). This decision in effect initiated the dispersal of the studio system through which classical Hollywood movies had flourished. As a consequence, independent filmmaking began its expansion (between 1946 and 1956 the number of independent films doubled to 150), and this growth of independence in turn encouraged the more active kind of relationship between writers, books, and movies that film noir and similar films were encouraging in other ways.

The second event struck directly at writers in Hollywood—the investigations of the House Un-American Activities Committee (HUAC) hearings. Adding to the tensions in the relationship between writing and film of this period, political conservatives, led by Senator Joseph McCarthy, sought out members of the Hollywood movie community—

most notably the screenwriters—whom they suspected of being communists. Dalton Trumbo and Bertolt Brecht are just two of the writers called before the committee that condemned some to serve jail time for refusing to cooperate with the hearings. Others, who were, or were not necessarily, part of the famous "Hollywood Ten" called before the committee, were blacklisted from working in Hollywood. Jules Dassin and Joseph Losey, two of the most creative writers to cross between theater and film, were casualties of this process and ended up doing most of their later work outside Hollywood (Losey in Europe as a renowned interpreter of Harold Pinter's plays). In 1949, Robert Rossen adapted Robert Penn Warren's *All the King's Men* as a bitter tale of political machinery and demagoguery, and, ironically or predictably, as a member of the "Hollywood Nineteen," he was subpoenaed by HUAC.

If the Hollywood studios were being forced to make way for more independent relations between writers and filmmaking, the HUAC hearings made clear the massive challenges facing independent and creative writing in Hollywood then. Two useful examples of this paradox and problem are *Sunset Blvd.* (1950) and *Native Son* (1951). With some irony, the winner of three Oscars in 1950 (including best screenplay), *Sunset Blvd.*, tells the gloomy and disturbing tale of a murdered screen-

Sunset Blvd. (1950) is a movie about a delusory movie queen and a dead screenwriter who paradoxically acts as the voice-over narrator of the story of his own death. Beyond the drama of the murder mystery, the film suggests a wry perspective on the turbulent role of the writer in a changing Hollywood. (*Photofest*)

writer from the voice-over perspective of that same writer, present but dead. In it the writer-protagonist cynically remarks that "audiences don't know [that] anyone writes a picture. They think the actors make it up as they go along." This contradictory position in which the writer is both acknowledged and denied (fictionally, politically, or industrially) becomes nearly an allegory of the "deauthorizing" of the writer that characterizes the relationship of film and literature during these years. A second illustration of this deauthorization of the writer of a literary tradition, as a twisted engagement with literary authority and tradition, is the saga of the adaptation of Richard Wright's 1940 novel *Native Son*. Given the novel's blistering attack on racism in the United States, Wright felt that it could be adequately adapted only outside Hollywood—specifically in Argentina, in 1951. The result, however, was a desperately lame film that even in its muted form, was banned and repressed when it first appeared in the United States, marginalizing outside the movie mainstream one of the central voices in African-American writing. Here, and in many other cases of new writing and the movies, a central irony appears: So many dramas of deauthorization occur, throughout the 1950s, just as the writer as an independent literary force becomes the model for a new creativity in a film industry undergoing major changes and looking for new directions

A similar deauthorizing and suspicion of the traditions of high culture informed the major changes that were occurring in film cultures around the world. In Europe, we see somewhat different versions of these dramas about film, literature, writing, and language. After World War II, many salient parts of European film culture seemed to turn sharply from the literary traditions that had supported the cinema since the beginning, but which now became suspect when viewed across the horrific products of Western culture. Most famously, Italian neorealism initiated a call for a depiction of the social realities left out of the grand fictions and theatrical displays of Hollywood films, and this movement would produce numerous decidedly unliterary and flatly realistic dramas of postwar life in Italy, such as Roberto Rossellini's *Rome, Open City* (1945) and Vittorio De Sica's *The Bicycle Thief* (1948). While film and literature were exploring their relationship most fruitfully and creatively in some corners of Europe and Hollywood, one of the celebrated spokespersons for Italian neorealism, Cesare Zavattini, called for the removal of the story from the screenplay. Even off the Italian screens, the postwar concern with the social realism of shattered lives produced stark literary landscapes in the writings of Elio Vittorini, Vasco Pratolini, Cesare Pavese, and later the fiction of Pasolini.

Besides the Italians, other European film cultures and literary movements participated in this call for a new realism sprung from the devastations and insecurities unleashed and recorded by World War II.

THE SCREENPLAY

As a kind of writing that precedes the filming of a topic or story, screenwriting is a practice between literary writing and a finished movie. While the first films rarely worked from a script or screenplay, this changed quickly, and movies today work from screenplays that have been revised many times. Within the studio system, the first stage of a screenplay is often a one- or two-page summary of an idea that comes from a "programming" or story department that is charged with developing potential material from newspapers or "literary properties." With a successful plot, this is followed by a thirty-to-sixty-page treatment, which is an extended summary and outline of the main idea and plot of a film. After this stage, a detailed screenplay may be developed through many stages (and sometimes by different screenwriters). A final shooting script will develop specific scenes with descriptions of the settings, actions, and dialogue.

The connections between a screenplay and a finished film can vary considerably. Some filmmakers work quite creatively and loosely from a screenplay, changing dialogue and action as they shoot the film or allowing actors to improvise (as with the films of John Cassavettes or Mike Leigh). Others insist that the script be followed strictly and often use a script that details precise camera angles and positions. In any case, a screenplay should rarely be seen as the verbal equivalent of the film images, and to study a screenplay as literature means perceiving it as a form of writing between literature and film.

Many of the most reputable literary figures of the twentieth century have worked as screenwriters, the movie industry hoping to take advantage of both their reputations and their abilities as writers: Gabriele D'Annunzio, William Faulkner, Marguerite Duras, and Peter Handke are a sampling. Although many writers consider screenwriting only a prelude to the real work of filmmaking, others, such as Pasolini, have argued that the screenplay is a literary work in its own right.

Indeed there may be some justification in considering the screenwriter as controlling the perspective and ideas of a film as much as the director. Thus screenwriters like Anita Loos (*Gentlemen Prefer Blondes* [1928, 1953]), Howard Koch (*Letter from an Unknown Woman* [1948]), or Garson Kanin (*Woman of the Year* [1942]) produced scripts that often have the textual consistencies and personal voice used to identify good literature and creative writers. A number of daring directors were, in fact, first scriptwriters who emerged from the turbulence of the forties and fifties to direct new kinds of movies: Richard Brooks (*The Blackboard Jungle* [1955]), Joseph Mankiewicz (*All about Eve* [1950]), Robert Rossen (*The Hustler* [1961]), and Samuel Fuller *Pickup on South Street* [1953]) dramatize the crucial creative links between writing and filming, especially during the 1950s (and in many other decades as well).

Recommended Readings Béla Balázs's "The Script," Pasolini's "The Screenplay as a Structure That Wants to Be Another Structure (in *Heretical Empiricism*), and Douglas Garrett Winston's *The Screenplay as Literature*. Also recommended is Pat McGilligan's *Backstory* series, which features interviews with screenwriters.

By the mid-fifties, for example, the British Free Cinema provided its own form of this realism in short documentary films. Later it would join the parallel work being done by the "angry young men" of the British theater and literary world, and produce filmmaker Tony Richardson's adaptation of John Osborne's play *Look Back in Anger* (1959) and Karel Reisz's version of Alan Sillitoe's novel *Saturday Night and Sunday Morning* (1960), both hugely successful literary accommodations of the tough realism that punctuated the fifties. These and other films of the British New Cinema of the 1960s would foster film/literary collaborations between Joseph Losey and Harold Pinter (*The Servant* [1963] and *The Accident* [1967]) and William Golding and Peter Brook (*Lord of the Flies* [1963]), among others.

One final and tangentially related instance of this renegotiation of authors, authority, and realism in the fifties is the spread of method acting in drama and film. Usually identified with the Actor's Studio of Elia Kazan and Lee Strasberg and derived to a large extent from Stanislavsky's work in the Moscow Art Theater, method acting altered acting on the stage and screen for the next several decades, as a tactic in which actors would intensely "inhabit" the role being played in order to forsake the authority of the actor's own personality and to recreate the full reality of the character. This encounter between a literary character and the filmic or dramatic performance of that character's reality quickly became the heart of much modern film or theater. One of the most powerful examples of it is Marlon Brando's performance in Kazan's screen version of Tennessee Williams's *A Streetcar Named Desire* (1951). In this particular example, not only does Williams's play become a literature confronting an illusory past to unveil the sordid realism of the present, but Brando's and Kazan's performances of that play (as a character and a film) permanently instantiate that work as a literature with particularly real bodies, actual movements, and historically determined spaces.

In an important sense, the film *A Streetcar Named Desire* deauthorizes and reauthorizes a literary character and work in terms of a more visceral and more historical realism. In this context, it shares a common ground with film performances from Orson Welles's remakings of Shakespeare's *Macbeth* (1948) and *Othello* (1952) to Akira Kurosawa's astonishingly original recreation of Shakespeare's *Macbeth* as *Throne of Blood* (1957). Whereas realism since the nineteenth century functions as a way of measuring the distance between film and literature, realism of the 1950s now appears—in the United States and other societies around the world—as a way of binding new filmmakers and new writers in a common effort to rethink and recreate, in terms of the *present historical reality*, the authorities and authors of both the literary and the cinematic past. Masters of literature now become very malleable material for the new authors of cinema.

More than simply adapting Tennessee Williams's play, Elia Kazan's *A Streetcar Named Desire* (1951) remakes that play as a singular cinematic achievement. The physical performances of Vivien Leigh and Marlon Brando, along with the creative realism of the sets and cinematography, help to establish Kazan's *A Streetcar Named Desire* as an important piece of film history and not merely a filmed version of a play. (*Photofest*)

Reauthoring Film

As a continuation of the unease that closed the 1940s, films in the 1950s marked a major shift in the rapport between film and literature. Literature began, decisively I believe, to loose its hierarchical control over film, and films began to claim their own rights and powers as an independent way of examining and employing the literary paradigms of the past and the harsh realities of a postwar world. Whether intentionally or not, the movies seem no longer to need the authority of a sanctioned literary work, and can now promote their own rebellious independence by choosing works of popular literary culture outside the respected literary mainstream, works that often provide enough intellectual space for the filmmaker to do what he or she wishes to do in filmic form. Despite being described as a filmmaker with "such a great reliance on literature, with such a pronounced affinity with his country's literary culture," the Swedish director Ingmar Bergman—one of the most singularly influential filmmakers to emerge from the 1950s—would claim "Film has nothing to do with literature; the character and substance of the two art forms are usually in conflict" (quoted in D. G. Winston, 96). Dismissing the authority of literature, other filmmakers, as well, would position themselves as the creative authors of the new cinema.

Like Bergman, many individuals behind the French New Wave (Jean-Luc Godard, Francois Truffaut, Alain Renais, Agnes Varda, and others) often argued that a dependence on literary sources was an uncreative and retrograde way to make films. This attitude became distilled in Francois Truffaut's famous attack on a "cinema of quality" and its dependence on the literal adaptation of well-known classics (in his essay "A Certain Tendency of the French Cinema"). In 1948, however, André Bazin, with typical prescience for the direction of film history, noted the contradictions and paradoxes in this claim, suggesting that even the Italian neorealists remained indebted to literature. Like several other postwar cinemas, Bazin argued, Italian neorealism sprang from a close rapport with the American novel as it developed decades earlier. Citing the novels of William Faulkner, John Dos Passos, and Ernest Hemingway specifically, he stressed a more creative notion of adaptation. For Bazin, these instances of adaptation worked across historical and cultural differences, allowing film to seek past literature which accorded with present times:

> So then, while Hollywood adapts bestseller after bestseller at the same time moving further away from the spirit of this literature, it is in Italy, naturally with an ease that excludes any notion of willful and deliberate imitation, that the cinema of American literature has become a reality.... It is a long while since the modern novel created its realist revolution, since it combined behaviorism, a reporter's technique, and the ethic of violence. Far from the cinema having the slightest effect on this revolution, as is commonly held today, a film like *Paisa* [*Paisan*] proves that the cinema was twenty years behind the contemporary novel. It is not the least of the merits of the Italian cinema that it has been able to find the truly cinematic equivalent for the most important literary revolution of our time. (II, 39–40)

In France as well, despite different filmmakers' denunciation of one literary tradition, the movies begin to reinvent themselves out of other literary paradigms and institutions. Poet, dramatist, and filmmaker Jean Cocteau is a well-known transitional figure in the appearance of the French New Wave. He had insisted, since his 1930 film *The Blood of the*

A collaboration between writer Marguerite Duras and filmmaker Alain Resnais, *Hiroshima Mon Amour* (1960) describes the affair of a French actress in Hiroshima as complex narrative about memory and communication. One of the early successes of the French New Wave, the film uses the technical resources of movies for new kinds of artistic freedoms, expressions, and communications. (*Movie Still Archives*)

Poet and through his 1946 *Beauty and the Beast*, that "poetry" encompassed many practices, including filmmaking. Historically related to popular ciné-clubs (where important, as well as obscure, films would be screened and discussed), Henri Langlois's Cinématheque Francais defines the 1950s in France (after going underground during World War II) by becoming a library of modern film culture, replacing books with the texts of films from different nations and historical eras. The cinématheque and those other ciné-clubs were bound up with a growing number of journals, including *La Revue du cinéma* (started in 1946), *Positif* (1952), and the *Cahiers du cinéma* (1951). These journals, mirroring the literary journals and reviews that had been arbitrators and promoters of literary culture since 1800, argued and educated a developing cinema culture that would see and discriminate about films as readers and critics do about literature.

Appropriately, the critical writer who fought for film in these journals became the cinematic auteur aspiring to use the camera like a pen. In 1959–1960, the landmark years for the French new cinema, three of these writer/critics would show the world what the revitalized authors of

---

AUTHORS AND AUTEURS

One central connection between literature and film is the writer. With literature, the place and function of the writer is fairly clear: He or she is the author who expresses and organizes a feeling, a perspective, an idea, or a story through words. Today we generally describe this authorial activity as creative, in part because this work is considered so personal and imaginative. This conception of the author has provided an immediate obstacle in finding a corresponding figure for the creative force in filmmaking where the literary writer has been compared to the screenwriter, the director, and even producers, stars, studios, and super-agents. That few, if any, of these movie creators have the independence and isolation associated with the activity of a literary author has invariably complicated the equation.

Of the many discussions of the filmmaker as *auteur*, Peter Wollen's is one of the more complex and discriminating. In 1969 he discusses auteurism, specifically in how it might relate to adaptation:

> What the *auteur* theory demonstrates is that the director is not simply in command of a performance of a pre-existing text.... Don Siegel was recently asked on television what he took from Hemingway's short story for his film, *The Killers*; Siegel replied that "the only thing taken from it was the catalyst that a man has been killed by somebody and he did not try to run away." The word Siegel chose—"catalyst"— could not be better. Incidents and episodes in the original screenplay or novel can act as catalysts; they are the agents which are introduced in the mind (conscious or unconscious) of the *auteur* and react there with the motifs and themes characteristic of his work. The director does not subordinate himself to another author; his source is only a pretext, which provides catalysts, scenes, which fuse with his own preoccupations to produce a radically new work. Thus the manifest process of performance, the treatment of a subject, conceals the latent production of a quite new text, the production of a director as a *auteur*." (Wollen 112–113)

Auteurism may become more complicated by recognizing that even literary authors rarely have the romantic independence imagined for them, and that only since the nineteenth century have writers and societies tried to hide or disguise the amount of social and commercial machinery and social activity that shapes the writing of a novel, play, or poem. Filmmaker Atom Egoyan is, for many, an example of a contemporary auteur whose relation to that label is complicated by industrial and commercial pressures. His attitude toward adaptation suggests some of the complications in seeing the film auteur as an author of personal expression and perspectives: On adapting a Russell Banks' novel for his 1997 *The Sweet Hereafter*, he says, "I'd become impatient with my own stylistic predispositions. How do you challenge yourself? By attaching yourself to an existing property" (Philadelphia Inquirer, p. C3).

Recommended Readings   John Caughie's *Theories of Authorship*, Timothy Corrigan's "The Commerce of Auteurism" (in *A Cinema without Walls*), and Dudley Andrew's "The Unauthorized Auteur Today."

the film image could bring forth: Francois Truffaut's *400 Blows*, an intensely personal story of a delinquent boy rebelling against encrusted traditions and a failed family, Alain Resnais and Marguerite Duras's *Hiroshima Mon Amour*, the struggle of two illicit lovers to find a language for their wartime memories in France and Japan, and Jean-Luc Godard's *Breathless*, a wry portrait of outlaw behavior in a equally wry and ironic play with the powers of cinematic idioms.

The idea that the movie camera can be used like a writer's pen becomes one of the most suggestive and inspiring metaphors for alternative film practices in this decade, both as a vehicle for a more "personal" cinema and as a pathway to more and more complex arguments for a language of the cinema comparable to a literary language. That film technology makes available a new lightweight Arriflex camera (and later other models) during this period dovetails with those other social shifts toward independent cinema and aesthetic claims for a more critical and creative cinema. With this more mobile equipment filmmakers could work more quickly and individually, as one might express oneself through words on a page.

Well removed from Hollywood, then, the attention to the language and writing of cinema received a more intellectual and less overtly social twist in the 1950s and 1960s. Whereas the first quarter-century saw movie culture working to absorb and accommodate literary traditions as a way of solidifying a respectable position in that culture, in the fifties and later, film cultures began to stress the distinctions of film and literature, or the more creative possibilities in that relationship, by emphasizing its unique artistic practices—modeled, somewhat paradoxically, after literary figures and paradigms. This argument about a distinctive cinematic language has appeared before—from the hieroglyphic idiom that many saw in early cinema to the defenders of the pure language of silent cinema. But now, that language of cinema is endowed with the power of personal expression. Alexandre Astruc's famous article "La Camera-Stylo" articulated this position most definitively in 1948: "The cinema is quite simply becoming a means of expression, just as all other arts have before it, and in particular painting and the novel ... cinema like literature is not so much a particular art as a language which can express any sphere of thought" (17, 19). In 1960, filmmaker Maya Deren goes even farther than Astruc's equation of literary language and a filmic language in asking film to break entirely with its literary heritages and to choose subjects and forms suited to its own unique language:

> If cinema is to take its place beside the others as a full-fledged art form, it must cease merely to record realities that owe nothing of their actual existence to the film instrument. Instead, it must create a total experience so much out of the very nature of the instrument as to be

inseparable from its means. It must relinquish the narrative disciplines it has borrowed from literature and its timid imitation of the causal logic of narrative plots, a form which flowered as a celebration of the earthbound, step-by-step concept of time, space and relationship which was part of the primitive materialism of the nineteenth century. Instead, it must develop the vocabulary of filmic images and evolve the syntax of filmic techniques which relate those. It must determine the disciplines inherent in the medium, discover its own structural modes, explore the new realms and dimensions accessible to it and so enrich our culture artistically as science has done in its own province. (70)

Situated between the deauthorization of literature and the reauthorization of themselves as authors, many other emerging and independent cinemas use language as a model for film, not, however, simply to underline the expressive possibilities of film but to expand its connections with the other "languages" of society, especially popular culture. In this way, the French New Wave articulates the paradox of film as and beyond literature. As T. Jefferson Kline remarks about this most influential of the new waves: "In usurping the place of the writer, these filmmakers simply recast the meta-literary concerns of the 1950s into meta-cinematic ones" (3–4). Using film as a language, but a more mobile and critical language than literary words, these filmmakers aim to call into question the classical claims of literature to transparently reveal reality and to replace that tradition and authority with a filmic language that, often through its association with popular culture, could create critical arguments about the dominant forms and languages of culture. The new writers of film, in short, would, like the Beat poets and other alternative literary movements of this time, work to create a language of cinema fully aware of its limitations and relativity, willfully enlisted with cultural fields and personal voices that avoid literary hierarchies and centers.

Works Cited

Astruc, Alexandre. "The Birth of the New Avant-Garde: La Canera-Stylo." In *The New Wave*. Ed. Peter Graham. New York: Doubleday, 1968.

Bazin, André. *What Is Cinema?* Vol. 2. Berkeley, CA: University of California Press, 1971.

Deren, Maya. "Cinematography: The Creative Use of Reality." In *Film Theory and Criticism*. 4th ed. Ed. Gerald Mast, Marshall Cohen, and Leo Braudy. New York: Oxford University Press, pp. 59–70.

"Interview with Atom Egoyan." *Philadelphia Inquirer*, February 21, 1996.

Kline, T. Jefferson. *Screening the Text: Intertextuality in New Wave French Cinema.* Baltimore, MD: The John Hopkins University. Press, 1992.

Winston, Douglas Garrett. *The Screenplay as Literature.* Rutherford, NJ: Fairleigh Dickinson University Press, 1973.

Wollen, Peter. *Signs and Meaning in the Cinema.* Rev. ed. Bloomington, IN: Indiana University Press, 1972.

5

ACADEMIC CINEMA
AND INTERNATIONAL
SPECTACLES, 1960–1980

What characterized the 1960s in most world cultures was a pervasive rattling of social cages: The Vietnam War, the Paris Student Riots, the Soviet invasion of Czechoslovakia in 1968, both the Black and Women's Liberation Movements, and youth cultures promoting the freedom of sexuality and drugs, all contribute to societies around the world questioning and reacting to rapid changes. As an extension of the anxieties, suspicions, and restlessness of the 1950s, traditional views about family and gender, race and religion, and education and entertainment are sometimes radically confronted during these times. One trend that figures most prominently in the relationship of film and literature is the continued internationalization of film as a language to be examined on both personal and ideological grounds. From it, however, three more specific directions appear: (1) Literature of the fifties and the sixties provides film with stories and other materials to challenge the status quo positions that, in the first half of the century, movies helped to establish; (2) as literature turns to film for structures and forms more in touch with modern experience, film declares not only its independence but to a certain extent its supremacy, recuperating and remaking both classic and contemporary literature as "intertextual arguments" or collaborations; and (3) Hollywood films particularly continue the imperative to transform big literature into big spectacles.

Fueling these changes in the relationship between film and literature are three demographic changes in the movie business (most visibly in the United States), all of which start in the 1950s and all of which relate to those three aesthetic patterns. First, the primary audience for the movies grows younger and younger, and this "teenaging" of the moviegoer leads to more youthful, energetic, restless, and often discontented films. Second, as an extension of the ciné-club tradition in France, film culture becomes a central part of colleges and universities, from unofficial film societies to regular film courses in the classrooms, and these academizations of movie culture more consciously shape intellectual audiences and practices at the movies. Third, the social and geographic movement of urban populations to the suburbs encouraged different types of moviegoing habits and different types of movies that must compete with television and draw audiences out of the isolation of their homes by casting movies as major, if not spectacular, events.

The Subversive Power of Literature as Film

Although movies in the 1960s describe other directions and activities, one prominent rapport between film and literature suggests a more pronounced stage in the historical reversals begun in the 1950s. Unlike the relationship in the first three decades of the twentieth century, literature during the sixties does not become a traditional source for textual and cultural respectability but rather the source for social and aesthetic challenges. Following those larger social trends, American movies during the fifties and sixties risk more confrontational and daring subject matter, which results in a particularly rich relationship with works of literature outside the mainstream and outside the classical traditions. In the expanding literature of the fifties and sixties, sexuality becomes a more explicit subject to be examined and celebrated; the sanctities of the family come into question; and political and historical flashpoints, scandals, and nightmares are exposed and derided.

Contemporary literature becomes, then, an invigorating source for a film culture dissatisfied with the status quo and mainstream. Movies like Joseph Strick's 1963 film of Jean Genet's play *The Balcony* and his shocking attempt in 1967 to adapt James Joyce's monumental *Ulysses* were two of several daring literary adaptations by Strick that struck an appropriately confrontational chord. *The Pawnbroker* (1965) and *Who's Afraid of Virginia Woolf?* (1966)—the first derived from Edward Lewis Wallant and the second from Edward Albee's play—are two notable examples of movies whose grating depictions of society failed to pass the censors and were released without an MPAA certificate. Even the 1963 *Tom Jones* turned the eighteenth-century novel into a gleefully scandalous celebration of sensual pleasures. Indeed, a contributing factor and an inevitable result of this outbreak of a new and subversive breed of literary adaptations was the revision of the MPAA rating system to allow more flexibility and experimentation with the matter and manner of movies. Faced with the image of unsettling but acclaimed literary works, even the censors seemed to acknowledge that literature should be allowed to provide film with ways to challenge middle-class perspectives rather than to comfort and secure that group the way classical literary adaptations once did.

Mike Nichols's 1966 adaptation of Edward Albee's *Who's Afraid of Virginia Woolf?* matches a new kind of literature and a new kind of film. Both are a confrontation with illusory and disintegrating social values—especially those associated with the family and sexuality. (*Mel Traxel/Motion Picture & Television Photo Archives*)

Collaborative Enterprises

One striking tendency in the late fifties that continued through the sixties was an increasing number of literary and film collaborations not only on the subject matter of the movies but also with the metaphors, tropes, perspectives, and structural organizations of the film. In those literature/film exchanges in the immediate postwar period, we identified a process of deauthorization and reauthorization, whereby filmmakers critically examined or rejected one literary tradition and rediscovered another in their films. Gradually, however, that pattern of exchange becomes more and more an equitable sharing in which each sees the other as participating in common theoretical and aesthetic concerns. Similar to the modernity that film brought to literature in the twenties and thirties, the imagistic structures of film in the sixties interacted with the verbal play of contemporary literature to create a shared project often called postmodernity, a vision of life and culture as a place of decentered, surface images.

During this period, film offered literature another way of perceiving the world, a visual rhetoric that captured the crisis and desires of a new

THE ESSAY FILM

One of the rarely acknowledged products of the collaboration between film and literature is the essay film. The essay as a literary form has its origins, for most historians, in the writings of Michel de Montaigne who wrote short personal reflections on the facts and idiosyncrasies of his everyday life. The term *essay* comes from the French word meaning "attempts" or "testings," and remains suggestive of the provisional and fragmentary perspectives of a prose writing practiced by Bacon, Samuel Johnson, William Hazlitt, Walter Pater, Virginia Woolf, and some of the best contemporary writers from James Baldwin to Joan Didion.

As a film practice it is usually identified with the documentary forms that extend back to the beginnings of cinema history and specifically to the Lumière brothers. In the 1950s, documentary practices experimented with numerous formal innovations, including the presence of the personal voice and perspective of the filmmaker as he or she reflects on the realities before the camera. In bringing these essayistic innovations to film, postwar European cinema offered the most recognizable essay films as a merger of that literary tradition and the new investigations of realism in the fifties.

While its most renowned practitioners in the 1950s included Chris Marker, Alain Renais, and Agnes Varda, it was Godard in the 1960s who described his own work during this period—*Made in the USA* (1966) and *La Chinoise* (1967) for example—as essayistic. According to Godard, "I consider myself an essayist; I do essays in the form of novels and novels in the form of essays: Simply I film them instead of writing them" (Giannetti 19). Variations on the essay film can also be found in the experimental documentaries of Jonas Mekas and later in the work of Raoul Ruiz, Wim Wenders, and Trinh T. Minh-ha.

Characteristic of the essay film are (1) a usually—but not necessarily—short documentary subject, (2) the lack of a dominant narrative organization (although narrative may provide one of several patterns in the film), and (3) the interaction of a personal voice or vision, sometimes in the form of a voice-over. In the essay film, the interaction of that subjective perspective and the reality before it becomes a testing or questioning of both, and the structure of the film, like the literary essay, follows the undetermined movement of that dialogue.

Recommended Readings Michael Renov's *"Lost, Lost, Lost*: Mekas as Essayist" and Bill Nichols's *Blurred Boundaries.*

"society of spectacle." One of the advocates of the so-called new novel, Alain Robbe-Grillet accepts this offer—in novels like *The Voyeur* (1955) and *Snapshots* (1962), in a theoretical study *For a New Novel* (1963), and a landmark film *Last Year in Marienbad* (1961), and makes both his films and novels exercises in external visual form and the imagistic constructions of presence without meaning. "Man looks at the world" he writes,

Helke Sander's *Redupers* is not quite a story and not quite a documentary. It alternates between documenting the daily struggles of a single woman and recording her reflections on those struggles, and so approximates the strategies of a literary essay.

"and the world does not look back at him" (58). Profoundly influenced by the new cinema of the fifties and sixties, poet Adrienne Rich writes poems that internalize the collage structures of alternative movies, explaining in her "Images for Godard":

> the mind of the poet is the only poem
> the poet is at the movies
> dreaming the film-maker's dream but differently
> free in the dark as if asleep (53)

Indicative of the fragmented, dislocated, and imagistic sensibility shared by writers and filmmakers during this time is this observation by the alienated protagonist of Walker Percy's 1961 *The Moviegoer*: "Other people treasure memorable moments in their lives.... What I remember is the time John Wayne killed three men with a carbine as he was falling to the dusty street in *Stagecoach*, and the time the kitten found Orson Welles in the doorway of *The Third Man*." About his 1960 novel *Laughter*

THE FILM NOVEL

W hat most obviously defines the film novel is that the action and events take place around movies or movie culture. This could mean a setting in a film center such as Hollywood or a character whose thoughts and experiences are determined by the movies. Although sometimes described more narrowly as "the Hollywood novel," novels of this kind have been written throughout this century with increasing frequency, several having both critical and commercial success: F. Scott Fitzgerald's *The Last Tycoon*, Nathaniel West's *The Day of the Locust*, Luigi Pirandello's *Shoot!*, and Vladimir Nabokov's *Laughter in the Dark* are only a sampling. In one sense, film novels are only a particular version of what other novels do when they assimilate the different social forms and discourses into their plots and backgrounds—in this case the settings and discourses of film culture.

As with many of the novels, film novels can go beyond simply using movie culture to surround and define characters. Film novels can use film and its techniques in a variety of other ways as well: (1) as measures of historical or cultural values that introduce debates about history, gender, or other social values, as does Michael Tolkin's *The Player* or, in less obvious ways, Thomas Pynchon's *Gravity's Rainbow*; (2) as part of a style and structure, in which the language and formal shapes of the novel mimic or approach the forms and structures used by the cinema; (3) as focal points for stories about seeing and the psychology of perception; and (4) as philosophical or epistemological touchstones for discussing the relationship between different registers of reality, as in both Manuel Puig's novel and Hector Babenco's film *Kiss of the Spider Woman* (1985).

Less prevalent are film theater or film poems, which raise similar questions. Not surprisingly, film novels are a favorite genre of literature for movies to adapt.

Recommended Reading   Gavriel Moses's *The Nickel Was for the Movie*.

---

in the Dark, Vladimir Nabokov says he tried to write "the entire book as if it were a film" (Appel 258).

More than the exchanges of themes, characters, and stories, and more than a logic according to which film would simply transfer the structures of literature to the screen (such as narrative forms), now film and literature offer each other textual and formal systems whose languages were compatible enough to create an "intertextual" dialogue on problems of representation and interpretation. Godard's 1962 *My Life to Live* transforms Émile Zola's novelistic Nana into a thoroughly modern techno-industrial image of the life of a prostitute in Paris. In Italy, Pasolini releases both the novel and the film *Teorema* (1968) the same year, with the assumption that they represent the same argument but with somewhat different textual idioms. As much as Michelangelo Antonio alters and expands the plot and characters of Julio Cortázar's short story for his 1967 film *Blow Up*, he maintains its obsession with dynamics of visuality and its indeterminancies. Stanley Kubrick's works with contemporaneous literature are, from the beginning of the decade with his *Lolita* (1962), creative dialogues with the novelists, but by the time of his 1971 version of Anthony Burgess's *A Clockwork Orange*, the filmmaker seems to work with novels whose imagistic textuality already approaches cinematic forms. In the same spirit, Austrian writer Peter Handke and German director Wim Wenders collaborate from 1969 through the seventies on films such as an adaptation of Handke's novel *The Goalie's Anxiety at the Penalty Kick* (1972); the full textual parity of this collaboration crystallizes in Handke's virtually simultaneous production and publication of a film and a novel titled *The Left-Handed Woman*, the story of a woman/translator isolated in the images around her.

The role of the universities and other educational institutions in this period of cinema history cannot be underestimated, especially since these institutions began to defend more vigorously than ever before the

The story of a woman translator living with her son, *The Left-Handed Woman* (1978) was directed as a film by Austrian novelist/screenwriter/filmmaker Peter Handke and almost simultaneously written by him as a novel. In this case, the film and the literature seem to share the same textual surface where the stark and flat images of the film coincide with the equally minimal verbal descriptions of the novel.

place of cinema as the cultural equal of literature, painting, and other traditional arts. While European (and particularly French) universities had occasionally introduced film studies into academia in the fifties, the sixties were the period when film studies began to proliferate in many Western countries, including the United States. That these new film courses are claimed more by English and comparative literature professors is not a trivial point. Film would no longer be presented simply as a question of industrial craft and production nor as an entertainment that students could learn to appreciate. Rather it grew rapidly as an aesthetic discipline whose histories and screenplays more often than not shared an office shelf with Shakespeare, George Eliot, Flaubert, and W. H. Auden. As part of this academic status in the sixties and seventies, film became a subject for theoretical studies that developed complex arguments for film as a sign system. Rooted in the structuralism of Levi-Strauss and the early semiotics of Umberto Eco, Roland Barthes, and others, these new theoretical models are instant allies of film (1) because they turn serious intellectual attention to culture at large, including popular cultural forms like the movies, and (2) because they offered rigorous models for discussing how shared "sign systems" (such as film and literature) could both differ and productively interact.

Movie Spectaculars and Cinematic Theatricality

Meanwhile, a very different relationship between film and literature has developed as another part of movie culture, mainly through mainstream commercial centers such as Hollywood. Here, literature maintains a more recognizable and traditional connection with the cinema; aiming to attract audiences (drifting into the suburbs or television), it provides materials to be transformed into movie spectacles in which images of literature are made even grander through the power of the cinema. This literature as spectacle describes a traditional merger of the literary and the cinematic as commercial theatrics. Alongside and counterpointing these commercial theatrics, however, is a very different sort of theatrical film during this same stretch of years: These are the variety of mostly noncommercial theatrical adaptations that foreground their theatricality in order to align themselves with the art film traditions that grew out of the fifties.

Revived in the late fifties and evolving into the contemporary blockbusters of today, movie spectaculars have existed since the silent films and have always had a close relationship with literary works. King Vidor made one of the most expensive films ever seen when he adapted *War and Peace* in 1956; Cecil B. DeMille returned his earlier biblical epic, *The Ten Commandments*, to an even bigger screen in the same year, now with

Franco Zeffirelli's *Romeo and Juliet* (1968) represents a major event in the history of Shakespearean adaptations for the screen. With its young stars, lavish sets, and themes of love and rebellion, the movie popularized the play as a movie spectacular aimed at the large youth audience of the 1960s. (*Motion Picture & Television Photo Archives*)

Oscar-winning special effects; and in 1959 the new three-and-one-half hour Cinemascope production of *Ben-Hur* added more momentum to a trend that would continue through the 1960s in huge box-office successes such as *Lawrence of Arabia* (1962) and *Doctor Zhivago* (1965). For many, Franco Zeffirelli's 1968 *Romeo and Juliet* epitomized both the directions and the larger goals of these modern literary spectacles: An international production (British and Italian), it successfully targeted the restless discontent of a large youth audience, while still managing a wonderfully operatic interpretation of the play, purporting to return Shakespeare to popular culture with artistic integrity. With the dissolution of the old studio system and the subsequent rising cost of making movies, blockbusters like these could draw audiences from their television sets through the scale of the movie production values (widescreens, Technicolor processes, and stars) and the aura of their literary values.

Paralleling these commercial theatrics, however, another more alternative kind of cinema turned to theater and its theatrics to create complex dialogues between film and drama, often with self-conscious political or aesthetic aims. After a number of extraordinary adaptations in the fifties, Orson Welles continued his work with theater and film in his 1966 version of Shakespeare's *Henry IV*, Part I and II, *Chimes at Midnight*, a curiously personal film in which Welles cast himself as Falstaffian collaborator and victim. Peter Brook's adaptation of Peter Weiss's *Marat Sade* (1966) used film to critique the political theatrics of modern life in his staging of Marquis de Sade's asylum revolutionaries; and Eric Rohmer's later adaptations—*The Marquise of O* (1976), based on Heinrich von Kleist's novella, and *Perceval* (1978), based on an unfinished twelfth-century poem, Chrétien de Troyes—abandon all vestiges of historical realism to create stunningly artificial sets, costumes, and acting styles as contemporary updatings of a theater of the mind. In Germany, R. W. Fassbinder's 1972 *The Bitter Tears of Petra Von Kant*, based on his own play, exhausts a single theatrical space as an exploration of the theatrics of gender and power; and his 1979 *Despair*, an English language collaboration with Nabokov's novel, playwright Tom Stoppard's screenplay, and global star Dirk Bogarde, ironically deconstructs the very logic of films as commercial spectacles whose pleasures and entertainments, for Fassbinder, often disguise a brutal politics.

After its heydays in the thirties, theater and drama return full force to film practice in the sixties, seventies, and eighties, but the situation is, of course, quite different from that in the thirties. For many of these alternative films (up through Robert Altman's *Come Back to the 5 & Dime Jimmy Dean, Jimmy Dean* [1982] and *Fool for Love* [1985]), theatricality now represents not a similar set of mechanisms with which to capture images of the world, but mechanisms and styles whose artificiality and spatial limitations could expose or critique the false realism of social identities, as well as the commodified realism of movies themselves.

Much of this energy and creative movement between film and literature during these decades is a consequence of an evolving audience for the cinema. By the early seventies, American and European film culture could assume an audience saturated from childhood through college with television and movies, and this audience is both more casually and more seriously familiar with media culture than ever before. Moviegoers are now able, if not always willing, to watch and follow films with remarkably sophisticated competencies, and in that sense the old tensions and showdowns over the cultural authority of literature or the movies have already dissipated significantly. One of the consequences of this matur-

Francis Coppola's *The Godfather* (1972) marks one of the high points in modern American cinema, both economically and artistically. Through elaborate film techniques, Coppola's film remakes Mario Puzo's popular novel into a complex epic of family, nation, and violence. The irony and social criticism that pervade the film seem clearly aimed at an audience perhaps more knowledgeable about film form and history than about literature. (*Archive Photos*)

ing film audience is an exceptionally dynamic and creative period in film's use of literature through the 1970s.

Indeed, this implicit presumption of an audience with a cinematic literacy perhaps comparable to high points of verbal literacy, an audience able to appreciate the complexities of film and its many relationships with literature, is a crucial backdrop for Francis Coppola's 1972 transformation of *The Godfather*, a best seller with quite unremarkable literary value, into a blockbuster art film. Mario Puzo's novel offers Coppola a confrontational subject that sometimes brutally questions the sacred cows of the American family and political system, but Coppola transforms that material into *The Godfather I* and *The Godfather II* (1974), with intricate cinematic texts and theatrical spectacles that fully overshadow the book. The *Godfather* films become one of the most celebrated achievements of modern cinema, involving all three of those salient motifs characterizing film and literature from the sixties through the seventies: subversive material, collaborative cinematics, and commercial theatrics. Following *The Godfather* and its new audiences, other movies from *The Exorcist* (1973) through *Jurassic Park* (1993), would take books and plays where they have never gone before—sometimes as finer artistic achievements and often with much larger economic success. Once highlighted as a textual issue, collaborations between film and literature are now becoming a much more transparently financial matter, which an ingenious director could sometimes work to an artistic advantage.

Works Cited

Appel, Alfred, Jr. *Nabokov's Dark Cinema*. New York: Oxford University Press, 1974.

Giannetti, Louis D. *Godard and Others: Essays on Film Form*. Rutherford, NJ: Fairleigh Dickinson University Press, 1975.

Rich, Adrienne. *Adrienne Rich's Poetry*. Ed. Barbara Charlesworth Gelpi and Albert Gelpi. New York: Norton, 1975.

Robbe-Grillet, Alain. *For a New Novel: Essays on Fiction*. Trans. Richard Howard. New York: Grove Press, 1965.

6

BOOKS AND MOVIES AS MULTIMEDIA
INTO THE 1990s

The films of Stanley Kubrick stand out as intricate and fascinating examples of the trends and changes that occur during the last decades of the twentieth century. From *Lolita* to *A Clockwork Orange*, Kubrick's adaptations through the sixties and early seventies align best with the auteurist experiments to collaborate with and creatively remake the literary as the filmic. In each of these movies, the literature provides a respected creative perspective that the filmmaker, often with the assistance of the novelist, transforms into a film. With his 1980 *The Shining*, based on the best seller by writer Stephen King, however, the relationship becomes a more antagonistic whirlpool of art and commerce. Whereas Nabokov revised *Lolita* as a screenplay for Kubrick and ultimately accepted the director's many changes as a "first-rate film with magnificent actors" (Phillips 105), King's relationship with Kubrick was more territorial and hostile from the outset. With scriptwriter Diane Johnson, Kubrick stripped down King's horror novel and largely reinvented it. Although initially flattered that Kubrick would adapt his novel, King quickly turned on Kubrick and his film; he was most horrified at Kubrick's intention to change the ending (in which Hallran would be shockingly killed) and by the choice of Jack Nicholson to play Jack Torrance. The choice of Nicholson, Kubrick explained, was economics—he was "bankable"—but for King the film became a beautiful image emptied of its inner meaning. This seems, however, hardly a question of literature versus film since King's novels were always films in the making, and in 1997 King would reclaim his novel with the ABC mini-series version of *The Shining*, an adaptation he produced, acted in, and even rewrote parts of the novel for. As this case suggests, in the 1980s and 1990s, film and literature battle mostly for the media image of a work, not for some untranslatable quality in the literature. One of the results is a prolif-

The choice of Jack Nicholson as the maniacal Jack in Stanley Kubrick's *The Shining* (1980) was one of many points of contention between the filmmaker and novelist Stephen King. The saga of that embattled adaptation, as Kubrick's brilliant film and King's own television version years later, suggests the growing importance of the multimedia in the marketing of literature and in complicating notions of authenticity. (*Photofest*)

eration of images of and from literature with little concern about authenticity or authority.

Through the 1970s and into the 1990s, within and outside Hollywood, film and literature paid more visible attention to their commercial and industrial terms. Whereas the decades immediately preceding this period promoted expressive powers, linguistic and textual structures, and a reimagining of the politics associated with those concerns, by the mid-seventies both film and literature were more blatantly enmeshed in the commercial shapes that determined their artistic possibilities. The value and meanings of both film and literature were increasingly determined by their status as saleable commodities, and what they shared as entertainment products began to overshadow the differences of the past. From this perspective, (1) the value and meaning of both forms are fundamentally determined by a marketplace economics rather than by aesthetic or social discourses, and (2) within this commodification of form and meaning, writers and filmmakers would, necessarily or by choice, learn to use the other's commodified textuality as the focus for a self-promotion, critique, or play for consumer choice. This dynamic of commerce would be part of many different corners of film culture in the United States and abroad: More blatantly than ever, commerce and its image would shape most mainstream filmmaking (such as George Lucas's use of the serial novel formula for his *Indiana Jones* films [1981–1989]); it would influence the inheritors of auteurist or alternative cinema (like Martin Scorsese's *The Age of Innocence* [1993] and Spike Lee's 1992 *Malcolm X*); and it would trouble many ambiguous positions in between (including films like Steven Spielberg's *The Color Purple* [1985] and Kenneth Branagh's 1993 *Much Ado About Nothing*).

Multimedia Conglomerates, Blockbusters, and Home Viewing

Recent decades in film history have been most significantly defined by two forces: the reorganization of the movie industry in the hands of multimedia conglomerates and the technological expansion of the ways movies are exhibited, most obviously through home video technologies. The first change begins in the sixties and early seventies when industrial giants such as Gulf & Western and Transamerica Corporation took over the studio production units like Paramount and United Artists in pursuit of the large profits promised by blockbuster films like *The Godfather* or *Jaws* (1975). The logic here is not too complicated: By investing more and more capital into fewer movies (including the investment of paying more money for a blockbuster novel or play), these conglomerates could generate from the movies the kinds of revenues they found in oil, hotels, and other holdings. By the late 1980s, however, another industrial change is afoot: The conglomerate powers behind the movies refocus and downsize as exclusively media empires. Directing their energies more exclusively toward television, movies, records, or book and magazine publication, Gulf & Western becomes Paramount Communications; in 1989 Kinney becomes the multimedia mogul Time Warner; Fox joins Rupert Murdoch's News Corporation in 1985; and Sony extends its media powers by buying Columbia in 1989.

Movies have been a commercial, industrial enterprise practically since their inception at the end of the nineteenth century; literature too, since at least the eighteenth century, has been inescapably connected to the economics and industry of publishing or theatrical production. But this restructuring of the film industry through conglomerate and media giants has major consequences for film and literature:

(1) Conglomerates encourage a continued transformation of literature into commodified spectacles in which movies reduce narrative and character; and (2) sharing the same spread sheets, books now must compete commercially, and fewer and fewer risky or experimental works of literature find their way through publishing houses. "High concept" became a buzz word for condensing the marketability of movie projects, and one of the most effective high concepts is to simply match a best seller or classic novel with a well-known star or director. Conversely, literary publishers and Broadway producers began to view manuscripts and plays for their potential as blockbusters—the common media ground for stage, literary, and film work—and, as the 1997 Broadway production of the movie *The Lion King* reminds us, neither traditional cultural value nor the traditional logic of the direction of adaptation dictates anymore the exchanges between literature and the movies. Even film cultures outside of Hollywood learned to use literature as part of high concept competition: From Volker Schlöndorff's *The Tin Drum* (1979) through Jean Paul Rappeneau's *Cyrano de Bergerac* (1990), literature can sell films and films can sell literature.

The rapid advance of home video technology has been the second important change from the mid-seventies to the present, creating a situation in which the majority of movies are now seen through home video players, cable networks, and computers. Watching movies on television is, of course, not an entirely new phenomenon, and literature on television is a kind of adaptation that has been prevalent since the 1950s. The recent explosion of VCR technologies and the recent expansion of ways to watch movies with computer technologies (through, for instance, DVD technologies) influence, however, the ways individuals and audiences watch films and bear significantly on the intersection of film and literature. Most obviously, watching movies is now more often a domestic or private experience that comes, in some ways, closer to the conditions of reading a work of literature. Unlike the experience of seeing a movie blockbuster in theater, the private control that a home viewer has over a film approaches that of reading at a certain pace or rereading certain lines or passages, and many original films and many recent adaptations seem geared toward this more readerly relationship between the film and the viewer, a relationship in which the spectator becomes a more active participant in the address and style of the movie. Peter Greenaway's *Prospero's Books*, David Cronenberg's 1991 version of William Burrough's novel *Naked Lunch*, and even the recent *Clueless* (adapted from Austen's *Emma*) may map a new field for the relationship between film and literature, where movies do not assimilate literature to their own visual theatrics but develop a unique relationship with their film audiences analogous to the more concentrated activity of private reading.

NOVELIZATIONS AND TIE-INS

One of the most striking products of the movie industry's assimilation by con-glomerates and media corporations has been the burgeoning business of tie-ins. Ancillary tie-ins have been a part of the film/literature relationship since the beginning of the twentieth century. They refer to the practice of marketing a vari-ety of merchandises around the release of a movie, and the tie-ins of contempo-rary film culture can mean anything from tee-shirts and hamburgers to toys and music compact discs. Today, most studios have their own merchandising units in their marketing departments. Responding to logic and the economics of tie-ins, publishers of literature would continue to take advantage of a successful adapta-tion to promote or redistribute a book, but especially in recent years, the connec-tion becomes more common since the studio and the publisher may work for the same media corporation. The Disney Corporation may be the most notorious and successful company in spreading a movie through merchandise from, for instance, the music and collectible figures of *Pocahontas* to novelizations of the story.

Novelization is one increasingly common version of ancillary marketing of a tie-in with a literary film or a film with literary potential. It is the process of turning the story of another work, such as a play, poem, or film, into a novel and can describe the practice of repackaging a successful movie as a novel or written narrative ver-sion of that movie. The 1944 film *To Have and Have Not* (scripted by William Faulkner and propelled by Humphrey Bogart and Lauren Bacall) generated three new printings of Hemingway's novel. But, in the last few decades, through the power of novelization, the process has grown more convoluted. After Arthur C. Clark's short story "The Sentinel" became the critically acclaimed movie *2001: A Space Odyssey* (1968), the same year Clark developed it into a novel with the same title. He wrote a sequel novel, *2010: Odyssey Two*, which was made into a film in 1984, and that was followed by yet another novel, *2061: Odyssey Three*, in a series of spin-offs and tie-ins binding the fiction and the films. In 1970, Eric Segal wrote a small novel based on Robert Evans's screenplay for the forthcoming movie *Love Story* (1970). After a major promotion campaign, the book topped the New York Times bestseller list just as the movie was released in December. Indeed, many popular novels today appear aimed at film adaptation even when they are first pub-lished as novels, and their style and structure could be considered already that of a novelization. In the 1990s it is rare not to see either a novelization or re-issue of a novel or play as a coordinated tie-in with the release of a movie.

In this context there are many implications for literature and the activity of read-ing: (1) The novelization usually becomes a reduction or literalization of the movie in which the traditional descriptive techniques and textual richness of narrative fic-tion are transformed into only action and character; (2) reading a novelization (or a traditional novel rereleased in the spotlight of a successful movie) usually means that the reading will be mediated by the film images, characters, and so on.

Recommended Reading   Justin Wyatt's *High Concept: Movies and Marketing in Hollywood* and Henry Jenkins's *Textual Poachers: Television Fans and Participatory Culture.*

The Return of the Classics: Choosing a Version

Even a casual viewer during the 1980s and 1990s would note the unusual proliferation of adaptations of classic novels and other classic literature. From the spate of Jane Austen and Henry James novels and Shakespeare plays to the less commonly adapted works of Thomas Hardy, Edith Wharton, and Virginia Woolf, reputable literature and canonized names compete vigorously today with blockbusters and action films for contemporary movie audiences around the world. From James Ivory's adaptation of Henry James's *The Europeans* (1979) through his version of E. M. Forster's *Howard's End* (1992), some of this fashion may be attributable to the usual industry problem of finding basic material to make into films or of finding sufficiently recognizable works of classic literature to make into a literary spectacle. There are, however, three other ways to view this widespread return of literary classics in the 1980s and 1990s: (1) as a reaction against contemporary filmmaking trends to diminish traditional plot and character; (2) as a conservative or at least therapeutic turn from cultural complexity; and (3) as a reflection of contemporary film audiences and their increasing concern with manner over matter.

The exceptional prevalence of nineteenth-century adaptations in the last two decades can, first, be seen as a reaction to certain tendencies in filmmaking today, a period when the force and reliability of narrative (as a way of knowing the world) has been devalued or marginalized. Since the 1970s and 1980s, even mainstream movies have tended to abandon or undermine complex or coherent characters, tight plot lines, and causal logics. In a range of movies from *Rambo* through Jim Jarmusch's *Mystery Train* (1989) and Oliver Stone's *Natural Born Killers* (1994), characters are, by choice or default, constructed more and more as surface images lacking much psychological depth; their frequently unmotivated actions create dynamic performances but are often based only on the slightest of plot lines as intentionally fragmented stories. In this context, literary masterpieces present the fresh, and ironically alternative, possibility of both full characters and classical narrative logics. Much of the fascination with nineteenth-century novels or Shakespearean drama may be, in short, what some have identified as a post-postmodern yearning for good plots and characters with depth.

There is, at the same time, more than a trace of a cultural conservatism in these literary reactions to unmoorings of plot and character in contemporary society. The subject matter alone might indicate a nostalgia for past worlds of coherency, romance, adventure, and some degree of psychological and social order. This should not be interpreted, however, to mean that a Jane Austen heroine or a Shakespearean society does not struggle with choices and balances. Nor is it to suggest that contemporary life is truly or factually more complex or violent than life in the eighteenth or nineteenth centuries. What does seem true is that media cultures of contemporary societies have inundated individuals with more information and more images than ever before and, as today's global perspective grows larger and more rapid, individual and social identities find themselves shaped by those fast and disorienting images. In contrast, movie adaptations of classic literature combine images of other times and places (with at least more civilized violence and articulate fears of race and gender) and the conceptual and imagistic reductions needed to make and market literary films today (as the "high concept" images of "great literature"). The result is a literary image that acts as a packageable and comprehensible alternative to the other, much less comprehensible, images audiences live through today. Beyond questions of fidelity to the Henry James novel, Jane Campion's Isabel Archer is the portrait of a lady who, like many women in the 1990s, moves through a cross-fire of social perspectives and desires; this *Portrait of a Lady* remains, however, a beautifully framed, historically past, and commercially finished image whose literary status assures it the stable meanings not available in most images today.

Finally, there is another attraction and activity embedded in the numerous classics offered up on the contemporary screens and monitors and in the numerous versions of the same work of literature that audiences can now watch. Today, literary classics on film are multiple and redundant in two ways. Not only are different versions of a novel or film sometimes produced by different filmmakers within a few years of each other (including several *Emmas* in the nineties or almost simultaneous versions of Laclos's *Dangerous Liaisons* by Stephen Frears [1988] and Milos Forman [the 1989 *Valmont*]) but home video and computer technologies have made it possible for viewers to watch and compare even more versions of an adaptation from other periods of film history. After seeing those different contemporary versions of Austen's and Laclos's novels, audiences today might have the option of watching on video Clarence Brown's 1932 *Emma* or Roger Vadim's 1960 *Dangerous Liaisons*, and these, of course, could be sampled next to the original novels and, in the case of *Dangerous Liaisons*, next to Christopher Hampton's play. Contemporary film culture offers more versions and more opportunities to see and compare the relationships between film and literature as historical practices and textual performances, and one consequence of this redistribution of literature through the media may be that questions of fidelity or authenticity

Stephen Frears's *Dangerous Liaisons* (1988) is one of many versions of Laclos's eighteenth-century novel. It is the story of a group of aristocrats who change and disguise their identities and motives in games of power and manipulation. Comparing the many variations and incarnations of this drama is one of the pleasures that VCR technology offers the contemporary viewer.

may be less and less a concern for both filmmakers and their audiences. As Scorsese's *Age Of Innocence* seems to suggest in its almost fetishistic obsession with the surface of gowns, wall coverings, and dinner table settings, audiences today may be more interested in the different textures of adaptation than in the textual accuracy of any one adaptation.

New directions in filmmaking already point to different kinds of literature and alternate relationships between film and literature in the 1990s. Especially in recent years, for example, movies have commercially expanded the cinematic potentials of comic book literatures and other unconventional literary forms (from *Popeye* [1980] to *Batman* [1989], *Dick Tracy* [1990], and *Crumb* [1994]). Developing countries, in Asia, Africa, and Arab cultures, offer extraordinary works that explore the connections between oral literatures and film (see Pines and Willemen; Malkmus and Armes). Following the example of the poet Maya Angelou's television film *Down in the Delta* (1998), television and video will doubtless attract and offer opportunities to literary figures in ways different from those historically provided by the cinema. Finally, if home video has already demanded a rethinking of how audiences watch film or read literature in both different and similar ways, these issues will only become more exciting and complicated as various computer technologies redefine future ways of seeing and reading.

SHAKESPEARE AND FILM

*"S*hakespeare on Film" is practically a genre in its own right. Since the years of silent movies, Shakespeare's plays have been regularly adapted by a wide range of directors. Besides the many short silent homages to Shakespeare (detailed in Robert Ball's *Shakespeare on Silent Film*), the major movements of film history become, from one point of view, a history of Shakespeare on film: Douglas Fairbanks's early Hollywood sound attempt at Shakespeare in *The Taming of the Shrew* (1929), Max Reinhardt's lavishly scenic 1935 *A Midsummer Night's Dream*, Laurence Olivier's celebrated *Henry V* (1945), Orson Welles's 1948 expressionistic *Macbeth*, Akira Kurosawa's remarkable 1957 cross-cultural translation of *Macbeth* as a samurai *Throne of Blood*, Franco Zefferelli's triumphant success with the youth market in his 1968 *Romeo and Juliet*, Liz White's 1980 racially charged production of *Othello*, Jean-Luc Godard's humorously self-referential *King Lear* (1988), Gus Van Sant's postmodern use of Shakespeare's Henry plays in *My Own Private Idaho*, Kenneth Branagh's many Shakespeares, and the recent *William Shakespeare's Romeo and Juliet* (with star Leonardo DiCaprio).

Shakespearean movies have used vastly different styles and cultural perspectives. Often these adaptations have tried to be faithful to Shakespeare's texts and the theatrical conventions of his times. At other times, these films have liberally reinterpreted the materials and the aesthetic or political intentions of the original play. Shakespeare has been put on film and television in attempts to popularize language and plots that often alienated audiences; films of his plays have also aimed to record definitively complete versions of those plays for scholarly or classroom use.

Many of the questions asked of adaptations in general apply to Shakespearean movies: Is the adaptation interested in a faithful or creative exchange with the play? What motivates certain omissions or changes in the film? Or, how does the time and place of the adaptation color or determine the film? Yet there are other important questions specific to Shakespearean adaptations: (1) How is Shakespearean language used or not used and at what cost? (2) What is the relation of the language, the acting, and the images? (3) How is the cultural or literary value of Shakespeare, as perhaps the greatest icon of Western literature, being drawn on or addressed?

Recommended Readings   Peter Donaldson's *Shakespearean Films/Shakespearean Directors*, Jack J. Jorgens's *Shakespeare on Film*, Lynda Boose and Richard Burt's *Shakespeare, The Movie*.

Certainly one of the most idiosyncratic films to engage Shakespeare, Jean-Luc Godard's *King Lear* (1987) leaves the Shakespeare play only barely visible. It uses the play mainly as a cultural reference to address issues of power and authority, issues which implicate the filmmaker Godard as well. (*Fotos International/Archive Photos*)

As in the past, the present and future intersections of film and literature are about more than just movies and books. The evolving relationship tells us not only about individual works of film and literature but also about how each works to change the other's meaning and value as part of complex historical and cultural ratios. To read a book, to attend a play, to hear a poem, to view a film, to watch a television broadcast today are experiences that offer discrete and particular meanings. Like all discrete experiences, they open up larger debates and questions—about history, about aesthetics, and about human value. When those experiences are visibly doubled as dual engagements in which film and literature regard each other, those debates and questions become, I think, more specific and more pressing—about cultural literacy, about the psychologies of different arts, about the social politics of entertainment, and about the varieties of human and technological expression. This is why the questions provoked by the dialogues between film and literature have been and will continue to be so central in their relentless particularity.

Baz Luhrmann's *William Shakespeare's Romeo and Juliet* (1996) is one of the most recent adaptations of Shakespeare, featuring stars Claire Danes and Leonardo DiCaprio. Updated with an urban setting and a pop-music soundtrack, this *Romeo and Juliet* outraged as many viewers as it delighted, and in the debates that surrounded it the relationship between film and literature once again raised concerns about the preservation and communication of culture. (*Phototest*)

Works Cited

Malkmus, Lizbeth, and Roy Armes. *Arab and African Film Making*. London: Zed, 1991.

Phillips, Gene. *Stanley Kubrick: A Film Odyssey*. New York: Popular Library, 1977.

Pines, Jim, and Paul Willemen. *Questions of Third Cinema*. London: BFI, 1989.

CRITICAL BORDERS AND BOUNDARIES
ANALYTICAL CATEGORIES
FOR FILM AND LITERATURE

Each of the seven categories in this section represents a basic introduction to techniques and structures used when thinking about, analyzing, or writing about film and literature. The categories are spread through two chapters, the first discussing important thematic and formal questions in works of film and literature and the second emphasizing larger analytical categories such as genres. Each category calls attention to ideas and forms that film and literature share, that they modify, and that they do not share.

The aim here in Part II is to develop a critical vocabulary that allows viewers and readers to think more carefully about how they understand individual works and how related works use certain techniques and structures to develop different perspectives and ideas. Any work of film or literature will use these forms in a particular way, and a critical vocabulary will grow more refined and insightful in response to those individual works.

7

THEMES, NARRATIVES, AND ELEMENTS OF STYLE

Themes and Motifs

Whether in film or literature, a *theme* or *motif* identifies the main idea or ideas developed in that work. This is not necessarily the same as a moral or message, although often themes and motifs are a way of focusing what the work is "about." Often themes will be consistent in moving between film and literature, so that a film version of *Hamlet*, for example, will retain and recreate Shakespeare's theme of the tragic isolation and indecision of the hero in a corrupt society. At other times, a movie may elaborate on or change the central theme of an original literary work, such as when Laurence Olivier emphasizes Hamlet's Oedipal sexual crisis in his 1948 adaptation or when Nathaniel Hawthorne's grim tale of repressed desire, penance, and social obligation becomes thematically transformed through the massive additions and upbeat conclusion of the 1995 *Scarlet Letter*.

Intricate works of films or literature, such as Mary Shelley's *Frankenstein*, can put several motifs into play that may relate to or diverge from the central theme. Always try to identify and refine a theme, so that you can recognize if it moves in several directions. Beyond the ambitious pride of Dr. Frankenstein, for instance, which other themes appear? Companionship and family? Male versus female perspectives on the world? How have the many adaptations of that novel altered the themes? Are the different thematic concerns connected to the time and place when the different works—of literature or film—were produced?

Characters

Some films and literary works do not have characters. Most, however, use one or more characters. Characters are those individuals that populate and propel stories, plays, movies, and even poems. Traditionally, characters have been designated as major or minor, as a *protagonist* (one with heroic or positive features) or an *antagonist* (one with villainous or negative features). How characters are depicted and what they contribute to the themes and meanings of different works can vary a great deal, depending on the perspective of the work and the medium being used: They may be realistic or cartoonish; they may be described only in terms of external appearance or by means of internal thoughts and psychological depth; a character may motivate actions and events or be passively subject to them. A novel, such as George Eliot's *Middlemarch*, may present such a vast number of major and minor characters that it would be difficult for a film to reproduce all of them; another, such as Albert Camus's *The Stranger*, may concentrate on a single character and the drama in his or her mind. Even with very personal poetry, a character or mask known as a *persona* provides some distance between the author and the ideas and feeling of the poem. It thus becomes common to identify the speaker of the poem not with the author but with a persona who mediates between the author and the perspectives of the poem.

When a film adapts a literary character, much is at stake. A character's appearance, which is originally grounded in words or in a reader's imagination, is made visible in a movie, and this is a frequent source of confusion or dissatisfaction in measuring a film against its literary source. In theater and film particularly, body types—short, thin, attractive, fidgety, and so on—can communicate a great deal about characters being interpreted by an actor; and gestures and movements can add much to the meaning of a play or film. The use of Tom Cruise in the 1994 adaptation of Anne Rice's *Interview with a Vampire*, for example, seems, to some, a flagrant case of either misreading the literary character or miscasting. Indeed, unlike literary characters, movie characters are often a product of a *star system* that commercially promotes the images and personalities of certain actors, and these star images can sometimes jar with the literary image that they must inhabit. Vladimir Nabokov was perfectly satisfied with his Lolita incarnated through actress Sue Lyon, while Stephen King was upset by Kubrick's choice of Jack Nicholson to play his character Jack Torrance. Ask questions about how characters are produced and about the choices made in adapting characters. What are the different ways that certain linguistic or narrative strategies produce literary characters? With many or few adjectives, for instance? How are movie characters a product of certain techniques and film materials? What advantages do the use of words and moving images have over a purely linguistic description of characters or even over the physical presence of a character on stage? What are the drawbacks in portraying characters this way? Which characters are added, omitted, or changed in an adaptation? In Luchino Visconti's 1971 adaptation of Thomas Mann's *Death in Venice*, the filmmaker changes the profession of the central character (from a writer to a composer). Why?

Point of View

Point of view is central to both visual arts and literary arts. It describes the position from which an individual views another person, object, or event, and often suggests how that point of view determines the meaning of what is seen. Thus, a tree seen from a plane window above a forest may seem rather insignificant or commonplace; seen by a girl perched amidst its branches, however, that same tree may be infinitely varied and endlessly fascinating. Drama usually presents itself to the objective or communal view of a large audience; lyric poetry frequently suggests the private view of, as John Stuart Mill put it, "an utterance overheard." Many sorts of literature, particularly novels, allow multiple points of view to interact, and this ability to mobilize multiple points of view has been a salient connection between novels and films that likewise create dramas from confrontations and exchanges across many points of view.

Just as a poem frequently organizes its points of view through a speaker/persona, so too do novels and movies present, explicitly or implicitly, their stories through a point of view: It may be a *first-person point of view*, in which events are seen through the eyes and mind of a single individual; it may be a *third-person omniscient point of view*, where there are seemingly no limitations to what can be seen, known, and presented; or it may be *a limited third-person point of view*, in which the point of view is objectively outside that of the characters but remains focused primarily on one or two characters.

A simple exercise would be to take a short section of a poem or novel or film and describe how the point of view controls the meaning of that passage: In Robert Browning's poem "His Last Duchess" the reader follows the speech of the Duke as he both distorts the life of his former wife and unwittingly reveals his own egomania. In a movie like Japanese director Akira Kurosawa's *Rashomon* (1950), a rape and murder are recounted in four different and conflicting versions from the points of view of a bandit, a priest, the wife, and a woodcutter. One must keep in mind, though, the distinctions of point of view in these different practices: Poetry, novels, and short stories rely on language; drama employs language and physical space; and film uses language and an imagistic space. Consider the following, for example: How does the imagistic point of view used in a movie expand or limit the power of linguistic point of view? What happens to the satirical linguistic perspectives of authors Henry Fielding or Evelyn Waugh when those literary works are recreated as images in *Tom Jones* (1963) or *The Loved Ones* (1965)?

Story/Plot/Narrative

Films borrow most heavily from the forms and practices of short stories, novels, and plays, all of which tend to tell stories. *Stories* are commonly what literature and movies might share, as they provide basic materials, from fact or fiction, about events, lives, characters, and their motivations. Where film and literature often part ways is in the narrative construction of those stories through a *plot*, which presents those events in a certain order (either chronological or not), and a *narration* that shapes and colors that plot with a certain point of view. David Lean's adaptation of *Great Expectations* (1946) remains quite close to the story found in Charles Dickens's novel and even recreates the narrative point of view of the main character Pip, yet many of the narrative subplots needed to be abandoned and the ending of the film narrative differs from both Dickens's original and revised endings. In this case, *narrative closure*, or how and where the story is clearly concluded or resolved, becomes one of many signs that the adapted cinematic narration has remade the literary narrative.

Many film plots inherit their structure from classical dramas that focused on a *dramatic conflict* between characters or between a character and society or other larger forces. This fundamental dramatic structure has evolved and developed through film and literature to feature other standard conventions of plots: *narrative causality* through which characters' needs and desires motivate events and actions (in *The Wizard of Oz*, the plot maps Dorothy's anxious desire to get home), or a *parallel narrative structure* in which the private lives of the characters entwine with more public or social events (in *Emma*, the protagonist's predicament involves both arranging relationships in her community and discovering the truth about her own emotions). Let these and other common narrative formulas guide your questioning of film adaptations. How has the narrative structure and logic changed or not changed in the conversion to a movie? Do the same causal motives drive the narrative in both versions, or have those motives been reduced or altered? To what extent does the ending determine the meaning of the story, and, if an adaptation changes that ending, how does that change the meaning of the story?

There are, of course, many literary and film structures that are not narratives and many works that deviate from those classical narrative patterns to create alternative narrative patterns. Various poetic forms, experimental work, and documentaries describe strategies that, in films and literature, eschew narrative conventions. Many literary and film narratives, moreover, aim at overturning or subverting those narrative expectations established through classical narrative literature and cinema. For instance, many of the films and novels of Alain Robbe-Grillet will undermine precisely those forms of narrative causality and closure that readers and viewers have come to expect. Sometimes, in fact, a filmmaker may remake a classical literary narrative in a way that undoes and questions the structural terms of the original narrative, as R. W. Fassbinder does when he refashions Theodor Fontane's nineteenth-century novel as his own *Effi Briest* (1974), a film in which the female protagonist seems, for Fassbinder, as trapped by narrative conventions as by social conventions. When you encounter a film or work of literature that intentionally plots and narrates a story in an unexpected or troubling way, begin by investigating the possible reasons for this alternative way of telling the story.

Settings/Sets/Mise-en-Scène

In one sense, all film and literature depends on a *setting* or a location in which to place the action and characters. Settings are more precisely the descriptive backgrounds used in novels, short stories, and some poetry, and, like the Mississippi River in Mark Twain's *Adventures of Huckleberry Finn*, settings can have realistic, cultural, historical, and symbolic meanings. *Sets* are specifically those props, backdrops, and other constructions used in theatrical productions, and can range from the minimal to the extravagant. In Tennessee Williams *A Streetcar Named Desire*, the sets that describe a dilapidated section of New Orleans reflect the collapse of the lives of some of the characters. With film criticism, settings and sets are part of the *mise-en-scène*, which also includes all the other theatrical and stage materials put in place before the camera begins filming. These are props, lighting, costumes, and so forth; even the actors can be considered part of a cinematic mise-en-scène.

With films, even an actual location, such as the city of San Francisco in Hitchcock's *Vertigo* (1958), functions as part of a mise-en-scène. Indeed, one complex issue for the film/literature debates is whether the mise-en-scène of a film that often seems so natural and realistic can carry the ideas and meanings conveyed by the conscious choices of sets and settings in dramas and novels. Do viewers of the film *A Streetcar Named Desire* simply take for granted a "natural" setting whose meanings they may be more sensitive to if it is constructed as the sets of the play? Do these audiences assume that props such as the light bulb, stair case, and the other metaphoric elements of sets and settings are merely naturalistic details in the film? If settings in novels and sets on a theatrical stage always imply a principle of selection that indicates some designated significance or meaning, how does the mise-en-scène of a filmic adaptation suggest, in a similar way, a metaphoric or other meaning for a location or background?

When the sets or settings of an original work are known, the changes in sets, settings, and mise-en-scène provide some of the most inventive moments in the cross-overs between film and literature. Witness the recent *William Shakespeare's Romeo and Juliet* (1996) where the Italian setting of a Renaissance Verona becomes a futuristic or post-modern landscape of urban decay. In Laurence Olivier's *Henry V* (1945), there is a famous shift early in the movie from a realistic reconstruction of Shakespeare's Elizabethan theater, in which stagehands move back-grounds props, to the wide views of a realistic location where Henry pre-pares to depart for France. Here Olivier dramatically calls attention to the different ways sets and settings function in theater and in films. Does that shift from stage to a realistic setting bear on the themes of the play?

Other Elements of Style and Structure

Even when they go unnoticed, stylistic strategies and conventions—which would include narrative styles and elements of sets, settings, and mise-en-scène—are sometimes the most important and distinguishing features in a work of literature or film. Ernest Hemingway's use of short declarative sentences in *The Sun Also Rises*, Bernard Shaw's aristocrat-ic drawing rooms or occasional long intellectual conversations in *Pygmalion*, or Martin Scorsese's extended and detailed takes of dinner tables and home furnishings in his *The Age of Innocence* (1993) all under-line and extend the complex meanings of the novel, the play, and the film. Of the many conventions of style in film and literature, here we will iso-late several formal and stylistic techniques that distinguish most promi-nently the different practices in film and literature.

Poetry, novels, and films (both silent and sound) use language in various ways. Language can be printed, spoken, or recorded, and in each of these separate materials and forms, language can be stylistically com-plex. From the intertitles of silent movies to the dialogue found in all forms of literature, linguistic styles can run the gamut from the sparsely prosaic to the elaborately poetic. Along this spectrum, *prose* can be described as the everyday or ordinary use of language, reflecting the way of speaking or writing in a specific historical time and place; *poetry* usu-ally employs the *rhythms* and sometimes the *rhymes* associated with intensified verse. When analyzing the rhetoric of literature, such as the poetic dialogue of Shakespeare or the prose style of D. H. Lawrence's *Women in Love*, we note how the rhythmic pace of different words or the syntactical arrangements of those words can indicate complicated states of minds or paradoxical perceptions and feelings. Of a related kind, listen to the remarkably rapid rhythms in the dialogue of Howard Hawks's 1940 *His Girl Friday* (remade from the play *The Front Page*). How are these rhythms important to the meaning of the play/film?

Whether poetic or prosaic, literary and filmic language will rely on movements between denotation and connotation, imagery and rhetorical figures such as similes, metaphors, and symbols. *Denotation* describes the dictionary meaning of a word, while *connotations* are those other meanings that common usage has added to words. Thus to refer to film as "a movie" or "the cinema" may have the same denotative meaning but different connotations (entertainment versus art perhaps). *Imagery* is the use of a descriptive image to imply an idea or emotional state: In two William Butler Yeats poems, the city of Byzantium suggests a lost world or exotic splendor and permanence to which that poem's persona longs to escape. How would a visual but realistic medium like film suggest these imagistic meanings? With a *metaphor*, the meaning of a term is transferred from one object it usually represents to another object, such as referring to "the bird of time" to encapsulate how fleeting time is. A *simile* explicitly points to the construction of this resemblance by using "like" or "as" ("time passes like a bird in flight"). A *symbol* will connect a word or image with an abstract meaning or larger idea, so that a flag might be a symbol for the beliefs of a country.

Reading and analyzing literature requires abilities to comprehend and interpret figurative uses of language such as these. The verbal play of language in film does as well. One may argue that a movie cannot possibly reconstruct the linguistic densities and turns that make up a single sentence in Henry James's *Wings of a Dove*. Yet, although clever adaptation like *Clueless* will change entirely the language of Jane Austen's characters, it can replace the ironies and precisions of the original with appropriately lively and witty sets of metaphors and similes that reflect the new social locale of Southern California. Attend not to just what words say, in short, but, for film as well as literature, to their many stylistic constructions.

In addition to sharing these literary forms, film has developed its own formal and stylistic units. These cinematic units can be classified as (1) those created by *the positioning and composition of the film image* and (2) those created by *the editing of sound and image on film*. In considering these units of filmic form and style, some writers have suggested a correlation between the film shot, scene, and sequence, and the literary word, sentence, and paragraph. Although this is more suggestive than accurate, the analogy does draw attention to the way film techniques can carry and inflect nuanced meanings in ways similar to but quite different from literary techniques and styles.

The *shot* describes a single, uncut segment of film, such as an early shot in Truffaut's *400 Blows* that shows a boy's hand writing on a pad. Some of the common stylistic techniques that add to the significance of the shot are: (1) the *shape of the frame* (which can have a standard rectangular ratio of 1.33:1, a widescreen shape, or be resized to fit a television screen), (2) the *perspective of the image* (which can range from a deep focus that clearly shows backgrounds, middlegrounds, and foregrounds to a very flat shallow focus), (3) the *film speed* (which creates slow, fast, or normal motion), (4) the *distance between the camera and the figure* being filmed (resulting in close-ups, long shots, and other relations), (5) the *angle* at which the shot captures the object or event (which results in low angle, high angle, or straight-on shots), (6) *camera movements* (such as sweeping *pans* of a horizon or *tracks* that follow the action on a cart), and (7) the use of *color* or *black and white* film (both of which can discriminate among a wide range of tones). All of these technical dimensions of a shot can be utilized as individually and creatively as the stylistic constructions of words. To recreate a literary passage that develops connotations, metaphors, and linguistic rhythms, a movie may frame a close-up of a man that simultaneously focuses on a floundering ship in the background and strewn furniture in the middleground along the beach; the frame then pans to an empty jungle horizon in which the forest creates an impenetrable flat surface image. When one or more shots like this are rhythmically linked or edited together to describe a single space or place, this is called a *scene*; a *sequence* describes a number of edited shots and scenes that are connected by a specific action or idea. In the previous example, the film may construct a scene of a number of shots as the man looks about him at the sea, sits in the waves beating against the sand, and explores the edges of the jungle; when surrounded by various other scenes of the man swimming from the ship and later salvaging cargo from it, these scenes then become part of a sequence about loss and determination, adapted from Daniel Defoe's *Robinson Crusoe*.

As our example indicates, scenes and sequences are usually constructed through *editing*, which is the linking together of two or more shots. Most mainstream or classical films attempt to edit shots and sequences in a way that makes the editing unnoticeable, which is referred to as *continuity editing* or *invisible editing*. This conventional kind of editing suggests a significantly different experience than that provided by the more or less discontinuous constructions found in the theater where changes in scenes are always noticeable. Continuity editing is frequently considered closer to the fluidity of the experience of reading traditional novels. Many films and works of literature can, however, choose a *discontinuous editing* style in which the editing calls attention to itself and to actions and perspectives that do not fit smoothly together. When a work of narrative or dramatic literature is adapted, editing can become a key indicator of how that work is being interpreted. Choose a single sequence or scene, such as the opening sequence of Peter Brook's 1963 *Lord of the Flies*, and analyze how the editing might try to recreate the same section of the William Golding's 1954 novel. If the comparable sections are significantly different, ask how and why the editing reshapes the material of the literature. Might a modern adaptation update a classic literary work by simply transforming a continuous narrative style into a discontinuous one?

Like literature (especially poetry), editing can create rhythms and even rhymes in the style of a film. This can be done, to take two popular strategies, by pacing the editing with *takes* (long takes hold a shot for an extended period of time, while short takes cut quickly) or generating a rhythm of *shot/reverse shot* exchanges (whereby the image might cut between a person looking and the person or thing being looked at). For example, an *establishing shot*, which introduces the place where the action will take place, may introduce the setting of a film, and then be rapidly followed by a series of reverse shots of individuals looking at that same scene. *Sound editing* is also a major part of film style and form, and can involve not only the editing of dialogue and other sounds that are part of the scene, but also *offscreen sounds*, whose source is outside the frame of the image, or *postdubbed sounds*, which are sounds extraneous to the action but which may work to support or counterpoint what is seen in the image. In the remake of Henry James's novella *The Turn of the Screw* as *The Innocents* (1961), the editing of sound becomes one of the most unsettling dimensions of this ghost story. How does this use of sound create a sense of an invisible world? Does it reflect the perspectives of James's story?

Formal parallels and analogies between film and literature are, of course, always imperfect, which may be why they are such productive grounds for analyzing adaptations and other exchanges between film and literature. Focus on these stylistic elements and investigate the meanings or responses that follow from them: Are long takes on the character of *Hamlet* meant to emphasize his inscrutability or his mental paralysis? Does the rapid editing of the battle sequence in Welles's *Chimes at Midnight* portray the energy and brutality of war more graphically than Shakespeare was able to accomplish when his *Henry IV* plays were staged?

Remember the following, however: These formal units found in film and literature represent only a suggestive sampling of the many stylistic possibilities available, pointing toward some of the shared, singular, and transformative techniques that cross between the two practices. There are, in addition, larger structural conventions that should be considered and investigated when thinking about or analyzing film and literature. Traditional theater organizes its dialogues, conflicts, and actions through scenes and acts, and novels usually develop according to chapters. Poetry can make use of an extraordinarily rich heritage of structures from sonnets and epics to numerous lyrical forms. The different expectations and experiences initiated by these and other formal or material distinctions in film and literature may seem obvious but can be the starting point for incisive discussions and writings about film and literature.

8

GENRES AND OTHER ASSUMPTIONS

Literature and film have always been dependent on genres and other paradigms to classify, organize, provoke, and challenge expectations of readers and audiences. Since film arrives historically later than literature, many of film's genres and types come directly or indirectly from literary precedents. Both literary and film genres spring from a social and aesthetic contract: They assume and address an audience's expectations about the conventions of certain kinds of expressions or stories (like a mystery or western), and, following the Hollywood studio system that promoted the production and success of genre films, genres have an important economic and commercial dimension since they prepare readers and audiences for similar or new works that writers and filmmakers want them to see, enjoy, and understand. Genres also contain a tension. On the one hand, they participate in conventions and archetypes that seem to transcend individual examples of that genre; on the other hand, genres continually evolve in terms of specific historical periods and practices.

From Archetypes to Parodies

In one sense, genres are versions of the *archetypes* that help to describe characters and imagery that pervade most literary and cinematic forms. As archetypes, the images of the desert, the lost child, the journey, or the garden often appear as repeatable models of experience, representing, perhaps, periods of crisis or stages in life. When these archetypes take the shape of a religious or cultural story describing central events in the history of that society, these are commonly referred to as *myths*, such as myths that tell of the founding of a country by one great man or woman. When those narratives emphasize an abstract idea or message, they can be characterized as *allegories*, so that the story of a trip into the desert and a triumphant return could be a moral allegory explaining that suffering and struggle will lead to a better life. Since archetypes, myths, allegories, and similar structures assume recognizable patterns and figures, they can easily be the object of *parody* and *irony*. Parody implies a humorous or sarcastic use of well-known models and stories, while irony describes a more complex set of structural or rhetorical maneuvers whereby the ironic phrase or work will create a critical distance between itself and the common or accepted use of the word or form. Irony aims to debunk the original form or fashion or to generate a different meaning from it. An ironic film like *Thelma & Louise* (1991) reverses an old archetype of women as passive and domestic; a parodic film like *This Is Spinal Tap* (1984) gleefully dismantles the myth of the rise of the superstar rock band.

The Evolutions of Genre

Generic classifications have traditionally disagreed about what the primary genres are, and genre is, to say the least, a malleable and changing way to classify films, literature, and our expectations about individual works. Some have claimed fiction, drama, and the lyric are the paramount generic types. Literary critic Northrop Frye has associated the main genres with the seasonal patterns of spring (comedy), summer (romance), fall (tragedy), and winter (satire). Still others have expanded the list of genres to include difficult-to-classify works such as autobiography, lyric fragments, or tragicomedies. Like all generic lists, the following clusters of common genres is a bit loose and in some places debatable, but, by concentrating on plot and dramatic structures, it attempts to highlight the historical paths of some of the primary literary genres as they have evolved into film practice. None of the lineages are, of course, quite so direct or separate.

   Comedy is a dramatic genre that is less about laughs than about the triumph of society and social consensus over the differences of individuals. Classical comedy will typically begin with some social disturbance, such as the separation of lovers, and, as in Shakespeare's *A Midsummer Night's Dream*, will move toward overcoming this crisis and eventually reestablishing harmony, as the lovers are united and society put in balance again. One of the literary descendants of this genre is the *sentimental comedy*: Frequently in the form of a novel or play, these romantic comedies also highlight the estrangement of an individual (from family or society) but the emphasis is more on the emotional alienation. Like all comedic structures, the tears of frustrated desires and social obstacles are eventually overcome and love, marriage, and laughter are the rewards.

In movie culture, there are three clear descendants of those literary genres: The *comedies* associated with laughs are still about the foibles and tribulations of outsiders, but the humor of the outsider's position (whether he is Jacque Tati or Bill Murray) is viewed sympathetically, allowing any eccentricities to be understood or reintegrated into the community. *Screwball comedies*—particularly visible in movies of the 1930s (like the 1939 *Bringing Up Baby*) but still popular today—replicate the plot structure of comedies but exaggerate the physical problems rather than the emotional or social problems of the characters (which is one reason the theater provides many of the literary sources for these movies). Perhaps the most common generic comedy in film today, *romantic comedies*, such as *Sleepless in Seattle* (1993), develop many of the themes and forms of those earlier variations, but usually adapt a more realistic balance between the physical, intellectual, and emotional problems of the individuals at the center; some kind of harmonious conclusion, reasserting a communal balance, remains a defining characteristic, although the standard heterosexual pairings are only one kind of happy couple now found at the movies.

Tragedy is usually presented as the generic opposite of comedy. In classical tragedy, the central character and leader (an Oedipus, a Hamlet) acts out a tragic flaw, which is normally related to pride and which directly affects the health of the community. Inevitably this flaw leads to the leader's suffering and downfall. Unlike the main comedic characters, the tragic figure is not reintegrated into the society but must be sacrificed and expelled, leaving greater knowledge in his or her wake. Many variations on this tragic pattern develop through the Renaissance theater of Shakespeare and other playwrights as it moves toward the realism of the eighteenth and nineteenth centuries. In these centuries *melodrama* emerges as one of the modern derivatives of tragedy. With melodrama too, the protagonist suffers a torment, but the powers that persecute him or her are less a consequence of spiritual fates than of the material forces found in patriarchal families, societies, or governments. Gothic novels use melodramatic plots to pit individuals against supernatural and political horrors, and during this period the classically tragic male frequently becomes the melodramatic female whose plight is often incomprehensible to her and inexpressible by her.

Across a historical leap with numerous variations, melodramas resurface as one of the main literary forms of even the earliest films. By the late 1940s and early 1950s melodrama takes the form of a prominent movie genre known as *women's films* (in films like *Mildred Pierce* [1945]), continuing the transformation of the tragic king into the middle-class woman; in the 1960s and 1970s, the melodramatic tragedy might be seen rematerializing in the *slasher film* (from the 1960 *Psycho* through the 1978 *Halloween*). In the first, an ambitious or passionate woman loses love, family, and economic achievements pursuing her overweening desires (and possibly learns from those experiences). In the second, one or more sexually liberated women ignore parental or social conventions and are violently and graphically slaughtered as an implied sacrifice to social normalcy.

Originating as medieval French tales, *romances* tell stories of chivalric, imaginary, or personal love and the search for fulfillment or completion. *Arthurian legends, quest narratives*, and *picaresque novels* (the kind parodied in works from Cervantes's *Don Quixote* to *Monty Python and the Holy Grail*) are part of this tradition, and it appears in the nineteenth century as variations on the *Bildüngsroman*, novels like Goethe's *Wilhelm Meister's Apprenticeship* or Dickens's *Oliver Twist* about growing up and the various quests associated with that maturation process. In the twentieth century, both the film and literary genres of the *hard-boiled detective stories*, as in the movie *The Big Sleep* (1946), are dark descendants of this genre as they entwine the complex search for truth and meaning with the search for love. Of postwar movie genres, the *road movie* represents another detour on this generic path: Here, the male questors of *Easy Rider* (1969), *Kings of the Road* (1976), or *The Living End* (1992) have little hope of permanent love and little sense of the goal of their travels, yet each makes the search for an undefined grail a way to learn about love and relationships.

Related to romances, *epic poetry* such as Homer's *Odyssey* or William Wordsworth's *The Prelude* depict the heroic adventures of an individual as he confronts and conquers physical and mental obstacles on journeys across the world or the land. Through these encounters, epics recount the originating history of a people and the beginnings of a culture or nation. In the nineteenth century, this originally poetic genre adapted the form of historical fiction, as practiced by writers like Sir Walter Scott, Alessandro Manzoni, and Leo Tolstoy. In these more modern literatures, epic journeys reflect actual historical events and backgrounds, and the hero becomes a more recognizably human character who survives as an emblem of a cultural or national memory. From *Stagecoach* to *Heaven's Gate* (1980) and *Dances with Wolves* (1990), *western movies* follow the epic genre in their emphasis on the hero who conquers the western wilderness and helps establish the history of the American identity. In contemporary *action films* (the *Rambo* sequels [1982–1988], *Die Hard* [1988], and so forth), this epic fight for a national identity takes place in a global environment where the narrative length and detail of classical epics has been replaced by visual spectacles.

Since the plays of Aristophanes (*Lysistrata*) and other Greek and Roman playwrights, *satire* has been a genre of literature that ridicules or exposes human and social follies and vices. Usually less concerned with private life than with public life, satires flourished in the late seventeenth century and eighteenth century in the plays of Molière (*Tartuffe*), the poetry of Alexander Pope ("The Rape of the Lock"), and the narrative prose of Jonathan Swift (*Gulliver's Travels*). By the end of the nineteenth century, playwrights like George Bernard Shaw (*Mrs. Warren's Profession*) and Oscar Wilde (*The Importance of Being Earnest*) debunk with scathing humor the pretensions of Victorian society, and in the twentieth century, literary satire ranges from the dour political attacks on technological society found in George Orwell's novel *1984* to Samuel Beckett's combination of cosmic despair and slapstick mockery (in *Waiting for Godot*, as well as in a minimalist film with Buster Keaton called *Film*). Indeed, the slapstick films of Charlie Chaplin, Keaton, and others represent an early and important connection between literary satire and films that continue to explore, wryly but sometimes severely, the predicament of the human individual caught in the machinery of the twentieth century. That the movies are such a public forum has, moreover, encouraged satiric films in numerous subgenres directly descended from the literary genre: *Comedic satires*, from the movies of the Marx Brothers to *Austin Powers: International Man of Mystery* (1997), poke light fun at human behavior and social rituals; *social satires*, from Erich von Stroheim's bitter portraits of married life in the 1922 *Foolish Wives* to Barry Levinson's *Wag the Dog* (1998), employ little, or only an uncomfortable, humor in leveling sharp criticisms at individuals and institutions; and *reflexive satires*, from Keaton's 1924 *Sherlock Jr.* to Robert Altman's *The Player* (1992), expose and ridicule the politics, individuals, and assumptions of filmmaking itself.

Finally, it is worth considering the *literary film* as a film genre in its own right (just as the movie novel could be considered a literary genre). The literary film can be defined most generally as a film in which a literary work or other literary connections function, like all genres, as part of the expectations it elicits from its audience. In that sense a literary film would include two kinds of movies: (1) adaptations in which the movie draws attention to the literary work from which it is derived, presuming either familiarity with that work or at least cultural recognition of its literary status (whether its 1929 audience had actually read *The Taming of the Shrew* or simply knew it as a celebrated Shakespeare play makes little difference in the generic definition of that Mary Pickford literary film); (2) films in which a prominent literary presence—such as a writer turned filmmaker or a script by a recognized novelist or playwright—shapes expectations about the literary qualities of those films (for instance, a film directed by writer Norman Mailer or the 1995 *Smoke* in which the screenwriting contribution of novelist Paul Auster is highlighted in the promotion of that movie).

Recognizing genres and the connections and differences between works of the same genres is a critical part of how we enjoy movies and literature and how we understand both. Generic models and their historical transformations help viewers appreciate innovations and alterations in, say, how epic films respond one to another. Examining generic subjects and forms as they evolve from literary practices to the cinema deepens and enriches that appreciation and our ability to analyze what a work inherits and how it reinvents that heritage. Some of those changes through the history of a genre are connected to historical and social changes, so that the elevated cosmic subjects of ancient Greek tragedies must give way to the domestic tragedies of a modern life; other changes respond to the different forms and vehicles for those generic structures, so that a romantic quest will take on different characteristics as a narrative poem and a feature film. When considering the generic assumptions that inform a particular literary or film practice, ask how both cultural history and the literary or film form determine its specific issues and styles. If classical epics assumed an omniscient narrative perspective (tantamount to that of a god) in order to acclaim heroes who were like gods, do modern westerns rely on long shots to emphasize how grand perspectives on nature are a significant part of the tales of more democratic nations? If eighteenth-century literary satires direct verbal ironies at the hypocrisy of different classes, do movie satires sometimes make the satire more a physical comedy about individual behavior? More generally, are there movie genres without a literary past?

MAJOR DOCUMENTS AND DEBATES

This section of the book features a wide selection of critical writings on film and literature. The writings represent various approaches to both specific and general questions about the relationships of film and literature. Some may be concerned with cultural issues and survey a large number of examples; others may use models derived from psychology, semiotics, or political science and may concentrate on a single film or filmmaker. Arranged chronologically, the following essays also represent various historical periods and cultures, and their arguments may implicitly or explicitly be responding to how the movies and literature interact in a particular period or particular culture—such as the silent film era in Europe or the field of contemporary popular culture in Hollywood. Across such variety, not surprisingly, some essays are easily accessible and others require more effort to read.

As a general rule through this section of the book, I recommend three guidelines. First, consider each essay as a product of a particular social and historical environment that generates specific issues about the relationship between film and literature. Second, see each argument as addressing and responding to certain films or kinds of film which determine the range of questions and answers available in writing about film and literature. Third, approach the argument of each essay as an open debate—as a point of departure for other questions and discussions about film and literature.

9

HISTORICAL POSITIONS

One of the early pioneers in serious discussions of the movies as an art, Vachel Lindsay was also a determined poet who saw film as a revolutionary vehicle for bringing the spirit of poetry to masses of individuals. The Art of the Moving Picture *was written in 1915 and revised in 1922, and many of its assumptions and arguments are a product of the silent films (especially the work of D. W. Griffith) that defined film culture at the time. Along with a number of sharp insights into a new way of telling stories, Lindsay's work represents a still resonant argument about the real and potential place of movies within society and, more specifically, their place on book shelves in universities and within other institutions of knowledge and culture. Here and at other points in his book, Lindsay demonstrates a sense of the universal potential of film language as it translates social ideas and poetic visions into pictorial terms that all audiences understand. Both this utopian faith in the new language of the cinema and its revolutionary power to claim a place in culture next to literature were shared by Griffith and other early filmmakers.*

"Progress and Endowment"
from *The Art of the Moving Picture*

Vachel Lindsay

The moving picture goes almost as far as journalism into the social fabric in some ways, further in others. Soon, no doubt, many a little town will have its photographic news-press. We have already the weekly world-news films from the big centres.

With local journalism will come devices for advertising home enterprises. Some staple products will be made attractive by having film-actors show their uses. The motion pictures will be in the public schools to stay. Text-books in geography, history, zoölogy, botany, physiology, and other sciences will be illustrated by standardized films. Along with these changes, there will be available at certain centres collections of films equivalent to the Standard Dictionary and the Encyclopædia Britannica.

And sooner or later we will have a straight-out capture of a complete film expression by the serious forces of civilization. The merely impudent motion picture will be relegated to the leisure hours with yellow journalism. Photoplay libraries are inevitable, as active if not as multitudinous as the book-circulating libraries. The oncoming machinery and expense of the motion picture is immense. Where will the money come from? No one knows. What the people want they will get. The race of man cannot afford automobiles, but has them nevertheless. We cannot run away into non-automobile existence or non-steam-engine or non-movie life long at a time. We must conquer this thing. While the more stately scientific and educational aspects just enumerated are slowly on their way, the artists must be up and about their ameliorative work.

Every considerable effort to develop a noble idiom will count in the final result, as the writers of early English made possible the language of the Bible, Shakespeare, and Milton. We are perfecting a medium to be used as long as Chinese ideographs have been. It will no doubt, like the Chinese language, record in the end massive and classical treatises, imperial chronicles, law-codes, traditions, and religious admonitions. All this by the *motion picture* as a recording instrument, not necessarily the *photoplay* [short film], a much more limited thing, a form of art.

...

High-minded graduates of university courses in sociology and schools of philanthropy, devout readers of The Survey, The Chicago Public, The Masses, The New Republic, La Follette's, are going to advocate increasingly, their varied and sometimes contradictory causes, in films. These will generally be produced by heroic exertions in the studio, and much passing of the subscription paper outside.

Then there are endowments already in existence that will no doubt be diverted to the photoplay channel. In every state house, and in Washington, DC, increasing quantities of dead printed matter have been turned out year after year. They have served to kindle various furnaces and feed the paper-mills a second time. Many of these routine reports will remain in innocuous desuetude. But one-fourth of them, perhaps, are capable of being embodied in films. If they are scientific demonstrations, they can be made into realistic motion picture records. If they are exhortations, they can be transformed into plays with a moral, brothers of the film Your Girl and Mine. The appropriations for public printing should include such work hereafter.

The scientific museums distribute routine pamphlets that would set the whole world right on certain points if they were but read by said world. Let them be filmed and started. Whatever the congressman is permitted to [be] frank to his constituency, let him send in the motion picture form when it is the expedient and expressive way.

When men work for the high degrees in the universities, they labor on a piece of literary conspiracy called a thesis which no one outside the university hears of again. The gist of this research work that is dead to the democracy, through the university merits of thoroughness, moderation of statement, and final touch of discovery, would have a chance to live and grip the people in a motion picture transcript, if not a photoplay. It would be University Extension. The relentless fire of criticism which the heads of the departments would pour on the production before they allowed it to pass would result in a standardization of the sense of scientific fact over the land. Suppose the film has the coat of arms of the University of Chicago along with the name of the young graduate whose thesis it is. He would have a chance to reflect credit on the university even as much as a foot-ball player.

Large undertakings might be under way, like those described in the chapter on Architecture-in-Motion. But these would require much more than the ordinary outlay for thesis work, less, perhaps, than is taken for Athletics. Lyman Howe and several other world-explorers have already set the pace in the more human side of the educative film. The list of Mr. Howe's offerings from the first would reveal many a one that would run the gantlet of a university department. He points out a new direction for old energies, whereby professors may become citizens.

Let the cave-man, reader of picture-writing, be allowed to ponder over scientific truth. He is at present the victim of the alleged truth of the specious and sentimental variety of photograph. It gives the precise edges of the coat or collar of the smirking masher and the exact fibre in the dress of the jumping-jack. The eye grows weary of sharp points and hard edges that mean nothing. All this idiotic precision is going to waste. It should be enlisted in the cause of science and abated everywhere else. The edges in art are as mysterious as in science they are exact.

Some of the higher forms of the Intimate Moving Picture play should be endowed by local coteries representing their particular region. Every community of fifty thousand has its group of the cultured who have heretofore studied and imitated things done in the big cities.

Some of these coteries will in exceptional cases become creative and begin to express their habitation and name. The Intimate Photoplay is capable of that delicacy and that informality which should characterize neighborhood enterprises.

The plays could be acted by the group who, season after season, have secured the opera house for the annual amateur show. Other dramatic ability could be found in the high-schools. There is enough talent in any place to make an artistic revolution, if once that region is aflame with a common vision. The spirit that made the Irish Players, all so racy of the soil, can also move the company of local photoplayers in Topeka, or Indianapolis, or Denver. Then let them speak for their town, not only in great occasional enterprises, but steadily, in little fancies, genre pictures, developing a technique that will finally make magnificence possible.

There was given not long ago, at the Illinois Country Club here, a performance of The Yellow Jacket by the Coburn Players. It at once seemed an integral part of this chapter.

The two flags used for a chariot, the bamboo poles for oars, the red sack for a decapitated head, etc., were all convincing, through a direct resemblance as well as the passionate acting. They suggest a possible type of hieroglyphics to be developed by the leader of the local group.

Let the enthusiast study this westernized Chinese play for primitive representative methods. It can be found in book form, a most readable work. It is by G. C. Hazelton, Jr., and J. H. Benrimo. The resemblance between the stage property and the thing represented is fairly close. The moving flags on each side of the actor suggest the actual color and progress of the chariot, and abstractly suggest its magnificence. The red sack used for a bloody head has at least the color and size of one. The dressed-up block of wood used for a child is the length of an infant of the age described and wears the general costume thereof. The farmer's hoe, though exaggerated, is still an agricultural implement.

The evening's list of properties is economical, filling one wagon, rather than three. Photographic realism is splendidly put to rout by powerful representation. When the villager desires to embody some episode that if realistically given would require a setting beyond the means of the available endowment, and does not like the near-Egyptian method, let him evolve his near-Chinese set of symbols.

The Yellow Jacket was written after long familiarity with the Chinese Theatre in San Francisco. The play is a glory to that city as well as to Hazelton and Benrimo. But every town in the United States has something as striking as the Chinese Theatre, to the man who keeps the eye of his soul open. It has its Ministerial Association, its boys' secret society, its red-eyed political gang, its grubby Justice of the Peace court, its free school for the teaching of Hebrew, its snobbish chapel, its fire-engine house, its milliner's shop. All these could be made visible in photoplays as flies are preserved in amber.

Edgar Lee Masters looked about him and discovered the village graveyard, and made it as wonderful as Noah's Ark, or Adam naming the animals, by supplying honest inscriptions to the headstones. Such stories can be told by the Chinese theatrical system as well. As many different films could be included under the general title: "Seven Old Families, and Why they Went to Smash." Or a less ominous series would be "Seven Victorious Souls." For there are triumphs every day under the drab monotony of an apparently defeated town: conquests worthy of the waving of sun-banners.

Above all, The Yellow Jacket points a moral for this chapter because there was conscience behind it. First: the rectitude of the Chinese actors of San Francisco who kept the dramatic tradition alive, a tradition that was bequeathed from the ancient generations. Then the artistic integrity of the men who readapted the tradition for western consumption, and their religious attitude that kept the high teaching and devout feeling for human life intact in the play. Then the zeal of the Drama League that indorsed it for the country. Then the earnest work of the Coburn Players who embodied it devoutly, so that the whole company became dear friends forever.

By some such ladder of conscience as this can the local scenario be endowed, written, acted, filmed, and made a real part of the community life. The Yellow Jacket was a drama, not a photoplay. This chapter does not urge that it be readapted for a photoplay in San Francisco or anywhere else. But a kindred painting-in-motion, something as beautiful and worthy and intimate, in strictly photoplay terms, might well be the flower of the work of the local groups of film actors.

Harriet Monroe's magazine, "Poetry" (Chicago), has given us a new sect, the Imagists:—Ezra Pound, Richard Aldington, John Gould Fletcher, Amy Lowell, F. S. Flint, D. H. Lawrence, and others. They are gathering followers and imitators. To these followers I would say: the Imagist impulse need not be confined to verse. Why would you be imitators of these leaders when you might be creators in a new medium? There is a clear parallelism between their point of view in verse and the Intimate-and-friendly Photoplay, especially when it is developed from the standpoint of the last part of chapter nine, *space measured without sound plus time measured without sound.*

There is no clan to-day more purely devoted to art for art's sake than the Imagist clan. An Imagist film would offer a noble challenge to the overstrained emotion, the overloaded splendor, the mere repetition of what are at present the finest photoplays. Now even the masterpieces are incontinent. Except for some of the old one-reel Biographs of Griffith's beginning, there is nothing of Doric restraint from the best to the worst. Read some of the poems of the people listed above, then imagine the same moods in the films. Imagist photoplays would be Japanese prints taking on life, animated Japanese paintings, Pompeian mosaics in kaleidoscopic but logical succession, Beardsley drawings made into actors and scenery, Greek vase-paintings in motion.

Scarcely a photoplay but hints at the Imagists in one scene. Then the illusion is lost in the next turn of the reel. Perhaps it would be a sound observance to confine this form of motion picture to a half reel or quarter reel, just as the Imagist poem is generally a half or quarter page. A series of them could fill a special evening.

The Imagists are colorists. Some people do not consider that photographic black, white, and gray are color. But here for instance are seven colors which the Imagists might use: (1) The whiteness of swans in the light. (2) The whiteness of swans in a gentle shadow. (3) The color of a sunburned man in the light. (4) His color in a gentle shadow. (5) His color in a deeper shadow. (6) The blackness of black velvet in the light. (7) The blackness of black velvet in a deep shadow. And to use these colors with definite steps from one to the other does not militate against an artistic mystery of edge and softness in the flow of line. There is a list of possible Imagist textures which is only limited by the number of things to be seen in the world. Probably only seven or ten would be used in one scheme and the same list kept through one production.

The Imagist photoplay will put discipline into the inner ranks of the enlightened and remind the sculptors, painters, and architects of the movies that there is a continence even beyond sculpture and that seas of realism may not have the power of a little well-considered elimination.

The use of the scientific film by established institutions like schools and state governments has been discussed. Let the Church also, in her own way, avail herself of the motion picture, wholeheartedly, as in mediaeval time she took over the marvel of Italian painting. There was a stage in her history when religious representation was by Byzantine mosaics, noble in color, having an architectural use, but curious indeed to behold from the standpoint of those who crave a sensitive emotional record. The first paintings of Cimabue and Giotto, giving these formulas a touch of life, were hailed with joy by all Italy. Now the Church Universal has an opportunity to establish her new painters if she will. She has taken over in the course of history, for her glory, miracle plays, Romanesque and Gothic architecture, stained glass windows, and the music of St. Cecilia's organ. Why not this new splendor? The Cathedral of St. John the Divine, on Morningside Heights, should establish in its crypt motion pictures as thoroughly considered as the lines of that building, if possible designed by the architects thereof, with the same sense of permanency.

This chapter does not advocate that the Church lay hold of the photoplays as one more medium for reillustrating the stories of the Bible as they are given in the Sunday-school papers. It is not pietistic simpering that will feed the spirit of Christendom, but a steady church-patronage of the most skilful and original motion picture artists. Let the Church follow the precedent which finally gave us Fra Angelico, Botticelli, Andrea del Sarto, Leonardo da Vinci, Raphael, Michelangelo, Correggio, Titian, Paul Veronese, Tintoretto, and the rest.

Who will endow the successors of the present woman's suffrage film, and other great crusading films? Who will see that the public documents and university researches take on the form of motion pictures? Who will endow the local photoplay and the Imagist photoplay? Who will take the first great measures to insure motion picture splendors in the church?

Things such as these come on the winds of to-morrow. But let the crusader look about him, and where it is possible, put in the diplomatic word, and coöperate with the Gray Norns.

Questions and Projects

- Compare an early D. W. Griffith film to a work of late nineteenth-century theater or fiction. How does the film fail to communicate all that the work of literature does? Are there ways, as Lindsay would claim, that the film expands or surpasses the literary work in communicating certain ideas or emotions?

- Examine a current issue or question regarding film and its relation to education, such as the use of film in science, literature, or history classrooms or the arguments about how movies affect the reading habits of children. How should Lindsay's great claims for the movies as education be tempered or challenged in these instances? Or, can one show, with some detailed analysis, how film does educate in its own manner?

- Select a striking image or series of images from a film, and compare them, as Lindsay suggests, to an Imagist poem by Ezra Pound, Hilda Doolittle (H. D.), or another poet of that school.

If Lindsay was primarily interested in the social force of movies as it advanced the spirit of traditional literature, Munsterberg, writing at about the same time (1916), approached the film/literature debate from a very different point of view: Using a psychology and aesthetics of perception, he investigates how film organizes human experience in a way that distinguishes it from other artistic and literary forms. For him, that unique organization is a function of film's intimate access to an internal movement and a psychological space that other literatures can only approach or describe. With these more abstract matters addressed in the first part of his book, he turns in the second part to a discussion of film as an art form distinguished from traditional literature and art. One of the significant historical points about the following excerpt from The Film: A Psychological Study *is that it practices film criticism and theory as rigorously as academic philosophy and social sciences, employing an interdisciplinary approach that assumes from the start that film is as complex as literature and theater. If Lindsay draws the debate about film and literature into a social arena, Munsterberg delineates a psychological aesthetic that would become, despite his archaic description of film as a "photoplay," a rich framework for discussion of the illusory forms of the art cinema—of German Expressionism, French Surrealism, and others—that flourished from 1917 to 1930.*

"The Means of Photoplay"
from *The Film: A Psychological Study*
Hugo Munsterberg

We have now reached the point at which we can knot together all our threads, the psychological and the esthetic ones. If we do so, we come to the true thesis of this whole book. Our esthetic discussion showed us that it is the aim of art to isolate a significant part of our experience in such a way that it is separate from our practical life and is in complete agreement within itself. Our esthetic satisfaction results from this inner agreement and harmony, but in order that we may feel such agreement of the parts we must enter with our own impulses into the will of every element, into the meaning of every line and color and form, every word and tone and note. Only if everything is full of such inner movement can we really enjoy the harmonious coöperation of the parts. The means of the various arts, we saw, are the forms and methods by which this aim is fulfilled. They must be different for every material. Moreover the same material may allow very different methods of isolation and elimination of the insignificant and reënforcement of that which contributes to the harmony. If we ask now what are the characteristic means by which the photoplay succeeds in overcoming reality, in isolating a significant dramatic story and in presenting it so that we enter into it and yet keep it away from our practical life and enjoy the harmony of the parts, we must remember all the results to which our psychological discussion in the first part of the book has led us.

We recognized there that the photoplay, incomparable in this respect with the drama, gave us a view of dramatic events which was completely shaped by the inner movements of the mind. To be sure, the events in the photoplay happen in the real space with its depth. But the spectator feels that they are not presented in the three dimensions of the outer world, that they are flat pictures which only the mind molds into plastic things. Again the events are seen in continuous movement; and yet the pictures break up the movement into a rapid succession of instantaneous impressions. We do not see the objective reality, but a product of our own mind which binds the pictures together. But much stronger differences came to light when we turned to the processes of attention, of memory, of imagination, of suggestion, of division of interest and of emotion. The attention turns to detailed points in the outer world and ignores everything else: the photoplay is doing exactly this when in the close-up a detail is enlarged and everything else disappears. Memory breaks into present events by bringing up pictures of the past: the photoplay is doing this by its frequent cut-backs, when pictures of events long past flit between those of the present. The imagination anticipates the future or overcomes reality by fancies and dreams; the photoplay is doing all this more richly than any chance imagination would succeed in doing. But chiefly, through our division of interest our mind is drawn hither and thither. We think of events which run parallel in different places. The photoplay can show in intertwined scenes everything which our mind embraces. Events in three or four or five regions of the world can be woven together into one complex action. Finally, we saw that every shade of feeling and emotion which fills the spectator's mind can mold the scenes in the photoplay until they appear the embodiment of our feelings. In every one of these aspects the photoplay succeeds in doing what the drama of the theater does not attempt.

If this is the outcome of esthetic analysis on the one side, of psychological research on the other, we need only combine the results of both into a unified principle: *the photoplay tells us the human story by overcoming the forms of the outer world, namely, space, time, and causality, and by adjusting the events to the forms of the inner world, namely, attention, memory, imagination, and emotion.*

We shall gain our orientation most directly if once more, under this point of view, we compare the photoplay with the performance on the theater stage. We shall not enter into a discussion of the character of the regular theater and its drama. We take this for granted. Everybody knows that highest art form which the Greeks created and which from Greece has spread over Asia, Europe, and America. In tragedy and in comedy from ancient times to Ibsen, Rostand, Hauptmann, and Shaw we recognize one common purpose and one common form for which no further commentary is needed. How does the photoplay differ from a theater performance? We insisted that every work of art must be somehow separated from our sphere of practical interests. The theater is no exception. The structure of the theater itself, the framelike form of the stage, the difference of light between stage and house, the stage setting and costuming, all inhibit in the audience the possibility of taking the action on the stage to be real life. Stage managers have sometimes tried the experiment of reducing those differences, for instance, keeping the audience also in a fully lighted hall, and they always had to discover how much the dramatic effect was reduced because the feeling of distance from reality was weakened. The photoplay and the theater in this respect are evidently alike. The screen too suggests from the very start the complete unreality of the events.

But each further step leads us to remarkable differences between the stage play and the film play. In every respect the film play is further away from the physical reality than the drama and in every respect this greater distance from the physical world brings it nearer to the mental world. The stage shows us living men. It is not the real Romeo and not the real Juliet; and yet the actor and the actress have the ringing voices of true people, breathe like them, have living colors like them, and fill physical space like them. What is left in the photoplay? The voice has been stilled: the photoplay is a dumb show. Yet we must not forget that this alone is a step away from reality which has often been taken in the midst of the dramatic world. Whoever knows the history of the theater is aware of the tremendous rôle which the pantomime has played in the development of mankind. From the old half-religious pantomimic and suggestive dances out of which the beginnings of the real drama grew to the fully religious pantomimes of medieval ages and, further on, to many silent mimic elements in modern performances, we find a continuity of conventions which make the pantomime almost the real background of all dramatic development. We know how popular the pantomimes were among the Greeks, and how they stood in the foreground in the imperial period of Rome. Old Rome cherished the mimic clowns, but still more the tragic pantomimics. "Their very nod speaks, their hands talk and their fingers have a voice." After the fall of the Roman empire the church used the pantomime for the portrayal of sacred history, and later centuries enjoyed very unsacred histories in the pantomimes of their ballets. Even complex artistic tragedies without words have triumphed on our present-day stage. *L'Enfant Prodigue* which came from Paris, *Sumurun* which came from Berlin, *Petroushka* which came from Petrograd, conquered the American stage; and surely the loss of speech, while it increased the remoteness from reality, by no means destroyed the continuous consciousness of the bodily existence of the actors.

Moreover the student of a modern pantomime cannot overlook a characteristic difference between the speechless performance on the stage and that of the actors of a photoplay. The expression of the inner states, the whole system of gestures, is decidedly different: and here we might say that the photoplay stands nearer to life than the pantomime. Of course, the photoplayer must somewhat exaggerate the natural expression. The whole rhythm and intensity of his gestures must be more marked than it would be with actors who accompany their movements by spoken words and who express the meaning of their thoughts and feelings by the content of what they say. Nevertheless the photoplayer uses the regular channels of mental discharge. He acts simply as a very emotional person might act. But the actor who plays in a pantomime cannot be satisfied with that. He is expected to add something which is entirely unnatural, namely a kind of artificial demonstration of his emotions. He must not only behave like an angry man, but he must behave like a man who is consciously interested in his anger and wants to demonstrate it to others. He exhibits his emotions for the spectators. He really acts theatrically for the benefit of the bystanders. If he did not try to do so, his means of conveying a rich story and a real conflict of human passions would be too meager. The photoplayer, with the rapid changes of scenes, has other possibilities of conveying his intentions. He must not yield to the temptation to play a pantomime on the screen, or he will seriously injure the artistic quality of the reel.

The really decisive distance from bodily reality, however, is created by the substitution of the actor's picture for the actor himself. Lights and shades replace the manifoldness of color effects and mere perspective must furnish the suggestion of depth. We traced it when we discussed the psychology of kinematoscopic perception. But we must not put the emphasis on the wrong point. The natural tendency might be to lay the chief stress on the fact that those people in the photoplay do not stand before us in flesh and blood. The essential point is rather that we are conscious of the flatness of the picture. If we were to see the actors of the stage in a mirror, it would also be a reflected image which we perceive. We should not really have the actors themselves in our straight line of vision; and yet this image would appear to us equivalent to the actors themselves, because it would contain all the depth of the real stage. The film picture is such a reflected rendering of the actors. The process which leads from the living men to the screen is more complex than a mere reflection in a mirror, but in spite of the complexity in the transmission we do, after all, see the real actor in the picture. The photograph is absolutely different from those pictures which a clever draughtsman has sketched. In the photoplay we see the actors themselves and the decisive factor which makes the impression different from seeing real men is not that we see the living persons through the medium of photographic reproduction but that this reproduction shows them in a flat form. The bodily space has been eliminated. We said once before that stereoscopic arrangements could reproduce somewhat this plastic form also. Yet this would seriously interfere with the character of the photoplay. We need there this overcoming of the depth, we want to have it as a picture only and yet as a picture which strongly suggests to us the actual depth of the real world. We want to keep the interest in the plastic world and want to be aware of the depth in which the persons move, but our direct object of perception must be without the depth. That idea of space which forces on us most strongly the idea of heaviness, solidity and substantiality must be replaced by the light flitting immateriality.

But the photoplay sacrifices not only the space values of the real theater; it disregards no less its order of time. The theater presents its plot in the time order of reality. It may interrupt the continuous flow of time without neglecting the conditions of the dramatic art. There may be twenty years between the third and the fourth act, inasmuch as the dramatic writer must select those elements spread over space and time which are significant for the development of his story. But he is bound by the fundamental principle of real time, that it can move only forward and not backward. Whatever the theater shows us now must come later in the story than that which it showed us in any previous moment. The strict classical demand for complete unity of time does not fit every drama, but a drama would give up its mission if it told us in the third act something which happened before the second act. Of course, there may be a play within a play, and the players on the stage which is set on the stage may play events of old Roman history before the king of France. But this is an enclosure of the past in the present, which corresponds exactly to the actual order of events. The photoplay, on the other hand, does not and must not respect this temporal structure of the physical universe. At any point the photoplay interrupts the series and brings us back to the past. We studied this unique feature of the film art when we spoke of the psychology of memory and imagination. With the full freedom of our fancy, with the whole mobility of our association of ideas, pictures of the past flit through the scenes of the present. Time is left behind. Man becomes boy; today is interwoven with the day before yesterday. The freedom of the mind has triumphed over the unalterable law of the outer world.

It is interesting to watch how playwrights nowadays try to steal the thunder of the photoplay and experiment with time reversals on the legitimate stage. We are esthetically on the borderland when a grandfather tells his grandchild the story of his own youth as a warning, and instead of the spoken words the events of his early years come before our eyes. This is, after all, quite similar to a play within a play. A very different experiment is tried in *Under Cover*. The third act, which plays on the second floor of the house, ends with an explosion. The fourth act, which plays downstairs, begins a quarter of an hour before the explosion. Here we have a real denial of a fundamental condition of the theater. Or if we stick to recent products of the American stage, we may think of *On Trial*, a play which perhaps comes nearest to a dramatic usurpation of the rights of the photoplay. We see the court scene and as one witness after another begins to give his testimony the courtroom is replaced by the scenes of the actions about which the witness is to report. Another clever play, *Between the Lines*, ends the first act with a postman bringing three letters from the three children of the house. The second, third, and fourth acts lead us to the three different homes from which the letters came and the action in the three places not only precedes the writing of the letters, but goes on at the same time. The last act, finally, begins with the arrival of the letters which tell the ending of those events in the three homes. Such experiments are very suggestive but they are not any longer pure dramatic art. It is always possible to mix arts. An Italian painter produces very striking effects by putting pieces of glass and stone and rope into his paintings, but they are no longer pure paintings. The drama in which the later event comes before the earlier is an esthetic barbarism which is entertaining as a clever trick in a graceful superficial play, but intolerable in ambitious dramatic art. It is not only tolerable but perfectly natural in any photoplay. The pictorial reflection of the world is not bound by the rigid mechanism of time. Our mind is here and there, our mind turns to the present and then to the past: the photoplay can equal it in its freedom from the bondage of the material world.

But the theater is bound not only by space and time. Whatever it shows is controlled by the same laws of causality which govern nature. This involves a complete continuity of the physical events: no cause without following effect, no effect without preceding cause. This whole natural course is left behind in the play on the screen. The deviation from reality begins with that resolution of the continuous movement which we studied in our psychological discussions. We saw that the impression of movement results from an activity of the mind which binds the separate pictures together. What we actually see is a composite; it is like the movement of a fountain in which every jet is resolved into numberless drops. We feel the play of those drops in their sparkling haste as one continuous stream of water, and yet are conscious of the myriads of drops, each one separate from the others. This fountainlike spray of pictures has completely overcome the causal world.

In an entirely different form this triumph over causality appears in the interruption of the events by pictures which belong to another series. We find this whenever the scene suddenly changes. The processes are not carried to their natural consequences. A movement is started, but before the cause brings its results another scene has taken its place. What this new scene brings may be an effect for which we saw no causes. But not only the processes are interrupted. The intertwining of the scenes which we have traced in detail is itself such a contrast to causality. It is as if different objects could fill the same space at the same time. It is as if the resistance of the material world had disappeared and the substances could penetrate one another. In the interlacing of our ideas we experience this superiority to all physical laws. The theater would not have even the technical means to give us such impressions, but if it had, it would have no right to make use of them, as it would destroy the basis on which the drama is built. We have only another case of the same type in those series of pictures which aim to force a suggestion on our mind. We have spoken of them. A certain effect is prepared by a chain of causes and yet when the causal result is to appear the film is cut off. We have the causes without the effect. The villain thrusts with his dagger—but a miracle has snatched away his victim.

While the moving pictures are lifted above the world of space and time and causality and are freed from its bounds, they are certainly not without law. We said before that the freedom with which the pictures replace one another is to a large degree comparable to the sparkling and streaming of the musical tones. The yielding to the play of the mental energies, to the attention and emotion, which is felt in the film pictures, is still more complete in the musical melodies and harmonies in which the tones themselves are merely the expressions of the ideas and feelings and will impulses of the mind. Their harmonies and disharmonies, their fusing and blending, is not controlled by any outer necessity, but by the inner agreement and disagreement of our free impulses. And yet in this world of musical freedom, everything is completely controlled by esthetic necessities. No sphere of practical life stands under such rigid rules as the realm of the composer. However bold the musical genius may be he cannot emancipate himself from the iron rule that his work must show complete unity in itself. All the separate prescriptions which the musical student has to learn are ultimately only the consequences of this central demand which music, the freest of the arts, shares with all the others. In the case of the film, too, the freedom from the physical forms of space, time, and causality does not mean any liberation from this esthetic bondage either. On the contrary, just as music is surrounded by more technical rules than literature, the photoplay must be held together by the esthetic demands still more firmly than is the drama. The arts which are subordinated to the conditions of space, time, and causality find a certain firmness of structure in these material forms which contain an element of outer connectedness. But where these forms are given up and where the freedom of mental play replaces their outer necessity, everything would fall asunder if the esthetic unity were disregarded.

This unity is, first of all, the unity of action. The demand for it is the same which we know from the drama. The temptation to neglect it is nowhere greater than in the photoplay where outside matter can so easily be introduced or independent interests developed. It is certainly true for the photoplay, as for every work of art, that nothing has the right to existence in its midst which is not internally needed for the unfolding of the unified action. Wherever two plots are given to us, we receive less by far than if we had only one plot. We leave the sphere of valuable art entirely when a unified action is ruined by mixing it with declamation, and propaganda which is not organically interwoven with the action itself. It may be still fresh in memory what an esthetically intolerable helter-skelter performance was offered to the public in *The Battlecry of Peace*. Nothing can be more injurious to the esthetic cultivation of the people than such performances which hold the attention of the spectators by ambitious detail and yet destroy their esthetic sensibility by a complete disregard or the fundamental principle of art, the demand for unity. But we recognized also that this unity involves complete isolation. We annihilate beauty when we link the artistic creation with practical interests and transform the spectator into a selfishly interested bystander. The scenic background of the play is not presented in order that we decide whether we want to spend our next vacation there. The interior decoration of the rooms is not exhibited as a display for a department store. The men and women who carry out the action of the plot must not be people whom we may meet tomorrow on the street. All the threads of the play must be knotted together in the play itself and none should be connected with our outside interests. A good photoplay must be isolated and complete in itself like a beautiful melody. It is not an advertisement for the newest fashions.

This unity of action involves unity of characters. It has too often been maintained by those who theorize on the photoplay that the development of character is the special task of the drama, while the photoplay, which lacks words, must be satisfied with types. Probably this is only a reflection of the crude state which most photoplays of today have not outgrown. Internally, there is no reason why the means of the photoplay should not allow a rather subtle depicting of complex character. But the chief demand is that the characters remain consistent, that the action be developed according to inner necessity and that the characters themselves be in harmony with the central idea of the plot. However, as soon as we insist on unity we have no right to think only of the action which gives the content of the play. We cannot make light of the form. As in music the melody and rhythms belong together, as in painting not every color combination suits every subject, and as in poetry not every stanza would agree with every idea, So the photoplay must bring action and pictorial expression into perfect harmony. But this demand repeats itself in every single picture. We take it for granted that the painter balances perfectly the forms in his painting, groups them so that an internal symmetry can be felt and that the lines and curves and colors blend into a unity. Every single picture of the sixteen thousand which are shown to us in one reel ought to be treated with this respect of the pictorial artist for the unity of the forms.

The photoplay shows us a significant conflict of human actions in moving pictures which, freed from the physical forms of space, time, and causality, are adjusted to the free play of our mental experiences and which reach complete isolation from the practical world through the perfect unity of plot and pictorial appearance.

Questions and Projects

- Choose a film made between 1900 and 1925 (perhaps F. W. Murnau's *Nosferatu* [1922] or *The Last Laugh* [1924] or an early Fritz Lang movie) and a work of literature written about the same time (August Strindberg's play *The Ghost Sonata*, the prose fiction of James Joyce, or a poem by T. S. Eliot, for example) that best demonstrates or that best refutes Munsterberg's position about the different capacities of film and literature to represent psychological experiences.

- Select a novel or other work of literature and demonstrate how it attempts to approximate psychological experiences as they are shown on film. To what extent do literary techniques such as "stream of consciousness" validate Munsterberg's argument about the psychological limitations of literature and advantages of film? Are there psychological experiences that literature can represent that the movies cannot?

A Chilean who spent much of her adult life in Spain, Mistral was an active and well-known poet. Her claims for the poetry of cinema here are both aesthetic and social, and this doubled polemic reflects the times when it was written (the middle of the 1930s): From the 1920s through the 1930s, many parts of society questioned both the social value of cinema and its ability to create truly imaginative forms. Clearly she believes in the power of cinema to do both, and her two-pronged argument that films can be as socially responsible and as imaginative as the best poetry might best be illustrated by the contemporaneous work of filmmaker Luis Buñuel, which blended social realism and poetic fantasy. Mistral's essay, however, is relevant to the works of other filmmakers, from Jean Renoir to Werner Herzog to Monty Python's Terry Gilliam, as well as to mainstream animation and cartoons. Besides questioning the importance of realism at the movies, Mistral points toward larger issues whereby the literary imagination finds a place in film: the poetry of children's movies, the relationship between literary masterpieces and big budgets, and the cinema as education, for example.

"The Poet's Attitude toward the Movies" from *The Movies on Trial*

Gabriela Mistral (Lucila Godoy)

Translated from the Spanish by Marion A. Zeitlin

The poet's attitude toward the movies is necessarily the same as that which he adopts toward all things; he demands of the movies that the reality of the world be reduced, translated, wrought by them into poetry. Even though it may sound strange, this demand is most natural.

For who is the poet but that one for whom poetry constitutes both the true outward semblance of things and creatures and their inmost heart? The poet, with the same voice as the mystic, names as appearance, phantasmagoria, chaff and dross, all the material, heaped up or scattered abroad in the world, which has not yet been exalted to, or has ceased to be, poetry.

NATURALISM

The invention of the moving picture caused the *Naturalist* or *Realist* hosts to leap with joy. With it the reign of the image was being stoutly inaugurated: we were coming to a kind of *Transfiguration* of photography; an art was making its appearance that could have no other support than matter.

This time, as ever, the rational Demon was wrong, and the advantage slipped out of his hands and into those of the gods.

Naturalism (we take that of Zola as the archetype) is a puny undertaking, a march that exhausts itself after a few steps. Never has there been a school that wore itself out more easily, that spent itself more rapidly. A school is, in a way, like maternity: its virtue resides in its being fertile and its being able to overspread several centuries with its descendants. But naturalism proved sadly lacking in maternity; within fifty years its generative powers were gone.

Before thirty years had passed, it became evident that naturalism had succeeded only in making odious that which the Master considered to be Nature, but which was in reality no more than the outer integument of the natural, and was projecting the soul again and with meteor-like violence in the direction of the most unbridled poetry. Nature had acted somewhat like a vaccine against itself.

The cinema has turned out to be an art that evolves more rapidly than any other, the livest branch on the good tree of the Arts, an art directed, even in its worst zones, by people of greater talent than literary patrons. This may be seen in the fact that the return to fancy has been much more rapid in the movies than in literature.

IMAGINATION

I believe in the future of the cinema as great art only in proportion as it packs itself with imagination, and I should believe in its vertical decline if I saw in it the symptoms (ever arteriosclerotic) of slavery to the fact, to the phenomenon, to immediate reality.

I am using the word *reality* here not with the meaning that I myself give it, but with that given it by people in general. Reality for me is all they hold it to be, plus all the unseen worlds with which reality is inextricably interlocked.

Let us consider the landscape, which should afford the naturalist his greatest success. I have just seen a short and very felicitous French film, built on the theme of *water*, which if one were to judge by the announcements, promises something like an elementary chapter in realism.

The most beautiful—and most real—parts of this film are those in which a horizontal—or a vertical—mass of free water takes on fantastic aspects, ceasing to be water and coming to suggest some other element.

I recall certain mountain scenes where those spots and those moments were sought in which the mere mountain, released from itself, was transformed into a phantasmagoria of mirrors or into a misty dreamland.

Man—poor Zola never understood—is surfeited with man, satiated and nauseated with man. And it seems that, like us, what we call Nature and believe to be the rational *par excellence*, loathes being only what it is, and is ever seeking modes and attitudes which free it from its rusty hinges and send it flying down heroically mad ways.

The other perfectly rational domain which the movies invaded, besides the landscape, was that of biography or historical fact. At first sight, it seems that here as well, it would be impossible to escape the exact, the veracious; that here too, the *genre* would give more and more pleasure to the spectator in the degree that it conformed with the arid truth. Nothing of the kind: the Napoleons, Ivan the Terribles, Mary Stuarts, seen through the eyes of the historian, presented in schoolmaster fashion, were flat, tedious, stupid, in short, the very opposite of what those splendid figures really were. Then there began to appear Napoleons and Marys transformed into phosphorescent myths, fashioned by truth and dreaming in collaboration. The public, that seems so stupid, but is in truth, like the child, who is never stupid—the public found a source of admiration and delight in those characters conceived in a cross-breeding of historical exactitude and beautiful fiction.

We shall go further yet in the future and weave our heroes of flesh and blood into the same tapestry of imagination and light as our *Parsifals* and *Lohengrins*.

Let us pass to another branch, in which the real is, to all appearances, triumphant: the scientific film, applied to botany, biology, or mineralogy.

We have seen the opening of a flower and its fertilization, witnessing the vegetable rite, an unadorned act of plant life; we have sliced away the disfiguring commentary and the auxiliary paraphernalia.

The flower, magnified so as to be enormously visible, is from the outset a very different flower from the one we knew; the stamens and pistil have become a forest; the calyx has been transformed into a kind of Roman fountain. The image takes hold of us, jolts us, carries us away, because of its metamorphosis, because it has ceased to be natural and has become fantastic. The same thing happens with the tissue of the human body, in which we are shown the circulation of the blood. We had never seen, nor even imagined, the wonder of the coursing of that mechanical and cunning fluid, which, at this very moment, is taking place within us; and when it is revealed to us in all its complexity, it all at once ceases to be looked upon by us as a natural (and, therefore, ordinary) function, and changes into wonder—that is, into food for the imagination rather than for the intellect.

What has been said applies equally well to the study of insects or the reactions of substances in a chemical experiment.

It still remains for us to cast a glance at the most fascinating portion of the movies of the past or the future: the juvenile movie. Let us make it clear that in using the word "juvenile," we have in mind the child, and not a certain moral zone which takes in all of us.

Without pretending to greatness—on the contrary, unconscious of being anything more than insignificant trifles—there appeared years ago, for the delight of children the whole series of "Mickies," "Felixes" and "Betty Boops." Prior to that, two other ways had been tried: that of the clown of flesh and blood, and that of the simple puppet or marionette. The clown wore out quickly: he lacked the piquant aid of verbal buffoonery, and without his jests, soon palled. The puppets made a much greater contribution, so much so that it may be said that the clever animated cartoon of today is another puppet show, conceived and made for children, and proving to be excellent for the adult seeker after carnal—and angelical—laughter.

I expressly say *angelical* to indicate a *genre* which is on the way, but has not yet arrived. Juvenile humor is being elaborated gradually from a curious mixture of the adult, the infantile, the zoological and the angelical. Time and space make it impossible for me to describe completely this attractive field with its interplay of mischievous, grotesque and beautiful elements. This simple indication is sufficient for anyone familiar with the subject.

GREAT THEMES

If motion-picture publications failed to signalize Wells' "The Invisible Man" as one of the successes of the year, it must have been because no great stars took part in this film, and because so worthwhile a work as this was not approached with all the emphasis on complete realization that it deserved.

Nevertheless, in spite of having been made with second-rate actors and with a niggardly outlay of money, this film, belonging to the imaginative type, pleased the crowd, and at the same time, afforded the cultivated a glimpse of the possibilities of the fantastic movie.

Here lies a dangerous fault in the moving-picture industry. With the exception of Germany, Russia, and, occasionally, the United States, the general rule is for it to spend large sums on silly stories, which are finally put over by means of great actors and outrageous extravagance in the settings.

On the other hand, it adopts masterly stories infrequently, intrusts them to mediocre actors, and expends money grudgingly for their production.

I shudder at the thought of someday seeing "The Divine Comedy" acted by bunglers with wretched pasteboard sets to represent Heaven and Hell; or "Hamlet," put on by gesticulating puppets and mumbling ghosts.

The masterpiece has not yet been given financial support in keeping with its dignity by an industry which stands today among the most opulent. Such works are either eliminated because they are still regarded as bogies terrible to face, or else they are produced by the overbold in a style that reminds one of the way they are presented in small towns in the tableaux of school children—that is, with the most beautiful of cynicism.

THE GENERAL PUBLIC AND FANCY

It is unbelievable how the people, generally looked upon as the Sancho Panza *par excellence*, a creature of sight, hearing and touch, a Herod that abhors and persecutes the creations of the imagination—it is unbelievable, I say, how they love imagination above the best reality, how they seek after it if the way is opened to them, and how, once they are in its realm, they are allured by it, partake of it, revel in it, and are loath to give it up.

Absurd though it may seem, it is the most natural thing in the world. Those masses of industrial workers and small functionaries lived imagination—if ever—in their first seven years. Afterwards, work cast them headlong into the blackest slime, into the foulest cloacas of the real. Here they vaguely long for the phosphorescence with which things glowed when they looked at them or touched them as children; each one dimly retains in his thoughts the memory of the man he was before becoming merely a stevedore, miner or garbage collector—that is, the memory of the child, the angel that consumes and produces wonder.

Neither the musician nor the poet went near this man, degraded by the "nobility" of labor and turned by it into the reverse of what he really is. It was necessary for the movies and the radio to come for poet, painter and musician to enter his life and reinstall all the old, holy illusions without which none of God's creatures can remain what he was intended to be.

I realize very well that through these two sluices, the radio and the movies, open now and forever upon the masses, there has poured forth also all the great stupidity, the tacky shoddiness, the crudity of poor art which plebeianizes as much as good art ennobles. But, at any rate, these sluices allow nobility to pass out along with the scum and the mud, and he who understands, little by little learns to separate them, tastes spirituality, and is saved.

It seems that there were no other channels than these dangerous ones of the radio and the movies through which art might flow out abundantly over popular life. We must accept them and be thankful for them, therefore, without wavering as we musicians and writers have in the past.

Each new discovery becomes a sort of autonomous being, and has, like us, its demons and its angels who attend it in legions, just as they did the Jew of the Zohar. Each invention scarcely sees the light when it must, like Adam, set about defending itself from those Satanical parasites which fall upon it as soon as it begins to grow, and seek to live on it and devour it, or to attach themselves to it.

Among the demons of the movies let us count *Realism*; and let us point to *Poetry* as its good genius.

For the first time since what is called "popular education" has existed, there might now be a chance to elevate the masses through the imaginative. The schools have *handled* the masses through the will and through the emotions—in a much smaller way, through the intellect—

using pedagogics that resolve themselves into little more than emotive, volitive and intellectual hocus-pocus.

The imagination, an aristocratic faculty if there ever was one, and the oldest of all, being the mother of two of those mentioned, has never constituted a serious interest, much less an acknowledged aim of any well-known pedagogy—inasmuch as the pedagogical leader is commonly the man most lacking in it that ever God set loose upon the earth.

The movies might take over this untouched field in popular education, that is, imagination on a huge scale, which is viewed with horror by incapable pedagogues and completely neglected by stupid parents.

REPROACHES

Three classes of well-intentioned people cry out against the movies from the four points of the compass: teachers, clergymen, and parents. The first want, more or less, a utilitarian cinema that would help them teach lessons—or replace them—and that would calm down the rather tragic tumult they have brought to the child's mind. The second want films that will not pervert the devout clientele of their churches, and that will aid, if possible, their soul-saving sermons. The third demand of the movies that they shall not go on inciting their children to lives of adventure with detective stories, gangsters, gypsies, etc.

Teachers may be answered by saying that the moving picture will be vertically educational only within the boundaries of the school, and that in Rome a certain International Educational Cinematographic Institute, to which they attach little importance, is engaged, under the auspices of the League of Nations, in supplying better and better—at times even perfect—material. But the extra-scholastic movie, the commercial spectacle, can never become more than obliquely educational, because children seek it as pure pleasure, as they seek water for their boats or wind for their kites.

To clergymen, it may be said that the struggle between church and cinema for the soul of the hearer and spectator is going to be won, not by the purer (alas!), but by the better judge of human nature, by the one that offers the more savory bait to the terrible prey, which is very worldly and demands, even of the Gospel, an insnaring eloquence.

The answer to parents is that they have so neglected to make their children read, to give them noble adventure in books and, more especially, in the nursery tale, in short, that they have been and are parents so Mosaic in their imperious dryness and doctrinal wearisomeness, that their very vital offspring have slipped away from them and tumbled over the precipice of the gangster film. Let them learn entrancingly to tell and repeat Homer or Shakespeare, let them become capable of gay puerilities, and it is possible that as in the mystery of homeopathy, they may cure the hopeless cancer with the white aconite of the bedtime story about dragons and goblins, which they have so long been omitting to tell.

The poet, at this point, can give his solemn assurance that imagination, great imagination, saves here too, and that it is moral for the very reason that it is not professionally so. The imagination, like things universally, has its underground cellars and its sunny chambers, and he who has not grown accustomed to live in the sunlight of balcony and terrace, must live among the musty odors of the basement, at home with bats and dampness. Great imagination, which is of starry essence, which is itself a firmament, does not vitiate palates, pollute bodies or communicate noxious fevers. Vitiation and fever are the portion of that gentleman so dear to the good *bourgeois*, who has gone by the name of *Naturalism*.

The Poet's Plea and Demand

We poets ask of the movies this thing which we have given up asking of the school because we are completely disillusioned with it. We must have at least as much right to be heard on this question as the Salvation Army has to demand sickly moralities, or Manufacturers' Associations to call for something that will "pep up" labor.

What we demand has already been indicated: that they should reproduce a state of childhood in the adult and prolong it in the child by means of the story of pure imagination; that they should, with the instrument of fancy, rejuvenate this world which goes limping along like a cripple with its broken limbs and its noble passions all awry. The theologians, exalted gentlemen, say of imagination that she gave birth to the world, God's imagining, and that since that divine phantasmagoria nothing tonic has ever happened in history that has not been brought forth by her, the one and only cause of miracles in this world.

Questions and Projects

- Find a work of literature in which the imagination plays a thematic role—*The Tempest* or *Wuthering Heights*, for example—and show how its film adaptation portrays that realm of imagination. Attempt to define and illustrate as concretely as possible what imagination means in both the literature and the film.

- To what extent might animation films provide the clearest link with the literary imagination and poetry specifically? Choose one or two animation films and argue for or against this point. Are there specific literary antecedents for this kind of "cinematic poetry," such as the nonsense verse of Lewis Carroll or the illogical flights of French symbolist poetry?

*W*ritten in 1935, Benjamin's "The Work of Art in the Age of Mechanical Reproduction" is one of the most widely cited and quoted essays in studies of film and studies of twentieth-century aesthetics. The reasons are many, but for students of the relationship between film and literature, this essay is especially central as it combines and extends some of the ideas introduced by Lindsay and Munsterberg: namely, that film offers a radical social relationship with modern audiences and this new relationship—supported by the technological differences of the cinema—is decidedly different from the one implied in classical art and literature. Literature itself is not discussed in much detail in this excerpt; Benjamin provides only suggestive remarks about the French poet Stéphane Mallarmé, Italian playwright Luigi Pirandello, Max Reinhardt's adaptation of A Midsummer Night's Dream, and the literature of Dadaism. Yet his concern with how audiences relate to and comprehend film, in what he considered a new age, opens enormously important questions about film culture versus literary culture. These questions not only reflect the changes in the 1930s in how the two arts looked at each other, but they have continued to influence debates about language, literacy, and literature/film discussions since then. Indeed, his comments on the vexed issue of "authenticity" provide a powerful starting point for arguments about adaptation. (Benjamin's essay is not reproduced here in its entirety; this excerpt begins with section III of the original essay. I have omitted the numerical divisions—i.e., section III, section IV, etc.—used in the original essay.)

"The Work of Art in the Age of Mechanical Reproduction" from *Illuminations*

Walter Benjamin

... During long periods of history, the mode of human sense perception changes with humanity's entire mode of existence. The manner in which human sense perception is organized, the medium in which it is accomplished, is determined not only by nature but by historical circumstances as well. The fifth century, with its great shifts of population, saw the birth of the late Roman art industry and the Vienna Genesis, and there developed not only an art different from that of antiquity but also a new kind of perception. The scholars of the Viennese school, Riegl and Wickhoff, who resisted the weight of classical tradition under which these later art forms had been buried, were the first to draw conclusions from them concerning the organization of

perception at the time. However far-reaching their insight, these scholars limited themselves to showing the significant, formal hallmark
which characterized perception in late Roman times. They did not
attempt—and, perhaps, saw no way—to show the social transformations expressed by these changes of perception. The conditions for an
analogous insight are more favorable in the present. And if changes in
the medium of contemporary perception can be comprehended as decay
of the aura, it is possible to show its social causes.

The concept of aura which was proposed above with reference to
historical objects may usefully be illustrated with reference to the aura
of natural ones. We define the aura of the latter as the unique phenomenon of a distance, however close it may be. If, while resting on a
summer afternoon, you follow with your eyes a mountain range on the
horizon or a branch which casts its shadow over you, you experience the
aura of those mountains, of that branch. This image makes it easy to
comprehend the social bases of the contemporary decay of the aura. It
rests on two circumstances, both of which are related to the increasing
significance of the masses in contemporary life. Namely, the desire of
contemporary masses to bring things "closer" spatially and humanly,
which is just as ardent as their bent toward overcoming the uniqueness
of every reality by accepting its reproduction.[4] Every day the urge
grows stronger to get hold of an object at very close range by way of its
likeness, its reproduction. Unmistakably, reproduction as offered by
picture magazines and newsreels differs from the image seen by the
unarmed eye. Uniqueness and permanence are as closely linked in the
latter as are transitoriness and reproducibility in the former. To pry an
object from its shell, to destroy its aura, is the mark of a perception
whose "sense of the universal equality of things" has increased to such
a degree that it extracts it even from a unique object by means of reproduction. Thus is manifested in the field of perception what in the theoretical sphere is noticeable in the increasing importance of statistics.
The adjustment of reality to the masses and of the masses to reality is
a process of unlimited scope, as much for thinking as for perception.

The uniqueness of a work of art is inseparable from its being
imbedded in the fabric of tradition. This tradition itself is thoroughly
alive and extremely changeable. An ancient statue of Venus, for example, stood in a different traditional context with the Greeks, who made
it an object of veneration, than with the clerics of the Middle Ages, who
viewed it as an ominous idol. Both of them, however, were equally confronted with its uniqueness, that is, its aura. Originally the contextual
integration of art in tradition found its expression in the cult. We know
that the earliest art works originated in the service of a ritual—first the
magical, then the religious kind. It is significant that the existence of
the work of art with reference to its aura is never entirely separated

from its ritual function.[5] In other words, the unique value of the "authentic" work of art has its basis in ritual, the location of its original use value. This ritualistic basis, however remote, is still recognizable as secularized ritual even in the most profane forms of the cult of beauty.[6] The secular cult of beauty, developed during the Renaissance and prevailing for three centuries, clearly showed that ritualistic basis in its decline and the first deep crisis which befell it. With the advent of the first truly revolutionary means of reproduction, photography, simultaneously with the rise of socialism, art sensed the approaching crisis which has become evident a century later. At the time, art reacted with the doctrine of *l'art pour l'art*, that is, with a theology of art. This gave rise to what might be called a negative theology in the form of the idea of "pure" art, which not only denied any social function of art but also any categorizing by subject matter. (In poetry, Mallarmé was the first to take this position.)

An analysis of art in the age of mechanical reproduction must do justice to these relationships, for they lead us to an all-important insight: for the first time in world history, mechanical reproduction emancipates the work of art from its parasitical dependence on ritual. To an ever greater degree the work of art reproduced becomes the work of art designed for reproducibility.[7] From a photographic negative, for example, one can make any number of prints; to ask for the "authentic" print makes no sense. But the instant the criterion of authenticity ceases to be applicable to artistic production, the total function of art is reversed. Instead of being based on ritual, it begins to be based on another practice—politics.

Works of art are received and valued on different planes. Two polar types stand out: with one, the accent is on the cult value; with the other, on the exhibition value of the work.[8] Artistic production begins with ceremonial objects destined to serve in a cult. One may assume that what mattered was their existence, not their being on view. The elk portrayed by the man of the Stone Age on the walls of his cave was an instrument of magic. He did expose it to his fellow men, but in the main it was meant for the spirits. Today the cult value would seem to demand that the work of art remain hidden. Certain statues of gods are accessible only to the priest in the cells; certain Madonnas remain covered nearly all year round; certain sculptures on medieval cathedrals are invisible to the spectator on ground level. With the emancipation of the various art practices from ritual go increasing opportunities for the exhibition of their products. It is easier to exhibit a portrait bust that can be sent here and there than to exhibit the statue of a divinity that has its fixed place in the interior of a temple. The same holds for the painting as against the mosaic or fresco that preceded it. And even though the public presentability of a mass originally may have been just as great as that of a symphony, the latter originated at the moment when its public presentability promised to surpass that of the mass.

With the different methods of technical reproduction of a work of art, its fitness for exhibition increased to such an extent that the quantitative shift between its two poles turned into a qualitative transformation of its nature. This is comparable to the situation of the work of art in prehistoric times when, by the absolute emphasis on its cult value, it was, first and foremost, an instrument of magic. Only later did it come to be recognized as a work of art. In the same way today, by the absolute emphasis on its exhibition value the work of art becomes a creation with entirely new functions, among which the one we are conscious of, the artistic function, later may be recognized as incidental.[9] This much is certain: today photography and the film are the most serviceable exemplifications of this new function.

In photography, exhibition value begins to displace cult value all along the line. But cult value does not give way without resistance. It retires into an ultimate retrenchment: the human countenance. It is no accident that the portrait was the focal point of early photography. The cult of remembrance of loved ones, absent or dead, offers a last refuge for the cult value of the picture. For the last time the aura emanates from the early photographs in the fleeting expression of a human face. This is what constitutes their melancholy, incomparable beauty. But as man withdraws from the photographic image, the exhibition value for the first time shows its superiority to the ritual value. To have pinpointed this new stage constitutes the incomparable significance of Atget, who, around 1900, took photographs of deserted Paris streets. It has quite justly been said of him that he photographed them like scenes of crime. The scene of a crime, too, is deserted; it is photographed for the purpose of establishing evidence. With Atget, photographs become standard evidence for historical occurrences, and acquire a hidden political significance. They demand a specific kind of approach; free-floating contemplation is not appropriate to them. They stir the viewer; he feels challenged by them in a new way. At the same time picture magazines begin to put up signposts for him, right ones or wrong ones, no matter. For the first time, captions have become obligatory. And it is clear that they have an altogether different character than the title of a painting. The directives which the captions give to those looking at pictures in illustrated magazines soon become even more explicit and more imperative in the film where the meaning of each single picture appears to be prescribed by the sequence of all preceding ones.

The nineteenth-century dispute as to the artistic value of painting versus photography today seems devious and confused. This does not diminish its importance, however; if anything, it underlines it. The dispute was in fact the symptom of a historical transformation the universal impact of which was not realized by either of the rivals. When the age of mechanical reproduction separated art from its basis in cult, the semblance of its autonomy disappeared forever. The resulting change in the function of art transcended the perspective of the century; for a long time it even escaped that of the twentieth century, which experienced the development of the film.

Earlier much futile thought had been devoted to the question of whether photography is an art. The primary question—whether the very invention of photography had not transformed the entire nature of art— was not raised. Soon the film theoreticians asked the same ill-considered question with regard to the film. But the difficulties which photography caused traditional aesthetics were mere child's play as compared to those raised by the film. Whence the insensitive and forced character of early theories of the film. Abel Gance, for instance, compares the film with hieroglyphs: "Here, by a remarkable regression, we have come back to the level of expression of the Egyptians.... Pictorial language has not yet matured because our eyes have not yet adjusted to it. There is as yet insufficient respect for, insufficient cult of, what it express- es."* Or, in the words of Séverin-Mars: "What art has been granted a dream more poetical and more real at the same time! Approached in this fashion the film might represent an incomparable means of expression. Only the most high-minded persons, in the most perfect and mysterious moments of their lives, should be allowed to enter its ambience."† Alexandre Arnoux concludes his fantasy about the silent film with the question: "Do not all the bold descriptions we have given amount to the definition of prayer?"‡ It is instructive to note how their desire to class the film among the "arts" forces these theoreticians to read elements into it—with a striking lack of discretion. Yet when these speculations were published, films like *L'Opinion publique* and *The Gold Rush* had already appeared. This, however, did not keep Abel Gance from adducing hieroglyphs for purposes of comparison, nor Séverin-Mars from speaking of the film as one might speak of paintings by Fra Angelico. Characteristically, even today ultrareactionary authors give the film a similar contextual significance—if not an out- right sacred one, then at least a supernatural one. Commenting on Max Reinhardt's film version of *A Midsummer Night's Dream*, Werfel states that undoubtedly it was the sterile copying of the exterior world with its streets, interiors, railroad stations, restaurants, motorcars, and beaches which until now had obstructed the elevation of the film

---

*Abel Gance, "Le Temps de l'image est venu," *L'Art cinématographique*, Vol. 2, pp. 94f, Paris, 1927, pp. 100–101.

†Séverin-Mars, quoted by Abel Gance, *op. cit.*, p. 100.

‡Alexandre Arnoux, *Cinéma pris*, 1929, p. 28.

to the realm of art. "The film has not yet realized its true meaning, its real possibilities ... these consist in its unique faculty to express by natural means and with incomparable persuasiveness all that is fairy-like, marvelous, supernatural."*

The artistic performance of a stage actor is definitely presented to the public by the actor in person; that of the screen actor, however, is presented by a camera, with a twofold consequence. The camera that presents the performance of the film actor to the public need not respect the performance as an integral whole. Guided by the cameraman, the camera continually changes its position with respect to the performance. The sequence of positional views which the editor composes from the material supplied him constitutes the completed film. It comprises certain factors of movement which are in reality those of the camera, not to mention special camera angles, close-ups, etc. Hence, the performance of the actor is subjected to a series of optical tests. This is the first consequence of the fact that the actor's performance is presented by means of a camera. Also, the film actor lacks the opportunity of the stage actor to adjust to the audience during his performance, since he does not present his performance to the audience in person. This permits the audience to take the position of a critic, without experiencing any personal contact with the actor. The audience's identification with the actor is really an identification with the camera. Consequently the audience takes the position of the camera; its approach is that of testing.[10] This is not the approach to which cult values may be exposed.

For the film, what matters primarily is that the actor represents himself to the public before the camera, rather than representing someone else. One of the first to sense the actor's metamorphosis by this form of testing was Pirandello. Though his remarks on the subject in his novel *Si Gira* were limited to the negative aspects of the question and to the silent film only, this hardly impairs their validity. For in this respect, the sound film did not change anything essential. What matters is that the part is acted not for an audience but for a mechanical contrivance—in the case of the sound film, for two of them. "The film actor," wrote Pirandello, "feels as if in exile—exiled not only from the stage but also from himself. With a vague sense of discomfort he feels inexplicable emptiness: his body loses its corporeality, it evaporates, it is deprived of reality, life, voice, and the noises caused by his moving about, in order to be changed into a mute image, flickering an instant on the screen, then vanishing into silence.... The projector will play with his shadow before the public, and he himself must be content to

---

*Franz Werfel, "Ein Sommernachtstraum, Ein Film von Shakespeare und Reinhardt," *Neues Wiener Journal*, cited in *Lu* 15, November, 1935.

play before the camera."* This situation might also be characterized as follows: for the first time—and this is the effect of the film—man has to operate with his whole living person, yet forgoing its aura. For aura is tied to his presence; there can be no replica of it. The aura which, on the stage, emanates from Macbeth, cannot be separated for the spectators from that of the actor. However, the singularity of the shot in the studio is that the camera is substituted for the public. Consequently, the aura that envelops the actor vanishes, and with it the aura of the figure he portrays.

It is not surprising that it should be a dramatist such as Pirandello who, in characterizing the film, inadvertently touches on the very crisis in which we see the theater. Any thorough study proves that there is indeed no greater contrast than that of the stage play to a work of art that is completely subject to or, like the film, founded in, mechanical reproduction. Experts have long recognized that in the film "the greatest effects are almost always obtained by 'acting' as little as possible...." In 1932 Rudolf Arnheim saw "the latest trend ... in treating the actor as a stage prop chosen for its characteristics and ... inserted at the proper place."[11] With this idea something else is closely connected. The stage actor identifies himself with the character of his role. The film actor very often is denied this opportunity. His creation is by no means all of a piece; it is composed of many separate performances. Besides certain fortuitous considerations, such as cost of studio, availability of fellow players, decor, etc., there are elementary necessities of equipment that split the actor's work into a series of mountable episodes. In particular, lighting and its installation require the presentation of an event that, on the screen, unfolds as a rapid and unified scene, in a sequence of separate shootings which may take hours at the studio; not to mention more obvious montage. Thus a jump from the window can be shot in the studio as a jump from a scaffold, and the ensuing flight, if need be, can be shot weeks later when outdoor scenes are taken. Far more paradoxical cases can easily be construed. Let us assume that an actor is supposed to be startled by a knock at the door. If his reaction is not satisfactory, the director can resort to an expedient: when the actor happens to be at the studio again he has a shot fired behind him without his being forewarned of it. The frightened reaction can be shot now and be cut into the screen version. Nothing more strikingly shows that art has left the realm of the "beautiful semblance" which, so far, had been taken to be the only sphere where art could thrive.

The feeling of strangeness that overcomes the actor before the

---

*Luigi Pirandello, *Si Gira*, quoted by Léon Pierre-Quint, "Signification du cinéma," *L'Art cinématographique, op. cit.*, pp. 14–15.

camera, as Pirandello describes it, is basically of the same kind as the estrangement felt before one's own image in the mirror. But now the reflected image has become separable, transportable. And where is it transported? Before the public.[12] Never for a moment does the screen actor cease to be conscious of this fact. While facing the camera he knows that ultimately he will face the public, the consumers who constitute the market. This market, where he offers not only his labor but also his whole self, his heart and soul, is beyond his reach. During the shooting he has as little contact with it as any article made in a factory. This may contribute to that oppression, that new anxiety which, according to Pirandello, grips the actor before the camera. The film responds to the shriveling of the aura with an artificial build-up of the "personality" outside the studio. The cult of the movie star, fostered by the money of the film industry, preserves not the unique aura of the person but the "spell of the personality," the phony spell of a commodity. So long as the movie-makers' capital sets the fashion, as a rule no other revolutionary merit can be accredited to today's film than the promotion of a revolutionary criticism of traditional concepts of art. We do not deny that in some cases today's films can also promote revolutionary criticism of social conditions, even of the distribution of property. However, our present study is no more specifically concerned with this than is the film production of Western Europe.

It is inherent in the technique of the film as well as that of sports that everybody who witnesses its accomplishments is somewhat of an expert. This is obvious to anyone listening to a group of newspaper boys leaning on their bicycles and discussing the outcome of a bicycle race. It is not for nothing that newspaper publishers arrange races for their delivery boys. These arouse great interest among the participants, for the victor has an opportunity to rise from delivery boy to professional racer. Similarly, the newsreel offers everyone the opportunity to rise from passer-by to movie extra. In this way any man might even find himself part of a work of art, as witness Vertoff's *Three Songs About Lenin* or Ivens' *Borinage*. Any man today can lay claim to being filmed. This claim can best be elucidated by a comparative look at the historical situation of contemporary literature.

For centuries a small number of writers were confronted by many thousands of readers. This changed toward the end of the last century. With the increasing extension of the press, which kept placing new political, religious, scientific, professional, and local organs before the readers, an increasing number of readers became writers—at first, occasional ones. It began with the daily press opening to its readers space for "letters to the editor." And today there is hardly a gainfully employed European who could not, in principle, find an opportunity to publish somewhere or other comments on his work, grievances, documentary reports, or that sort of thing. Thus, the distinction between author and public is about to lose its basic character. The difference becomes merely functional; it may vary from case to case. At any moment the reader is ready to turn into a writer. As expert, which he had to become willy-nilly in an extremely specialized work process, even if only in some minor respect, the reader gains access to authorship. In the Soviet Union work itself is given a voice. To present it verbally is part of a man's ability to perform the work. Literary license is now founded on polytechnic, rather than specialized training and thus becomes common property.

All this can easily be applied to the film, where transitions that in literature took centuries have come about in a decade. In cinematic practice, particularly in Russia, this change-over has partially become established reality. Some of the players whom we meet in Russian films are not actors in our sense but people who portray *themselves*—and primarily in their own work process. In Western Europe the capitalistic exploitation of the film denies consideration to modern man's legitimate claim to being reproduced. Under these circumstances the film industry is trying hard to spur the interest of the masses through illusion-promoting spectacles and dubious speculations.

...

One of the foremost tasks of art has always been the creation of a demand which could be fully satisfied only later.[17] The history of every art form shows critical epochs in which a certain art form aspires to effects which could be fully obtained only with a changed technical standard, that is to say, in a new art form. The extravagances and crudities of art which thus appear, particularly in the so-called decadent epochs, actually arise from the nucleus of its richest historical energies. In recent years, such barbarisms were abundant in Dadaism. It is only now that its impulse becomes discernible: Dadaism attempted to create by pictorial—and literary—means the effects which the public today seeks in the film.

Every fundamentally new, pioneering creation of demands will carry beyond its goal. Dadaism did so to the extent that it sacrificed the market values which are so characteristic of the film in favor of higher ambitions—though of course it was not conscious of such intentions as here described. The Dadaists attached much less importance to the sales value of their work than to its uselessness for contemplative immersion. The studied degradation of their material was not the least of their means to achieve this uselessness. Their poems are "word salad" containing obscenities and every imaginable waste product of language. The same is true of their paintings, on which they mounted buttons and tickets. What they intended and achieved was a relentless destruction of the aura of their creations, which they branded as reproductions with the very means of production. Before a painting of Arp's or a poem by August Stramm it is impossible to take time for contemplation and evaluation as one would before a canvas of Derain's or a poem by Rilke. In the decline of middle-class society, contemplation became a school for asocial behavior; it was countered by distraction as a variant of social conduct.[18] Dadaistic activities actually assured a rather vehement distraction by making works of art the center of scandal. One requirement was foremost: to outrage the public.

From an alluring appearance or persuasive structure of sound the work of art of the Dadaists became an instrument of ballistics. It hit the spectator like a bullet, it happened to him, thus acquiring a tactile quality. It promoted a demand for the film, the distracting element of which is also primarily tactile, being based on changes of place and focus which periodically assail the spectator. Let us compare the screen on which a film unfolds with the canvas of a painting. The painting invites the spectator to contemplation; before it the spectator can abandon himself to his associations. Before the movie frame he cannot do so. No sooner has his eye grasped a scene than it is already changed. It cannot be arrested. Duhamel, who detests the film and knows nothing of its significance, though something of its structure, notes this circumstance as follows: "I can no longer think what I want to think. My thoughts have been replaced by moving images."* The spectator's process of association in view of these images is indeed interrupted by their constant, sudden change. This constitutes the shock effect of the film, which, like all shocks, should be cushioned by heightened presence of mind.[19] By means of its technical structure, the film has taken the physical shock effect out of the wrappers in which Dadaism had, as it were, kept it inside the moral shock effect.[20]

The mass is a matrix from which all traditional behavior toward works of art issues today in a new form. Quantity has been transmuted into quality. The greatly increased mass of participants has produced a change in the mode of participation. The fact that the new mode of participation first appeared in a disreputable form must not confuse the spectator. Yet some people have launched spirited attacks against precisely this superficial aspect. Among these, Duhamel has expressed himself in the most radical manner. What he objects to most is the kind of participation which the movie elicits from the masses. Duhamel calls the movie "a pastime for helots, a diversion for uneducated, wretched, worn-out creatures who are consumed by their worries..., a spectacle which requires no concentration and presupposes no intelligence..., which kindles no light in the heart and awakens no hope other than the

---

*Georges Duhammel, *Scénes de la vie future*, Paris, 1930, p. 52.

ridiculous one of someday, becoming a 'star' in Los Angeles."* Clearly, this is at bottom the same ancient lament that the masses seek distraction whereas art demands concentration from the spectator. That is a commonplace. The question remains whether it provides a platform for the analysis of the film. A closer look is needed here. Distraction and concentration form polar opposites which may be stated as follows: A man who concentrates before a work of art is absorbed by it. He enters into this work of art the way legend tells of the Chinese painter when he viewed his finished painting. In contrast, the distracted mass absorbs the work of art. This is most obvious with regard to buildings. Architecture has always represented the prototype of a work of art the reception of which is consummated by a collectivity in a state of distraction. The laws of its reception are most instructive.

Buildings have been man's companions since primeval times. Many art forms have developed and perished. Tragedy begins with the Greeks, is extinguished with them, and after centuries its "rules" only are revived. The epic poem, which had its origin in the youth of nations, expires in Europe at the end of the Renaissance. Panel painting is a creation of the Middle Ages, and nothing guarantees its uninterrupted existence. But the human need for shelter is lasting. Architecture has never been idle. Its history is more ancient than that of any other art, and its claim to being a living force has significance in every attempt to comprehend the relationship of the masses to art. Buildings are appropriated in a twofold manner: by use and by perception—or rather, by touch and sight. Such appropriation cannot be understood in terms of the attentive concentration of a tourist before a famous building. On the tactile side there is no counterpart to contemplation on the optical side. Tactile appropriation is accomplished not so much by attention as by habit. As regards architecture, habit determines to a large extent even optical reception. The latter, too, occurs much less through rapt attention than by noticing the object in incidental fashion. This mode of appropriation, developed with reference to architecture, in certain circumstances acquires canonical value. For the tasks which face the human apparatus of perception at the turning points of history cannot be solved by optical means, that is, by contemplation, alone. They are mastered gradually by habit, under the guidance of tactile appropriation.

The distracted person, too, can form habits. More, the ability to master certain tasks in a state of distraction proves that their solution has become a matter of habit. Distraction as provided by art presents a covert control of the extent to which new tasks have become soluble by apperception. Since, moreover, individuals are tempted to avoid such tasks, art will tackle the most difficult and most important ones where

---

*Duhamel, *op. cit.*, p. 58.

it is able to mobilize the masses. Today it does so in the film. Reception in a state of distraction, which is increasing noticeably in all fields of art and is symptomatic of profound changes in apperception, finds in the film its true means of exercise. The film with its shock effect meets this mode of reception halfway. The film makes the cult value recede into the background not only by putting the public in the position of the critic, but also by the fact that at the movies this position requires no attention. The public is an examiner, but an absent-minded one.

Notes

...

4. To satisfy the human interest of the masses may mean to have one's social function removed from the field of vision. Nothing guarantees that a portraitist of today, when painting a famous surgeon at the breakfast table in the midst of his family, depicts his social function more precisely than a painter of the 17th century who portrayed his medical doctors as representing this profession, like Rembrandt in his "Anatomy Lesson."

5. The definition of the aura as a "unique phenomenon of a distance however close it may be" represents nothing but the formulation of the cult value of the work of art in categories of space and time perception. Distance is the opposite of closeness. The essentially distant object is the unapproachable one. Unapproachability is indeed a major quality of the cult image. True to its nature, it remains "distant, however close it may be." The closeness which one may gain from its subject matter does not impair the distance which it retains in its appearance.

6. To the extent to which the cult value of the painting is secularized the ideas of its fundamental uniqueness lose distinctness. In the imagination of the beholder the uniqueness of the phenomena which hold sway in the cult image is more and more displaced by the empirical uniqueness of the creator or of his creative achievement. To be sure, never completely so; the concept of authenticity always transcends mere genuineness. (This is particularly apparent in the collector who always retains some traces of the fetishist and who, by owning the work of art, shares in its ritual power.) Nevertheless, the function of the concept of authenticity remains determinate in the evaluation of art; with the secularization of art, authenticity displaces the cult value of the work.

7. In the case of films, mechanical reproduction is not, as with literature and painting, an external condition for mass distribution. Mechanical reproduction is inherent in the very technique of film production. This technique not only permits in the most direct way but virtually causes mass distribution. It enforces distribution because the production of a film is so expensive that an individual who, for instance, might afford to buy a painting no longer can afford to buy a film. In 1927 it was calculated that a major film, in order to pay its way, had to reach an audience of nine million. With the sound film, to be sure, a setback in its international distribution occurred at first: audiences became limited by language barriers. This coincided with the Fascist emphasis on national interests. It is more important to focus on this connection with Fascism than on this setback, which was soon minimized by synchronization.

The simultaneity of both phenomena is attributable to the depression. The same disturbances which, on a larger scale, led to an attempt to maintain the existing property structure by sheer force led the endangered film capital to speed up the development of the sound film. The introduction of the sound film brought about a temporary relief, not only because it again brought the masses into the theaters but also because it merged new capital from the electrical industry with that of the film industry. Thus, viewed from the outside, the sound film promoted national interests, but seen from the inside it helped to internationalize film production even more than previously.

8. This polarity cannot come into its own in the aesthetics of Idealism. Its idea of beauty comprises these polar opposites without differentiating between them and consequently excludes their polarity. Yet in Hegel this polarity announces itself as clearly as possible within the limits of Idealism. We quote from his Philosophy of History:

"Images were known of old. Piety at an early time required them for worship, but it could do without *beautiful* images. These might even be disturbing. In every beautiful painting there is also something nonspiritual, merely external, but its spirit speaks to man through its beauty. Worshipping, conversely, is concerned with the work as an object, for it is but a spiritless stupor of the soul.... Fine art has arisen ... in the church..., although it has already gone beyond its principle as art."

Likewise, the following passage from *The Philosophy of Fine Art* indicates that Hegel sensed a problem here.

"We are beyond the stage of reverence for works of art as divine and objects deserving our worship. The impression they produce is one of a more reflective kind, and the emotions they arouse require a higher test...."—G. W. F. Hegel, *The Philosophy of Fine Art*, trans., with notes, by F. P. B. Osmaston, Vol. I, p. 12, London, 1920.

The transition from the first kind of artistic reception to the second characterizes the history of artistic reception in general. Apart from that, a certain oscillation between these two polar modes of reception can be demonstrated for each work of art. Take the Sistine Madonna. Since Hubert Grimme's research it has been known that the Madonna originally was painted for the purpose of exhibition. Grimme's research was inspired by the question: What is the purpose of the molding in the foreground of the painting which the two cupids lean upon? How, Grimme asked further, did Raphael come to furnish the sky with two draperies? Research proved that the Madonna had been commissioned for the public lying-in-state of Pope Sixtus. The Popes lay in state in a certain side chapel of St. Peter's. On that occasion Raphael's picture had been fastened in a nichelike background of the chapel, supported by the coffin. In this picture Raphael portrays the Madonna approaching the papal coffin in clouds from the background of the niche, which was demarcated by green drapes. At the obsequies of Sixtus a pre-eminent exhibition value of Raphael's picture was taken advantage of. Some time later it was placed on the high altar in the church of the Black Friars at Piacenza. The reason for this exile is to be found in the Roman rites which forbid the use of paintings exhibited at obsequies as cult objects on the high altar. This regulation devalued Raphael's picture to some degree. In order to obtain an adequate price nevertheless, the Papal See resolved to add to the bargain the tacit toleration of the picture above the high altar. To avoid attention the picture was given to the monks of the far-off provincial town.

9. Bertolt Brecht, on a different level, engaged in analogous reflections: "If the concept of 'work of art' can no longer be applied to the thing that emerges once the work is transformed into a commodity, we have to eliminate this concept with cautious care but without fear, lest we liquidate the function of the very thing as well. For it has to go through this phase without mental reservation, and not as noncommittal deviation from the straight path; rather, what happens here with the work of art will change it fundamentally and erase its past to such an extent that should the old concept be taken up again—and it will, why not?—it will no longer stir any memory of the thing it once designated."

10. "The film ... provides—or could provide—useful insight into the details of human actions.... Character is never used as a source of motivation; the inner life of the persons never supplies the principal cause of the plot and seldom is its main result." (Bertolt Brecht, *Versuche*, "Der Dreigroschen-prozess," p. 268.) The expansion of the field of the testable which mechanical equipment brings about for the actor corresponds to the extraordinary expansion of the field of the testable brought about for the individual through economic conditions. Thus, vocational aptitude tests become constantly more important. What matters in these tests are segmental performances of the individual. The film shot and the vocational aptitude test are taken before a committee of experts. The camera director in the studio occupies a place identical with that of the examiner during aptitude tests.

11. Rudolf Arnheim, *Film als Kunst*, Berlin, 1932, pp. 176f. In this context certain seemingly unimportant details in which the film director deviates from stage practices gain in interest. Such is the attempt to let the actor play without make-up, as made among others by Dreyer in his *Jeanne d'Arc*. Dreyer spent months seeking the forty actors who constitute the Inquisitors' tribunal. The search for these actors resembled that for stage properties that are hard to come by. Dreyer made every effort to avoid resemblances of age, build, and physiognomy. If the actor thus becomes a stage property, this latter, on the other hand, frequently functions as actor. At least it is not unusual for the film to assign a role to the stage property. Instead of choosing at random from a great wealth of examples, let us concentrate on a particularly convincing one. A clock that is working will always be a disturbance on the stage. There it cannot be permitted its function of measuring time. Even in a naturalistic play, astronomical time would clash with theatrical time. Under these circumstances it is highly revealing that the film can, whenever appropriate, use time as measured by a clock. From this more than from many other touches it may clearly be recognized that under certain circumstances each and every prop in a film may assume important functions. From here it is but one step to Pudovkin's statement that, "the playing of an actor which is connected with an object and is built around it ... is always one of the strongest methods of cinematic construction." (W. Pudovkin, *Filmregie und Filmmanuskript*, Berlin, 1928, p. 126.) The film is the first art form capable of demonstrating how matter plays tricks on man. Hence, films can be an excellent means of materialistic representation.

12. The change noted here in the method of exhibition caused by mechanical reproduction applies to politics as well. The present crisis of the bourgeois democracies comprises a crisis of the conditions which determine the public presentation of the rulers. Democracies exhibit a member of government directly and personally before the nation's representatives. Parliament is his public. Since the innovations of camera and recording equipment make it possible for the orator to become audible and visible to an unlimited number of persons, the presentation of the man of politics before camera and recording equipment becomes paramount. Parliaments, as much as theaters, are deserted. Radio and film not only affect the function of the professional actor but likewise the function of those who also exhibit themselves before this mechanical equipment, those who govern. Though their tasks may be different, the change affects equally the actor and the ruler. The trend is toward establishing controllable and transferrable skills under certain social conditions. This results in a new selection, a selection before the equipment from which the star and the dictator emerge victorious.

. . .

17. "The work of art," says André Breton, "is valuable only in so far as it is vibrated by the reflexes of the future." Indeed, every developed art form intersects three lines of development. Technology works toward a certain form of art. Before the advent of the film there were photo booklets with pictures which flitted by the onlooker upon pressure of the thumb, thus portraying a boxing bout or a tennis match. Then there were the slot machines in bazaars; their picture sequences were produced by the turning of a crank.

Secondly, the traditional art forms in certain phases of their development strenuously work toward effects which later are effortlessly attained by the new ones. Before the rise of the movie the Dadaists' performances tried to create an audience reaction which Chaplin later evoked in a more natural way.

Thirdly, unspectacular social changes often promote a change in receptivity which will benefit the new art form. Before the movie had begun to create its public, pictures that were no longer immobile captivated an assembled audience in the so-called *Kaiserpanorama*. Here the public assembled before a screen into which stereoscopes were mounted, one to each beholder. By a mechanical process individual pictures appeared briefly before the stereoscopes, then made way for others. Edison still had to use similar devices in presenting the first movie strip before the film screen and projection were known. This strip was presented to a small public which stared into the apparatus in which the succession of pictures was reeling off. Incidentally, the institution of the *Kaiserpanorama* shows very clearly a dialectic of the development. Shortly before the movie turned the reception of pictures into a collective one, the individual viewing of pictures in these swiftly outmoded establishments came into play once more with an intensity comparable to that of the ancient priest beholding the statue of a divinity in the cella.

18. The theological archetype of this contemplation is the awareness of being alone with one's God. Such awareness, in the heyday of the bourgeoisie, went to strengthen the freedom to shake off clerical tutelage. During the decline of the bourgeoisie this awareness had to take into account the hidden

tendency to withdraw from public affairs those forces which the individual draws upon in his communion with God.

19. The film is the art form that is in keeping with the increased threat to his life which modern man has to face. Man's need to expose himself to shock effects is his adjustment to the dangers threatening him. The film corresponds to profound changes in the apperceptive apparatus—changes that are experienced on an individual scale by the man in the street in big-city traffic, on a historical scale by every present-day citizen.

20. As for Dadaism, insights important for Cubism and Futurism are to be gained from the movie. Both appear as deficient attempts of art to accommodate the pervasion of reality by the apparatus. In contrast to the film, these schools did not try to use the apparatus as such for the artistic presentation of reality, but aimed at some sort of alloy in the joint presentation of reality and apparatus. In Cubism, the premonition that this apparatus will be structurally based on optics plays a dominant part; in Futurism, it is the premonition of the effects of this apparatus which are brought out by the rapid sequence of the film strip.

Questions and Projects

- From the late 1920s through the 1930s there were many superior film adaptations of literary works: from Marcel L'Herbier's updating of an Émile Zola novel as *L'Argent* (1929) to George Cukor's (1937) *Camille*. Do these provoke the new ways of "reading" and understanding that Benjamin hopes for? How or how not? Are there better examples of films that achieve Benjamin's aims, such as Russian director Alexander Dovzhenko's *Earth* (1930) or Eisenstein's aborted project with American novelist Upton Sinclair, *Qué viva Mexico!* (1933)?

- Are Benjamin's arguments still valid today? Does literature, in short, participate in a cultural "aura" that the movies are free of? Choose a particularly good contemporary example of a film that transforms a literary work into an experience that is more politically accessible or socially relevant. Analyze how this is accomplished in terms of the style of the film and the audience's relation to it.

After decades of arguments about what distinguishes film as an art form, this 1944 essay by Russian filmmaker Eisenstein (director of Potemkin *[1925],* Alexander Nevsky *[1938], and other films) reclaims the crucial connections between literature and film but only as films create an historical and critical engagement with their literary forerunners. He specifically credits the novels of Charles Dickens as anticipating the editing methods that Griffith transposed to film—which he calls montage. Yet, keeping with the general trends of the 1940s, Eisenstein's historical perspective on the connections is more complex than arguments about what film shares with literature or how it differs from literature. He is quick to argue that film evolves from the social and industrial traditions that redefined space and time for the individual in the nineteenth century, but for him—as he argues in other sections of this essay—film offers possibilities of moving beyond the heritage of Western individualism shared by Dickens and Griffith and, through montage, of creating the new, more liberating visions of the individual in society.*

"Dickens, Griffith, and the Film Today" from *Film Form*

Sergei Eisenstein

People talked as if there had been no dramatic or descriptive music before Wagner; no impressionist painting before Whistler; whilst as to myself, I was finding that the surest way to produce an effect of daring innovation and originality was to revive the ancient attraction of long rhetorical speeches; to stick closely to the methods of Moliére; and to lift characters bodily out of the pages of Charles Dickens.

—George Bernard Shaw[1]

"THE KETTLE began it...."
Thus Dickens opens his *Cricket on the Hearth.*
"The kettle began it...."
What could be further from films! Trains, cowboys, chases ... and *The Cricket on the Hearth*? "The kettle began it!" But, strange as it may seem, movies also were boiling in that kettle. From here, from Dickens, from the Victorian novel stem the first shoots of American film esthetic, forever linked with the name of David Wark Griffith.

Although at first glance this may not seem surprising, it does appear incompatible with our traditional concepts of cinematography, in particular with those associated in our minds with the American cinema. Factually, however, this relationship is organic, and the "genetic" line of descent is quite consistent.

...

In order to understand Griffith, one must visualize an America made up of more than visions of speeding automobiles, streamlined trains, racing ticker tape, inexorable conveyor-belts. One is obliged to comprehend this second side of America as well—America, the traditional, the patriarchal, the provincial. And then you will be considerably less astonished by this link between Griffith and Dickens.

The threads of both these Americas are interwoven in the style and personality of Griffith—as in the most fantastic of his own parallel montage sequences.

What is most curious is that Dickens appears to have guided *both* lines of Griffith's style, reflecting both faces of America: Small-Town America, and Super-Dynamic America.

This can be detected at once in the "intimate" Griffith of contemporary or past American life, where Griffith is profound, in those films about which Griffith told me, that "they were made for myself and were invariably rejected by the exhibitors."

But we are a little astonished when we see that the construction of the "official," sumptuous Griffith, the Griffith of tempestuous tempi of dizzying action, of breathtaking chases—has also been guided by the same Dickens! But we shall see how true this is.

First the "intimate" Griffith, and the "intimate" Dickens.

The kettle began it....

As soon as we recognize this kettle as a typical close-up, we exclaim: "Why didn't we notice it before! Of course this is the purest Griffith. How often we've seen such a close-up at the beginning of an episode, a sequence, or a whole film by him!" (By the way, we shouldn't overlook the fact that one of Griffith's earliest films was based on *The Cricket on the Hearth!**)

Certainly, this kettle is a typical Griffith-esque close-up. A close-up saturated, we now become aware, with typically Dickens-esque "atmosphere," with which Griffith, with equal mastery, can envelop the severe face of life in *Way Down East*, and the icy cold moral face of his characters, who push the guilty Anna (Lillian Gish) onto the shifting surface of a swirling ice-break.

Isn't this the same implacable atmosphere of cold that is given by Dickens, for example, in *Dombey and Son*? The image of Mr. Dombey is revealed through cold and prudery. And the print of cold lies on every-

---

*Released On May 27, 1909, with Herbert Pryor, Linda Arvidson Griffith, Violet Mersereau. Owen Moore, this film followed the dramatic adaptation of the *Cricket* made by Albert Smith with Dickens's approval.

one and everything—everywhere. And "atmosphere"—always and everywhere—is one of the most expressive means of revealing the inner world and ethical countenance of the characters themselves.

We can recognize this particular method of Dickens in Griffith's inimitable bit-characters who seem to have run straight from life onto the screen. I can't recall who speaks with whom in one of the street scenes of the modern story of *Intolerance*. But I shall never forget the mask of the passer-by with nose pointed forward between spectacles and straggly beard, walking with hands behind his back as if he were manacled. As he passes he interrupts the most pathetic moment in the conversation of the suffering boy and girl. I can remember next to nothing of the couple, but this passer-by, who is visible in the shot only for a flashing glimpse, stands alive before me now—and I haven't seen the film for twenty years!

Occasionally these unforgettable figures actually walked into Griffith's films almost directly from the street: a bit-player developed in Griffith's hands to stardom; the passer-by who may never again have been filmed; and that mathematics teacher who was invited to play a terrifying butcher in *America*—the late Louis Wolheim—who ended the film career thus begun with his incomparable performance as "Kat" in *All Quiet on the Western Front*.

These striking figures of sympathetic old men are also quite in the Dickens tradition; and these noble and slightly one-dimensional figures of sorrow and fragile maidens; and these rural gossips and sundry odd characters. They are especially convincing in Dickens when he uses them briefly, in episodes.

> The only other thing to be noticed about [Pecksniff] is that here, as almost everywhere else in the novels, the best figures are at their best when they have least to do. Dickens's characters are perfect as long as he can keep them out of his stories. Bumble is divine until a dark and practical secret is entrusted to him.... Micawber is noble when he is doing nothing; but he is quite unconvincing when he is spying on Uriah Heep.... Similarly, while Pecksniff is the best thing in the story, the story is the worst thing in Pecksniff....[2]

Free of this limitation, and with the same believability, Griffith's characters grow from episodic figures into those fascinating and finished images of living people, in which his screen is so rich.

Instead of going into detail about this, let us rather return to that more obvious fact—the growth of that second side of Griffith's creative craftsmanship—as a magician of tempo and montage; a side for which it is rather surprising to find the same Victorian source.

When Griffith proposed to his employers the novelty of a parallel "cut-back" for his first version of *Enoch Arden* (*After Many Years*, 1908), this is the discussion that took place, as recorded by Linda Arvidson Griffith in her reminiscences of Biograph days:

> When Mr. Griffith suggested a scene showing Annie Lee waiting for her husband's return to be followed by a scene of Enoch cast away, on a desert island, it was altogether too distracting. "How can you tell a story jumping about like that? The people won't know what it's about."
> "Well," said Mr. Griffith, "doesn't Dickens write that way?"
> "Yes, but that's Dickens; that's novel writing; that's different."
> "Oh, not so much, these are picture stories; not so different."[3]

But, to speak quite frankly, all astonishment on this subject and the apparent unexpectedness of such statements can be ascribed only to our—ignorance of Dickens.

All of us read him in childhood, gulped him down greedily, without realizing that much of his irresistibility lay not only in his capture of detail in the childhoods of his heroes, but also in that spontaneous, child-like skill for story-telling, equally typical for Dickens and for the American cinema, which so surely and delicately plays upon the infantile traits in its audience. We were even less concerned with the technique of Dickens's composition: for us this was non-existent—but captivated by the effects of this technique, we feverishly followed his characters from page to page, watching his characters now being rubbed from view at the most critical moment, then seeing them return afresh between the separate links of the parallel secondary plot.

As children, we paid no attention to the mechanics of this. As adults, we rarely re-read his novels. And becoming film-workers, we never found time to glance beneath the covers of these novels in order to figure out what exactly had captivated us in these novels and with what means these incredibly many-paged volumes had chained our attention so irresistibly.

Apparently Griffith was more perceptive ...

But before disclosing what the steady gaze of the American film-maker may have caught sight of on Dickens's pages, I wish to recall what David Wark Griffith himself represented to us, the young Soviet film-makers of the twenties.

To say it simply and without equivocation: a revelation.

...

What enthralled us was not only these films, it was also their possibilities. Just as it was the possibilities in a tractor to make collective cultivation of the fields a reality, it was the boundless temperament and tempo of these amazing (and amazingly useless!) works from an unknown country that led us to muse on the possibilities of a profound, intelligent, class-directed use of this wonderful tool.

The most thrilling figure against this background was Griffith, for it was in his works that the cinema made itself felt as more than an entertainment or pastime. The brilliant new methods of the American cinema were united in him with a profound emotion of story, with human acting, with laughter and tears, and all this was done with an astonishing ability to preserve all that gleam of a filmically dynamic holiday, which had been captured in *The Gray Shadow* and *The Mark of Zorro* and *The House of Hate*. That the cinema could be incomparably greater, and that this was to be the basic task of the budding Soviet cinema—these were sketched for us in Griffith's creative work, and found ever new confirmation in his films.

Our heightened curiosity of those years in *construction and method* swiftly discerned wherein lay the most powerful affective factors in this great American's films. This was in a hitherto unfamiliar province, bearing a name that was familiar to us, not in the field of art, but in that of engineering and electrical apparatus, first touching art in its most advanced section—in cinematography. This province, this method, this principle of building and construction was *montage*.

This was the montage whose foundations had been laid by American film-culture, but whose full, completed, conscious use and world recognition was established by our film. Montage, the rise of which will be forever linked with the name of Griffith. Montage, which played a most vital rôle in the creative work of Griffith and brought him his most glorious successes.

Griffith arrived at it through the method of parallel action. And, essentially, it was on this that he came to a standstill. But we mustn't run ahead. Let us examine the question of how montage came to Griffith or—how Griffith came to montage.

Griffith arrived at montage through the method of parallel action, and he was led to the idea of parallel action by—Dickens!

To this fact Griffith himself has testified, according to A. B. Walkley, in *The Times* of London, for April 26, 1922, on the occasion of a visit by the director to London. Writes Mr. Walkley:

> He [Griffith] is a pioneer, by his own admission, rather than an inventor. That is to say, he has opened up new paths in Film Land, under the guidance of ideas supplied to him from outside. His best ideas, it appears, have come to him from Dickens, who has always been his favorite author.... Dickens inspired Mr. Griffith with an idea, and his employers (mere "business" men) were horrified at it; but, says Mr. Griffith, "I went home, re-read one of Dickens's novels, and came back next day to tell them they could either make use of my idea or dismiss me."

Mr. Griffith found the idea to which he clung thus heroically in Dickens. That was as luck would have it, for he might have found the same idea almost anywhere. Newton deduced the law of gravitation from the fall of an apple; but a pear or a plum would have done just as well. The idea is merely that of a "break" in the narrative, a shifting of the story from one group of characters to another group. People who write the long and crowded novels that Dickens did, especially when they are published in parts, find this practice a convenience. You will meet with it in Thackeray, George Eliot, Trollope, Meredith, Hardy, and, I suppose, every other Victorian novelist.... Mr. Griffith might have found the same practice not only in Dumas *père*, who cared precious little about form but also in great artists like Tolstoy, Turgeniev, and Balzac. But, as a matter of fact it was not in any of these others, but in Dickens that he found it; and it is significant of the predominant influence of Dickens that he should be quoted as an authority for a device which is really common to fiction at large.

Even a superficial acquaintance with the work of the great English novelist is enough to persuade one that Dickens may have given and did give to cinematography far more guidance than that which led to the montage of parallel action alone.

Dickens's nearness to the characteristics of cinema in method, style, and especially in viewpoint and exposition, is indeed amazing. And it may be that in the nature of exactly these characteristics, in their community both for Dickens and for cinema, there lies a portion of the secret of that mass success which they both, apart from themes and plots, brought and still bring to the particular quality of such exposition and such writing.

What were the novels of Dickens for his contemporaries, for his readers? There is one answer: they bore the same relation to them that the film bears to the same strata in our time. They compelled the reader to live with the same passions. They appealed to the same good and sentimental elements as does the film (at least on the surface); they alike shudder before vice,* they alike mill the extraordinary, the unusual, the fantastic, from boring, prosaic and everyday existence. And they clothe this common and prosaic existence in their special vision.

Illumined by this light, refracted from the land of fiction back to life, this commonness took on a romantic air, and bored people were

---

*As late as April 17, 1944, Griffith still considered this the chief social function of film-making. An interviewer from the Los Angeles *Times* asked him, "What is a good picture?" Griffith replied, "One that makes the public forget its troubles. Also, a good picture tends to make folks think a little, without letting them suspect that they are being inspired to think. In one respect, nearly all pictures are good in that they show the triumph of good over evil." This is what Osbert Sitwell, in reference to Dickens, called the "Virtue *v.* Vice Cup-Tie Final."

grateful to the author for giving them the countenances of potentially romantic figures.

This partially accounts for the close attachment to the novels of Dickens and, similarly, to films. It was from this that the universal success of his novels derived. In an essay on Dickens, Stefan Zweig opens with this description of his popularity:

> The love Dickens's contemporaries lavished upon the creator of Pickwick is not to be assessed by accounts given in books and biographies. Love lives and breathes only in the spoken word. To get an adequate idea of the intensity of this love, one must catch (as I once caught) an Englishman old enough to have youthful memories of the days when Dickens was still alive. Preferably it should be someone who finds it hard even now to speak of him as Charles Dickens, choosing, rather, to use the affectionate nickname of "Boz." The emotion, tinged with melancholy, which these old reminiscences call up, gives us of a younger generation some inkling of the enthusiasm that inspired the hearts of thousands when the monthly installments in their blue covers (great rarities, now) arrived at English homes. At such times, my old Dickensian told me, people would walk a long way to meet the postman when a fresh number was due, so impatient were they to read what Boz had to tell.... How could they be expected to wait patiently until the letter-carrier, lumbering along on an old nag, would arrive with the solution of these burning problems? When the appointed hour came round, old and young would sally forth, walking two miles and more to the post office merely to have the issue sooner. On the way home they would start reading, those who had not the luck of holding the book looking over the shoulder of the more fortunate mortal; others would set about reading aloud as they walked; only persons with a genius for self-sacrifice would defer a purely personal gratification, and would scurry back to share the treasure with wife and child.
>
> In every village, in every town, in the whole of the British Isles, and far beyond, away in the remotest parts of the earth where the English-speaking nations had gone to settle and colonize, Charles Dickens was loved. People loved him from the first moment when (through the medium of print) they made his acquaintance until his dying day....[4]

Dickens's tours as a reader gave final proof of public affection for him, both at home and abroad. By nine o'clock on the morning that tickets for his lecture course were placed on sale in New York, there were two lines of buyers, each more than three-quarters of a mile in length:

> The tickets for the course were all sold before noon. Members of families relieved each other in the queues; waiters flew across the streets and squares from the neighboring restaurant, to serve par-

ties who were taking their breakfast in the open December air; while excited men offered five and ten dollars for the mere permission to exchange places with other persons standing nearer the head of the line![5]*

Isn't this atmosphere similar to that of Chaplin's tour through Europe, or the triumphant visit to Moscow of "Doug" and "Mary," or the excited anticipation around the première of *Grand Hotel* in New York, when an airplane service assisted ticket buyers on the West Coast? The immense popular success of Dickens's novels in his own time can be equaled in extent only by that whirlwind success which is now enjoyed by this or that sensational film success.

Perhaps the secret lies in Dickens's (as well as cinema's) creation of an extraordinary plasticity. The observation in the novels is extraordinary—as is their optical quality. The characters of Dickens are rounded with means as plastic and slightly exaggerated as are the screen heroes of today. The screen's heroes are engraved on the senses of the spectator with clearly visible traits, its villains are remembered by certain facial expressions, and all are saturated in the peculiar, slightly unnatural radiant gleam thrown over them by the screen.

It is absolutely thus that Dickens draws his characters—this is the faultlessly plastically grasped and pitilessly sharply sketched gallery of immortal Pickwicks, Dombeys, Fagins Tackletons, and others.

Just because it never occurred to his biographers to connect Dickens with the cinema, they provide us with unusually objective evidence, directly linking the importance of Dickens's observation with our medium.

> [John] Forster speaks of Dickens's recollections of his childhood sufferings, and notes, as he could hardly fail to note, Dickens's amazingly detailed memory. He does not note, as he should, how this super-acuteness of physical vision contributed a basic element to Dickens's artistic method. For with that acuteness of physical

---

*Dickens himself witnessed a modern by-product of popular success—speculators: "At Brooklyn I am going to read in Mr. Ward Beecher's chapel: the only building there available for the purpose. You must understand that Brooklyn is a kind of sleeping-place for New York, and is supposed to be a great place in the money way. We let the seats pew by pew! The pulpit is taken down for my screen and gas! and I appear out of the vestry in canonical form!... The sale of tickets there was an amazing scene. The noble army of speculators have now furnished (this is literally true, and I am quite serious) each man with a straw mattress, a little bag of bread and meat, two blankets, and a bottle of whiskey.... It being severely cold at Brooklyn, they made an immense bonfire in the street—a narrow street of wooden houses—which the police turned out to extinguish. A general fight then took place; from which the people furthest off in the line rushed bleeding when they saw any chance of owning others nearer the door, put their mattresses in the spots so gained, and held on by the iron rails...."[6]

vision, and that unerring recollection of every detail in the thing seen, went an abnormally complete grasp of the thing in the totality of its natural connections....

And if ever a man had the gift of the eye—and not merely of the eye but of the ear, and of the nose—and the faculty of remembering with microscopic accuracy of detail everything ever seen, or heard, or tasted, smelled, or felt, that man was Charles Dickens.... The whole picture arises before us in sight, sound, touch, taste, and pervading odour, just exactly as in real life, and with a vividness that becomes positively uncanny.

To readers less sensitive than Dickens, this very vividness with which he visualizes plain things in plain everyday life appears to be "exaggeration." It is no such thing. The truth is that Dickens always sees instantly, and in every last, least, tiny detail, *all* that there is to be seen; while lesser mortals see only a part, and sometimes a trifling part at that.[7]

Zweig continues the case:

He cuts through the fog surrounding the years of childhood like a clipper driving through the waves. In *David Copperfield*, that masked autobiography, we are given reminiscences of a two-year-old child concerning his mother with her pretty hair and youthful shape, and Peggotty with no shape at all; memories which are like silhouettes standing out from the blank of his infancy. There are never any blurred contours where Dickens is concerned; he does not give us hazy visions, but portraits whose every detail is sharply defined.... As he himself once said, it is the little things that give meaning to life. He is, therefore, perpetually on the watch for tokens, be they never so slight; a spot of grease on a dress, an awkward gesture caused by shyness. a strand of reddish hair peeping from beneath a wig if its wearer happens to lose his temper. He captures all the nuances of a handshake, knows what the pressure of each finger signifies; detects the shades of meaning in a smile.

Before he took the career of a writer, he was parliamentary reporter for a newspaper. In this capacity he became proficient in the art of summary, in compressing long-winded discussions; as shorthand writer he conveyed a word by a stroke, a whole sentence by a few curves and dashes. So in later days as an author he invented a kind of shorthand to reality, consisting of little signs instead of lengthy descriptions, an essence of observation distilled from the innumerable happenings of life. He has an uncannily sharp eye for the detection of these insignificant externals: he never overlooks anything; his memory and his keenness of perception are like a good camera lens which, in the hundredth part of a second, fixes the least expression, the slightest gesture, and yields a perfectly precise negative. Nothing escapes his notice. In addition, this perspicacious observation is enhanced by a marvellous power of refraction which, instead of presenting an object as merely reflected in its ordinary proportions from the surface of a mirror, gives us an image clothed in an excess of characteristics. For he invariably underlines the personal attributes of his characters....

This extraordinary optical faculty amounted to genius in Dickens.... His psychology began with the visible; he gained his insight into character by observation of the exterior—the most delicate and fine minutiae of the outward semblance, it is true, those utmost tenuosities which only the eyes that are rendered acute by a superlative imagination can perceive. Like the English philosophers, he does not begin with assumptions and suppositions, but with characteristics.... Through traits he discloses types: Creakle had no voice, but spoke in a whisper; the exertion cost him, or the consciousness of talking in that feeble way, made his angry face much more angry, and his thick veins much thicker. Even as we read the description, the sense of terror the boys felt at the approach of this fiery blusterer becomes manifest in us as well. Uriah Heep's hands are damp and cold; we experience a loathing for the creature at the very outset as though we were faced by a snake. Small things? Externals? Yes, but they invariably are such as to recoil upon the soul.[8]

The visual images of Dickens are inseparable from aural images. The English philosopher and critic, George Henry Lewes,[9] though puzzled as to its significance, recorded that "Dickens once declared to me that every word said by his characters was distinctly *heard* by him....

We can see for ourselves that his descriptions offer not only absolute *accuracy of detail*, but also an absolutely *accurate drawing of the behavior* and actions of his characters. And this is just as true for the most trifling details of behavior—even gesture, as it is for the basic generalized characteristics of the image. Isn't this piece of description of Mr. Dombey's behavior actually an exhaustive regisseur-actor directive?

He had already laid his hand upon the bell-rope to convey his usual summons to Richards, when his eye fell upon a writing-desk, belonging to his deceased wife, which had been taken, among other things, from a cabinet in her chamber. It was not the first time that his eye had lighted on it. He carried the key in his pocket; and he brought it to his table and opened it now—having previously locked the room door—with a well-accustomed hand.[10]

Here the last phrase arrests one's attention: there is a certain awkwardness in its description. However, this "inserted" phrase: *having previously locked the room door*, "fitted in" as if recollected by the author in the middle of a later phrase, instead of being placed where it apparently should have been, in the consecutive order of the description, that is, before the words, *and be brought it to his table*, is found exactly at this spot for quite *un*fortuitous reasons.

In this deliberate "montage" displacement of the time-continuity of the description there is a brilliantly caught rendering of the *transient thievery* of the action, slipped between the preliminary action and the act of reading another's letter, carried out with that absolute "correctness" of gentlemanly dignity which Mr. Dombey knows how to give to any behavior or action of his.

This very (montage) arrangement of the phrasing gives an exact direction to the "Performer," so that in defining this decorous and confident opening of the writing-desk, he must "play" the closing and locking of the door with a hint of an entirely different shade of conduct. And it would be this "shading" in which would also he played the unfolding of the letter; but in this part of the "performance" Dickens makes this shading more precise, not only with a significant arrangement of the words, but also with an exact description of characteristics.

> From beneath a heap of torn and cancelled scraps of paper, he took one letter that remained entire. Involuntarily holding his breath as he opened this document, and 'bating in the stealthy action something of his arrogant demeanour, he sat down, resting his head upon one hand, and read it through.

The reading itself is done with a shading of absolutely gentlemanly cold decorum:

> He read it slowly and attentively, and with a nice particularity to every syllable. Otherwise than as his great deliberation seemed unnatural, and perhaps the result of an effort equally great, he allowed no sign of emotion to escape him. When he had read it through, he folded and refolded it slowly several times, and tore it carefully into fragments. Checking his hand in the act of throwing these away, he put them in his pocket, as if unwilling to trust them even to the chances of being reunited and deciphered; and instead of ringing, as usual, for little Paul, he sat solitary all the evening in his cheerless room.

This scene does not appear in the final version of the novel, for with the aim of increasing the tension of the action, Dickens cut out this passage on Forster's advice; in his biography of Dickens Forster preserved this page to show with what mercilessness Dickens sometimes "cut" writing that had cost him great labor. This mercilessness once more emphasizes that sharp clarity of representation towards which Dickens strove by all means, endeavoring with purely cinematic laconism to say what he considered necessary. (This by the way, did not in the least prevent his novels from achieving enormous breadth.)

I don't believe I am wrong in lingering on this example, for one need only alter two or three of the character names and change Dickens's name to the name of the hero of my essay, in order to impute literally almost everything told here to the account of Griffith.

...

I don't know how my readers feel about this, but for me personally it is always pleasing to recognize again and again the fact that our cinema is not altogether without parents and without pedigree, without a past, without the traditions and rich cultural heritage of the past epochs. It is only very thoughtless and presumptuous people who can erect laws and an esthetic for cinema, proceeding from premises of some incredible virgin-birth of this art!

Let Dickens and the whole ancestral array, going back as far as the Greeks and Shakespeare, be superfluous reminders that both Griffith and our cinema prove our origins to be not solely as of Edison and his fellow inventors, but as based on an enormous cultured past; each part of this past in its own moment of world history has moved forward the great art of cinematography. Let this past be a reproach to those thoughtless people who have displayed arrogance in reference to literature, which has contributed so much to this apparently unprecedented art and is, in the first and most important place: the art of viewing—not only the *eye*, but *viewing*—both meanings being embraced in this term.

This esthetic growth from the *cinematographic eye* to the *image of an embodied viewpoint on phenomena* was one of the most serious processes of development of our Soviet cinema in particular; our cinema also played a tremendous rôle in the history of the development of world cinema as a whole, and it was no small rôle that was played by a basic understanding of the principles of film-montage, which became so characteristic for the Soviet school of film-making.

None the less enormous was the rôle of Griffith also in the evolution of the system of Soviet montage: a rôle as enormous as the rôle of Dickens in forming the methods of Griffith. Dickens in this respect played an enormous rôle in heightening the tradition and cultural heritage of preceding epochs; just as on an even higher level we can see the enormous rôle of those social premises, which inevitably in those pivotal moments of history ever anew push elements of the montage method into the center of attention for creative work.

...

Notes

1. George Bernard Shaw, *Back to Methuselah* (Preface). London, 1921.

2. Gilbert Keith Chesterton, *Charles Dickens, The Last of the Great Men.* New York, The Readers Club, 1942, p. 107.

3. Mrs. D. W. Griffith, *When the Movies Were Young.* New York, E. P. Dutton & Company, 1925, p. 66.

4. Stefan Zweig, *Three Masters: Balzac, Dickens, Dostoyevsky,* translated by Eden and Cedar Paul. New York, The Viking Press, 1930, pp. 51–53.

5. A Philadelphia newspaper, New York correspondent, December 1867.

6. Letters of January 5 and 9, 1868; quoted in John Forster, *The Life of Charles Dickens.* London, Chapman and Hall, 1892.

7. T. A. Jackson, *Charles Dickens; The Progress of a Radical.* New York, International Publishers, 1938, pp. 250–251, 297–298.

8. Zweig, *op. cit.*

9. George Henry Lewes, "Dickens in Relation to Criticism," *The Fortnightly Review,* February 1, 1872, p. 149

10. Quoted in Forster, *op. cit.*, p. 364.

Questions and Projects

- Analyze in detail how a specific literary work (say, from another Victorian novel like Thackeray's *Vanity Fair*) and a specific film (say, Rouben Mamoulian's 1935 version of the novel retitled as *Becky Sharp*) juxtapose and contrast images or scenes. Do these juxtapositions correspond to Eisenstein's model of montage? Or is there some other, more appropriate way to describe the logic and ideas behind how these works construct and edit actions, images, and scenes?

- Besides montage and editing techniques, which other film forms have their sources in literature (or vice versa)? Voice-over narration? Chapter breaks? Narrative frames? Examine a film that may self-consciously use one of these literary techniques (such as Kenneth Branagh's use of a narrative frame in his 1994 *Mary Shelley's Frankenstein*). What is gained and what is lost?

In both the silent and sound film eras, Hungarian Béla Balázs directed films, wrote scripts, taught cinema courses, and formulated film theory. The volume in which the following chapter appears was first published in 1945. Even at this late date, however, there had not been much serious attention to the script or screenplay as literature, and in that sense Balázs's argument here first reacts to views which for the first three decades of film history saw film and especially the screenplay as largely derivative of literary writing and, second, anticipates the postwar recognition of film as a literary-like form with powers of authorial expression.

"The Script"
from *Theory of Film: Character and Growth of a New Art*
Béla Balázs

Not so very long ago it was still difficult to convince the Philistines that the film was an independent, autonomous new art with laws of its own. Today this is scarcely ever questioned and it is also admitted that the literary foundation of the new art, the script, is just as much a specific, independent literary form as the written stage play. The script is no longer a technical accessory, not a scaffolding which is taken away once the house is built, but a literary form worthy of the pen of poets, a literary form which may even be published in book form and read as such. Of course scripts can be good or bad, like any other literary work, but there is nothing to prevent them from being literary masterpieces. That the literary form of the film script has not yet had a Shakespeare, a Calderón, Molière, an Ibsen is no matter—it will have some day. In any case, we do not even know whether there may or may not have been some great masterpiece lost among the thousands of film scripts to which we paid not the slightest attention. We never searched for masterpieces among them, often even denied the very possibility of one being found in such an unlikely place.

Most cinema-goers do not realize that what they are watching is the staging of a film script, very much as they would be watching the staging of a play in the theatre. And even in the theatre, how many spectators think of this? If the newspaper reviews did not discuss the play itself and the performance of it as two distinct subjects, few theatre-goers would think of the literary creative work that has to precede every stage performance of a play.

That public opinion distinguishes more easily between play and stage performance than between script and screened film is due to the fact that a play can be performed in many ways in many theatres, thus demonstrating that the play has an existence of its own apart from the performance. The film on the contrary mostly absorbs the script completely so that it is not preserved as an independent object which could be used again for a different film production. In most cases it is not available in print; it is not yet an accepted custom to publish scripts for reading.

The film script is an entirely new literary form, newer even than the film itself, and so it is scarcely surprising that no books on the æsthetics of literature mention it as yet. The film is fifty years old, the script as a literary form only twenty-five at most. It was in the twenties of this century, in Germany, that specially interesting scripts first began to be published.

In this again the film slavishly copied the development of the stage. There had been highly developed and popular theatre, there had been great playwrights for centuries before plays began to be written down and made available for reading outside the theatre. In ancient Greece, in the Middle Ages and in the Renaissance the written play was always a product of a later differentiation. The drama began with ritual or improvisation, or was born on the stage itself out of the permanent characters of the *commedia dell' arte*. The stage is a much older thing than the play. It is well known that Shakespeare's plays were pieced together later from the parts written out for the actors

In the same way the film is much older than the script. 'Much' here means about twenty years—but that is nearly half of the whole history of the film.

When the film began, there was no script: the director improvised each scene on the set, telling each actor what to do during the next shot. The sub-titles were written and cut in later.

The film script was born when the film had already developed into an independent new art and it was no longer possible to improvise its new subtle visual effects in front of the camera; these had to be planned carefully in advance. The film script became a literary form when the film ceased to aim at literary effects, planted itself firmly on its own feet and thought in terms of visual effects. The picture sequences of the photographed theatre could be written down in the form of a stereotyped stage play; but a film using specific visual effects could no longer be pressed into the form of the drama, nor of the novel. A new form was needed. Its terms of reference and its novelty were determined by the paradoxical task it had to fulfill, which was to present in words the visual experiences of the silent film, that is, something that could not be adequately expressed in words.

The first scripts were in fact mere technical aids, nothing but lists of the scenes and shots for the convenience of the director. They merely indicated what was to be in the picture, and in what order, but said nothing about how it was to be presented.

In the days of the silent film the importance of the literary script grew in the same measure in which the adventurous film stories were simplified and the films themselves given a deeper meaning. The type of imagination the adventure-story writers possessed was no longer suitable; a special filmic imagination was required, subtle visual ideas without intricate plots. The intensity of the close-up drove out the complicated story and brought a new literary form into being.

Such a simplification of the story did not, however, simplify the film at all. There was less adventure, but more psychology. The development turned inward and script-writing was now a task worthy of the pen of the best writers.

It should be said here that this decline of the adventure story was not the only trend in the development of the silent film. There was at the same time a leaning towards the most exotic romanticism—and both these trends can be traced to the same origins. They were both escapist trends, but running in opposite directions. On the one hand the film provided escape into exotic, romantic adventure, on the other escape to some particle of reality entirely isolated from the rest.

With the birth of the talkie the script automatically came to be of paramount importance. It needed dialogue, as a play did, but it needed very much more than that. For a play is only dialogue and nothing else, it is dialogue spoken, as it were, in a vacuum. The stage, though indicated by directions, is not presented in literary form. In the abstract spiritual space of the drama the visual surroundings of the *dramatis personae* were a mere background which could not influence their state of mind and hence could not take part in the action. But in the film visible and audible things are projected on to the same plane as the human characters and in that pictorial composition common to them all they are all equivalent participants in the action. For this reason the script-writer cannot deal with the scene of action by means of a few stage directions. He must present, characterize, depict the visual aspect as well as the rest, express it by literary means, but in much greater detail than for instance the novelist, who may leave a great deal to the imagination of his readers. In the script the script-writer must define the part played by the images of things every bit as carefully as all the other parts, for it is through them that the destinies of the human characters fulfill themselves.

Thus the now fully developed and mature film art had borne a new fruit, a new literary form, the film script. By now many scripts are available in print and soon they may be more popular reading than the more abstract stage play. It is difficult to say how much time must elapse before our literary critics finally notice this new phenomenon born before their eyes; for this reason we shall try to define the laws governing this new literary form.

The problem is: in what respect does the film script differ from the stage play or the novel? The question is put in this form because it will be easiest to define the specific principles and laws of the script by defining the essential qualities which distinguish it from the other forms most closely related to it.

The present-day script is not an unfinished sketch, not a ground-plan, not a mere outline of a work of art, but a complete work of art in itself. The script can present reality, give an independent, intelligible picture of reality like any other form of art. True, the script puts on paper scenes and dialogues which later are to be turned into a film: but so does the drama put on paper the stage performance. And yet the latter is regarded as a literary form superior to the former.

Written music is only a symbol of the music to be produced by the instruments, but nevertheless no one would call a Beethoven sonata 'unfinished' or a 'sketch' because of this. We even have film scripts now which are intended for reading and could not be shot—just as there are 'book' plays which could never be staged. Nevertheless such scripts are not novels or short stories or stage plays—they are film scripts. They belong to a new literary form.

The basic fact which underlies every form of film and determines the laws governing the script is that the film is an audible spectacle, a motion picture, i.e. an action played out in the present, before our eyes.

One of the things that follows from this basic fact is that the script, like the drama, can present only 'real time.' The author cannot speak for himself in the script, just as he cannot in the drama. The author cannot say 'meanwhile time passed...,' he cannot say '... after many years...' or '... after this....' The script cannot refer to the past, cannot tell us about something that happened long ago or in some other place, it cannot summarize events, as the epic forms can. The script can only present what can be enacted before our eyes, in the present, in a space and time accessible to our senses; in this it is similar to the drama.

How, then, does the script differ from the drama?

In the film, as on the stage, the action is visible and audible, but on the stage it is enacted in real space (the space of the stage) by live human beings (the actors). The film on the other hand shows only pictures, images of that space and of those human beings. The film does not present some action played out in the imagination of a poet, but an actual event enacted in real space by real human beings in nature or in a studio, but presents only a picture, a photograph of these events. Thus it is neither a figment of the brain nor immediate reality.

The upshot of this is that the script as a literary form can contain only what is visible and audible on the screen. This appears to be a truism if we do not examine the bounds set by this rule. But it is on this that everything turns.

In one of the finest Soviet films, *Chapayev*, the political commissar attached to Chapayev's partisan troop arrests one of the partisan leaders for stealing a pig. But why lock him up on the farm where they are staying? There is only a dilapidated barn with a broken door that cannot be locked. We see this because the giant partisan more than once pushes his tiger-like head through the door. He could of course come out at will. What prevents him from kicking down the whole tumbledown contraption? That Furmanov, the political commissar, has placed a sentry to guard the door? But the sentry is even more decrepit than the barn; he is a hollow-chested short-sighted, pitiful little figure, a clerk who scarcely knows one end of his rifle from the other. The giant, savage partisan could blow the funny little man away with a breath of his mighty lungs. But he does not do so. It is thus made obvious that what holds the giant captive is not physical force but a moral influence. And we can *see* this moral influence, it is quite unmistakably manifested in a pictorial effect.

Then Chapayev himself comes to release his friend. But the ridiculous, miserable little private who is guarding the prisoner, bars his way. Whose way? The way of the commander, the tremendously strong, fierce, dangerous Chapayev, who rages, flings his sword away—but does not shove the ridiculous little soldier out of the way. Why? Here again it is not physical force that stops Chapayev, but a moral power rendered evident by the visible, pictorial presentation; a moral force incarnated in the hollow-chested, short-sighted, clumsy little man put there on guard by the representative of the Party. It is the authority of the Communist Party which even the undisciplined, unruly, fierce partisans respect and which endows the ridiculous little sentry with a conscious dignity.

Here the authority of the Party, although it may seem an abstract idea, has been rendered visible in a dramatic scene, and thus something that can be photographed. It is to be particularly noted that in this example there are no symbolic or 'metaphorical' shots. they are all quite real, ordinary, pictures with nothing improbable about them and yet they radiate a 'deeper meaning.'

Lessing and the Film

In analyzing the basic difference between the drama and its stage presentation, Lessing outlined the difference between the film script and the film a century and a half before their time. His definition of the nature and laws governing the stage were so brilliant that now, 150 years later, they helped us to define the different laws and the different nature of a different although not entirely unrelated art.

At the beginning of his *Hamburgische Dramaturgie* he speaks of plays made from novels and says: 'It is not at all difficult ... to expand single emotions into scenes ... but to be able to transpose oneself from the point of view of a narrator to the true point of view of each character and instead of describing their passions make these come into existence under the eyes of the spectator and develop without a break in an illusory continuity—that is what is needed here.' In this passage all is said about the most essential difference between drama and epic. The same difference exists between the film script and the epic. Like the drama, the script does not describe the passions but makes them come into being, and develop under the eyes of the spectator. But in this same passage Lessing also defined the difference between the drama and the film script and has helped us to understand one of the basic principles of film art. He says that the drama presents the passions without a break, in an illusory continuity. And truly this is the specific quality of the drama; such continuity is a necessary consequence of the fact that the drama is written for the stage. For a character coming on to the stage is under our eyes in uninterrupted continuity, without a break, until it leaves the stage again.

Parallel Actions

The novelist can take his readers into a large gathering and then deal with only one person of all the company. He can tell the whole life-story of that one person without informing the reader of what the other people present were doing all that time. The reader may easily forget that they are there at all. In the epic forms such 'jumps' are possible and the illusion of an unbroken continuity of scene is not imperative as it is on the stage. This is the basic difference between epic and dramatic forms.

In this respect, however, the film script is related to the epic rather than the dramatic form. The film, like the epic, is not bound to maintain the illusion of unbroken continuity,—such continuity is not even possible. In a film scene all the persons present at the same place not only need not all be visible in every shot but to show them all, all the time, would even be contrary to the style and technique of the film. The public has the illusion that the participants in the scene are present, but they are not always all of them visible. In ceaselessly changing short shots and close-ups we see only those whose face or words happen to be needed just then. The film can lift such a figure out of the greatest crowd and devote special attention to it, penetrate deeply into its emotions and psychology. In this the film and the film script are related to the epic.

The film can interrupt the continuity of a scene not only by not showing all the persons in a scene all the time—the whole scene itself can be interrupted, the film show a different scene enacted in quite a different place, and then the previously interrupted scene can be continued. This is inconceivable on the stage. The possibility of showing in parallel sequence more than one simultaneous action is a quite specific feature of the film and hence a specific possibility of the film script as an art form.

The unity of space thus binds the film even less than the least form-bound of dramas. For the drama cannot in the middle of a scene show another scene enacted in quite a different place and then return to continue the original scene. The law of the unity of space does not apply to the film at all. But the unity of time all the more so. For even if we interrupt a scene and the interpolated scene is enacted *elsewhere*, it must not be enacted at another *time*. It must happen neither sooner nor later, but at the same time, else the audience would either not understand what was going on or would not believe it.

Technical Conditions and Artistic Principles

The question now arises: if there are several characters on the stage but only one or two of them are really engaged in speech or action, do not the others pale into mere lifeless properties? (This is what the technique of the film enables us to avoid.) In a good play this cannot happen, because a good play always has a central problem which organically binds together all the *dramatis personae*. Whatever is said on the stage, whoever says it, always concerns questions vital to all the characters and therefore they all remain alive and interesting. Thus the technical requirements of the stage determine the literary structure of the drama.

As we have seen, the technical requirements of the film are different and therefore the literary structure of the script is different too. The single central problem, the grouping around a single central conflict, which characterizes the structure of the drama, is contrary to the nature of the film, the technical conditions of which are different. The visual nature of the film does not tolerate a structure consisting of a few long scenes. The reason for this is that while long scenes without a change of setting are possible if they are full of internal movement and people can talk in a room for hours if their words express some internal movement or internal struggle, the film, in which the decisive element is always the visible, cannot be content with such long-drawn, merely internal—and hence non-visible—events. The film requires an external, visible, 'shootable' picture for every internal happening. For this reason the film script—again like the novel—does not centralize the conflicts but faces the characters with a series of problems in the course of the story.

One of the laws governing the form of the film script is its prescribed length. In this it resembles the drama, the length of which is determined by the duration feasible on the stage. Of course there are also dramas which are not intended to be performed and which disregard this condition. In the same way it is possible to write fine film scripts intended only for reading and not for shooting as a film.

The film, too, has by now developed a standard length, partly for business reasons, to enable the motion picture theatres to give several shows daily; but there are also physiological reasons which have limited the length of films. For the time being, films longer than ten thousand feet tire the eye.

These are merely external, technical considerations. But it often happens in art that external technical conditions harden into laws governing the internal artistic composition of the work. The short story was created by the predetermined length of the newspaper feature and this art form then brought forth such classics as the short stories of Maupassant or Chekhov. Architectural forms dictated many a composition of sculpture.

The predetermined length may also determine the content. The prescribed length of the sonnet determines its style. No one is forced to write sonnets or film scripts. But if one does, the predetermined length must not become a bed of Procrustes which curtails or draws out the required content. The theme, content and style of the film script must be inspired by the predetermined length of it. This predetermined length is in itself a style, which the script-writer must master.

By now the script has come to be an independent literary form. It was born of the film as the drama was born of the stage play. In the course of time the drama gained precedence over the stage play and now it is the drama that prescribes the tasks and style of the stage, and the history of the stage has long been merely an appendage to the history of the drama.

In the film there is as yet no trace of a similar development. But it will come in time. Up to now the history of the film script has been merely a chapter in the history of the film. But soon the script may in its turn determine the history of the film. Present developments certainly point in this direction.

In discussing the specific laws of the film script as a literary form there is, however, need for some further remarks. No art and no art form consist exclusively of specific elements, because the reproduction of reality has certain basic principles which are universally valid for every art. These principles, however, can be readily found in any text-book on aesthetics. Nevertheless, all things can be characterized the most precisely by means of the specific peculiarities which differentiate them from all other things. It is this specific trait which determines the varying forms of manifestation taken in each art by elements basically common to them all. For instance, painting can express not only experiences 'purely' and 'absolutely' pertaining only to the art of painting—it can also express motives borrowed from literature, philosophy, psychology—in fact every kind of thought and emotion. But whatever may be the content it expresses, such content will have to be made apparent in the specific material of painting, that is, in the form of visual impressions—otherwise it would not be made manifest at all. Hence if we talk of painting, we must first define its specific material.

The art of the film does not consist solely of specific film effects (any more than painting consists of colour effects alone)—however fiercely the fanatics of the absolute film championed such a limitation. In it, as in other art forms, we can find elements of dramatic presentation and of psychological characterization. But one thing is certain: in the film these elements can appear only in the form of moving and talking pictures, that is, they must conform to the specific laws of film art.

It has been said that the content determines the form. But things are not quite so simple as all that, and one need not take this rule to mean that for ages writers had been hatching film themes, film stories and film characters which could not be presented in novels or plays; that these poor authors had to wait decade after decade for the possibility of visual expression, until finally they went to the Lumière brothers and ordered a cinematograph, the new form to fit the new content.

History tells us that the reverse is what actually happened. Lumière had been photographing stage performances for a dozen years before a truly filmic, genuinely specific film story could be born. The hammer and the chisel were not invented by sculptors for their own ends. The technique of the film was known for some time. But it did not develop into a new form-language until a new content, a new and different message was added to it. The hammer and chisel would have for ever remained the tools of the stonemason, if there had been no human being who had experiences which could be best expressed by hewing stone into shape with hammer and chisel. But if a form of art has once developed, then its specific laws determine by dialectic interaction the suitable, specific themes and contents. The script-writers must make their contents conform to the laws governing the fully developed art form of the film.

Then new contents, too, may for a long time be contained in older forms, setting up tensions and causing slight changes in them until after a certain, perhaps a long, time, the new content bursts the old form and creates a new one. But this, too, is done within the bounds of the art form in question. The drama still remains drama, the novel novel, the film film. Only once in our history have we experienced the birth of a completely new art—the art of the film.

The dialectic interrelation of form and content can be compared with the interrelation of a river and its bed. The water is the content, the river-bed the form. Without a doubt it was the water that at one time dug itself this bed—the content created the form. But once the river bed is made it collects the waters of the surrounding countryside and gives them shape. That is, the form shapes the content. The power of mighty floods is required before the waters, over-flowing the old bed, dig an entirely new bed for themselves.

Questions and Projects

- Use published screenplays from different historical periods to analyze the significant changes in this kind of writing. Do these changes in script writing reflect the literature of the times, the movies, or both?
- Select a movie adaptation for which the screenplay is available. Examine and try to explain the alterations that occur between a work of literature, a screenplay, and a finished film. To what extent do these differences allow you to describe the screenplay as a kind of writing with its own aesthetic structures and styles?

This 1948 essay by Alexandre Astruc is considered by many to be a seminal statement in the appearance of New Wave directors in France, other European countries, and eventually the United States. It is a dramatic and compelling assertion that filmmakers could use the camera as a writer uses a pen or as an essayist expresses thoughts. The analogy is a fragile one, given the collaborative teamwork necessary to make a film and the economic and technological obstacles that stand between an individual's idea and its filmic expression. Yet, the timing of the statement is historically precise: Film and filmmakers were positioning themselves on separate but equal terms with literature; the industrial monolith of Hollywood cinema was beginning to give way to alternative practices; and camera technology would soon introduce more mobile, lightweight equipment that could be used by individuals rather than teams. Following Astruc, the debates about film and literature would include notions of film as personal expression, the filmmakers as author or auteur, and an increasingly complex sense of what the "language" of film is or is not.

"The Birth of a New Avant-Garde: La Caméra-Stylo"
from *The New Wave*
Alexandre Astruc

What interests me in the cinema is abstraction.

—Orson Welles

One cannot help noticing that something is happening in the cinema at the moment. Our sensibilities have been in danger of getting blunted by those everyday films which, year in year out, show their tired and conventional faces to the world.

The cinema of today is getting a new face. How can one tell? Simply by using one's eyes. Only a film critic could fail to notice the striking facial transformation which is taking place before our very eyes. In which films can this new beauty be found? Precisely those which have been ignored by the critics. It is not just a coincidence that Renoir's *La Règle du Jeu*, Welles's films, and Bresson's *Les Dames du Bois de Boulogne*, all films which establish the foundations of a new future for the cinema, have escaped the attention of critics, who in any case were not capable of spotting them.

But it is significant that the films which fail to obtain the blessing of the critics are precisely those which myself and several of my friends all agree about. We see in them, if you like, something of the prophetic.

That's why I am talking about *avant-garde*. There is always an *avant-garde* when something new takes place....

To come to the point: the cinema is quite simply becoming a means of expression, just as all the other arts have been before it, and in particular painting and the novel. After having been successively a fairground attraction, an amusement analogous to boulevard theatre, or a means of preserving the images of an era, it is gradually becoming a language. By language I mean a form in which and by which an artist can express his thoughts, however abstract they may be, or translate his obsessions exactly as he does in the contemporary essay or novel. That is why I would like to call this new age of cinema the age of *caméra-stylo* (camera-pen). This metaphor has a very precise sense. By it I mean that the cinema will gradually break free from the tyranny of what is visual, from the image for its own sake, from the immediate and concrete demands of the narrative, to become a means of writing just as flexible and subtle as written language. This art, although blessed with an enormous potential, is an easy prey to prejudice; it cannot go on for ever ploughing the same field of realism and social fantasy* which has been bequeathed to it by the popular novel. It can tackle any subject, any genre. The most philosophical meditations on human production, psychology, ideas, and passions lie well within its province. I will even go so far as to say that contemporary ideas and philosophies of life are such that only the cinema can do justice to them. Maurice Nadeau wrote in an article in the newspaper *Combat*: 'If Descartes lived today, he would write novels.' With all due respect to Nadeau, a Descartes of today would already have shut himself up in his bedroom with a 16mm camera and some film, and would be writing his philosophy on film: for his *Discours de la Méthode* would today be of such a kind that only the cinema could express it satisfactorily.

It must be understood that up to now the cinema has been nothing more than a show. This is due to the basic fact that all films are projected in an auditorium. But with the development of 16mm and television, the day is not far off when everyone will possess a projector, will go to the local bookstore and hire films written on any subject, of any form, from literary criticism and novels to mathematics, history, and general science. From that moment on, it will no longer be possible to speak of *the* cinema. There will be *several* cinemas just as today there are several literatures, for the cinema, like literature, is not so much a particular art as a language which can express any sphere of thought.

This idea of the cinema expressing ideas is not perhaps a new one. Feyder has said: 'I could make a film with Montesquieu's *L'Esprit des Lois*.' But Feyder was thinking of illustrating it 'with pictures' just as

---

*Carné liked to use these terms when referring to his pre-war films (Ed.).

Eisenstein had thought of illustrating Marx's *Capital* in book fashion. What I am trying to say is that cinema is now moving towards a form which is making it such a precise language that it will soon be possible to write ideas directly on film without even having to resort to those heavy associations of images that were the delight of the silent cinema. In other words, in order to suggest the passing of time, there is no need to show falling leaves and then apple trees in blossom; and in order to suggest that a hero wants to make love there are surely other ways of going about it than showing a saucepan of milk boiling over on the stove, as Clouzot does in *Quai des Orfèvres*.

The fundamental problem of the cinema is how to express thought. The creation of this language has preoccupied all the theoreticians and writers in the history of the cinema, from Eisenstein down to the scriptwriters and adaptors of the sound cinema. But neither the silent cinema, because it was the slave of a static conception of the image, nor the classical sound cinema, as it has existed right up to now, has been able to solve this problem satisfactorily. The silent cinema thought it could get out of it through editing and the juxtaposition of images. Remember Eisenstein's famous statement: 'Editing is for me the means of giving movement (i.e., an idea) to two static images.' And when sound came, he was content to adapt theatrical devices.

One of the fundamental phenomena of the last few years has been the growing realization of the dynamic, i.e., significant, character of the cinematic image. Every film, because its primary function is to move, i.e., to take place in time, is a theorem. It is a series of images which, from one end to the other, have an inexorable logic (or better even, a dialectic) of their own. We have come to realize that the meaning which the silent cinema tried to give birth to through symbolic association exists within the image itself, in the development of the narrative, in every gesture of the characters, in every line of dialogue, in those camera movements which relate objects to characters and characters to objects. All thought, like all feeling, is a relationship between one human being and another human being or certain objects which form part of his universe. It is by clarifying these relationships, by making a tangible allusion, that the cinema can really make itself the vehicle of thought. From today onwards, it will be possible for the cinema to produce works which are equivalent, in their profundity and meaning, to the novels of Faulkner and Malraux, to the essays of Sartre and Camus. Moreover we already have a significant example: Malraux's *L'Espoir*, the film which he directed from his own novel, in which, perhaps for the first time ever, film language is the exact equivalent of literary language.

Let us now have a look at the way people make concessions to the supposed (but fallacious) requirements of the cinema. Script-writers who adapt Balzac or Dostoievsky excuse the idiotic transformations they impose on the works from which they construct their scenarios by pleading that the cinema is incapable of rendering every psychological or metaphysical overtone. In their hands, Balzac becomes a collection of engravings in which fashion has the most important place, and Dostoievsky suddenly begins to resemble the novels of Joseph Kessel, with Russian-style drinking-bouts in night-clubs and troika races in the snow. Well, the only cause of these compressions is laziness and lack of imagination. The cinema of today is capable of expressing any kind of reality. What interests us is the creation of this new language. We have no desire to rehash those poetic documentaries and surrealist films of twenty-five years ago every time we manage to escape the demands of a commercial industry. Let's face it: between the pure cinema of the 1920s and filmed theatre, there is plenty of room for a different and individual kind of film-making.

This of course implies that the scriptwriter directs his own scripts; or rather that the scriptwriter ceases to exist, for in this kind of film-making the distinction between author and director loses all meaning. Direction is no longer a means of illustrating or presenting a scene, but a true act of writing. The film-maker/author writes with his camera as a writer writes with his pen. In an art in which a length of film and sound-track is put in motion and proceeds, by means of a certain form and a certain story (there can even be no story at all—it matters little), to evolve a philosophy of life, how can one possibly distinguish between the man who conceives the work and the man who writes it? Could one imagine a Faulkner novel written by someone other than Faulkner? And would *Citizen Kane* be satisfactory in any other form than that given to it by Orson Welles?

Let me say once again that I realize the term *avant-garde* savours of the surrealist and so-called abstract films of the 1920s. But that *avant-garde* is already old hat. It was trying to create a specific domain for the cinema; we on the contrary are seeking to broaden it and make it the most extensive and clearest language there is. Problems such as the translation into cinematic terms of verbal tenses and logical relationships interest us much more than the creation of the exclusively visual and static art dreamt of by the surrealists. In any case, they were doing no more than make cinematic adaptations of their experiments in painting and poetry.

So there we are. This has nothing to do with a school, or even a movement. Perhaps it could simply be called a tendency: a new awareness, a desire to transform the cinema and hasten the advent of an exciting future. Of course, no tendency can be so called unless it has something concrete to show for itself. The films will come, they will see the light of day—make no mistake about it. The economic and material difficulties of the cinema create the strange paradox whereby one can talk about something which does not yet exist; for although we know what we want, we do not know whether, when, and how we will be able to do it. But the cinema cannot but develop. It is an art that cannot live by looking back over the past and chewing over the nostalgic memories of an age gone by. Already it is looking to the future; for the future, in the cinema as elsewhere, is the only thing that matters.

Questions and Projects

- Choose a specific filmmaker (say, Marguerite Duras, Rainer Werner Fassbinder, or David Lynch) whose films seem to be about personal expression. What are the most important textual or thematic signs of this personal expression? Does that work also suggest differences between literary writing and filmmaking?

- How has the idea and image of a film director as a literary writer or auteur changed over the last four decades? Contrast the films of two or three filmmakers from different periods or places, and compare the different ways they use the cinema to position themselves as versions of the writer expressing his or her thoughts or perspectives.

*O*riginally published in French in 1951 and translated into English in 1967, the following and other essays in Bazin's What Is Cinema? represent highly energized and imaginative thinking about film in general and film and literature in specific. One of the leaders of serious film study in France, Bazin introduces crucial terms and distinctions about the relationships—past, present, and future—between film and drama, about canned theater, drama versus theater, the textuality of drama, and so forth. He also identifies the distinctive powers of the cinema to create a unique and powerful identification and presence for audiences through the use of spatial realism. While Bazin remains committed to the cinema as a unique artistic form, he clearly respects the powers of traditional literature and drama. He ultimately urges a creative evolution whereby cinema builds on its literary precedents as an exchange through which the two practices continually reinvigorate each other.

"Theater and Cinema" from *What Is Cinema?*

André Bazin

Part One

While critics often draw attention to the resemblances between the cinema and the novel, "filmed theater" still frequently passes for heresy. So long as its advocates and its prime examples were the statements and the plays of Marcel Pagnol it was reasonable enough to explain his one or two successes as flukes resulting from an unusual combination of circumstances. "Filmed theater" was bound up with recollections, in retrospect so farcical, of the *film d'art* or the boulevard hits in the "style" of Berthomieu.... The wartime failure of the screen adaptation of that admirable play *Le Voyageur sans baggages*, the subject of which would seem to have been suitably cinematic, apparently clinched the matter for the opponents of "filmed theater." It took a run of recent successes, from *The Little Foxes* to *Macbeth* by way of *Henry V*, *Hamlet*, and *Les Parents terribles*, to show that the cinema is a valid medium for a wide variety of dramatic works.

Truthfully speaking, those prejudiced against filmed theater would not have so many examples from the past to point to if the question were confined to films that were avowedly adaptations of plays. There is then some justification for looking over the history of films not according to titles but on the basis of their dramatic structure and direction.

A Brief Historical Note

While the critics were busy damning filmed theater without recourse, they were at the same time showering praise on certain forms of cinema that a closer analysis would have revealed to be the very embodiment of the art of the drama. Their vision obscured by the *film d'art* and its off-spring, the customs were letting by, stamped as "pure cinema," various examples of cinematographic theater beginning with American comedy. If you look at this comedy closely you will see that it is no less "theatrical" than the adaptation of any boulevard or Broadway play. Built on comedy of dialogue and situation, most of the scenes are interiors while the editing uses the device of shot-and-reverse-shot to point up the dialogue. Here one should perhaps expound on the sociological background that made possible the brilliant development of the American comedy over a decade. The effect of this I believe would be to confirm the existence of a working relationship between theater and cinema. The cinema had, so to speak, dispensed theater from any need for prior existence. There was no such need since the authors of these plays could sell them directly to the screen. But this is a purely accidental phenomenon historically related to a combination of sociological and economic conditions now seemingly on their way out. For the past fifteen years we have seen, along with the decline of a certain type of American comedy, an increasing number of filmed Broadway comedy successes.

In the realm of psychological drama and the drama of manners, Wyler had no hesitation in taking the play by Lillian Hellman, *The Little Foxes*, lock, stock and barrel, and bringing it to the screen virtually in its theatrical entirety. Actually there has never been any prejudice against filmed theater in the United States. But the circumstances of production in Hollywood, at least up to 1940, were not the same as in Europe. It was a matter there of a cinematographic theater restricted to certain specific genres and at least during the first decade of sound, of borrowing little from the stage. The present crisis in screen material in Hollywood has sent it looking for help more frequently to written theater. But in American comedy the theater, albeit invisible, was always potentially there.*

*In his book of reminiscences covering 50 years of cinema, entitled *The Public Is Always Right*, Adolph Zukor, creator of the star system, also tells us how the cinema in America even more than in France used its nascent awareness to plunder the theater. Realizing that the commercial future of the cinema depended on the quality of the subject matter and the prestige of the cast, Zukor bought up as many film adaptation rights as he could and enticed big names away from the theater. His salary scales, relatively high for the times, did not however always overcome the reluctance of the actors to become a part of this despised industry with its fairground flavor. Very soon, after the break with the theater, the phenomenon of the "star" peculiar to the cinema emerged, the public chose its favorites from among the famous theater names, and this elect rapidly acquired a glory with which stage fame could not be compared. Similarly, the earlier theatrical scenarios were abandoned in favor of stories adapted to the new mythology. Still, it was by copying the theater that the start had been made.

There is no question that we in Europe can lay no claim to an achievement comparable to the American comedy. With the exception of the special case of Marcel Pagnol, which needs a special study, boulevard comedies have failed lamentably on the screen.

Filmed theater, however, does not begin with sound. Let us go a little farther back, specifically to the time when the *film d'art* was demonstrably failing. That was the heyday of Méliès who saw the cinema as basically nothing more than a refinement of the marvels of the theater. Special effects were for him simply a further evolution of conjuring. The greater part of French and American comedians come from the music hall or from the boulevard theater. One need only look at Max Linder to see how much he owes to his theatrical experience. Like most comics of his time he plays directly to the audience, winks at them and calls on them to witness his embarrassment, and does not shrink from asides. As for Charlie Chaplin, apart from his indebtedness to the English school of mime, it is clear that his art consists in perfecting, thanks to the cinema, his skill as a music-hall comic. Here the cinema offers more than the theater but only by going beyond it, by relieving it of its imperfections. The economics of the gag are governed by the distance between the stage and the audience and above all by the length of the laughs which spur the actor to protract his effect to the point of its extinction. The stage, then, eggs him on, forces him indeed to exaggerate. Only the screen could allow Charlie to attain mathematical perfection of situation and gesture whereby the maximum effect is obtained in the minimum of time.

When one sees again the really old slapstick films, the *Boireau* or *Onésime* series, for example, it is not only the acting which strikes one as belonging to the theater, it is also the structure of the story. The cinema makes it possible to carry a simple situation to its ultimate conclusions which on the stage would be restricted by time and space, that is, to what might be called a larval stage. What makes it possible to believe that the cinema exists to discover or create a new set of dramatic facts is its capacity to transform theatrical situations that otherwise would never have reached their maturity. In Mexico there is a kind of salamander capable of reproduction at the larval stage and which develops no further. By injecting it with hormones, scientists have brought it to maturity. In like fashion we know that the continuity of animal evolution presented us with incomprehensible gaps until biologists discovered the laws of *paidomorphosis* from which they learnt not only to place embryonic forms in the line of evolution of the species but also to recognize that certain individuals, seemingly adult, have been halted in their evolutionary development. In this sense certain types of theater are founded on dramatic situations that were congenitally atrophied prior to the appearance of the cinema. If theater is, as Jean Hytier says it is, a metaphysic of the will, what is one to think of a burlesque like *Onésime et le beau voyage*—where an obstinate determination to proceed in spite of the most ludicrous obstacles, with a not too clearly explained sort of honeymoon trip which ceases to make any sense after certain early mishaps, borders on a kind of metaphysical insanity, a delirium of the will, a cancerous regeneration of action from out of itself against all reason.

Has one even the right here to use the terminology of the psychologist and speak of will? The majority of these burlesques are an endlessly protracted expression of something that cries from within the character. They are a kind of phenomenology of obstinacy. The domestic Boireau will continue to do the housework till the house collapses in ruins. Onésime, the migratory spouse, will continue on his honeymoon trip to the point of embarking for the horizon in his wicker trunk. The action here no longer calls for plot, episodes, repercussions, misunderstandings, or sudden reversals. It unfolds implacably to the point at which it destroys itself. It proceeds unswervingly towards a kind of rudimentary catharsis of catastrophe like a small child recklessly inflating a rubber balloon to the point where it explodes in his face—to our relief and possibly to his.

For the rest, when one examines the history of the characters, situations, and routines of classical farce it is impossible to avoid the conclusion that slapstick cinema gave it a sudden and dazzling rebirth. The "flesh and blood farce," on its way out since the seventeenth century, survived, highly specialized and transformed, only in the circus and in certain kinds of music hall. That is to say precisely in these places where the Hollywood producers of slapstick films went for their actors. The routines of this genre combined with the resources of the cinema added widely to their technical repertory. It made possible a Max Linder, a Buster Keaton, a Laurel and Hardy, a Chaplin. Between 1903 and 1920 it reached a peak unique in its history. I am referring to the tradition of farce as it has been perpetuated since the days of Plautus and Terence and even including the *Commedia dell'Arte* with its special themes and techniques. Let me take just one example. The "vat routine" turns up spontaneously in an old Max Linder around 1912 or 1913 in which we see the sprightly Don Juan seducer of the dyer's wife forced to take a header into a vat full of dye to escape the vengeance of the cheated husband. In a case like this there is no question of imitation, or of influence or of a remembered routine, just the spontaneous linking up of a genre with its tradition.

The Text! The Text!

It is clear from these few recollections from the past that the relations between theater and cinema are much older and closer than is generally thought to be the case and that they are certainly not limited to what is generally and deprecatingly called "filmed theater." We have also seen that the influence, as unconscious as it was unavowed, of the repertory and traditions of theater has been very marked on that class of film considered purely and specifically cinematic.

But the problem of the adaptation of a play as we generally use the term is something different again. We must begin, before going any further, by distinguishing between theatrical reality and dramatic reality.

Drama is the soul of the theater but this soul sometimes inhabits other bodies. A sonnet, a fable of La Fontaine, a novel, a film can owe their effectiveness to what Henri Gouhier calls *"the dramatic categories."* From this point of view it is useless to claim autonomy for the theater. Either that, or we must show it to be something negative. That is to say a play cannot not be dramatic while a novel is free to be dramatic or not. *Of Mice and Men* is simultaneously a novel and a model tragedy. On the other hand, it would be very hard to adapt *Swann's Way* for the theater. One would not praise a play for its novel-like qualities yet one may very well congratulate a novelist for being able to structure an action.

Nevertheless, if we insist that the dramatic is exclusive to theater, we must concede its immense influence and also that the cinema is the least likely of the arts to escape this influence. At this rate, half of literature and three quarters of the existing films are branches of theater. It is equally true that this is not the way to state the problem. The problem only came alive by virtue of the incarnation of the theatrical work not in the actor but in the text.

Phèdre was written to be played but it also exists as a work and as a tragedy for the student as he labors the year round at his classics. "Armchair theater," having only imagination to rely on, is lacking as theater, but it is nevertheless still theater. On the contrary *Cyrano de Bergerac* or *Le Voyageur sans baggages* as filmed are *not*, in spite of the text and of a generous dose of spectacle into the bargain.

If it were permissible to take just one single action from *Phèdre*, to reconstruct it according to the requirements of the novel or of cinematic dialogue, we would find ourselves back with our earlier hypothesis, namely of the theatrical reduced to the dramatic. Now while, metaphysically speaking, there is nothing to prevent one from doing this, there are a number of historical and purely practical arguments against it. The simplest of them is a salutary fear of the ridiculous, while the most forceful is our modern attitude towards a work of art which demands respect for the text and for the rights of authorship, and which is morally binding even after the author's death. In other words, only Racine has the right to make an adaptation of *Phèdre*. But here, over and above the fact that even so there is no guarantee that it would be any good (Anouilh himself adapted *Le Voyageur sans baggages*) there is also another fact to consider. Racine happens to be dead.

Some will hold that the situation is not the same during an author's lifetime, since he can himself revise his work and remodel his material. André Gide did this recently although in an opposite direction, namely from novel to screen with *Les Caves du Vatican*. At least he can keep an eye on the result and guarantee the adaptation. A closer examination however shows that this is a matter rather of jurisdiction than of aesthetics. In the first place talent, and still less genius, are not to be found everywhere, and nothing can guarantee that the original and the adaptation will be of the same standard even if they are the work of the same author. Furthermore, the usual reason for wanting to make a film out of a contemporary play is its commercial success in the theater. In the course of its successful run, the text, as tried out, has become crystallized so to speak as to its essentials and it is this text that the film audience will be looking for. So here we are, by way of a more or less honorable detour, back at our respect for the written text.

Finally it may be argued that the greater the dramatic quality of a work the more difficult it is to separate off the dramatic from the theatrical element, a synthesis of the two having been achieved in the text. It is significant that while novels are often dramatized, a novel is rarely made from a play. It is as if the theater stood at the end of an irreversible process of aesthetic refinement.

Strictly speaking one could make a play out of *Madame Bovary* or *The Brothers Karamazov*. But had the plays come first it would be impossible to derive from them the novels as we know them. In other words, when the drama is so much a part of the novel that it cannot be taken from it, reciprocally the novel can only be the result of a process of induction which in the arts means purely and simply a new creation. Compared with the play, the novel is only one of the many possible syntheses derivable from the simple dramatic element.

I am comparing for the moment novel and theater but there is every reason to suppose that the argument applies with greater force to the cinema. For we have one of two things to choose from. The film is either the photographed play, text and all, in which case we have our famous "filmed theater." Or the play is adapted to the requirements of the cinema and we are back with the composite that we spoke of above and it is a question of a new work. Jean Renoir drew his inspiration for *Boudu sauvé des eaux* from the play by René Fauchois but he made a superior thing of it, which in all probability eclipsed the original.* This is, incidentally, an exception that definitely proves the rule.

However one approaches it, a play whether classic or modern is unassailably protected by its text. There is no way of adapting the text

---

*He took no less a liberty with *La Carosse du S. Sacrement* by Merimée.

without disposing of it and substituting something else, which may be better but is not the play. This is a practice, for that matter, restricted of necessity to second-class authors or to those still living, since the masterpieces that time has hallowed demand, as a postulate, that we respect their texts.

The experience of the last ten years bears this out. If the problem of filmed theater has taken on a new lease of aesthetic life it is thanks to films like *Hamlet, Henry V,* and *Macbeth* among the classics, and among contemporary works films like *The Little Foxes* by Lillian Hellman and Wyler, *Les Parents terribles, Occupe-toi d'Amélie, Rope.* Jean Cocteau had written an adaptation of *Les Parents terribles* prior to the war. When he took up the project again in 1946 he decided to go back to the original text. As we shall see, a little later he also virtually preserved the original stage settings. Whether it has been in the United States, England, or France, both with the classics and the contemporary plays, the evolution of filmed theater has been the same. It has been characterized by an increasingly exacting demand for fidelity to the text as originally written. It is as if all the various experiments of the sound film had converged on this point.

Previously the first concern of a filmmaker was to disguise the theatrical origins of his model, to adapt it and to dissolve it in cinema. Not only does he seem to have abandoned this attitude, he makes a point of emphasizing its theatrical character. It could not be otherwise from the moment we preserve the essentials of the text. Conceived with a view to the potentialities of the theater, these are already embodied in the text. The text determines the mode and style of the production; it is already potentially the theater. There is no way at one and the same time of being faithful to it and of turning it aside from the direction it was supposed to go.

Hide That Theater Which I Cannot Abide!

We shall find a confirmation of this in an example borrowed from classical theater. It is a film that may still, perhaps, be creating havoc in French schools and lycées and which pretends to offer a method of teaching literature through cinema. I refer to *Le Médecin malgré lui.* It was brought to the screen, with the help of a doubtlessly well-intentioned teacher, by a director whose name we will not disclose. This film has a dossier, as laudatory as it is depressing, from professors and headmasters of lycées who are delighted by its fine qualities. In reality it is an unbelievable collection of all the faults guaranteed to make an end of film and theater alike, to say nothing of Molière himself. The first scene, with the bundles of wood, set in a real forest, opens with an interminable travelling shot through the underbrush, destined obviously to allow us to enjoy the effects of sunlight on the underside of the branches before showing us two clownlike characters who are presumably gathering mushrooms and whose stage costumes, in this setting, look like nothing so much as grotesque disguises. Real settings are used as much as possible throughout the film. The arrival of Sganarelle for a consultation is seized upon as an opportunity to show us a small country manor house of the seventeenth century. And what of the editing? In the first scene it moves from medium full-shot to full-shot, cross cutting with each piece of dialogue. One has the feeling that if the text, much against the director's will, had not dictated the length of film, he would have presented the flow of dialogue in that speeded-up form of editing we associate with Abel Gance. Such as it is, the editing sees to it that the students, through the use of shot-and-reverse-shot in close-up, miss nothing of the miming of the cast from the Comédie Française, which unquestionably takes us back to the heyday of the *film d'art*.

If by cinema we understand liberty of action in regard to space, and freedom to choose your angle of approach to the action, then filming a play should give the setting a breadth and reality unattainable on the stage. It would also free the spectator from his seat and by varying the shots give an added quality to the acting.

Faced with productions of this kind, one must agree that every argument against filmed theater is a valid one. But the problem is not with the production at all. What was actually done was to inject the power of "cinema" into the theater. The original drama and the text even more so have been turned out of house and home, so to speak. The duration of the action on the stage and on screen are obviously not the same. The dramatic primacy of the word is thrown off center by the additional dramatization that the camera gives to the setting. Finally and above all, a certain artificiality, an exaggerated transformation of the decor, is totally incompatible with that realism which is of the essence of the cinema. The text of Molière only takes on meaning in a forest of painted canvas and the same is true of the acting. The footlights are not the autumn sun. If it comes to that, the scene of the bundles of wood could be played in front of a curtain. It no longer calls for the foot of a tree.

This failure is a good example of what may be considered the major heresy of filmed theater, namely the urge "to make cinema." By and large this is responsible for the majority of adaptations of successful plays. If the action is supposed to take place on the Côte d'Azur, the lovers, instead of chatting in a nook of a bar, will be kissing at the wheel of an American car as they drive along the Corniche against a back projection showing the rocks of the Cap d'Antibes. As for editing, the contracts of Raimu and Fernandel being the same will assure us of a reasonably equal number of close-ups favoring now one and now the other. Besides, the preconceptions of the public in these matters serve to confirm those of the film-makers. People in general do not give much thought to the cinema. For them it means vast decor, exteriors, and plenty of action. If they are not given at least a minimum of what they call cinema, they feel cheated. The cinema must be more lavish than the theater. Every actor must be a somebody and any hint of poverty or meanness in the everyday surrounding contributes, so they say, to a flop. Obviously then, a director or a producer who is willing to challenge the public prejudice in these matters needs courage. Especially if they do not have too much faith in what they are doing. The heresy of filmed theater is rooted in an ambivalent complex that cinema has about the theater. It is an inferiority complex in the presence of an older and more literary art, for which the cinema proceeds to overcompensate by the "superiority" of its technique—which in turn is mistaken for an aesthetic superiority.

Canned or Supertheater?

Would you like to see these errors disproved? Two successful films like *Henry V* and *Les Parents terribles* will do the job perfectly.

When the director of *Le Médecin malgré lui* opened on a travelling shot in the forest, it was with the naive and perhaps unconscious hope that it would help us swallow the unfortunate scene with the bundles of wood like a sugar-coated pill. He tried to give us a little environment of reality, to give us a ladder onto the stage. His awkward tricks had, unfortunately, the opposite effect. They underlined the unreality of both the characters and the text.

Now let us see how Laurence Olivier succeeded in resolving the dialectic between cinematic realism and theatrical convention. His film also begins with a travelling shot, but in this case its purpose is to plunge us into the theater, the courtyard of an Elizabethan inn. He is not pretending to make us forget the conventions of the theater. On the contrary he affirms them. It is not with the play *Henry V* that the film is immediately and directly concerned, but with a performance of *Henry V*. This we know from the fact that the performance here given is not supposed to be an actual one, as when the play is given in the theater. It is supposed to be taking place in Shakespeare's day and we are even shown the audience and the backstage areas. There is no mistake about it, the act of faith usually required of a spectator as the curtain rises is not needed here for the enjoyment of the spectacle. We are not in the play, we are in an historical film about the Elizabethan theater, that is to say, we are present at a film of a kind that is widely accepted and to which we are quite used. Our enjoyment of the play however is not of the kind we would get from an historical documentary. It is in fact the pleasure to be derived from a Shakespearean performance. In other words the aesthetic strategy of Laurence Olivier was a trick to escape from the "miracle of the curtain," that is, from the need for the usual suspension of disbelief.

In making his film out of a play by showing us, from the opening, by a cinematic device that we are concerned here with theatrical style and conventions instead of trying to hide them, he relieved realism of that which makes it the foe of theatrical illusion. Once assured of a psychological hold on the complicity of the spectator, Olivier could then perfectly well allow himself the switch in pictorial style to the battle of Agincourt. Shakespeare invited it by his deliberate appeal to the imagination of the spectator; here again Olivier had a perfect excuse. This recourse to the cinematic, difficult to justify if the film was just a reproduction of the play, finds its justification in the play itself. Naturally he still had to honor his promise and we know that he did this. Let us simply remark here that the color, which may eventually come to seem an essentially unrealistic element, helps to justify the transition to the realm of the imaginary and once there to make it possible to accept a continuity which passes from miniatures to a realistic reconstruction of the battle of Agincourt. Never for one moment is *Henry V* really "filmed theater." The film exists so to speak side by side with the theatrical presentation, in front of and behind the stage. Both Shakespeare and the theater however are truly its prisoners, hemmed in on all sides by cinema.

The boulevard theater of today does not appear to make quite such obvious use of the conventions of theater. The *"Théâtre Libre"* and the theories of Antoine might even lead one to believe in the existence at one time of a "realist" theater, a kind of pre-cinema.* This is an illusion that no longer fools anybody. If there is such a thing, it is again only something that relates to a system of less obvious conventions, less explicit but just as absolute. There is no such thing as a "slice of life" in the theater. In any case, the mere fact that it is exposed to view on the

---

*A comment here might not come amiss. We must first of all recognize that melodrama and drama stirred up a realist revolution at the very core of the theater: the ideal stendhalian spectator fires a revolver at the traitor in the play (Orson Welles was later to do the opposite on Broadway and turn a machinegun on the orchestra stalls). A hundred years later, Antoine will stage a realist text by way of realist *mise-en-scène*. If Antoine subsequently made films it was not just a coincidence. The fact is that if one goes back a little into history, one must agree that an elaborate attempt at "theater-cinema" had already preceded "cinema-theater." Dumas *fils* and Antoine were the precursors of Marcel Pagnol. It could very well be that the renaissance in theater spurred by Antoine was greatly aided by the existence of cinema, which had taken upon its own head the heresy of realism and limited the theories of Antoine to a reasonable and effective reaction against symbolism. The choice that the Vieux Colombier had made during the revolution of the Théâtre Libre (leaving realism to the Grand Guignol), reasserting the value of stage conventions, might not have been possible without the competition of the cinema. It was a perfect example of competition which, whatever happens, has finally laughed dramatic realism out of court. Nobody can pretend today that even the most bourgeois of boulevard dramas is without its full share of theatrical conventions.

stage removes it from everyday existence and turns it into something seen as it were in a shop window. It is in a measure part of the natural order but it is profoundly modified by the conditions under which we observe it.

Antoine might decorate the stage with real joints of meat but, unlike the cinema, he could not show a whole flock of sheep passing by. If he wanted to plant a tree on the stage he had first to uproot it and in any case he had to give up any idea of showing the entire forest. So really his tree still derives from the Elizabethan placard which in the end is only a signpost. If we bear these undoubted truths in mind we will then admit that the filming of a melodrama like *Les Parents terrible* presents problems very little different from filming a classic play. What we here call realism does not at all place the play on the same footing as the cinema. It does not do away with the footlights. To put it simply, the system of conventions that govern the production and hence the text are, so to speak, at the initial level. The conventions of tragedy with their procession of odd-looking properties and their alexandrines are but masks and cothurni that confirm and emphasize the basic convention which is theater.

Cocteau was well aware of this when he filmed his *Parents terribles*. Again, since his play was markedly realist, Cocteau the film-maker understood that he must add nothing to the setting, that the role of the cinema was not to multiply but to intensify ... if the room of the play became an apartment in the film, thanks to the screen and to the camera it would feel even more cramped than the room on the stage. What it was essential to bring out was a sense of people being shut in and living in close proximity. A single ray of sunlight, any other than electric light, would have destroyed that delicately balanced and inescapable coexistence. The crowded coach too may travel to the other end of Paris, to Madeleine's house. We leave it at the door of one apartment to discover it at the door of the other. We do not have here the example of the classical editing short-cut but a positive part of the direction, which the cinema did not impose on Cocteau and who thereby went beyond the expressive possibilities of the theater. The latter, being restricted, cannot therefore produce the same effect. A hundred examples could be adduced to confirm the respect of the camera for the stage setting, its concern being only to increase the effectiveness of the settings and never to attempt to interfere with their relation to the characters of the play. All the annoyances of theater are not so easily disposed of. Having to show each room in succession and meanwhile to lower the curtain is without doubt a pointless imposition. Thanks to its mobility, it is the camera that is responsible for the real unity of time and place. The theater needed the cinema before it could freely express what it had to say and *Les Parents terribles* could be shown to be a tragedy of an apartment in which a door left ajar could take on more significance than a monologue on a bed. Cocteau never lets his work down, his respect for what are the essential requirements being the greater in proportion as he is able to separate them from those happenings which are not essential. The function of the cinema is to reveal, to bring to light certain details that the stage would have left untreated.

The problem of the decor having been solved, the most difficult one still remained, namely the editing. Here Cocteau gave proof of his ingenious imagination. The notion of "shot" is finally disposed of. There remains henceforth only the question of framing the fleeting crystallization of a reality of whose environing presence one is ceaselessly aware. Cocteau likes to tell how he thought his film through in 16mm. "Thought it through," is right. He would have been hard put to direct it in anything less than 35mm. What is important here is for the spectator to have a feeling of being totally present at what is going on, not as in Welles' pictures (or in Renoir's) through depth of focus but by virtue of a diabolic speed of vision which seems for the first time to be wedded here to the pure rhythm of attention. Undoubtedly all good editing takes this into consideration. The traditional device of shot-reverse-shot divides up the dialogue according to an elementary syntax of interest. The close-up of a telephone that rings at a pathetic moment is the equivalent of a concentration of attention. It seems to us however that normal editing is a compromise between three ways of possibly analyzing reality.

(1) *A purely logical and descriptive analysis* (the weapon used in the crime lying beside the corpse). (2) *A psychological analysis* from within the film, namely one that fits the point of view of one of the protagonists in a given situation. An example of this would be the glass of milk that may possibly be poisoned which Ingrid Bergman has to drink in *Notorious*, or the ring on the finger of Theresa Wright in *The Shadow of a Doubt*. (3) *Finally, a psychological analysis from the point of view of spectator interest*, either a spontaneous interest or one provoked by the director thanks precisely to this analysis. An example of this would be the handle of a door turning unseen by the criminal who thinks he is alone. ("Look out," the children used to shout to the Guignol whom the policeman is about to surprise.)

These three points of view which combined together constitute the synthesis of cinematographic events in most films are felt to be unique. Actually they imply at once a psychological heterogeneity and a material discontinuity. They are basically the same as those peddled by the traditional novelist—which, as we know, brought down the wrath of J. P. Sartre on the head of François Mauriac. The importance of depth of focus and the fixed camera in the films of Orson Welles and William Wyler springs from a reluctance to fragment things arbitrarily and a desire instead to show an image that is uniformly understandable and that compels the spectator to make his own choice.

Although he remains faithful to the classic pattern of cutting—his film includes a fair number of shots above medium—Cocteau gives it a special significance by using, practically exclusively, shots from category number three above. Logical and descriptive analysis together with points of view of the actor are virtually eliminated. There remain those of the witness. The subjective camera finally becomes a reality but in an opposite sense, that is to say not as in *The Lady in the Lake*, thanks to a puerile kind of identification of the spectator and the character by means of a camera trick but, on the contrary, through the pitiless gaze of an invisible witness. The camera is at last a spectator and nothing else. The drama is once more a spectacle. It was indeed Cocteau who said that cinema is an event seen through a keyhole. The impression we get here from the keyhole is of an invasion of privacy, the quasi-obscenity of "viewing." Let us take a highly significant example of this position of "exteriority." It is one of the final shots of the picture when Yvonne de Bray, poisoned, is withdrawing backwards into her own room, her eyes on the busy group around the happy Madeleine. The camera pulls back to accompany her. But the movement of the camera, no matter how great the temptation, is never confused with the subjective viewpoint of "Sophie." The shock of the travelling shot would be certainly more violent if we were in the position of the actress and were looking with her eyes. But Cocteau carefully avoided this false move. He keeps Yvonne de Bray "as bait" and pulls back, retreating a little, behind her. The purpose of the shot is to show not that she is looking, not even her gaze, it is to *see her actually looking*. It is done doubtless over her shoulder as is the privilege of cinema—one which Cocteau hastens to restore to the theater.

He thus returned to the principle of audience-stage relations. While the cinema allowed him to seize upon the drama from many angles, he deliberately chose to adopt the viewpoint of the spectator, the one denominator common to stage and screen.

So Cocteau maintains the essentially theatrical character of his play. Instead of trying like so many others to dissolve it in cinema, on the contrary he uses the resources of the camera to point up, to underline, to confirm the structure of the scenes and their psychological corollaries. The specific help given here by the cinema can only be described as an added measure of the theatrical.

As a result he joins ranks with Laurence Olivier, Orson Welles, Wyler, and Dudley Nichols. This is borne out by an analysis of *Macbeth*, *Hamlet*, *The Little Foxes*, and *Mourning Becomes Electra*, to say nothing of a film like *Occupe-toi d'Amélie* where Claude Autant-Lara does with vaudeville something comparable to what Olivier does with *Henry V*. All these very characteristic successes of the past fifteen years illustrate a paradox. One is no longer adapting a subject. One is staging a play by means of cinema. The problem of "canned" theater, whether it is a naive or an impudent question, has certainly taken on a new lease of life as a result of these recent successes. We have tried to see how it happened. Now, more ambitious than ever, will we be able to find out why?

Part Two

The leitmotiv of those who despise filmed theater, their final and apparently insuperable argument, continues to be the unparalleled pleasure that accompanies the presence of the actor. "What is specific to theater," writes Henri Gouhier, in *The Essence of Theater*, "is the impossibility of separating off action and actor." Elsewhere he says "the stage welcomes every illusion except that of presence; the actor is there in disguise, with the soul and voice of another, but he is nevertheless there and by the same token space calls out for him and for the solidity of his presence. On the other hand and inversely, the cinema accommodates every form of reality save one—the physical presence of the actor." If it is here that the essence of theater lies then undoubtedly the cinema can in no way pretend to any parallel with it. If the writing, the style, and the dramatic structure are, as they should be, rigorously conceived as the receptacle for the soul and being of the flesh-and-blood actor, any attempt to substitute the shadow and reflection of a man on the screen for the man himself is a completely vain enterprise. There is no answer to this argument. The successes of Laurence Olivier, of Welles, or of Cocteau can only be challenged—here you need to be in bad faith—or considered inexplicable. They are a challenge both to critics and philosophers. Alternatively one can only explain them by casting doubts on that commonplace of theatrical criticism "the irreplaceable presence of the actor."

The Concept of Presence

At this point certain comments seem called for concerning the concept of "presence," since it would appear that it is this concept, as understood prior to the appearance of photography, that the cinema challenges.

Can the photographic image, especially the cinematographic image, be likened to other images and in common with them be regarded as having an existence distinct from the object? Presence, naturally, is defined in terms of time and space. "To be in the presence of someone" is to recognize him as existing contemporaneously with us and to note that he comes within the actual range of our senses—in the case of cinema of our sight and in radio of our hearing. Before the arrival of photography and later of cinema, the plastic arts (especially portraiture) were the only intermediaries between actual physical presence and absence. Their justification was their resemblance which stirs the imagination and helps the memory. But photography is something else again. In no sense is it the image of an object or person, more correctly it is its tracing. Its automatic genesis distinguishes it radically from the other techniques of reproduction. The photograph proceeds by means of the lens to the taking of a veritable luminous impression in light—to a mold. As such it carries with it more than mere resemblance, namely a kind of identity—the card we call by that name being only conceivable in an age of photography. But photography is a feeble technique in the sense that its instantaneity compels it to capture time only piecemeal. The cinema does something strangely paradoxical. It makes a molding of the object as it exists in time and, furthermore, makes an imprint of the duration of the object.

The nineteenth century with its objective techniques of visual and sound reproduction gave birth to a new category of images, the relation of which to the reality from which they proceed requires very strict definition. Even apart from the fact that the resulting aesthetic problems cannot be satisfactorily raised without this introductory philosophical inquiry, it would not be sound to treat the old aesthetic questions as if the categories with which they deal had in no way been modified by the appearance of completely new phenomena. Common sense—perhaps the best philosophical guide in this case—has clearly understood this and has invented an expression for the presence of an actor, by adding to the placards announcing his appearance the phrase "in flesh and blood." This means that for the man in the street the word "presence," today, can be ambiguous, and thus an apparent redundancy is not out of place in this age of cinema. Hence it is no longer as certain as it was that there is no middle stage between presence and absence. It is likewise at the ontological level that the effectiveness of the cinema has its source. It is false to say that the screen is incapable of putting us "in the presence of" the actor. It does so in the same way as a mirror—one must agree that the mirror relays the presence of the person reflected in it—but it is a mirror with a delayed reflection, the tin foil of which retains the image.* It is true that in the theater Molière can die on the

---

*Television naturally adds a new variant to the "pseudopresences" resulting from the scientific techniques for reproduction created by photography. On the little screen during live television the actor is actually present in space and time. But the reciprocal actor-spectator relationship is incomplete in one direction. The spectator sees without being seen. There is no return flow. Televised theater, therefore, seems to share something both of theater and of cinema: of theater because the actor is present to the viewer, of cinema because the spectator is not present to the actor. Nevertheless, this state of not being present is not truly an absence. The television actor has a sense of the millions of ears and eyes virtually present and represented by the electronic camera. This abstract presence is most noticeable when the actor fluffs his lines. Painful enough in the theater, it is intolerable on television since the spectator who can do nothing to help him is aware of the unnatural solitude of the actor. In the theater in similar circumstances a sort of understanding exists with the audience, which is a help to an actor in trouble. This kind of reciprocal relationship is impossible on television.

stage and that we have the privilege of living in the biographical time of the actor. In the film about Manolete however we are present at the actual death of the famous matador and while our emotion may not be as deep as if we were actually present in the arena at that historic moment, its nature is the same. What we lose by way of direct witness do we not recapture thanks to the artificial proximity provided by photographic enlargement? Everything takes place as if in the time-space perimeter which is the definition of presence. The cinema offers us effectively only a measure of duration, reduced but not to zero, while the increase in the space factor reestablishes the equilibrium of the psychological equation.

Opposition and Identification

An honest appraisal of the respective pleasures derived from theater and cinema, at least as to what is less intellectual and more direct about them, forces us to admit that the delight we experience at the end of a play has a more uplifting, a nobler, one might perhaps say a more moral, effect than the satisfaction which follows a good film. We seem to come away with a better conscience. In a certain sense it is as if for the man in the audience all theater is "Corneillian." From this point of view one could say that in the best films something is missing. It is as if a certain inevitable lowering of the voltage, some mysterious aesthetic short circuit, deprived us in the cinema of a certain tension which is a definite part of theater. No matter how slight this difference it undoubtedly exists, even between the worst charity production in the theater and the most brilliant of Olivier's film adaptations. There is nothing banal about this observation and the survival of the theater after fifty years of cinema, and the prophecies of Marcel Pagnol, is practical proof enough. At the source of the disenchantment which follows the film one could doubtless detect a process of depersonalization of the spectator. As Rosenkrantz wrote in 1937, in *Esprit*, in an article profoundly original for its period, "The characters on the screen are quite naturally objects of identification, while those on the stage are, rather, objects of mental opposition because their real presence gives them an objective reality and to transpose them into beings in an imaginary world the will of the spectator has to intervene actively, that is to say, to will to transform their physical reality into an abstraction. This abstraction being the result of a process of the intelligence that we can only ask of a person who is fully conscious." A member of a film audience tends to identify himself with the film's hero by a psychological process, the result of which is to turn the audience into a "mass" and to render emotion uniform. Just as in algebra if two numbers equal a third, then they are equal to one another, so here we can say, if two individuals identify themselves with a third, they identify themselves with one another. Let us compare chorus girls on the stage and on the screen. On the screen they satisfy an unconscious sexual desire and when the hero joins them he satisfies the desire of the spectator in the proportion to which the latter has identified himself with the hero. On the stage the girls excite the onlooker as they would in real life. The result is that there is no identification with the hero. He becomes instead an object of jealousy and envy. In other words, Tarzan is only possible on the screen. The cinema calms the spectator, the theater excites him. Even when it appeals to the lowest instincts, the theater up to a certain point stands in the way of the creation of a mass mentality.* It stands in the way of any collective representation in the psychological sense, since theater calls for an active individual consciousness while the film requires only a passive adhesion.

These views shed a new light on the problem of the actor. They transfer him from the ontological to the psychological level. It is to the extent to which the cinema encourages identification with the hero that it conflicts with the theater. Put this way the problem is no longer basically insoluble, for it is a fact that the cinema has at its disposal means which favor a passive position or on the other hand, means which to a greater or lesser degree stimulate the consciousness of the spectator. Inversely the theater can find ways of lessening the psychological tension between spectator and actor. Thus theater and cinema will no longer be separated off by an unbridgeable aesthetic moat, they would simply tend to give rise to two attitudes of mind over which the director maintains a wide control.

Examined at close quarters, the pleasure derived from the theater not only differs from that of the cinema but also from that of the novel. The reader of a novel, physically alone like the man in the dark movie house, identifies himself with the character.† That is why after reading for a long while he also feels the same intoxication of an illusory intimacy with the hero. Incontestably, there is in the pleasure derived from cinema and novel a self-satisfaction, a concession to solitude, a sort of betrayal of action by a refusal of social responsibility.

The analysis of this phenomenon might indeed be undertaken from a psychoanalytic point of view. It is not significant that the psychiatrists took the term catharsis from Aristotle? Modern pedagogic research on psychodrama seems to have provided fruitful insights into the cathartic process of theater. The ambiguity existing in the child's mind between play and reality is used to get him to free himself by way

---

*Crowd and solitude are not antinomies: the audience in a movie house is made up of solitary individuals. Crowd should be taken here to mean the opposite of an organic community freely assembled.

†Cf. Cl. E. Magny, *L'Age du roman américain,* ed. Du Seuil.

of improvised theater from the repressions from which he suffers. This
technique amounts to creating a kind of vague theater in which the
play is of a serious nature and the actor is his own audience. The action
that develops on these occasions is not one that is divided off by footlights, which are undoubtedly the architectural symbol of the censor
that separates us from the stage. We delegate Oedipus to act in our
guise and place him on the other side of a wall of fire—that fiery fron-
tier between fantasy and reality which gives rein to Dionysiac monsters
while protecting us from them.* These sacred beasts will not cross this
barrier of light beyond which they seem out of place and even sacrile-
gious—witness the disturbing atmosphere of awe which surrounds an
actor still made up, like a phosphorescent light, when we visit him in
his dressing room. There is no point to the argument that the theater
did not always have footlights. These are only a symbol and there were
others before them from the cothurnus and mask onwards. In the seventeenth century the fact that young nobles sat up on the stage is no
denial of the role of the footlights, on the contrary, it confirms it, by way
of a privileged violation so to speak, just as when today Orson Welles
scatters actors around the auditorium to fire on the audience with
revolvers. He does not do away with the footlights, he just crosses them.
The rules of the game are also made to be broken. One expects some
players to cheat.† With regard to the objection based on presence and
on that alone, the theater and the cinema are not basically in conflict.
What is really in dispute are two psychological modalities of a performance. The theater is indeed based on the reciprocal awareness of the
presence of audience and actor, but only as related to a performance.
The theater acts on us by virtue of our participation in a theatrical
action across the footlights and as it were under the protection of their
censorship. The opposite is true in the cinema. Alone, hidden in a dark
room, we watch through half-open blinds a spectacle that is unaware of

---

*Cf. P. A. Touchard, *Dionysos*, ed. Du Seuil.

†Here is a final example proving that presence does not constitute theater except in so
far as it is a matter of a performance. Everyone either at his own or someone else's
expense has known the embarrassment of being watched without knowing it or in spite
of knowing it. Lovers who kiss on public benches offer a spectacle to the passerby, but
they do not care. My concierge who has a feeling for the *mot juste* says, when she sees
them, that it is like being at the movies. Each of us has sometimes found himself forced
to his annoyance to do something absurd before other people. On those occasions we experience a sense of shame which is the very opposite of theatrical exhibitionism. Someone
who looks through a keyhole is not at the theater; Cocteau has rightly demonstrated in
Le sang d'un poète that he was already at the cinema. And nevertheless there are such
things as "shows," when the protagonists are present to us in flesh and blood but one of
the two parties is ignorant of the fact or goes through with it reluctantly. This is not
"play" in the theatrical sense.

our existence and which is part of the universe. There is nothing to prevent us from identifying ourselves in imagination with the moving world before us, which becomes *the* world. It is no longer on the phenomenon of the actor as a person physically present that we should concentrate our analysis, but rather on the ensemble of conditions that constitute the theatrical play and deprive the spectator of active participation. We shall see that it is much less a question of actor and presence than of man and his relation to the decor.

Behind the Decor

The human being is all-important in the theater. The drama on the screen can exist without actors. A banging door, a leaf in the wind, waves beating on the shore can heighten the dramatic effect. Some film masterpieces use man only as an accessory, like an extra, or in counterpoint to nature which is the true leading character. Even when, as in *Nanook* and *Man of Aran,* the subject is man's struggle with nature, it cannot be compared to a theatrical action. The mainspring of the action is not in man but nature. As Jean-Paul Sartre, I think it was, said, in the theater the drama proceeds from the actor, in the cinema it goes from the decor to man. This reversal of the dramatic flow is of decisive importance. It is bound up with the very essence of the *mise-en-scène*. One must see here one of the consequences of photographic realism. Obviously, if the cinema makes use of nature it is because it is able to. The camera puts at the disposal of the director all the resources of the telescope and the microscope. The last strand of a rope about to snap or an entire army making an assault on a hill are within our reach. Dramatic causes and effects have no longer any material limits to the eye of the camera. Drama is freed by the camera from all contingencies of time and space. But this freeing of tangible dramatic powers is still only a secondary aesthetic cause, and does not basically explain the reversal of value between the actor and the decor. For sometimes it actually happens that the cinema deliberately deprives itself of the use of setting and of exterior nature—we have already seen a perfect instance of this in *Les Parents terribles*—while the theater in contrast uses a complex machinery to give a feeling of ubiquity to the audience. Is *La Passion de Jeanne d'Arc* by Carl Dreyer, shot entirely in close-up, in the virtually invisible and in fact theatrical settings by Jean Hugo, less cinematic than *Stagecoach*? It seems to me that quantity has nothing to do with it, nor the resemblance to certain theater techniques. The ideas of an art director for a room in *Les Dames aux camélias* would not noticeably differ whether for a film or a play. It's true that on the screen you would doubtless have some close-ups of the blood-stained handkerchief, but a skillful stage production would also know how to make some play with the cough and the handkerchief. All the close-ups in *Les Parents terribles* are taken directly from the theater where our attention would spontaneously isolate them. If film direction only differed from theater direction because it allows us a closer view of the scenery and makes a more reasonable use of it, there would really be no reason to continue with the theater and Pagnol would be a true prophet. For it is obvious that the few square yards of the decor of Vilar's *La Danse de la mort* contributed as much to the drama as the island on which Marcel Cravene shot his excellent film. The fact is that the problem lies not in the decor itself but in its nature and function. We must therefore throw some light on an essentially theatrical notion, that of the dramatic place.

There can be no theater without architecture, whether it be the cathedral square, the arena of Nîmes, the palace of the Popes, the trestle stage on a fairground, the semicircle of the theater of Vicenza that looks as if it were decorated by Bérard in a delirium, or the rococo amphitheaters of the boulevard houses. Whether as a performance or a celebration, theater of its very essence must not be confused with nature under penalty of being absorbed by her and ceasing to be. Founded on the reciprocal awareness of those taking part and present to one another, it must be in contrast to the rest of the world in the same way that play and reality are opposed, or concern and indifference, or liturgy and the common use of things. Costume, mask, or make-up, the style of the language, the footlights, all contribute to this distinction, but the clearest sign of all is the stage, the architecture of which has varied from time to time without ever ceasing to mark out a privileged spot actually or virtually distinct from nature. It is precisely in virtue of this *locus dramaticus* that decor exists. It serves in greater or less degree to set the place apart, to specify. Whatever it is, the decor constitutes the walls of this three-sided box opening onto the auditorium, which we call the stage. These false perspectives, these façades, these arbors, have another side which is cloth and nails and wood. Everyone knows that when the actor "retires to his apartment" from the yard or from the garden, he is actually going to his dressing room to take off his make-up. These few square feet of light and illusion are surrounded by machinery and flanked by wings, the hidden labyrinths of which do not interfere one bit with the pleasure of the spectator who is playing the game of theater. Because it is only part of the architecture of the stage, the decor of the theater is thus an area materially enclosed, limited, circumscribed, the only discoveries of which are those of our collusive imagination.

Its appearances are turned inward facing the public and the footlights. It exists by virtue of its reverse side and of anything beyond, as the painting exists by virtue of its frame.* Just as the picture is not to be confounded with the scene it represents and is not a window in a wall. The stage and the decor where the action unfolds constitute an aesthetic microcosm inserted perforce into the universe but essentially distinct from the Nature which surrounds it.

It is not the same with cinema, the basic principle of which is a denial of any frontiers to action.

The idea of a *locus dramaticus* is not only alien to, it is essentially a contradiction of the concept of the screen. The screen is not a frame like that of a picture but a mask which allows only a part of the action to be seen. When a character moves off screen, we accept the fact that he is out of sight, but he continues to exist in his own capacity at some other place in the decor which is hidden from us. There are no wings to the screen. There could not be without destroying its specific illusion, which is to make of a revolver or of a face the very center of the universe. In contrast to the stage the space of the screen is centrifugal. It is because that infinity which the theater demands cannot be spatial that its area can be none other than the human soul. Enclosed in this space the actor is at the focus of a two-fold concave mirror. From the auditorium and from the decor there converge on him the dim lights of conscious human beings and of the footlights themselves. But the fire with which he burns is at once that of his inner passion and of that focal point at which he stands. He lights up in each member of his audience an accomplice flame. Like the ocean in a sea shell the dramatic infinities of the human heart moan and beat between the enclosing walls of the theatrical sphere. This is why this dramaturgy is in its essence human. Man is at once its cause and its subject.

On the screen man is no longer the focus of the drama, but will become eventually the center of the universe. The impact of his action may there set in motion an infinitude of waves. The decor that sur-

---

*The ideal historical example of this theory of theater architecture and its relations to the stage and the decor is provided by the Palladium with the extraordinary Olympic Theater of Vicenza, making of the ancient amphitheater open to the sky a purely architectural *trompe-l'oeil*. There is not a single element, including the entrance to the auditorium, which is not an affirmation of its essentially architectural nature. Built in 1590, inside an old barracks donated by the town, outwardly the Olympic Theater appears to be just red-brick walls, that is, a purely utilitarian piece of architecture which one might describe as amorphous in the sense in which chemists distinguish between the amorphous state and the crystal state of the same body. The visitor going in by what appears to be a hole in the wall cannot believe his eyes when he finds himself all of a sudden in the extraordinary hollowed-out grotto which constitutes the semicircle of the theater. Like those blocks of quartz or amethyst which outwardly look like common stones whereas inside they are a composite of pure crystal, secretly oriented inward, the theater of Vicenza is conceived according to the laws of an aesthetic and artificial space polarized exclusively towards the center.

rounds him is part of the solidity of the world. For this reason the actor as such can be absent from it, because man in the world enjoys no a priori privilege over animals and things. However there is no reason why he should not be the mainspring of the drama, as in Dreyer's *Jeanne d'Arc*, and in this respect the cinema may very well impose itself upon the theater. As actions *Phèdre* or *King Lear* are no less cinematographic than theatrical, and the visible death of a rabbit in *La Règle du jeu* affects us just as deeply as that of Agnès' little cat about which we are merely told.

But if Racine, Shakespeare, or Molière cannot be brought to the cinema by just placing them before the camera and the microphone, it is because the handling of the action and the style of the dialogue were conceived as echoing through the architecture of the auditorium. What is specifically theatrical about these tragedies is not their action so much as the human, that is to say the verbal, priority given to their dramatic structure. The problem of filmed theater at least where the classics are concerned does not consist so much in transposing an action from the stage to the screen as in transposing a text written for one dramaturgical system into another while at the same time retaining its effectiveness. It is not therefore essentially the action of a play which resists film adaptation, but above and beyond the phases of the intrigue (which it would be easy enough to adapt to the realism of the screen) it is the verbal form which aesthetic contingencies or cultural prejudices oblige us to respect. It is this which refuses to let itself be captured in the window of the screen. "The theater," says Baudelaire, "is a crystal chandelier." If one were called upon to offer in comparison a symbol other than this artificial crystal-like object, brilliant, intricate, and circular, which refracts the light which plays around its center and holds us prisoners of its aureole, we might say of the cinema that it is the little flashlight of the usher, moving like an uncertain comet across the night of our waking dream, the diffuse space without shape or frontiers that surrounds the screen.

The story of the failures and recent successes of theater on film will be found to be that of the ability of directors to retain the dramatic force of the play in a medium that reflects it or, at least, the ability to give this dramatic force enough resonance to permit a film audience to perceive it. In other words, it is a matter of an aesthetic that is not concerned with the actor but with decor and editing. Henceforth it is clear that filmed theater is basically destined to fail whenever it tends in any manner to become simply the photographing of scenic representation even and perhaps most of all when the camera is used to try and make us forget the footlights and the backstage area. The dramatic force of the text, instead of being gathered up in the actor, dissolves without echo into the cinematic ether. This is why a filmed play can show due respect to the text, be well acted in likely settings, and yet be completely worthless. This is what happened, to take a convenient example, to *Le Voyageur sans baggages*. The play lies there before us apparently true to itself yet drained of every ounce of energy, like a battery dead from an unknown short. But over and beyond the aesthetic of the decor we see clearly both on the screen and on the stage that in the last analysis the problem before us is that of realism. This is the problem we always end up with when we are dealing with cinema.

The Screen and the Realism of Space

The realism of the cinema follows directly from its photographic nature. Not only does some marvel or some fantastic thing on the screen not undermine the reality of the image, on the contrary it is its most valid justification. Illusion in the cinema is not based as it is in the theater on convention tacitly accepted by the general public; rather, contrariwise, it is based on the inalienable realism of that which is shown. All trick work must be perfect in all material respects on the screen. The "invisible man" must wear pyjamas and smoke a cigarette.

Must we conclude from this that the cinema is dedicated entirely to the representation if not of natural reality at least of a plausible reality of which the spectator admits the identity with nature as he knows it? The comparative failure of German expressionism would seem to confirm this hypothesis, since it is evident that *Caligari* attempted to depart from realistic decor under the influence of the theater and painting. But this would be to offer an oversimplified explanation for a problem that calls for more subtle answers. We are prepared to admit that the screen opens upon an artificial world provided there exists a common denominator between the cinematographic image and the world we live in. Our experience of space is the structural basis for our concept of the universe. We may say in fact, adapting Henri Gouhier's formula, "the stage welcomes every illusion except the illusion of presence," that "the cinematographic image can be emptied of all reality save one—the reality of space."

It is perhaps an overstatement to say "all reality" because it is difficult to imagine a reconstruction of space devoid of all reference to nature. The world of the screen and our world cannot be juxtaposed. The screen of necessity substitutes for it since the very concept of universe is spatially exclusive. For a time, a film is the Universe, the world, or if you like, Nature. We will see how the films that have attempted to substitute a fabricated nature and an artificial world for the world of experience have not all equally succeeded. Admitting the failure of *Caligari* and *Die Nibelungen* we then ask ourselves how we explain the undoubted success of *Nosferatu* and *La Passion de Jeanne d'Arc*, the criterion of success being that these films have never aged.

Yet it would seem at first sight that the methods of direction belong to the same aesthetic family, and that viewing the varieties of temperament and period, one could group these four films together as expressionist as distinct from realist. However, if we examine them more closely we see that there are certain basic differences between them. It is clear in the case of R. Weine and Murnau. *Nosferatu* plays, for the greater part of the time, against natural settings whereas the fantastic qualities of *Caligari* are derived from deformities of lighting and decor. The case of Dreyer's *Jeanne d'Arc* is a little more subtle since at first sight nature plays a nonexistent role. To put it more directly, the decor by Jean Hugo is no whit less artificial and theatrical than the settings of *Caligari*, the systematic use of close-ups and unusual angles is well calculated to destroy any sense of space. Regular cinéclub goers know that the film is unfailingly introduced with the famous story of how the hair of Falconetti was actually cut in the interests of the film and likewise, the actors, we are told, wore no make-up. These references to history ordinarily have no more than gossip value. In this case, they seem to me to hold the aesthetic secret of the film; the very thing to which it owes its continued survival. It is precisely because of them that the work of Dreyer ceases to have anything in common with the theater, and indeed one might say, with man. The greater recourse Dreyer has exclusively to the human "expression," the more he has to reconvert it again into Nature. Let there be no mistake, that prodigious fresco of heads is the very opposite of an actor's film. It is a documentary of faces. It is not important how well the actors play, whereas the pockmarks on Bishop Cauchon's face and the red patches of Jean d'Yd are an integral part of the action. In this drama-through-the-microscope the whole of nature palpitates beneath every pore. The movement of a wrinkle, the pursing of a lip are seismic shocks and the flow of tides, the flux and reflux of this human epidermis. But for me Dreyer's brilliant sense of cinema is evidenced in the exterior scene which every other director would assuredly have shot in the studio. The decor as built evoked a Middle Ages of the theater and of miniatures. In one sense, nothing is less realistic than this tribunal in the cemetery or this drawbridge, but the whole is lit by the light of the sun and the gravedigger throws a spadeful of real earth into the hole.*

It is these "secondary" details, apparently aesthetically at odds with the rest of the work, which give it its truly cinematic quality.

---

*This is why I consider the graveyard scene in *Hamlet* and the death of Ophelia bad mistakes on Olivier's part. He had here a chance to introduce sun and soil by way of counterpoint to the setting of Elsinore. Does the actual shot of the sea during the soliloquy of Hamlet show that he had sensed the need for this? The idea, excellent in itself, is not well handled technically.

If the paradox of the cinema is rooted in the dialectic of concrete and abstract, if cinema is committed to communicate only by way of what is real, it becomes all the more important to discern those elements in filming which confirm our sense of natural reality and those which destroy that feeling. On the other hand, it certainly argues a lack of perception to derive one's sense of reality from these accumulations of factual detail. It is possible to argue that *Les Dames du Bois de Boulogne* is an eminently realistic film, though everything about it is stylized. Everything, except for the rarely noticeable sound of a windshield-wiper, the murmur of a waterfall, or the rushing sound of soil escaping from a broken vase. These are the noises, chosen precisely for their "indifference" to the action, that guarantee its reality.

The cinema being of its essence a dramaturgy of Nature, there can be no cinema without the setting up of an open space in place of the universe rather than as part of it. The screen cannot give us the illusion of this feeling of space without calling on certain natural guarantees. But it is less a question of set construction or of architecture or of immensity than of isolating the aesthetic catalyst, which it is sufficient to introduce in an infinitesimal dose, to have it immediately take on the reality of nature.

The concrete forest of *Die Nibelungen* may well pretend to be an infinite expanse. We do not believe it to be so, whereas the trembling of just one branch in the wind, and the sunlight, would be enough to conjure up all the forests of the world.

If this analysis be well founded, then we see that the basic aesthetic problem of filmed theater is indeed that of the decor. The trump card that the director must hold is the reconversion into a window onto the world of a space oriented toward an interior dimension only, namely the closed and conventional area of the theatrical play.

It is not in Laurence Olivier's *Hamlet* that the text seems to be rendered superfluous or its strength diminished by directorial interpretations, still less in Welles' *Macbeth*, but paradoxically in the stage productions of Gaston Baty, to the precise extent that they go out of their way to create a cinematographic space on the stage; to deny that the settings have a reverse side, thus reducing the sonority of the text simply to the vibration of the voice of the actor who is left without his "resonance box" like a violin that is nothing else but strings. One would never deny that the essential thing in the theater is the text. The latter conceived for the anthropocentric expression proper to the stage and having as its function to bring nature to it cannot, without losing its raison d'être, be used in a space transparent as glass. The problem then that faces the filmmaker is to give his decor a dramatic opaqueness while at the same time reflecting its natural realism. Once this paradox of space has been dealt with, the director, so far from hesitating to bring theatrical conventions and faithfulness to the text to the screen will find himself now, on the contrary, completely free to rely on them. From that point on it is no longer a matter of running away from those things which "make theater" but in the long run to acknowledge their existence by rejecting the resources of the cinema, as Cocteau did in *Les Parents terribles* and Welles in *Macbeth*, or by putting them in quotation marks as Laurence Olivier did in *Henry V*. The evidence of a return to filmed theater that we have had during the last ten years belongs essentially to the history of decor and editing. It is a conquest of realism—not, certainly, the realism of subject matter or realism of expression but that realism of space without which moving pictures do not constitute cinema.

An Analogy from Play-Acting

This progress in filmed theater has only been possible insofar as the opposition between them did not rest on the ontological category of presence but on a psychology of "play." In passing from one to the other, one goes from the absolute to the relative, from antinomy to simple contradiction. While the cinema cannot offer the spectator the community feeling of theater, a certain knowledge of direction will allow him finally, and this is a decisive factor, to preserve the meaning and force of the text. The grafting of the theatrical text onto the decor of cinema is an operation which today we know can be successful. There remains that awareness of the active opposition existing between the spectator and the actor which constitutes the "play" of theater and is symbolized by scenic architecture. But there is a way of reducing even this to the psychology of the cinematic.

The reasoning of Rosenkrantz concerning opposition and identification requires in effect an important correction. It carries with it, still, a measure of equivocation. Rosenkrantz seems to equate identification with passivity and escape—an accepted fact in his time because of the condition of the cinema but less and less so in its present stage of evolution. Actually the cinema of myth and dream is now only one variety of production and one that is less and less frequent. One must not confuse an accidental and historical social condition with an unalterable psychological one—two activities, that is to say, of the spectator's consciousness that converge but are not part of one another. I do not identify equally with Tarzan and Bresson's curé. The only denominator common to my attitude to these two heroes is that I believe that they really exist, that I cannot refuse, except by staying away from the film, to share their adventures and to live them through with them, inside their universe, a universe that is not metaphorical and figurative but spatially real. This interior sharing does not exclude, in the second example, a consciousness of myself as distinct from the person from whom I chose to be alienated in the first example. These factors originating in the affective order are not the only ones that argue against passive identification; films like *L'Espoir* or *Citizen Kane* require in the spectator an intellectual alertness incompatible with passivity. The most that one can suggest is that the psychology of the cinematographic image offers a natural incline leading towards a sociology of the hero characterized by a passive identification. But in the arts as in morals, inclines are also made to be climbed. While the contemporary man of the theater often tries to lessen the sense of theatricality in a performance by a kind of realism in the production— just as those who love to go to the Grand Guignol play at being frightened but hold on at the very height of the horror to a delicious awareness of being fooled—the film director discovers on his side means of exciting the awareness of the spectator and of provoking him to reflection. This is something which would set up a conflict at the very heart of the identification. This private zone of consciousness, this self-awareness at the height of illusion, creates a kind of private footlights. In filmed theater it is no longer the microcosm of the play which is set over against nature but the spectator who is conscious of himself. On the screen *Hamlet* and *Les Parents terribles* cannot nor should they escape from the laws of cinematic perception; Elsinore and "La Roulotte" really exist but I pass through them unseen, rejoicing in that equivocal freedom which certain dreams allow us. I am walking but moving backwards.

Certainly the possibility of a state of intellectual self-awareness at the moment of psychological identification should never be confused with that act of the will which constitutes theater, and that is why it is foolish to identify stage and screen as Pagnol does. No matter how conscious of myself, how intelligent a film can make me, it is not to my will that it appeals—only at most to my good will. A film calls for a certain effort on my part so that I may understand and enjoy it, but it does not depend on me for its existence. Nevertheless it would certainly seem, from experience, that the margin of awareness allowed by the cinema is enough to establish an acceptable equivalent to the pleasure given by theater, at least enough to preserve what is essential to the artistic values of the play. The film, while it cannot pretend to be a complete substitute for the stage performance, is at least capable of assuring the theater a valid artistic existence and can offer us a comparable pleasure. There can never be question of anything more than a complex mechanical aesthetic where the original theatrical effectiveness is almost never directly applied, rather it is preserved, reconstituted, and transmitted thanks to a system of circuits, as in *Henry V*, of amplification as for example in *Macbeth*, of induction or interference. The true filmed theater is not the phonograph, it is its Martenot wave.

Morality

Thus the practice (certain) like the theory (possible) of successful filmed theater reveals the reasons for former failures. Straightforward animated photography of theater is a childish error recognized as such these thirty years and on which there is no point in insisting further. The heresy of film adaptation has taken longer to smoke out. It will continue to have its dupes but we now know where it leads—to aesthetic limbos that belong neither to film nor to theater, to that "filmed theater" justly condemned as the sin against the spirit of cinema. The true solution, revealed at last, consists in realizing that it is not a matter of transferring to the screen the dramatic element—an element interchangeable between one art and another—of a theatrical work, but inversely the theatrical quality of the drama. The subject of the adaptation is not that of the play, it is the play precisely in its scenic essence. This truth, apparent at last, will allow us to reach a conclusion concerning three propositions seemingly paradoxical at first, but which on reflection are seen to be quite evident.

(1) Theater an Aid to Cinema

The first proposition is that so far from being a corruption of cinema, filmed theater serves on the contrary to enrich and elevate it. Let us first look at the matter of theater. It is alas only too certain that the level of film production is intellectually much below, if not that of current dramatic production—think of Jean de Létraz and Henry Bernstein—at least of the living heritage of theater, even if only because of its great age. True, our century is no less that of Charlie Chaplin than was the seventeenth century that of Racine and Molière, but after all the cinema has only half a century of literature behind it while the theater has twenty-five. What would the French theater be like today if, as is the case with the cinema, it had nothing to offer but the production of the past decade? Since the cinema is undeniably passing through a crisis of subject matter it is not risking anything by employing screen writers like Shakespeare or even Feydeau. Let us not labor the subject. The case is only too clear. However, the inferiority is less evident in the realm of form. If the cinema is a major art with its own laws and language, what can it gain by submitting to the laws and language of another art? A great deal! And precisely to the extent to which, laying aside all its vain and puerile tricks, it is seriously concerned to subordinate itself and render a service. To justify this point of view completely, one should really discuss it within the framework of the aesthetic history of influence in art in general. This would almost certainly reveal, we feel, that at some stage in their evolution there has been a definite commerce between the technique of the various arts. Our prejudice about "pure art" is a critical development of relatively recent origin. But the authority of these precedents is not indispensable to our argument. The art of direction, the mechanics of which in relation to certain major films, as we have had to explain earlier, more even than our theoretical hypotheses, supposes on the part of the director a grasp of the language of cinematography equalled only by his knowledge of what theater is. If the *film d'art* failed where Olivier and Cocteau have succeeded, it is first of all because they have at their disposal a much more developed means of expression, but they also know how to use it more effectively than their contemporaries. To say of *Les Parents terribles* that it is perhaps an excellent film but that it is not cinema because it follows the play step by step is critical nonsense. On the contrary, it is precisely for this reason that it is cinema. It is *Topaze* by Marcel Pagnol—in its most recent style—which is not cinema, precisely because it is no longer theater. There is more cinema, and great cinema at that, in *Henry V* alone than in 90% of original scripts. Pure poetry is certainly not that which has nothing to say, as Cocteau has so well demonstrated: all the examples of pure poetry given by the Abbé Brémond illustrate the exact opposite. *La Fille de Minos et Pasiphae* is as informative as a birth certificate. There is likewise a way, unfortunately not yet practiced, of reciting this poem on the screen which would be pure cinema because it would respect, in the most intelligent way, its true theatrical value.

The more the cinema intends to be faithful to the text and to its theatrical requirements, the more of necessity must it delve deeper into its own language. The best translation is that which demonstrates a close intimacy with the genius of both languages and, likewise, a mastery of both.

(2) The Cinema Will Save the Theater

That is why the cinema will give back to the theater unstintingly what it took from her, if it has not already done so. For if the success of filmed theater supposes that dialectical progress had been made with the cinematic form, it implies both reciprocally and a fortiori a reevaluation of the essentially theatrical. The idea exploited by Marcel Pagnol according to which the cinema will replace the theater by "canning it" is completely false. The screen cannot replace the stage as the piano has supplanted the clavichord. And to begin with, replace the theater for whom? Not for the film-going public that long ago deserted the theater. The divorce between public and theater does not date, so far as I know, from that historic evening at the Grand Café in 1895. Are we talking then about the privileged minority of culture and wealth which actually makes up the theater audiences? But we see that Jean de Létraz is not bankrupt and that the visitor to Paris from the provinces does not confuse the breasts of Françoise Arnoul that he has seen on the screen with those of Nathalie Nattier at the Palais-Royal, although the latter may be covered by a brassière; but they are there, if I may say so, "in the flesh." Ah! The irreplaceable presence of the actor! As for the "serious" theaters, say the Marigny or the Français, it is clearly a question of a public that for the most part, does not go to the cinema and, for the others, of people who go to both without confusing the pleasure to be derived from each. The fact is, if any ground has been taken over it is not the territory of the theatrical spectacle as it exists, it is much more the taking over of the place abandoned long ago by the now-defunct forms of popular theater. So far from being a serious rival to the stage, the cinema is in process of giving back, to a public that had lost it, a taste and feeling for theater.*

It is possible that canned theater had something to do at the time with the disappearance of touring companies from the road. When Marcel Pagnol makes a film of *Topaze*, there is no doubt about his intentions, namely to make his play available to the provinces with a "Paris cast" at the price of a cinema seat. It is often the same with the boulevard plays. Their successful run finished, the film is distributed to those who were unable to see the play. In those areas where the Baret touring companies performed with a second-rate cast, the film offers at a very reasonable price not only the original cast, but even more magnificent sets. But this illusion was really successful for only a few years and we now see provincial tours on the road again, the better for their experience. The public they have recaptured, made blasé by the cinema and its glamorous casting and its luxurious sets, has, "come to," as they say, and is looking for something that is, more or less, theater.

But the popularizing of Paris successes is still not the ultimate end of the theatrical revival nor is it the chief merit of the "competition" between screen and stage. One might even say that this improvement in the situation of the touring companies is due to badly filmed theater. It is the defects of these films that have finally turned the stomachs of a section of the public and sent them back into the theaters.

It was the same situation with regard to photography and painting. Cinema dispensed photography from what was aesthetically least essential to it: likeness and anecdote. The high standard and the lower

---

*The case of the Théâtre Nationale Populaire offers another unexpected and paradoxical example of support for the theater by the cinema. I presume that Jean Vilar would not dispute the undoubted help his enterprise gets from the film fame of Gérard Philipe. Actually in doing this the cinema is only paying back to the theater a part of the capital it borrowed some forty years ago in the heroic period when the infant film industry, an object of contempt, had recourse to stage celebrities who could provide the artistic discipline and prestige it needed before it could be taken seriously. Certainly the situation was soon enough reversed. The Sarah Bernhardt of the years between the wars went by the name of Greta Garbo and it is now the theater that is willing to advertise the name of a film star on its marquees.

cost of photography and the ease with which pictures are taken, has at last contributed to the due evaluation of painting and to establishing it unalterably in its proper place. But this is not the end of the benefits derived from their coexistence. The photographers have not just served as the helots of the painters. At the same time, as it became more conscious of itself, painting absorbed something of photography. It is Degas and Toulouse-Lautrec, Renoir and Manet, who have understood from the inside, and in essence, the nature of the photographic phenomenon and, prophetically, even the cinematographic phenomenon. Faced with photography, they opposed it in the only valid way, by a dialectical enriching of pictorial technique. They understood the laws of the new image better than the photographers and well before the movie-makers, and it is they who first applied them.

Nevertheless this is not all and photography is in process of rendering services to the plastic arts that are even more decisive still. Their fields henceforth clearly known and delimited, the automatic image multiplies and renews our knowledge of the pictorial image. Malraux has said what needed to be said on this. If painting has been able to become the most individual of arts, the most onerous, the most independent of all compromise while at the same time the most accessible, it is thanks to color photography.

The same process applies to the theater; bad "canned theater" has helped true theater to become aware of its own laws. The cinema has likewise contributed to a new concept of theatrical production. These are results henceforth firmly established. But there is a third result which good filmed theater permits us to look for, namely the remarkable increase in breadth of understanding of theater among the general public. What then is a film like *Henry V*? First of all, it is Shakespeare for everybody. Furthermore, and supremely, it is a blazing light thrown onto the dramatic poetry of Shakespeare—the most effective and brilliant of theater lessons. Shakespeare emerges from the process twice himself. Not only does the adaptation of the play multiply his potential audience in the same way that the adaptation of novels makes the fortune of publishers, but also, the public is far better prepared than before to enjoy the stage play. Laurence Olivier's *Hamlet* must obviously increase the audience for Jean-Louis Barrault's *Hamlet* and sharpen the critical sense. Just as there is a difference that can never be bridged between the finest modern reproduction of a painting and the pleasure of owning the original, seeing *Hamlet* on the screen cannot take the place of a performance of the play by, say, a group of English students. But you need a genuine education in theater to appreciate the real-life performance by amateurs, that is to be able truly to share in what they are doing. So the more successful the filmed theater, the deeper it probes into the essence of theater, the better to serve it, the more clearly it will reveal the unbridgeable gulf between stage and screen. It is, on the contrary, the canned theater on the one hand and mediocre popular theater on the other that give rise to the confusion. *Les Parents terribles* never misleads its audience. There is not a sequence in it that is not more effective than its stage counterpart, while there is not one which does not allude by implication to that indefinable pleasure that I would have had from the real thing. There is no better propaganda for the real theater than well-filmed theater. These truths are henceforth indisputable and it would have been ridiculous of me to have spent so much time on them if the myth about filmed theater did not still survive too frequently in the form of prejudice, of misunderstanding, and of minds already made up.

(3) From Filmed Theater to Cinematographic Theater

My last argument, I realize, will be the boldest. So far we have considered the theater as an aesthetic absolute to which the cinema can come close in a more or less satisfactory fashion, but only in all circumstances and under the best possible conditions, as its humble servant. However, the earlier part of our study allowed us to see in slapstick the rebirth of dramatic forms that had practically disappeared, such as farce and the *Commedia dell'Arte*. Certain dramatic situations, certain techniques that had degenerated in the course of time, found again, in the cinema, first the sociological nourishment they needed to survive and, still better, the conditions favorable to an expansive use of their aesthetic, which the theater had kept congenitally atrophied. In making a protagonist out of space, the screen does not betray the spirit of farce, it simply gives to the metaphysical meaning of Scarpin's stick its true dimensions, namely those of the whole universe. Slapstick is first and foremost, or at least is also, the dramatic expression of the tyranny of things, out of which Keaton even more than Chaplin knew how to create a tragedy of the Object. But it is true that the forms of comedy create something of a special problem in the history of filmed theater, probably because laughter allows the audience to become aware of itself and to use this to experience a measure of the opposition that theater creates between actor and audience. In any case, and that is why we have not gone farther into the study of it, the grafting together of cinema and comedy-theater happened spontaneously and has been so perfect that its fruit has always been accepted as the product of pure cinema.

Now that the screen can welcome other kinds of theater besides comedy without betraying them, there is no reason to suppose that it cannot likewise give the theater new life, employing certain of the stage's own techniques. Film cannot be, indeed must not be, as we have seen, simply a paradoxical modality of theater production, but stage structures have their importance and it is not a matter of indifference whether *Julius Caesar* is played in the arena at Nîmes or in a studio; but certain dramatic works, and by no means the least of them, have suffered in a very material way these thirty to fifty years from a discord between contemporary taste and the style of the staging that they call for. I am thinking particularly of tragedy. There, the handicap we suffer from is due especially to the disappearance of the race of traditional tragedians of the old school—the Mounet-Sullys and the Sarah Bernhardts, that is, who disappeared at the beginning of the century like prehistoric creatures of the secondary period. By a stroke of irony, it is the cinema that has preserved their bones, fossilized in the *films d'art*. It has become a commonplace to attribute their disappearance to the cinema and for two converging reasons: one aesthetic, the other sociological. The screen has certainly modified our feeling about verisimilitude in interpretation. It is enough to see one of the little films of Bernhardt or Bargy to understand that this type of actor was still trussed up to all intents and purposes in cothurnus and mask. But the mask is simply an object of laughter while a close-up can drown us in a tear, and the megaphone is ridiculous when the microphone can produce at will a roar from the feeblest vocal chords. Thus we are accustomed to the inner naturalness which only allows the stage actor a slender margin of stylization beyond verisimilitude. The sociological factor is probably even more decisive. The success and effectiveness of a Mounet-Sully was undoubtedly due to his talent but helped on by the consenting complicity of the public. It was the phenomenon of the *monstre sacré* which is today diverted almost exclusively to the cinema. To say that the classes at the Conservatory do not produce any more tragedians doesn't by any means imply that no more Sarah Bernhardts are being born, only that their gifts and the times do not consort well. Thus, Voltaire wore out his lungs plagiarizing the tragedy of the seventeenth century because he thought that it was only Racine who had died when actually it was tragedy itself. Today we see not the slightest difference between Mounet-Sully and a ham from the provinces because we could not recognize a tragedian of the old school when we saw one. Only the "monster" survives in the *film d'art* for a young man today. The sacred quality has departed.

In the circumstances it is not surprising that Racine's tragedy is in a period of eclipse. Thanks to its conservative attitude, the Comédie Française is in the fortunate position of being able to guarantee him a reasonable life, but no longer a triumphal one.* Furthermore, this is

---

*Triumph is precisely what *Henry V* is, thanks to color film. If one were searching through *Phèdre* for an example of cinematic potentiality, the recital of Theramine, a verbal reminiscence of the *tragicomédie à machines*, considered as a dramatically literary piece, dramatically out of place, would find, visually, a new raison d'être on the screen.

only because of an interesting filtering-through of traditional values, their delicate adaptation to modern tastes, and not by a radical renewal straight out of the period. As for ancient tragedy, it is paradoxically to the Sorbonne and to the archeological enthusiasm of students that it owes the fact that it moves us once more. But it is important to see in these experiments by amateurs an extremely radical reaction against the actor's theater.

Thus, is it not natural to think that if the cinema has completely turned to its own advantage the aesthetic and the sociology of the sacred monster, that it might return them if the theater came looking for them? It is reasonable enough to dream what an Athalie could have been with Yvonne de Bray and Jean Cocteau directing!

But doubtless it would not be just the style of the interpretation of tragedy that would find its raison d'être once more on the screen. One could well imagine a corresponding revolution on the stage which, without ceasing to be faithful to the spirit of the theater, would offer it new forms in keeping with modern taste and especially at the level of a great mass audience. Film theater is waiting for a Jean Cocteau to make it a cinematographic theater.

Thus not only is theater on film from now on aesthetically founded in truth and fact, not only do we know that henceforth there are no plays that cannot be brought to the screen, whatever their style, provided one can visualize a reconversion of stage space in accordance with the data. But it may also be that the only possible modern theatrical production of certain classics would be on the screen. It is no chance matter that some of the best filmmakers are also the best stage directors. Welles and Olivier did not come to the cinema out of cynicism, snobbery, or ambition, not even, like Pagnol, to popularize theatrical works. Cinema is for them only a complementary form of theater, the chance to produce theater precisely as they feel and see it.

Questions and Projects

- Examine Shakespeare's *Henry V* and Laurence Olivier's adaptation in light of Bazin's argument. Where does he seem most correct and where might there be omissions or problems with his analysis of that play? Are there other useful ways of comparing the two?
- Select two or three of Bazin's central claims and test them on more recent adaptations of theater on film such as Tom Stoppard's *Rosencrantz and Guildenstern Are Dead* (1990), Kenneth Branagh's *Henry V* (1989), or Wallace Shawn's *Vanya on 42nd Street* (1994).

*G*eorge Bluestone's 1957 study is one of the first of the new and mounting wave of academic books to bring the study of film up to the present. It uses a historical perspective that builds on a growing body of research on film and a cultural sentiment that is willing to accept film as an art form with its own properties and laws. Those textual properties, separated from other social issues or theoretical concerns, are the focus of this study. More specifically, Bluestone examines the two "modes of consciousness" that describe, respectively, novels and films; within those modes he looks at how the novel and film represent time according to the formal laws of their respective materials.

"The Limits of the Novel and the Limits of the Film" from *Novels in Film*

George Bluestone

The Two Ways of Seeing

Summing up his major intentions in 1913, D. W. Griffith is reported to have said, "The task I'm trying to achieve is above all to make you see."[1] Whether by accident or design, the statement coincides almost exactly with an excerpt from Conrad's preface to *Nigger of the Narcissus* published sixteen years earlier: "My task which I am trying to achieve is, by the power of the written word, to make you hear, to make you feel—it is, before all, to make you see."[2] Aside from the strong syntactical resemblance, the coincidence is remarkable in suggesting the points at which film and novel both join and part company. On the one hand, that phrase "to make you see" assumes an affective relationship between creative artist and receptive audience. Novelist and director meet here in a common intention. One may, on the other hand, see visually through the eye or imaginatively through the mind. And between the percept of the visual image and the concept of the mental image lies the root difference between the two media.

Because novel and film are both organic—in the sense that aesthetic judgments are based on total ensembles which include both formal and thematic conventions—we may expect to find that differences in form and theme are inseparable from differences in media. Not only are Conrad and Griffith referring to different ways of seeing, but the "you's" they refer to are different. Structures, symbols, myths, values which might be comprehensible to Conrad's relatively small middle-class reading public would, conceivably, be incomprehensible to Griffith's mass public. Conversely, stimuli which move the heirs of Griffith's audience to tears, will outrage or amuse the progeny of

Conrad's "you." The seeming concurrence of Griffith and Conrad splits apart under analysis, and the two arts turn in opposite directions. That, in brief, has been the history of the fitful relationship between novel and film: overtly compatible, secretly hostile.

On the face of it, a close relationship has existed from the beginning. The reciprocity is clear from almost any point of view: the number of films based on novels; the search for filmic equivalents of literature; the effect of adaptations on reading; box-office receipts for filmed novels; merit awards by and for the Hollywood community.

The moment the film went from the animation of stills to telling a story, it was inevitable that fiction would become the ore to be minted by story departments. Before Griffith's first year as a director was over, he had adapted, among others, Jack London's *Just Meat (For Love of Gold)*, Tolstoy's *Resurrection*, and Charles Reade's *The Cloister and the Hearth*. Sergei Eisenstein's essay, "Dickens, Griffith, and the Film Today,"[3] demonstrates how Griffith found in Dickens hints for almost every one of his major innovations. Particular passages are cited to illustrate the dissolve, the superimposed shot, the close-up, the pan, indicating that Griffith's interest in literary forms and his roots in Victorian idealism[4] provided at least part of the impulse for technical and moral content.

From such beginnings, the novel began a still unbroken tradition of appearing conspicuously on story conference tables. The precise record has never been adequately kept. Various counts range from 17 to almost 50 per cent of total studio production. A sampling from RKO, Paramount, and Universal motion picture output for 1934–35 reveals that about one-third of all full-length features were derived from novels (excluding short stories).[5] Lester Asheim's more comprehensive survey indicates that of 5,807 releases by major studios between 1935 and 1945, 976 or 17.2 per cent were derived from novels.[6] Hortense Powdermaker reports, on the basis of *Variety*'s survey (June 4, 1947) that of 463 screenplays in production or awaiting release, slightly less than 40 per cent were adapted from novels.[7] And Thomas M. Pryor, in a recent issue of the *New York Times*, writes that the frequency of the original screenplay, reaching a new low in Hollywood, "represented only 51.8 per cent of the source material of the 305 pictures reviewed by the Production Code office in 1955." Appropriate modifications must be made in these calculations, since both Asheim and Powdermaker report that the percentage of novels adapted for high-budgeted pictures was much higher than for low-budgeted pictures.[8]

The industry's own appraisal of its work shows a strong and steady preference for films derived from novels, films which persistently rate among top quality productions. Filmed novels, for example, have made consistently strong bids for Academy Awards. In 1950, *Time* reported the results of *Daily Variety*'s poll of 200 men and women who had been working in the industry for more than twenty-five years. *Birth of a Nation* was considered the best silent film; *Gone with the Wind* the best sound film and the best "all time film."[9] Originally, both were novels. The choice of *Gone with the Wind* was a happy meeting of commercial and artistic interests. For when, some five years later, *Time* reported *Variety*'s listing of Hollywood's "all time money makers," Miss Mitchell's title stood ahead of all others with earnings of some $33.5 million. More important, of the ten most valuable film properties, five had been adapted from novels.[10] The high percentage of filmed novels which have been financially and artistically successful may be more comprehensible when we remember how frequently Pulitzer Prize winners, from *Alice Adams* to *All the King's Men*, have appeared in cinematic form.[11]

Just as one line of influence runs from New York publishing house to Hollywood studio, another line may be observed running the other way. Margaret Farrand Thorp reports that when *David Copperfield* appeared on local screens, the demand for the book was so great that the Cleveland Public Library ordered 132 new copies; that the film premier of *The Good Earth* boosted sales of that book to 3,000 per week; and that more copies of *Wuthering Heights* have been sold since the novel was screened than in all the previous ninety-two years of its existence. Jerry Wald confirms this pattern by pointing out, more precisely, that after the film's appearance, the Pocket Book edition of *Wuthering Heights* sold 700,000 copies; various editions of *Pride and Prejudice* reached a third of a million copies; and sales for *Lost Horizon* reached 1,400,000.[12] The appearance, in 1956, of such films as *Moby Dick* and *War and Peace*, accompanied by special tie-in sales of the novels, has continued this pattern.

But when Jean Paul Sartre suggests that for many of these readers, the book appears "as a more or less faithful commentary" on the film,[13] he is striking off a typically cogent distinction. Quantitative analyses have very little to do with qualitative changes. They tell us nothing about the mutational process, let alone how to judge it. In the case of film versions of novels, such analyses are even less helpful. They merely establish the fact of reciprocity; they do not indicate its implications for aesthetics. They provide statistical, not critical data. Hence, from such information the precise nature of the mutation cannot be deduced.

Such statements as: "The film is true to the spirit of the book"; "It's incredible how they butchered the novel"; "It cuts out key passages, but it's still a good film"; "Thank God they changed the ending"—these and similar statements are predicated on certain assumptions which blur the mutational process. These standard expletives and judgments assume, among other things, a separable content which may be detached and reproduced, as the snapshot reproduces the kitten; that incidents and characters in fiction are interchangeable with incidents and characters in the film; that the novel is a norm and the film deviates at its peril; that deviations are permissible for vaguely defined reasons—exigencies of length or of visualization, perhaps—but that the extent of the deviation will vary directly with the "respect" one has for the original; that taking liberties does not necessarily impair the quality of the film, whatever one may think of the novel, but that such liberties are somehow a trick which must be concealed from the public.

What is common to all these assumptions is the lack of awareness that mutations are probable the moment one goes from a given set of fluid, but relatively homogeneous, conventions to another; that changes are *inevitable* the moment one abandons the linguistic for the visual medium. Finally, it is insufficiently recognized that the end products of novel and film represent different aesthetic genera, as different from each other as ballet is from architecture.

The film becomes a different *thing* in the same sense that a historical painting becomes a different thing from the historical event which it illustrates. It is as fruitless to say that film A is better or worse than novel B as it is to pronounce Wright's Johnson's Wax Building better or worse than Tchaikowsky's *Swan Lake*. In the last analysis, each is autonomous, and each is characterized by unique and specific properties. What, then, are these properties?

...

The Modes of Consciousness

It is a commonplace by now that the novel has tended to retreat more and more from external action to internal thought, from plot to character, from social to psychological realities. Although these conflicting tendencies were already present in the polarity of Fielding and Sterne, it was only recently that the tradition of *Tristram Shandy* superseded the tradition of *Tom Jones*. It is this reduction of the novel to experiences which can be verified in the immediate consciousness of the novelist that Mendilow has called modern "inwardness" and E. M. Forster the "hidden life." Forster suggests the difference when he says that "The hidden life is, by definition, hidden. The hidden life that appears in external signs is hidden no longer, has entered the realm of action. And it is the function of the novelist to reveal the hidden life at its source." But if the hidden life has become the domain of the novel, it has introduced unusual problems.

In a recent review of Leon Edel's *The Psychological Novel: 1900–1950*, Howard Mumford Jones sums up the central problems which have plagued the modern novelist: the verbal limitations of nonverbal experience; the dilemma of autobiographical fiction in which the novelist must at once evoke a unique consciousness and yet communicate it to others; the difficulty of catching the flux of time in static language. The summary is acutely concise in picking out the nerve centers of an increasingly subjective novel where "after images fished out of the stream of past time ... substitute a kind of smoldering dialectic for the clean impact of drama."[77]

Béla Balázs has shown us how seriously we tend to underestimate the power of the human face to convey subjective emotions and to suggest thoughts. But the film, being a presentational medium (except for its use of dialogue), cannot have direct access to the power of discursive forms. Where the novel discourses, the film must picture. From this we ought not to conclude like J. P. Mayer that "our eye is weaker than our mind" because it does not "*hold*" sight impressions as our imagination does."[78] For sense impressions, like word symbols, may be appropriated into the common fund of memory. Perceptual knowledge is not necessarily different in strength; it *is* necessarily different in kind.

The rendition of mental states—memory, dream, imagination—cannot be as adequately represented by film as by language. If the film has difficulty presenting streams of consciousness, it has even more difficulty presenting states of mind which are defined precisely by the absence in them of the visible world. Conceptual imaging, by definition, has no existence in space. However, once I cognize the signs of a sentence through the conceptual screen, my consciousness is indistinguishable from nonverbal thought. Assuming here a difference between *kinds* of images—between images of things, feelings, concepts, words—we may observe that conceptual images evoked by verbal stimuli can scarcely be distinguished in the end from those evoked by nonverbal stimuli. The stimuli, whether they be the signs of language or the sense data of the physical world, lose their spatial characteristics and become components of the total ensemble which is consciousness.

On the other hand, the film image, being externalized in space, cannot be similarly converted through the conceptual screen. We have already seen how alien to the screen is the compacted luxuriance of the trope. For the same reasons, dreams and memories, which exist nowhere but in the individual consciousness, Cannot be adequately represented in spatial terms. Or rather, the film, having only arrangements of space to work with, cannot render thought, for the moment thought is externalized it is no longer thought. The film, by arranging external signs for our visual perception, or by presenting us with dialogue, can lead us to *infer* thought. But it cannot show us thought directly. It can show us characters thinking, feeling, and speaking, but it cannot show us their thoughts and feelings. A film is not thought, it is perceived.[79]

That is why pictorial representations of dreams or memory on the screen are almost always disappointing. The dreams and memories of *Holiday for Henrietta* and *Rashomon* are spatial referents to dreams and memories, not precise renditions. To show a memory or dream, one must balloon a separate image into the frame (Gypo remembering good times with Frankie in *The Informer*); or superimpose an image (Gypo daydreaming about an ocean voyage with Katie); or clear the frame entirely for the visual equivalent (in *Wuthering Heights*, Ellen's face dissolving to the house as it was years ago). Such spatial devices are always to some degree dissatisfying. Acting upon us perceptually, they cannot render the conceptual feel of dreams and memories. The realistic tug of the film is too strong. If, in an effort to bridge the gap between spatial representation and nonspatial experience, we accept such devices at all, we accept them as cinematic conventions, not as renditions of conceptual consciousness.

Given the contrasting abilities of film and novel to render conceptual consciousness, we may explore further the media's handling of time.

Chronological Time

The novel has three tenses; the film has only one. From this follows almost everything else one can say about time in both media. By now, we are familiar with Bergson's distinction between two kinds of time: chronological time measured in more or less discrete units (as in clocks and metronomes); and psychological time, which distends or compresses in consciousness, and presents itself in continuous flux. What are the comparative abilities of novel and film to render these types of time?

To begin with, Mendilow describes language as "a medium consisting of consecutive units constituting a forward-moving linear form of expression that is subject to the three characteristics of time—transience, sequence, and irreversibility." But we must remember that Mendilow is here referring to chronological time only. And chronological time in the novel exists on three primary levels: the chronological duration of the reading; the chronological duration of the narrator's time; and the chronological span of the narrative events. That the three chronologies may harmonize in the fictive world is due entirely to the willingness of the reader to suspend disbelief and accept the authority of convention. As long as the novelist is not troubled by the bargain into which he enters with his reader, the three levels do not come into any serious conflict.

But Laurence Sterne saw a long time ago the essential paradox of the convention. If the novelist chooses to chronicle a series of events up to the present moment, he discovers that by the time he commits a single event to paper, the present moment has already slipped away. And if the novelist discovers that it takes a chronological year to record a single fictional day, as Sterne did, how is one ever to overcome the durational lag between art and life? If the present moment is being constantly renewed, how can prose, which is fixed, ever hope to catch it? Whenever a novelist chooses for his province a sequence of events which cannot be completed until the present moment, the three levels come into open conflict. In Sterne and Gide, that conflict becomes more central than conflicts between the characters.

The film is spared at least part of this conflict because one of the levels is omitted. Since the camera is always the narrator, we need concern ourselves only with the chronological duration of the viewing and the time-span of the narrative events. Even when a narrator appears in the film, the basic orientation does not change. When Francis begins to tell the story of Dr. Caligari, the camera shows his face; then the camera shifts to the scene of the story and there takes over the telling. What has happened is not so much that Francis has turned over the role of narrator to the omniscient camera as that the omniscient camera has included Francis as part of the narrative from the beginning.

The ranges of chronological time for reader and viewer are rather fluid, yet more or less fixed by convention. Where a novel can be read in anywhere from two to fifty hours, a film generally runs for one or two. *Intolerance* runs over two hours; the uncut version of *Les Enfants du Paradis* over three; and *Gone with the Wind* and *War and Peace* slightly less than four. Since the fictional events depicted in both novel and film may range anywhere from the fleeting duration of a dream (*Scarlet Street* and *Finnegans Wake*) to long but finite stretches of human history (*Intolerance* and *Orlando*), the sense of passing time is infinitely more crucial than the time required for reading or viewing.

We may note, of course, that a fifty-hour novel has the advantage of being able to achieve a certain density, that "solidarity of specification" which James admired, simply because the reader has lived with it longer. Further, because its mode of beholding allows stops and starts, thumbing back, skipping, flipping ahead, and so lets the reader set his own pace, a novel can afford diffuseness where the film must economize. Where the mode of beholding in the novel allows the reader to control his rate, the film viewer is bound by the relentless rate of a projector which he cannot control. The results, as may be expected, are felt in the contrast between the loose, more variegated conventions of the novel and the tight, compact conventions of the film.

Sometimes, to be sure, the conventions governing quantity do affect the end product. The silent version of *Anna Karenina* with Garbo (called *Love*) and the subsequent sound versions (the first with Garbo and Fredric March; the second with Vivien Leigh and Ralph Richardson) dropped the entire story of Levin and Kitty. And Philip

Dunne, the veteran screen writer, tells us that the boy in the film *How Green Was My Valley* never grew up, thus leaving out half the novel; that the *Count of Monte Cristo* contained no more than 5 per cent of its original; that *The Robe* and *The Egyptian* used less than a third of theirs.[80] While such quantitative deletions do alter the originals, it is, in the last analysis, the qualitative rather than the quantitative differences that militate against film adaptations of the novel.

If, as Mendilow says, "Fictional time is an ineluctable element in the novel," and fictional time treats of both kinds of time, then we discover that the moment we shift from chronological to psychological time, certain special problems arise.

Psychological Time: Variability in Rate

We speak of psychological time here in at least two roughly defined ways. The first suggests that the human mind is capable of accelerating and collapsing the "feel" of time to the point where each individual may be said to possess his own "time-system." The second suggests, beyond this variability in *rate*, the kind of flux which, being fluid and interpenetrable, and lacking in sharp boundaries, can scarcely be measured at all.

As long as the kind of time we are talking about in any sense implies discrete units in a series, language seems roughly adequate to the task. For example, the observation that chronological time crowded with activity, the sense of time passing quickly, seems "long" in retrospect, whereas chronological time taken up with dull and undifferentiated activity (the sense of time passing slowly) seems "short" in retrospect still has built into it a concept of measurement. It assumes the clock as a standard of measurement, for this kind of psychological time seems "long" or "short" in terms of certain normative expectancies. It assumes a normative "feel" for chronological time which may be distended or compressed by the stress of the moment, or by memory.

Here language is still appropriate to its task. Mendilow points out, for example, that in *Tom Jones* each book draws on a progressively greater length of the reader's clock time to cover a progressively shorter period of fictional time. So that where Book Three covers five years, Book Nine and Ten cover twelve hours each. The implication is that both for Tom and the reader, the events of the five weeks which occupy the last two thirds of the novel will seem "longer" than the events of the twenty years which occupy the first third.

Compression and distension of time has its exact equivalent in the film's use of speed-up and slow-motion. We have already noted how Pudovkin found the creative element of film in "the discovered, deeply imbedded detail." But that the deeply imbedded detail is in constant motion has further implications for filmic structure. Like the principles of editing, the principles of movement seem to collect around centers of gravity dictated by the film's persistent and almost willful self-assertion. "A sure folk instinct was shown," writes Panofsky, "when the photoplay immediately became known as the movies." Lawson extends this insight by making movement the pivotal element in film structure: "The conflict of individuals or groups projected on the screen has one characteristic that is not found in other story structures. *The conflict is in constant motion.*"

From this there develops a new kind of artistic reality, what Pudovkin calls filmic time and filmic space; what Panofsky calls the Dynamization of Space, and the Spatialization of Time. The theatrical producer, says Pudovkin,

> ... works with real actuality which though he may always remould, yet forces him to remain bound by the laws of real space and real time. The film director, on the other hand, has as his material the finished recorded celluloid.... The elements of reality are fixed on those pieces; by combining them in his selected sequence according to his desire, the director builds up his own "filmic" time and "filmic" space.[81]

The director, then, creates a new reality, and the most characteristic and important aspect of this process is that laws of space and time which are ordinarily invariable or inescapable become "tractable and obedient." Hollywood's silent comedians made use of this freedom in their own unique way. James Agee has noted how Mack Sennett, realizing "the tremendous drumlike power of mere motion to exhilarate,"[82] gave inanimate objects a mischievous life of their own, "*broke every law of nature* the tricked camera could serve him for and made the screen dance like a witches' Sabbath" (italics mine). And other comedians, energized by the liberation of untrammeled movement, "zipped and caromed about the pristine world of the screen." No previous narrative art has been able to achieve such graphic effects.

Not only is space liberated, but *because* it is liberated, time is, too. In thirty seconds, we see shoot, stem, bud, and blossom grow gracefully one from the other, a process that takes weeks in ordinary time. Just as space can be molded, time can be arrested and quickened. Anyone who has seen the remarkable slow-motion sequence in *Zéro de Conduite* can attest to the dramatic power of distended time. By interfering and only by interfering with natural time was Jean Vigo able to render the dream-like essence of the pillow fight.

Similarly, it is easy to find innumerable examples of accelerated motion in Hollywood where the emphasis has always been, for example, on the murderous pace of the comic chase. Chaplin out-races the Keystone cops. W. C. Fields dodges in and out of traffic at eighty miles an hour. Time is distorted in the opposite direction, but the principle remains the same. Spatial mobility makes time more flexible. A man is trying to find a job without success. The film may suggest the dreary routine of job-hunting by intercutting shots of the man's feet walking along asphalt streets with close-ups of other men shaking their heads, saying no. Four or five such alternate shots, taking a few seconds of running time, can suggest a process taking months, or even years. Thus the film is able, in an instant, to suggest the sense of monotonous events that seem "short" in retrospect, even though the duration of those events is "long" by clock time.

As for the kind of rhythmic progression one finds in music, the film has an exact parallel in the thoroughly discussed theory of montage. Not only does each shot take its meaning both from preceding shots and future expectations, but the use of sound (music, dialogue) provides a complex system of counterpoint.

Psychological Time: The Time-Flux

As soon as we enter the realm of time-in-flux, however, we not only broach all but insoluble problems for the novel but we also find a sharp divergence between prose and cinema. The transient, sequential, and irreversible character of language is no longer adequate for this type of time experience. For in the flux past and present lose their identity as discrete sections of time. The present becomes "specious" because on second glance it is seen as fused with the past, obliterating the line between them.

Discussing its essential modernity, Mendilow lends support to the idea that the whole of experience is implicit in every moment of the present by drawing from Sturt's *Psychology of Time*. For Sturt tries to work out the sense in which we are caught by a perpetual present permeated by the past:

> One of the reasons for the feeling of pastness is that we are familiar with the things or events that we recognize as past. But it remains true that this feeling of familiarity is a *present* experience, and therefore logically should not arouse a concept of the past. On the other hand, a present impression (or memory) of something which is past is different from a present impression of something which is present but familiar from the past.[83]

How this seeming contradiction operates in practice may be seen when we attempt to determine precisely which of two past events is prior, and in what manner the distinction between the memory of a past thing and the impression of a present thing is to be made. At first glance, we seem perfectly able to deduce which of two remembered events is prior. For example, on the way to the store this morning, I met a group of children going to school. I also mailed my letter just as the postman came by. I know that ordinarily the children go to school at nine o'clock and the postman comes by at eleven. Therefore, I deduce that I went to the store *before* I mailed my letter. Although I have not been able to give the act of my going to the store an exact location in the past, I have been able to establish its priority.

On second thought, however, it seems as if (apart from the deductions one makes by deliberate attention to relationships) the memory of a past event comes to me with its pastness already intended. The image I have of my friend *includes* the information that this is the way he looked the year before he died. Similarly, if I have a mental image of myself on a train to Kabul, then summon up an image of myself eating chestnuts, I know that the first is an image of a past thing and the second an image of a present thing because the image of myself on the train includes the information that the event took place last year. At the same time, I know that I am eating chestnuts right now. Here the perceptual witnessing of my present action checks and defines my mental images, confirming both the priority of the train ride and the presentness of the eating.

But suppose I bring my attention to bear on an object which is present now and which was also present yesterday at the same time, in the same place, in the same light. If, for example, I look at the lamp in my room which fulfills all these requirements, then close my eyes and behold the mental image, how am I to know if that image refers to the lamp which was there yesterday or to the lamp which is there today? In this instance, which is tantamount to fusing a thing's past with its present, my present image, for all practical purposes, no longer respects the distinction between past and present. It offers me no way of knowing the exact location of its temporal existence.

This obliteration between past and present is precisely the problem which faces the novelist who wishes to catch the flux in language. If he is faced with the presentness of consciousness on the one hand, and the obliteration of the discrete character of past and present on the other, how is he to express these phenomena in a language which relies on tenses?

Whether we look at William James' "stream of consciousness," Ford Madox Ford's "chronological looping," or Bergson's "*durée*," we find the theorists pondering the same problem: language, consisting as it does of bounded, discrete units cannot satisfactorily represent the unbounded and continuous. We have a sign to cover the concept of a thing's "becoming"; and one to cover the concept of a thing's "having become." But "becoming" is a *present* participle, "become" a *past* participle, and our language has thus far offered no way of showing the continuity between them.

So elusive has been the *durée* that the novelist has submitted to the steady temptation of trying to escape time entirely. But here, too, the failure has served to dramatize the medium's limitations. Speaking of Gertrude Stein's attempt to emancipate fiction from the tyranny of time, E. M. Forster notes the impasse: "She fails, because as soon as fiction is completely delivered from time it cannot express anything at all."

To be sure, there seem to be intuitive moments of illumination in Proust and Wolfe during which a forgotten incident floats up from oblivion in its pristine form and seems thereby to become free of time. Proust's involuntary memory fuses the experience of his mother's madeleine cake with the former experience of Aunt Léonie's, and the intervening time seems, for the moment, obliterated. But it is the precise point of Proust's agonizing effort that—despite our ability, through involuntary memory, to experience simultaneously events "with countless intervening days between"—there is always a sense in which these events remain "widely separated from one another in Time." The recognition of this conflict helps us understand why every formulation which attempts to define a "timeless" quality in a novel seems unsatisfactory, why Mendilow's attempt to find an "ideal time" in Kafka seems to say little more than that Kafka was not plagued by the problem. In the end, the phrase "timeless moment" poses an insuperable contradiction in terms.

We can see the problem exemplified concretely in a passage from Thomas Wolfe's *The Hills Beyond*. The passage describes Eugene Gant's visit to the house in St. Louis where his family had lived thirty years before. Eugene can remember the sights, shapes, sounds, and smells of thirty years ago, but something is missing—a sense of absence, the absence of his brother Grover, of his family away at the fair:

> And he felt that if he could sit there on the stairs once more, in solitude and absence in the afternoon, he would be able to get it back again. Then would he be able to remember all that he had seen and been—that brief sum of himself, the universe of his four years, with all the light of time upon it—that universe which was so short to measure, and yet so far, so endless, to remember. Then would he be able to see his own small face again, pooled in the dark mirror of the hall, and discover there in his quiet three years' self the lone integrity of "I," knowing: "Here is the House, and here House listening; here is Absence, Absence in the afternoon; and here in this House, this Absence, is my core, my kernel—here am I!"[84]

The passage shows the characteristic, almost obsessive longing of the modern novel to escape the passage of time by memory; the recognition that the jump, the obliteration, cannot be made; the appropriation of non-space as a reality in the novel—not the feeling of absence alone, but the absence of absence.

We arrive here at the novel's farthest and most logical remove from the film. For it is hard to see how any satisfactory film equivalents can be found for such a paragraph. We can show Eugene waiting in the house, then superimpose an image of the boy as he might have looked thirty years before, catch him watching a door as if waiting for Grover to return. But as in all cinematic attempts to render thought, such projection would inevitably fail. How are we to capture that combination of past absence and present longing, if both are conditions contrary to spatial fact?

The film-maker, in his own and perhaps more acute way, also faces the problem of how to render the flux of time. "Pictures have no tenses," says Balázs. Unfolding in a perpetual present, like visual perception itself, they cannot express either a past or a future. One may argue that the use of dialogue and music provides a door through which a sense of past and future may enter. Dialogue, after all, is language, and language does have referential tenses. A character whose face appears before us may *talk* about his past and thereby permeate his presence with a kind of pastness. Similarly, as we saw in our discussion of sound in editing, music may be used to counterpoint a present image (as in *High Noon* and *Alexander Nevsky*) and suggest a future event. In this way, apparently, a succession of present images may be suffused with a quality of past or future.

At best, however, sound is a secondary advantage which does not seriously threaten the primacy of the spatial image. When Ellen, the housekeeper, her withered face illumined by the fire, begins telling her story to Lockwood in *Wuthering Heights*, we do sense a certain tension between story-teller and story. But in the film we can never fully shake our attention loose from the teller. The image of her face has priority over the sound of her voice. When Terry Malone tells Edie bout his childhood in *On the Waterfront*, the present image of his face so floods our consciousness that his words have the thinnest substance only. The scars around his eyes tell us more about his past than any halting explanation. This phenomenon is essentially what Panofsky calls the "principle of coexpressibility," according to which a moving picture—even when it has learned to talk—remains a picture that moves, and does not convert itself into a piece of writing that is enacted. That is why Shakespearian films which fail to adapt the fixed space of the stage to cinematic space so often seem static and talky.

In the novel, the line of dialogue stands naked and alone; in the film, the spoken word is attached to its spatial image. If we try to convert Marlon Brando's words into our own thought, we leave for a moment the visual drama of his face, much as we turn away from a book. The difference is that, whereas in the book we miss nothing, in the film Brando's face has continued to act, and the moment we miss may be crucial. In a film, according to Panofsky, "that which we hear remains, for good or worse, inextricably fused with that which we see." In that fusion, our seeing (and therefore our sense of the present) remains primary.

If, however, dialogue and music are inadequate to the task of capturing the flux, the spatial image itself reveals two characteristics which at least permit the film to make a tentative approach. The first is the quality of familiarity which attaches itself to the perceptual image of a thing after our first acquaintance. When I first see Gelsomina in *La Strada*, I see her as a stranger, as a girl with a certain physical disposition, but without a name or a known history. However, once I identify her as a character with a particular relationship to other characters, I am able to include information about her past in the familiar figure which now appears before me. I do not have to renew my acquaintance at every moment. Familiarity, then, becomes a means of referring to the past, and this past reference fuses into the ensemble which is the present Gelsomina. The spatial image of Gelsomina which I see toward the end of the film includes, in its total structure, the knowledge that she has talked to the Fool and returned to Zampano. In a referential sense, the pastness is built in.

That the film is in constant motion suggests the second qualification of film for approximating the time-flux. At first glance, the film seems bound by discrete sections, much as the novel is bound by discrete words. At the film's outer limit stands the frame; and within the frame appear the distinct outlines of projected objects, each one cut as by a razor's edge. But the effect of running off the frames is startlingly different from the effect of running off the sentence. For whether the words in a novel come to me as nonverbal images or as verbal meanings, I can still detect the discrete units of subject and predicate. If I say, "The top spins on the table," my mind assembles first the top, then the spinning, then the table. (Unless, of course, I am capable of absorbing the sentence all at once, in which case the process may be extended to a paragraph composed of discrete sentences.) But on the screen, I simply perceive a shot of a top spinning on a table, in which subject and predicate appear to me as *fused*. Not only is the top indistinguishable from its spinning, but at every moment the motion of the top seems to contain the history of its past motion. It is true that the top-image stimulated in my mind by the sentence resembles the top-image stimulated by the film in the sense that both contain the illusion of continuous motion. Yet this resemblance does not appear in the *process* of cognition. It appears only after the fact, as it were, only after the component words have been assembled. Although the mental and filmic images do meet in rendering the top's continuity of motion, it is in the mode of apprehending them that we find the qualitative difference.

In the cinema, for better or worse, we are bound by the forward

looping of the celluloid through the projector. In that relentless unfolding, each frame is blurred in a total progression. Keeping in mind
Sturt's analysis of the presentness of our conceptions, a presentness
permeated by a past and therefore hardly ruled by tense at all, we note
that the motion in the film's *present* is unique. Montage depends for its
effects on instantaneous successions of different spatial entities which
are constantly exploding against each other. But a succession of such
variables would quickly become incomprehensible without a constant to
stabilize them. In the film, that constant is motion. No matter how
diverse the moving spaces which explode against each other, movement
itself pours over from shot to shot, binding as it blurs them, reinforcing
the relentless unrolling of the celluloid.

Lindgren advances Abercrombie's contention that completeness in
art has no counterpart in real life, since natural events are never complete: "In nature nothing at any assignable point begins and nothing at
any assignable point comes to an end: all is perfect continuity." But
Abercrombie overlooks both our ability to perceive spatial discreteness
in natural events and the film's ability to achieve "perfect continuity."
So powerful is this continuity, regardless of the *direction* of the motion,
that at times we tend to forget the boundaries of both frame and projected object. We attend to the motion only. In those moments when
motion alone floods our attention and spatial attributes seem forgotten,
we suddenly come as close as the film is able to fulfilling one essential
requirement of the time-flux—the boundaries are no longer perceptible.
The transience of the shot falls away before the sweeping permanence
of its motion. Past and present seem fused, and we have accomplished
before us a kind of spatial analogue for the flux of time.

If the film is incapable of maintaining the illusion for very long, if
its spatial attributes, being primary, presently assert themselves, if the
film's spatial appeal to the eye overwhelms its temporal appeal to the
mind, it is still true that the film, above all other non-verbal arts, comes
closest to rendering the time-flux. The combination of familiarity, the
film's linear progression, and what Panofsky calls the "Dynamization of
Space" permits us to intuit the *durée* insofar as it can, in spatial art, be
intuited at all.

The film, then, cannot render the attributes of thought (metaphor,
dream, memory); but it can find adequate equivalents for the kind of
psychological time which is characterized by variations in rate (distension, compression; speed-up, *ralenti*); and it approaches, but ultimately
fails, like the novel, to render what Bergson means by the time-flux.
The failure of both media ultimately reverts to root differences between
the structures of art and consciousness.

Our analysis, however, permits a usable distinction between the
two media. Both novel and film are time arts, but whereas the forma-

tive principle in the novel is time, the formative principle in the film is space. Where the novel takes its space for granted and forms its narrative in a complex of time values, the film takes its time for granted and forms its narrative in arrangements of space. Both film and novel create the illusion of psychologically distorted time and space, but neither destroys time or space. The novel renders the illusion of space by going from point to point in time; the film renders time by going from point to point in space. The novel tends to abide by, yet explore, the possibilities of psychological law; the film tends to abide by, yet explore, the possibilities of physical law.

Where the twentieth-century novel has achieved the shock of novelty by explosions of words, the twentieth-century film has achieved a comparable shock by explosions of visual images. And it is a phenomenon which invites detailed investigation that the rise of the film, which preëmpted the picturing of bodies in nature, coincides almost exactly with the rise of the modern novel which preëmpted the rendition of human consciousness.

Finally, to discover distinct formative principles in our two media is not to forget that time and space are, for artistic purposes, ultimately inseparable. To say that an element is contingent is not to say that it is irrelevant. Clearly, spatial effects in the film would be impossible without concepts of time, just as temporal effects in the novel would be impossible without concepts of space. We are merely trying to state the case for a system of priority and emphasis. And our central claim—namely that time is prior in the novel, and space prior in the film—is supported rather than challenged by our reservations.

Notes

1. Lewis Jacobs, *The Rise of the American Film* (New York, 1939), p. 119.

2. Joseph Conrad, *A Conrad Argosy* (New York, 1942), p. 83.

3. Sergei Eisenstein, *Film Form*, trans. Jay Leyda (New York, 1949), pp. 195–255.

4. Jacobs, pp. 98–99.

5. In Marguerite G. Ortman, *Fiction and the Screen* (Boston, 1935).

6. In Lester Asheim, "From Book to Film" (Ph.D. dissertation, University of Chicago, 1949).

7. In Hortense Powdermaker, *Hollywood: The Dream Factory* (Boston, 1950), p. 74.

8. For example, Asheim reports that of the "Ten Best" films listed in the *Film Daily Yearbook* for 1935–45, fifty-two or 47 percent were derived from established novels.

9. *Time*, LV (March 6, 1950), 92. From the point of view of thematic conventions, there may be further significance in the fact that both films deal with the Civil War and that both are sympathetic to the secessionists. To what extent has the Southern defeat haunted our national consciousness?

10. *Time*, LXV (January 17, 1955), 74. The figures are quoted from *Variety's* forty-ninth anniversary issue. The filmed novels were: *Gone with the Wind, From Here to Eternity, Duel in the Sun, The Robe,* and *Quo vadis.*

11. Among other filmed Pulitzer Prize winners: *The Good Earth, Gone with the Wind, The Late George Apley, The Yearling, The Grapes of Wrath, A Bell for Adano, The Magnificent Ambersons, So Big, Arrowsmith, The Bridge of San Luis Rey, Alice Adams.*

12. Jerry Wald, "Screen Adaptation," *Films in Review*, v (February, 1954), 66.

13. Jean-Paul Sartre, *What Is Literature?* trans. Bernard Frechman (New York, 1949), p. 245.

...

77. *Saturday Review*, XXXVIII (April 25, 1955), p. 19.

78. J. P. Mayer, *Sociology of Film* (London, 1946), p. 278.

79. See Maurice Merleau-Ponty, "Le Cinéma et la Nouvelle Psychologie," *Les Temps Modernes*, No. 26 (November, 1947), pp. 930–943.

80. Wald, p. 65.

81. Pudovkin, p. 53. See, too, A. Nicholas Vardac, *Stage to Screen* (Cambridge, Mass., 1949) for the influence of nineteenth-century theater on early American cinema.

82. Agee, p. 74.

83. Quoted in Mendilow, p. 98.

84. Thomas Wolfe, *The Hills Beyond* (New York, 1941), pp. 37–38. In *Thomas Wolfe: The Weather of His Youth* (Baton Rouge, 1955), pp. 28–53, Louis D. Rubin, Jr. analyzes in some detail Wolfe's handling of time.

Questions and Projects

- Select a novel with an unusual way of organizing or representing time as a scheme (such as Emily Bronte's *Wuthering Heights*, Albert Camus's *The Stranger* or Franz Kafka's *The Trial*) and use Bluestone's argument to compare the way it structures time with a film version of that novel (such as Luis Buñuel's 1954 *Wuthering Heights*, Orson Welles's 1946 *The Stranger*, Luchino Visconti's 1967 *The Stranger* or Welles's 1963 *The Trial*).

- In addition to the way in which the novel and film depict temporality, are there other experiences or dimensions to experience—such as the complexity of emotions, the description of nature, or the depiction of the physical features of a character—that film represents differently from the novel? Pair a recent novel and film and analyze how each accomplishes such a specific task to suggest what is at stake in the different artistic forms.

P. *Adams Sitney's focus is on the experimental or avant-garde films of the New American Cinema that developed after World War II. First published in 1974, this work aligns certain films first with a revolutionary poetic tradition associated with William Blake and other Romantic poets. Concentrating on the films of Stan Brakhage, Sitney argues a connection with those lyrical revolutions in vision and image, as well as with the literary techniques of traditional poetry such as rhythm and metaphor. Although this selection concentrates on one filmmaker, the connection between poetic techniques and creative processes should point toward the variety of experimental film practices.*

"The Lyrical Film"
from Visionary Film: The American Avant-Garde, 1943–1978
P. Adams Sitney

... In his aesthetics Brakhage has revived and revised the Romantic dialectics of sight and imagination which had been refocused in American abstract expressionistic painting and American poetry (particularly in the work of Wallace Stevens) during the film-maker's intellectual formation. The history of that argument is worth consideration at this time. William Blake championed the imagination against the prevailing epistemology of John Locke, who maintained that both thought and imagination were additive aspects of the verbal and visual memory. Blake wrote, "I assert for My Self that I do not behold the outward Creation & that to me it is a hindrance & not Action"—a forecast of the phraseology of Abstract Expressionism. "It is as the dirt upon my feet, No part of me.... I question not my Corporeal or Vegative Eye any more than I would Question a Window concerning a Sight. I look thro' it & not with it." Wordsworth too writes of the tyranny of sight:

> I speak in recollection of a time
> When the bodily eye, in every stage of life
> The most despotic of our senses, gained
> Such strength in me as often held my mind
> In absolute dominion
> —Prelude, XII, 127ff

Our philosophies and psychologies have shifted from the naturalism of Locke and his confidence in the senses. For some artists in the tradition of Blake and Wordsworth the eye now had a renewed and redemptive value. As Wallace Stevens puts it,

The eye's plain version is a Thing apart,
The vulgate of experience.
                —"An Ordinary Evening in New Haven," 1–2

Harold Bloom has observed that "Modernist poetry in English has organized itself, to an excessive extent, as a supposed revolt against Romanticism, in the mistaken hope of escaping [Romanticism's] inwardness (though it was unconscious of this as its prime motive)."[8] The eye which both Stevens and Brakhage enlist in the service of the imagination confirms while striving to reconcile, as Bloom's view would have it, the Romantic divorce of consciousness and nature.

Brakhage claims to see through his eyes, with his eyes, and even the electrical patterns on the surface of his eyes. When he decided to become a film-maker he threw away his eyeglasses. At the beginning of his book he argues with the way language constricts vision and with the idea of sight built into the film-maker's tools. In "The Camera Eye," he writes:

> And here, somewhere, we have an eye (I'll speak for myself) capable of any imagining (the only reality). And there (right there) we have the camera eye (the limitation of the original liar) ... its lenses ground to achieve 19th Century Western compositional perspective (as best exemplified by the 'classic' ruin) ... its standard camera and projector speed for recording movement geared to the feeling of the ideal slow Viennese waltz, and even its tripod head ... balled with bearings to permit it that Les Sylphides motion (ideal to the contemplative romantic and virtually restricted to horizontal and vertical movements) ... and its color film manufactured, to produce that picture post card effect (salon painting) exemplified by those oh so blue skies and peachy skins.[9]

He proceeds with a program for bringing the camera into the twentieth century by distorting its lens, obliterating perspective, discarding the tripod, altering camera speeds, and changing film stocks. He calls for these home-made modifications in the name of the eye, demanding of the film-maker (actually of himself) a dedication to what he actually sees, not what he has been taught to see or thinks he should see. That the resulting version of space corresponds to that of Abstract Expressionism, whose motivations are away from the physical eye, seems not to have occurred to Brakhage. His sense of vision presumes that we have been taught to be unconscious of most of what we see. For him, seeing includes what the open eyes view, including the essential movements and dilations involved in that primary mode of seeing, as well as the shifts of focus, what the mind's eye sees in visual memory and in dreams (he calls them "brain movies"), and the perpetual play of shapes and colors on the closed eyelid and occasionally on the eye surface ("closed-eye vision"). The imagination, as he seems to define it, includes the simultaneous functioning of all these modes. Thus Brakhage argues both with Blake and Locke, but his sympathies are with the former. Like the Romantics themselves, Brakhage's work attempts to refine the visionary tradition by correcting its errors.

The Romantic strain in Brakhage emerges with the creation of the lyrical film and culminates in his essay in mythopoeia, *Dog Star Man*, and its extended version, *The Art of Vision*, which will be discussed in the following chapter. Brakhage began to shoot his epic two years after finishing *Anticipation of the Night*. In the meantime, and through the shooting of that long film, he continued to make short lyrical films that mark one of the great periods in American avant-garde film. In this series of films—*Window Water Baby Moving* (1959), *Cat's Cradle* (1959), *Sirius Remembered* (1959), *The Dead (1960)*, *Thigh Line Lyre Triangular* (1961), *Mothlight* (1963), *Vein* (1964), *Fire of Waters* (1965), *Pasht* (1965)—Brakhage invented a form in which the film-maker could compress his thoughts and feelings while recording his direct confrontation with intense experiences of birth, death, sexuality, and the terror of nature. These works have transformed the idea of film-making for most avant-garde artists who began to make films in the late sixties.

Window Water Baby Moving and *Thigh Line Lyre Triangular* record the births of the film-maker's first and third children respectively. Between the two, finished only two years apart, there is a great shift in style: the former treats the occasion almost dramatically, although the montage attempts to relieve the drama which Brakhage obviously felt while shooting the film and seeing his first child born; the latter film centers itself more fully in the eyes of the film-maker as a visual and visionary experience. The difference between them is not simply a measure of experience (seeing a third child born as opposed to the first), but that is part of it.

There is an interplay between the film-maker and his wife in *Window Water Baby Moving* that disappears in *Thigh Line Lyre Triangular*. The poetic fulfillment of that interplay comes at the moment late in the film when we see the excited face of Brakhage just after the child has been born. His wife, still on the delivery table, took the camera from him to get these shots. Earlier, they had photographed each other during an argument, which Brakhage intercut with negative images of them making love in the film *Wedlock House: An Intercourse* (1959).

In no other film does Brakhage make as much of the reorganization of chronological time; for the most part, his lyrical films exist outside sequential time in a realm of simultaneity or of disconnected time spans of isolated events. *Window Water Baby Moving* begins with images of late pregnancy. The first shots are of a window, framed diagonally, intercut with flashes of blackness. Throughout the film Brakhage uses black and white leader to affirm the screen and the cinematic illusion as one of several tactics for relieving the dramatic tension built up as the moment of birth approaches.

A rhythmic montage moves from the window to the light cast on the water in a bathtub where the pregnant wife is bathing. The camera is static, and the shots remain on the screen longer here than in other films of the same period. After a longish pause of blackness, we see Jane for the first time on the delivery table. At a painful moment in her labor, he cuts from her screams to her smiling face from the earlier episode and follows it with a recapitulation of the window and water shots. He flashes back to the earlier scene nine times, always showing it in a group of shots and always passing from one scene to the other on a plastic cut, as the glimpse of a window behind the held-up placenta, near the end of the film, initiates another cut to the window of the opening and a recapitulation of the sunlit images that follow it. *Window Water Baby Moving* ends with shots of the parents and the baby spaced amid flashes of white leader following the rhythmic pattern at the film's opening.

In *Thigh Line Lyre Triangular* we see a radically transformed space. The passages of black and white leader are more insistent; there are twisting, anamorphic shots of Jane in labor; the montage mixes the birth with flaring shots of animals, a flamingo, and a polar bear from the out-takes of *Anticipation of the Night*. The entire film is painted over with colored dots, smears, and lines. The film begins with a painted stripe which seems to open up on a scene of childbirth with labor already under way. Underneath the rapidly changing, painted surface, we see the doctor, the birth, the placenta, the smiling mother, but in an elliptical flow completely devoid of the suspense of the earlier film. Where Brakhage used plastic cutting to switch from present to past or future in his first birth film, he uses the painted surface to smooth out and elide the transitions from the birth to the strange upside-down appearance of the polar bear or the shot of the flamingo.

Although we do not see him in this film there is no doubt that we are looking at the birth through the eyes of the artist, whose eccentric vision is ecstatic to the point of being possessed. At the time of the birth he was sufficiently self-composed to pay close attention to the subtleties of his seeing while watching his wife give birth. In the interview at the beginning of *Metaphors on Vision*, he explains that

> only at a crisis do I see both the scene as I've been trained to see it (that is, with Renaissance perspective, three-dimensional logic—colors as we've been trained to call a color a color, and so forth) and patterns that move straight out from the inside of the mind through the

optic nerves. In other words, in intensive crisis I can see from the inside out and the outside in.... I see patterns moving that are the same patterns I see when I close my eyes; and can also see the same kind of scene I see when my eyes are open.... What I was seeing at the birth of Neowyn most clearly, in terms of this "brain movie" recall process, were symbolic structures of an animal nature.[10]

In the first chapter of his book Brakhage observes, "This is an age which has no symbol for death other than the skull and bones of one stage of decomposition ... and it is an age which lives in total fear of annihilation." In *Sirius Remembered* and *The Dead* he searches for a deeper image of death. When his family's dog Sirius died, his wife did not want it buried. They left the body in the woods where it froze in the winter and rotted in the spring. Brakhage made periodic visits to it and filmed the stages of its decomposition. The title of his film puns on the memory and the reconstruction of the dog's members.

Formally, *Sirius Remembered* is the densest of his films in the repetitive, Steinian style of *Anticipation of the Night*, and it introduces a new style, which finds its purest expression in *The Dead*. The opening passage resembles a fugue, as one sweep of the camera is followed by another, beginning a little earlier and going a little further, while the third carries on from the first. The speed of these alternations and the sudden changes they make by a reversal of direction, the injection of a brighter still image, or the occurrence of a long pan suggest that the fugue has been transposed to the micro-rhythms of post-Stravinskian music. The similarity of the shots and their reduction through movement to two-dimensional abstractions fixes the attention on their rhythmic structure.

The pattern of rhythms established in the opening shots continues throughout the film as its visual material becomes more complex. The film proceeds through fall to winter to spring, with some reversals and overlapping of the seasons. Brakhage arrests the movement of the winter scenes with flashes of whiteness when the dog is covered by a layer of snow, to affirm the flat screen and puncture the illusion, but here also to suggest an emanation from the dog of pure white light.

Midway the already complex rhythmic structure becomes compounded by superimposition. The second half of the film elaborates an intricate harmonics as the two layers of fugue-like rhythms play against one another.

In this film Brakhage views death as the conquest of the antagonist, nature, over consciousness. He illustrated this antagonism with a story of the visit of two friends during the making of the film:

Suddenly I was faced in the center of my life with the death of a loved being which tended to undermine all my abstract thoughts of death.

I remember one marvelous time which gave me the sense of how others could avoid it. [P. T.] and [C. B.] came to visit us and C. wanted to go out into the fields to gather a little nature," as he put it. "Nature" was such a crisis to me at this time that I was shocked at that statement. [C.] made some martinis, handed me one; and [P. and C.], and I all went out into Happy Valley where they toasted the new buds of spring that were beginning to come up, etc., and marched right straight past the body of Sirius either without seeing it at all (any more than they can see my film *Sirius Remembered*) or else they saw it and refused to recognize it. [C.] was envaled in the ideal of toasting the budding spring and here was this decaying, stinking corpse right beside the path where we had to walk, and he literally did not, could not, or would not see it.[11]

In the same interview be describes in detail how a mystical illumination helped him edit the film.

The skeletal head of the dog in *Sirius Remembered* was the first of several conventional images which Brakhage has attempted to redeem from the realm of the cliché by looking at them freshly and presenting them in a novel form. Others are the image of the tombstone as a significant image of death (*The Dead*), the heart as an image of love (*Dog Star Man: Part Three*), and flowers as an image of sexuality (*Song XVI*).

While passing through Paris to work on a commercial project (for a long time Brakhage supported himself and his art by taking commercial assignments), he sneaked his camera into the Père-Lachaise cemetery to film the monumental tombs in black-and-white. During the same trip he filmed people walking along the Seine in color from a slow-moving tourist boat on the river. At the end of a black-and-white roll, he took a shot of Kenneth Anger sitting in a café.

When he returned to America, Brakhage associated Europe, Anger, and the two traditional images, the river and the tomb, with his thoughts on death. He says:

I was again faced with death as a concept; not watching death as physical decay, or dealing with the pain of the death of a loved one, but with the concept of death as something that man casts into the future by asking, "What is death like?" And the limitation of finding the images for a concept of death only in life itself is a terrible torture, i.e., Wittgenstein's *Tractatus Logico-Philosophicus* 6.4311: "Death is not an event of life. Death is not lived through. If by eternity is understood not endless temporal duration but timelessness, then he lives eternally who lives in the present. Our life is endless in the way that our visual field is without limit."[12]

He put the three images together—Anger, the tombs, and the Seine—to make *The Dead*.

Nearly every image in the film appears in superimposition, which serves several formal functions which I shall enumerate as they appear, and one poetic function: to make a spectral light emanate from people and things, as if the spirit showed through the flesh and burst through the cracks in marble tombs. Visually, Brakhage relates this effect to a thermal light sometimes visible to the trained eye, and to the Anglo-Saxon allusions to *aelf-scin*, a fairy light that hovers on the horizon at dusk.

The film opens with a pan up a Gothic statue, interrupted by flashes of negative. The black-and-white positive and negative have been printed on color stock, giving them a green-gray tint. From the color footage, only the blues of the water and occasional reds (sweaters, the oars of a rowboat) registered on the composite film. A quick image of Anger in the café changes to a double image of him as the negative is placed over the positive with left/right orientation reversed. The camera moves with fragments of rocking pans among gravestones and crypts upon which sporadic superimpositions briefly appear. This part of the film contains frequent sudden solarizations (the simultaneous printing of negative and positive, causing an instant flash or leap of the image on the screen).

A quick movement toward a crypt blackens the screen. Out of that darkness come deep blue images of the Seine, in a rapid montage, followed by a leisurely pan of the cemetery in tinted black-and-white. Another variation on the opening passage (Anger, Gothic ornamentation, the statue) ends in a white-out.

People, in blue and red, strolling along the banks of the river, appear over pans, sometimes upside-down, of the tombs. In this introduction of the theme of "the walking dead," as Brakhage calls these strollers, the tempo changes from slow, to staccato, to slow again, to staccato again, until the scene almost imperceptibly shifts from the superimposition of people with graves to a flow of superimposed cemetery images, a few frames out of synchronization, with its solarizing negative. The negative echoes the slow rocking of the positive images and pursues them like a ghost.

The shifting of visual themes and their gradual evolution through synthesis and elaboration constitute a meditation on death and the spirit in which thoughts, in the form of images, are tested, then refined, and finally passed over. A persistent idea of the light behind the objects of sight haunts the mind's eye of the film-maker and the structure of his film. Through the medium of the river, the stress shifts from positive to negative.

By overexposure of the film the graves appear almost washed out by the light of day. Another montage of water shots introduces a multiple-layered positive shot of the graves so white that only faint images in the corners of the screen indicate what they are. The movement on the river is contrasted with that of the cemetery through intercutting and superimposition until flashes, then long holds of pure white, break up the river shots.

The climax of the film is its breakthrough into negative following the flashes of whiteness. Brilliant, pure white trees in a black sky and dark crypts with cracks of brightness rock across the screen, paced with black leader. The long rocking motions move first in one direction, then another, shifting with the black shots. There is a long movement containing four black pauses as the camera passes so close to large tombs that the light is completely cut off. The second of these is so long that one thinks the film might have ended. But sudden flashes of solarization revive the ending structure, like final optimistic surges of sound before the end of many symphonies. A short finale brings us back to the Seine and the film ends on a slow movement across the shadow-marked marble wall of the river bank.

Like *Sirius Remembered*, some of the rhythmic texture of *The Dead* comes from the opposition, repetition, and superimposition of different movements of the camera. But here, rhythmic intricacy is less essential to the form of the film. *The Dead* uses superimposition organically, eliding the transitions from theme to theme or from one tempo to another. The abrupt element in the film is solarization. Finally the passages of pure whiteness and blackness act as poles in the spectrum from positive to negative and from black and white to color; they seldom interrupt the texture of the meditation. The best example of this is the long black passage in the pan of graves. The viewer can imagine the continuity of movement as he believes the camera is passing behind a large tomb. The shot a few seconds earlier prepared him for this. But gradually the overtone of movement evaporates, and the viewer is confronted with the presence of the black screen—another, most pessimistic, image of death. That too is denied the authority of a final image as the movement does eventually continue after this unnatural pause.

In *The Dead* Brakhage uses the vicissitudes of his raw materials— different kinds of film stock, the imperfect printing of black-and-white on color material, the washout effect of certain bright superimpositions—as metaphysical illuminations. Out of the specifically cinematic quality of light as it passes through these materials, he moulds his vision of the light of death. In *The Dead* Brakhage mastered the strategy he had employed limitedly in *Anticipation of the Night* of presenting and rejecting tentative images of the essence he seeks to penetrate. The traditional symbols of the tombs and river and the absolute poles of blackness, whiteness, and negativity are the primary metaphors for death which he tests, varies, and rejects. In the course of the film the process of testing, contemplating, and rejecting becomes more important than the images in themselves.

His most radical exploration into the inflection of light through his raw materials initially occurred in response to his oppressive economic situation. When he had no money to buy film stock, he conceived the idea of making a film out of natural material through which light could pass. The clue to this came from his observing the quantity of glue and paint which Stephen Lovi had put on his film *A Portrait of the Lady in the Yellow Hat* (1962). Brakhage collected dead moths, flowers, leaves, and seeds. By placing them between two layers of Mylar editing tape, a transparent, thin strip of 16mm celluloid with sprocket holes and glue on one side, he made *Mothlight* (1963), "as a moth might see from birth to death if black were white."

The passing of light through, rather than reflecting off, the plants and moth wings reveals a fascinating and sometimes terrifying intricacy of veins and netlike structures, which replaces the sense of depth in the film with an elaborate lateral complexity, flashing by at the extreme speed of almost one natural object to each frame of the three minute film. The original title of this visual lyric, when the film-maker began to construct it, had been *Dead Spring*. True to that original but inferior title the film incarnates the sense of the indomitable division between consciousness and nature, which was taking a narrative form at the same time in Brakhage's epic, *Dog Star Man*.

The structure of *Mothlight*, as the film maker observes in a remarkable letter to Robert Kelly printed in "Respond Dance," the final chapter of *Metaphors on Vision*, is built around three "Round-dances" and a coda. Three times the materials of the moths and plants are introduced on the screen, gain speed as if moving into wild flight, and move toward calm and separation; then in the coda a series of bursts of moth wings occurs in diminishing power, interspersed with passages of white (the whole film is fixed in a matrix of whiteness as the wings and flora seldom fill the whole screen). The penultimate burst regains the grandeur of the first in the series, but it is a last gasp, and a single wing, after the longest of the white passages, ends the film.

Significantly, in Brakhage's description of his interest in the moth's flight, sight, and functioning as oracular events in his life, he attributes to the appearance of a moth during the editing of an earlier film a liberation from a slump into self-consciousness that stalled his work:

> I was sty-my-eyed sinking into sty-*meed* in all self possession when suddenly Jane appeared holding a small dried plant which she put down on the working table, and without a word, left me—I soon began working again ... in the midst of attempts to work, what must surely have been the year's last moth began fluttering about me and

along the work table, the wind of its wings shifting the plant from time to time and blowing away all speculations in my mind as to movements of dead plants and to enable me to continue working.[13]

For Brakhage, extreme self-consciousness and the seduction of natural objects are equivalents (which can, as in the present case, cancel each other) since they both inhibit the working process, which is his ultimate value.

In "Respond Dance," Brakhage, adapting Robert Duncan's view of the poet's role as a medium working for the Poet to the situation of the filmmaker, writes:

Of necessity I become instrument for the passage of inner vision, thru all my sensibilities, into its external form. My most active part in this process is to increase all my sensibilities (so that all films arise out of some total area of being or full life) and, at the given moment of possible creation to act only out of necessity. In other words, I am principally concerned with revelation. My sensibilities are art-oriented to the extent that revelation takes place, naturally, within the given historical context of specifically Western aesthetics. If my sensibilities were otherwise oriented, revelation would take an other external form—perhaps a purely personal one. As most of what is revealed, thru my given sensibilities clarifies itself in relationship to previous (and future, possible) works of art, I offer the given external form when completed for public viewing. As you should very well know, even when I lecture at showing of past Brakhage films I emphasize the fact that I am not artist except when involved in the creative process and that I speak as viewer of my own (no—damn that "my own" which is just what I'm trying, do try in all lectures, letters, self-senses-of, etc., to weed out)—I speak (when speaking, writing, well—that, is with respect to deep considerations) as viewer of The Work (not of ... but By-Way-Of Art), and I speak specifically to the point of What has been revealed to me and, by way of describing the work-process, what I, as artist-viewer, understand of Revelation—that is: how to be revealed and how to be revealed to (or 2, step 2 and/or—the viewing process).[14]

What he reveals in the introductory interview, as the critic and explicator of his own work, is always illuminating and usually pertinent to our analysis of his films. But in the case of *Cat's Cradle*, the film does not support his expression of its theme. Brakhage recounts there how shortly after his marriage he took his wife to visit two friends, James Tenney and Carolee Schneemann, whom he had filmed in *Loving*. The film he shot of that encounter was to contain his observations on the tensions, identifications, and jealousies that it engendered. Yet the film itself effaces psychology and develops through its lightning montage of flat surfaces and gestures in virtually two-dimensional space an almost cubistic suggestion of the three-dimensional arena in which the four characters and one cat might interact, if only the furious pace of editing could be retarded and the synecdochic framing expanded.

The camera does not move. Like the montage at the opening of *Window Water Baby Moving*, the cutting at times follows an imaginary path of sunlight from the back of the cat, to a bedspread, to a bowl of flowers, to the opening of a door, etc. When there is movement within the frame, its direction and pace influence how it is cut. The various gestures of the film (a bare foot on the bedspread, Brakhage walking while buttoning his shirt, Carolee Schneemann painting and washing dishes, Tenney writing, Jane undressing) never seem complete; they are spread out evenly and often seen upside-down or simultaneously through the whole film without sequence or internal development. For the most part these activities are framed to obscure who the performer is so that together with the speed of the editing they tend to fuse the two men and two women together and even to create one androgynous being out of all four.

Floral wallpaper, an embroidered pillow, an amber bottle, and the cat's fur mix freely with the human gestures and with recurrent flashes of white leader and emphasize the flatness of the images. Off-screen looks of the human figures and changes of angle in a single subject establish axes of geometrical positioning, but with the rapidity of shot changes these axes spin wildly and eccentrically. The 700 shots in this five-minute film (remember there were some 3000 in the fifty minutes of the highly-edited *Twice a Man*) vary from two frames ($\frac{1}{12}$ of a second) to 48 (two seconds) with by far the greater number of images under half a second screen time.

Cat's Cradle suggests statis through, and despite, the speed of the colliding shots. In *Pasht*, made six years later, he again used a very rapid montage (one frame to sixty frame shots—mostly five or six frames), in a five-minute film for an even more stationary impression. In his blurb for the film in the catalogue of the Film-Makers Cooperative Brakhage tells us that the title comes from the name of a pet cat, named for the Egyptian goddess ruling cats. He shot the film while she was giving birth and edited it after her death. Without this guide the viewer would not know specifically what is happening in the film. It begins in black and soon shows a red furry image in the center of the screen—edgeless, undefined, and not filling the entire screen rectangle. Bits of black leader intercut with it make the image flicker like hot coals. The movement within the frame is slight, except for fragmentary glimpses of the discontinuous twisting of the fur by an anamorphic lens. The montage unites tiny bits of very similar images.

Sometimes a moving orange spot of light appears, reminding the viewer of the cat in *Cat's Cradle.*

The whole screen seems to pulse with variations in the light intensity of the image, the degree of movement, the clarity of the fur, the time of a shot on the screen, and the number of elements in burst-of-image between passages of blackness. A typical passage has one black frame followed by six of soft focused fur, another frame of black, three of focused fur, six of blurred fur ending in a flash of light, another black, one bright orange, and three black. As the film nears its end the bursts become longer and the hairs of fur more clearly focused and at times larger images fill the borders of the screen, almost identifiable as very close views or anamorphic views of a cat scratching or giving birth.

Pasht presents a vision of an organism simultaneously seeming to die and regenerate. It is clearly animal but liberated from the specifics of species and character. The difference in rhythm between *Pasht* and the lyrical films of 1959 and 1960 indicates the general, but not absolute, shift in the film-maker's approach to the lyrical film before and after the making of *Dog Star Man. Pasht* and many of the films that follow it substitute an organic, retarded pulse for the earlier counterpoint and micro-rhythmic dynamics. In this later phase of the lyrical form, Brakhage seems to want to still the filmic image and catch the shimmering vibrations of the forces that inspire and terrify him.

Fire of Waters operates within a structure similar to that of *Pasht.* Here the matrix is gray instead of black, and its black-and-white images are grainy and thin, with an ascetic denial of visual contrast. The film begins with static lights at night—for again the camera does not move—and flares toward whiteness. The image seems to wait, while a house light or a streetlamp sits on the depthless surface of the screen, for single-frame occurrences of summer lightning. With these flashes the silhouettes of trees, house, and clouds appear. At times only a portion of the screen is dimly lit by the lightning, and at other times the whole screen flashes. The duration of the illuminations varies from one to five frames toward the middle of the film, and when the lightning explosion extends beyond the single frame, there is always a slight variation in each of the frames in which it occurs.

The change of streetlamps, car light, or house lights prefigures each new flash and makes the viewer expectant. A flare introduces a scene of suburban houses in the quivering daylight of a gray sky. Three slow tones are heard on the soundtrack, which had previously been silent. When the film reverts to night, the lightning flashes are edited to follow one another more quickly than in the first section. A final change to daylight accompanies the sound of fast panting.

In a previously unpublished interview with the author, Brakhage describes his thematic and formal concerns in making this film:

Fire of Waters, as its title suggests, is inspired by a little postcard that Robert Kelly sent me when we were searching into the concerns of Being, Matter and Subject Matter, and Source. He sent a card which cut through all my German windiness about it. It said, The truth of the matter is this, that man lives in a fire of waters and will live eternally in the first taste." That haunted me. First I couldn't make any sense out of it at all, other than that "fire of waters" would refer to cells, in that the body is mostly water and is firing constantly to keep itself going.

That summer we were living at that abandoned theater. I had got a lot of lightning and streetlights on black-and-white film. I took a lot of daytime shots of the houses that surrounded us. There seemed to be an awful foreboding about that kind of neighborhood in which we were then living, which was a typical suburban neighborhood. I remember referring to it and saying "These houses look like inverted bomb craters." I had a sense of imminent disaster which I always seem to get more mysteriously and in a more sinister way in an American suburban area than I do even in New York City.

When I finally came to edit that, which was just before Christmas '64, I was inspired by Kelly's card and I had the sense that the opening shot would come out of pure white leader and then be a streetlight blinking. The blink of the streetlight would set a rhythm which then I could repeat in flashes of both other streetlights and of lightning flashes, and that blink would be source for the whole rhythm structure of the film. I wanted to see how far I could depart from that rhythm exactly and still retain that rhythm as source.

Then, as the whole concept deepened, I showed the actual source of those night house lights and house shadows by showing the daylight scenes of them. Then I could throw it back into the night with a build-up of the night structure, and then finally end with that one single house that dominated most of my concerns, directly across the street from us.

Then I felt the need for sound. For years I had imposed the discipline on myself that if ever a single sound was needed anywhere on a track to go with an image I would put that sound in even if no other sound was needed in the whole film. That permitted me when I felt the need of slowed-down bird sounds (that is a bird's cry slowed down so that it became like a western musical instrument), to put it in where I felt it was needed. Then that caused me to feel the need of a sound of wind rising to a certain pitch at the very beginning. At the end then the speeded-up sound of Jane giving birth to Myrenna occurs on two levels in the last shot of the house. It definitely sounds like a dog in somebody's backyard in the drama sense of that scene, yelping in pain. It does actually carry the sense of a terror beyond that. That's how the sound come into it and balanced out.[15]

Brakhage had made one other sound film since *Anticipation of the Night*. *Blue Moses* (1962) uses strategies from the lyrical film without itself being a meditation firmly postulated in the eye of the film-maker. For this one time in his career he employed synchronous speech. The existence of this film within Brakhage's filmography is very curious; there is nothing else like it in his work. It explicitly postulates an epistemological principle: that there can be no cinematic image without a film-maker to take it and that the presence, or even the existence, of the film-maker transforms what he films. Formally, *Blue Moses* anticipates the participatory film that calls upon or addresses itself directly to the audience, a form that emerged in the early 1970s on the tail of the structural film. We have encountered its embryonic manifestation already in Anger's *Invocation of My Demon Brother*.

The single actor of *Blue Moses* hollers to the audience when he first appears from his cave. He is the merchant of metaphysical fear Melville knew as "The Lightning Rod Man." He tries to scare us by proposing to quiet our fears: "Don't be afraid. We're not alone. There's the cameraman ... or was ... once." Then in an elliptical way he informs us of what we should be afraid of. He points to mysterious tracks, in a desolate place, left by a man who must have been running. That narrative hint, recurring throughout the film, hovers on the edge of parody of the devices used in novels and films to draw us into illusionism and suspense. In a fugal structure of leap-frogging episodes interrupted by dissolves to the same actor in different costumes, Brakhage lets his actor assume different guises from the history of acting (a classical Greek mask is painted on his face, in robes he strikes "Shakespearean" postures), and his language, usually that of the confidence man, veers to sing-song and melodrama.

The leap-frogging counterpoint of scenes at the beginning of the film is recapitulated in superimposition, both of picture and sound, near the end. The actor pulls off a false beard and, in a Pirandelloistic cliché, reveals himself to the audience. "Look," he says, "this is ridiculous. I'm an actor. You see what I mean?... You're my audience, my captive audience. I'm your entertainment, your player. This whole film is about us." In the course of the speech, the superimposition becomes footage from earlier in the film, projected over his chest. When he turns his back to the projector, the film images cease, and he is framed in a white rectangle of the projector operating without film.

In the middle of his speech in front of the interior film screen he repeats his consolation: "But don't be afraid. There's a film-maker behind *every scene*, in back of every word I speak, behind you, too, so to speak." When the camera suddenly swings around into the darkness, glimpsing the hand signals of the director, he adds, as if a spectator had turned his head to the projection booth: "No. Don't turn around. It's useless." It is at this point that he himself turns toward his screen and the images change to pure white light on his body.

Blue Moses ends as it began with a series of dissolves of the protagonist returning to his cave and gesturing ceremonially. In its form and substance *Blue Moses* attacks the dramatic film as an untenable convention. Brakhage temporarily accepts the principles of the realists of film theory who argue that cinema arises from the interaction of the artist with exterior reality in front of the camera. But he rebuts them with a demonstration of how fragile their sense of exterior reality is. At one point the actor of *Blue Moses* gestures to the sun and cries, "an eclipse," at which point an obvious, messy splice throws the image into blackness, and he adds, "manufactured, but not yet patented, for your pleasure." *Blue Moses* is a negative polemic, an attack on the modified Realism of the European cinema of the early sixties (Godard, Resnais, Fellini, Antonioni, etc.). In its place he proposed the investigation of the consciousness confronting (and constructing) external nature in the form of the lyrical film....

Notes

...

8. Bloom, "The Internalization of the Quest-Romance," p. 6.
9. *Metaphors on Vision*, p. 26.
10. *Ibid.*, p. 19.
11. *Ibid.*, pp. 9–10.
12. *Ibid.*, p. 14.
13. *Ibid.*, p. 80.
14. *Ibid.*, p. 77.
15. An unpublished interview with the author in the spring of 1965. A transcript is in the library of the Anthology Film Archives.

...

Questions and Projects

- Is it possible to give stricter definition of Sitney's use of the word "lyrical" as it applies to film? Might it involve questions of poetic "voice," "fragmented form," or "private communication"? Demonstrate one or more of these other defining features of lyric form in a poem, and then show how it transfers (or doesn't transfer) to a Brakhage film or to one by another experimental filmmaker (such as Kenneth Anger, Myra Deren, or others).

- Are there other poetic traditions, besides the Romantic one (which occurred in the early nineteenth century) that relate to the cinema? The ballad tradition? Concrete poetry? Does a film like Ingmar Bergman's *The Seventh Seal* resemble certain older poetic forms? Compare a particular film with a poem or poetic form that it seems to resemble or approximate in style or perspective.

German filmmaker, novelist, and theoretician, Alexander Kluge (with his co-authors) argues—at times broadly and at times precisely—the differences between a literature of words and a cinema of images. He relates the conceptual and material differences in the two practices to social and industrial problems in contemporary filmmaking (particularly in Germany in 1965). Central to the perspective is a vision of both film and literature as part of a large public and cultural dynamic (or "public sphere") that perceives film neither as derivative (as an adaptation) nor as isolated from literature (as an auteurist art on its own). Kluge envisions a "utopian" cinema that would assimilate literary techniques and languages as a new hybrid form of seeing and thinking. The complex interaction between literary and cinematic forms that results would lead, ideally, to a more active viewer who would see and interpret film in ways that reflected his or her life experience.

"Word and Film"*
from *October*, vol. 46

Alexander Kluge, Edgar Reitz, and Wilfried Reinke

I

Experts and publicists have proposed a whole series of views on film and language. These views resemble and contradict each other.[1] Statements chosen at random, corresponding to various conceptions of film, have one thing in common: they proceed from a fixed notion of film as well as an established, or presumably established, notion of language. The issue at hand, however, requires going beyond such general definitions. As trivial as it may sound, words can interact with film in a hundred different ways. Add to this the diversity of conceptions of film. For every one of these conceptions, for every kind of literary expression, the issue presents itself differently and demands a different answer. Walter Hagemann argues that film does not raise any new questions, "because it does not speak a new language; rather it conveys the old language through a new medium. This is the real reason for the backlash which the language of film suffered with the advent of sound."[2] We have to examine how the old language relates to the old film, how new forms of language available today relate to new concepts

---

*This essay was originally published as "Wort und Film," in *Sprache imtechnischen Zeitalter*, no. 13 (1965), pp. 1015–1030; this version, translated by Miriam Hansen, is reprinted from *October*, vol. 46, pp. 179–198 with the permission of the Massachusetts Institute of Technology. The authors are teachers at the Hochschule für Gestaltung at Ulm, where Kluge and Reitz founded the Film Department in 1965.

of film, and how the interplay of word and film may produce new, non-literary forms of language. Given the essay format, we can only outline a set of problems, we cannot offer any solutions. The following speculations, therefore, are merely intended as examples.

II

In the cultural history of the cinema, the transition to sound marks a radical break. In the beginning of the silent era, films often consisted of lengthy shots of theatrically staged scenes. This method proved problematic when making the transitions from one scene to the next. The principle of montage was the answer to this problem of transition, which could not have been solved otherwise. Montage, in turn, set free a whole range of forms of filmic expression. Without montage, neither the German, nor the Russian, nor the French cinema of the 1920s would have been conceivable. With the introduction of sound, however, film—or rather, commercial film—reverted to the naturalism towards which it had aspired in its early stages. Thus, the addition of sound actually entailed an impoverishment rather than the extraordinary opportunity that it could have been and should be today; this is why Chaplin, in his first sound films, used sound so sparingly, if at all.

As Walter Benjamin has shown, film works on the principle of attention without concentration; the viewer is distracted. This disposition permits film images to move along by association, which involves temporal gaps between shots as well as leaps of logic. The introduction of sound, then, makes it possible to create polyphonic effects which before could only have been deployed successively. François Truffaut, for instance, uses verbal effects like adjectives in conjunction with particular images; other films utilize various registers of sound and thus achieve an epic[3] multiplicity of layers. The current movement in film-making, which can be observed on an international level, points toward an emancipation of film sound, in particular of verbal language. These films make it difficult to determine whether speech is subordinated to action, image to speech, or action to theme, or vice versa. The films as they are elude this kind of hierarchical definition.

Why are such innovations so hard to accomplish in Germany? Why does the emancipation of film encounter such powerful obstacles? A major reason for this is the intellectual indifference of German film productions—they just have not contained an idea in years. Apart from the particular conditions in Germany, however, two other reasons have been important. (1) The pressures of naturalism: Allegedly, audiences who are interested in nothing but "sitting and staring" do not wish to be disturbed by language they have not heard a hundred times before in the media and everyday life. (2) The demand for coherence and superficial continuity makes every film conform to the model of the novella. "Pure entertainment and what it implies," as Adorno and Horkheimer say, "the relaxed abandoning of the self to diverse associations and happy nonsense, is cut short by what is currently marketed as entertainment; it is impeded by the surrogate of a coherent meaning by means of which the culture industry insists on ennobling its products, while actually misusing them admittedly as a pretext for the presentation of stars."[4] This procedure is typical of conventional commercial films, but it can also be found in films produced with artistic intentions. Cinema is hampered in this regard by modelling itself on the genre of the novella, which prevents cinema from developing its epic possibilities. Only in the epic ranges of film, however, could language fully unfold. As far as the construction of plots is concerned, even silent film, with its limited registers, could do better than the multi-level sound film.

III

Let us compare film and literature as modes of expression, choosing two examples at random. Is film capable of condensation? Can film attain the same expressive effects as highly differentiated language? Can film be precise? Helmut Heissenbüttel recently quoted the following sentences from Barbey d'Aurevilly's *The She-Devils* [1874]: "and to all this fury she replied like the female of the species [*Frauenzimmer*], who no longer has any reason to care, who knows the man she lives with down to his bones, and who knows that at the bottom of this pigsty of a common household lies eternal warfare. She was not as coarse as he, but more atrocious, more insulting, and more cruel in her coldness than he was in his anger."[5] With prose of such a high degree of figuration, film cannot compete.

Film cannot form metaphoric concepts [*Oberbegriffe*] (pigsty of a common household, fits of fury) or clichés (the female of the species); it is not capable of antithetical discourse on such a level of abstraction; it can never condense in such a manner; finally, film does not have the means to imitate the internal movement of language—which is what distinguishes this text—unless the filmmaker decides to quote the text. It might be interesting to imagine ways in which the event described could be rendered in filmic terms. This would probably require a short film of about twenty minutes, which could be broken down into the following sequences:

- study of the argument between husband and wife;
- study of irritated, reactive behavior of this woman and of women in general;
- study of marital habits;
- study of the habit of loving someone "down to the bones";
- the helplessness of both in the course of a long marriage, largely on the part of the husband;

- the history of the bourgeois marriage over the past two hundred years;
- the condition of eternal warfare;
- the biological superiority of the woman, her coldness;
- visual analysis of the conflict by means of a montage sequence which alternates, over an extended period of time, between the facial expression of the woman and that of the man, thus conveying the disproportionate and asynchronic nature of their struggle.

This filmic treatment would attempt, with great effort, to destroy the superficial sense of precision which film conveys on account of its excessive visual presence [*Anschauung*]; likewise, one would have to recover the degree of abstraction inherent in language by accumulating details. Only then would a film be capable of achieving any degree of conceptual precision.

As is well known, language has an advantage over film, owing to several thousand years of tradition. Modern Western languages derive from the differentiated languages of antiquity, which in turn are influenced by more archaic languages. If the cinema were to cultivate the narrative forms necessary to cope with the Barbey text over a longer period of history, at a later date a whole range of filmic metaphors would be available to filmmakers, allowing them to achieve the same economy of narration as is now available in the figurative and conceptual ranges of language. Even today we can discern developments in this direction. Louis Malle, for instance, alludes to individual films by Chaplin and thus evokes the aura of Chaplin's oeuvre as a whole. Another instance would be the conventions of a genre like the western, which can be quoted and repeated with figurative brevity. Most of the more recent westerns are animated by allusions to the old clichés of western narratives. The stagecoach, the entry into the saloon, the beginning of the showdown, the new sheriff, the almost masochistic position of the drunk judge, the iconography of the western hero, and the code of honor that binds all participants—through all these elements the accumulated aura of the genre is present in each individual western. This opens up a space for ambiguity, polyphony, and variation, which, as is well known, has often made the western a vehicle for political, social, and psychoanalytic messages; it might just as well encourage poetic modes of expression. Only when the cinema will have sufficiently enlarged its tradition of figuration will it be able to develop abstractions and differentiations comparable to those of literature. Because it already includes language anyway, film would actually have the capacity to articulate meanings that elude the grasp of verbal expression. Contemporary cinema, however, is not prepared for this project, since neither film production nor the spectator has as yet realized film's verbal and visual possibilities. The cinema, as we see it at this point, is not merely in the hands of the film authors (just as literature is not the product of writers alone), but is a form of expression which depends as much upon the receptivity of a social formation as on the imagination of its authors. A truly sophisticated film language requires a high level of filmic imagination on the part of spectators, exhibitors, and distributors alike.

Such a project, however, meets with almost total opposition from the cultural establishment, which regards the contamination of human minds by filmic images as a disastrous development. Instead, there is a tendency to impose upon the cinema the aesthetic ideals of the classical arts (which, in this context, could be said to include still photography). This creates a kind of visual "culture" which, in effect, robs film of its specific means of expression. The misleading ideal of the priority of image over word derives from a contemplative, purist position whose proponents dismiss filmic expression or content as merely secondary, a position that ultimately results in formalism. A cinema split between, on the one hand, the formalism of experimental film (whose experiments do not seek any new experience but rather aim to perpetuate a metaphysical "state of transition") and, on the other, the superficial naturalism of narrative film will never be able to compete with the great tradition of literary language.

Would a twenty-minute adaptation of the two sentences by Barbey have a substantially different, or even more complex, meaning than those two sentences? The film would have to use language, over and above the image track. Language in this case would not be literature, but an integrated part of the film. Compared to the literary source, the film would probably fall short of the precision achieved there; in terms of visual detail, however, it would be superior to the written text. At first sight, this would produce an effect similar to that which would have been produced if Marcel Proust had used the Barbey text to satisfy his own narrative proclivities for fifty to three hundred pages. The film would still remain on the side of visual presence. Yet the analytic capability of the camera might afford additional perspectives on the subject matter which would go beyond subjective experience. Thus we would have an accumulation of subjective and objective, of literary, auditory, and visual moments which would preserve a certain tension in relation to each other. This tension would make itself felt, among other places, in the gaps which montage created between the disparate elements of filmic expression. In layering expressive forms in such a manner, the film would succeed in concentrating its subject matter in the spaces between the forms of expression. For the material condensation of expression does not happen in the film itself but in the spectator's head, in the gaps between the elements of filmic expression. This kind of film does not posit a passive viewer "who just wants to sit and stare." Obviously such a conception of cinema remains a utopian project, given the limited ambitions of both film producers and audiences today; in the future, however, cinema could surpass even the tradition of literature, at least in certain aspects. The combination of verbal, auditory, and visual forms and their integration through montage enable film to strive for a greater degree of complexity than any of these forms in isolation. At the same time, the multiplication of materials harbors all the dangers of the *Gesamtkunstwerk* [total work of art].[6]

The relatively greater precision available to literary language is not merely a blessing. Centuries of tradition have endowed language with such polish and refinement that it has become immune to large areas of reality. Every expression, according to Kant, oscillates between concept [*Begriff*] and sensuous perception [*Anschauung*]. "Perception without concept is blind; concept without perception remains empty." Throughout most of its metaphors and expressions, language has settled into a compromise between these two poles; it is neither concrete nor really abstract. Film, by contrast, combines the radical concreteness of its materials with the conceptual possibilities of montage; thus it offers a form of expression which is as capable of a dialectical relationship between concept and perception as is verbal language without, however, stabilizing this relationship, as language is bound to do. This opens up particular opportunities for the insertion of literary language into film, especially because it might help rid that language of some of its literary constraints.

Let us raise the question from the reverse angle. Is film capable of controlling its degree of precision? Can film refract or deconstruct [*auflösen*] a given expression? How can it maintain a sufficient degree of indeterminacy? Does film have the option of remaining imprecise? Literary language can easily do so by using a conventional expression as a stylistic device. "When the secretary opened the door, a young lady, pretty as a picture and dressed to tease, entered the room"—such a phrase could not be reproduced in filmic terms. Film does not grant the variety of impressions that words like *pretty as a picture* and *dressed to tease* or *young lady* may provoke in the imagination of different readers; the image always refers to an individual instance. This could be counteracted somewhat by devices such as an extreme long shot or close-up, both of which introduce a high degree of indeterminacy. Likewise, iconic information can be reduced by means of shallow focus, high contrast, shots of extreme brevity or duration, transgressions of chronological order, multiple exposure, negation of the image track through sound or written text. All these, and other devices that one might use to achieve the effect of indeterminacy, are devices that interfere with reality and that question the apparent concreteness of iconic information. If a film were to give its viewers conceptual instructions as they are implied in phrases like *dressed to tease*, for instance, or *pretty as a picture*, it would have to resort to concrete clichés—which is what Hollywood films tend to do. We conclude, therefore, that film, insofar as it uses its resources legitimately, cannot convey any really precise mental images.

We cannot ignore the fact that producers of commercial films, like those of dime novels, have no intention whatsoever of disturbing the massive circulation of their products by anything that resembles precise description. The empty shells of literary commonplaces, such as abound in bad novels, are ideally suited for deploying narrative clichés. In the course of its history, conservative narrative cinema has succeeded in amalgamating the prefabricated forms of imagination with prefabricated vernacular language, so that people have come to expect this amalgam from any narrative film. If the pretty young lady above actually were to appear in a film, this event would be read in a way similar to its literary equivalent. Nonetheless, commercial cinema has to keep reestablishing the basis of these conventions. While literary commonplaces may have a certain degree of legitimacy, since they appeal to something in the reader's imagination which is not yet totally absorbed by cliché, and while such commonplaces may even be stylistically necessary, as for instance in Madame de Lafayette's *Princess of Clève* or in Brecht's plays, film inevitably distorts reality when it typifies. For film allows inference from the concrete only in the direction of a cliché; yet it is incapable of creating a general image of concrete multiplicity. The question remains whether or not individual films can avoid this dilemma through particular uses of language, for instance by speaking about things on the sound track which will not appear on the image track.

IV

There are no rules for combining word and image in film. We can roughly distinguish between modes of dialogue, modes of commentary, and more independent combinations of word and image.

Dialogue

Narrative cinema promotes the fictitious ideal of realistic dialogue. This type of dialogue is supposed to accompany the image track in a "natural" manner. Dialogue is motivated by narrative action, or all too often substitutes for action. Such is the case not only in commercial films, but also in films that simply adopt stage conventions to the screen, for example, *Twelve Angry Men* [1957; directed by Sidney Lumet, based on a play by Reginald Rose], *Les jeux sont faits* [1947; directed by Jean Delannoy, based on a play by Sartre], *The Time of Your Life* [1948; directed by H. C. Potter, based on a play by William Saroyan]. In either case, both language and the image track are subject to the regime of narrative. Such a concept of dialogue hinges on the belief that narrative events relate to each other as an organic whole, that drama is still possible. Take a film like *Password: Heron* [*Kennwort: Reiher*, Rudolf Jugert, 1964], recently awarded the Federal Film Prize; consider, for instance, the moment at which the characters note, via dialogue, that they "have been waiting here for hours." Immediately following the accidental killing of a patriot, a man emerges from a completely different chain of dramatic events and happens to identify the dead "comrade," whom he had not seen in twenty years, and thus the enigma gets resolved. The entanglement comes about, in the first place, because the hero stumbles into the very center of the French Resistance, led by an old man who, on the basis of a parallel chain of events dating back to World War I, is bound to misunderstand the hero. If measured against a strictly realistic standard, such dramaturgy (unlike that of Ibsen, who first invented this kind of dramaturgical incest) would collapse. At the same time, such films are defined by a grotesque effort to make the illusion appear realistic. Realism in this sense extends only to the detail; the film as a whole remains in the realm of fiction. It is a realism without enlightenment, a realism intended to cover up the fact that once more we have been cheated out of reality.

It has become apparent that, as a rule of thumb, dialogue is not a suitable means for advancing action. Moreover, dialogue is a specialized branch of film production, which is to say that the texts are written by specialists as mere supplements to the image track. As we see in the work of Antonioni, however, the function of dialogue can just as well be taken over by the image track, while spoken dialogue is carried along like a shell or fossil. Spoken dialogue in this case does not tell us anything about the actual inner movements of the film; dialogue loses its function as dialogue. "We have replaced dialogue with the communiqué," as Camus says. One might add that, precisely because it no longer serves any narrative purpose, dialogue is now available as a medium of reflection. When the prostitutes in Jean-Luc Godard's *Vivre sa vie* [1962] quote Montaigne, when Zazie and the other characters in Louis Malle's film *Zazie dans le métro* [1960] spout argot, their speech no longer has anything to do with Ionesco or Samuel Beckett; on the contrary, moments like these, when dialogue is actually not needed, allow for the development of specifically cinematic forms of expression. Godard and other film authors realize this opportunity when they apply to dialogue the same principles of montage as to the image track.

Voice-Over Commentary

Voice-over commentary is usually reserved for documentary film. It has the reputation of being "uncinematic," not only because it seems to be tied to a particular subject matter, but also because it assumes a certain autonomy in coordinating text and image and because it is often merely superimposed over live sound. There seems to be a general injunction against using voice-over in a way that would merely duplicate the events on the image track. This injunction presumes that commentary and a sequence of images are identical if they refer to one and the same thing; as a rule, however, this is not the case. A documentary on industrial work processes, for instance, shows a worker taking a scoop of liquid metal from one container and pouring it into another; voice-over: "The worker removes a small amount of liquid alloy for testing purposes to ensure a consistent quality in the final product." Or, in another film, the voice-over explains: "The extract can be obtained from the abdominal cavity of the dead mouse without difficulty"; the image shows a dead animal laid out on a red surface and rubber-gloved hands manipulating a syringe in its belly.[7] In both instances, the image would remain illegible without the voice-over, and it would take a considerable amount of demonstration to produce the same meaning.

Voice-over commentary is not limited to documentary film; it may also be used in fictional genres—as, indeed, it has been—with interesting effects. Narrative events tend to come across in different ways depending on whether they are enacted on the image track or narrated by a voice-over. A double-track description may stylize an event and produce a mutual distancing effect [*Verfremdungseffekt*], as it calls attention to the material difference of verbal and visual expression. The voice-over in this case may be identifiable as that of a particular character within the diegesis—and thus associated with a particular narrative function—or the voice could be altogether foreign to the narrative.

A special case in this context is the insertion of written titles. This practice has a tradition of its own dating back to the silent era. Whereas at that time written titles were the only way of confronting image and language, their special effect today is one of muteness. The result is an overlay of filmic events with the inner voice of the reading spectator—the spectator has to assume a more active role. The language of written titles, which does not assume any particular voice and thus cannot really be attached to characters within the diegesis, is even further removed from the filmic events than any conceivable form of voice-over. This greater distance, however, gives it an affinity with literary language. The increased participation of the spectator, in turn, creates a peculiar identification of the meaning of this language with the visually concretized events of the film (a recent impressive example in this respect is Godard's *Vivre sa vie*). Written language may enter a film in a variety of shapes and combinations: e.g., text superimposed upon moving images, inserts of written text, or text superimposed upon background images [*Stehkader*]. Writing may even push images aside completely; whole passages of film could consist of writing; written and spoken texts could be interwoven in many different ways.

Language at Liberty

Under this rubric, we are dealing with language that, detached from narrative events, accompanies and colors the image track, language that is not motivated by any subjective or objective point of view as is the case with dialogue or commentary. Examples of such use of language can be found in *Hiroshima mon amour* [1959] by Marguerite Duras and Alain Resnais, in *The Parallel Street* [*Parallelstrasse*, 1961] by Ferdinand Khittl, in *Moderato cantabile* by Peter Brook [1960; text by Duras], and in other films. Its mode may be recitation, poetic mediation, or "nonsense language," as in *Zazie*. In the cinema, words may be used more freely than in their usual syntactic or grammatical configurations. Film permits the disruption of the linear sequence of scenes, as well as of individual shots. In the field of literature, an author like Hans G. Helms tries to liberate language from the conventions of grammar and existing vocabulary. Nonetheless, his writing depends upon elements of literary language. If he abandoned even those tenuous semantic links, he would lose the last means of conveying expression, an objective to which even a writer like Helms is still committed. We could imagine, however, an experimental film (albeit one of extreme artistic intensity) which forcefully utilizes the oscillation between literary, visual, and auditory elements as well as the gaps between these elements; such a film might succeed in producing clusters of expression which are not required to yield meaning down to the last detail, which can be understood without having to be prefabricated or historically reconstructed. In a world in which everyone else conforms to rational reason, someone at least could be unreasonable. Since the totalizing quest for meaning has itself become irrational, literary language should be shifted to areas in which it is not totally subjected to the imperative of meaning, as it is in its proper field. Language in film may be blind.

V

We have been speaking of possibilities; let us now focus on actual instances and develop some criteria for the combination of language and film.

(1) Michelangelo Antonioni, *L'Avventura* (1959), scene 3

Text:

SANDRO: Would you like me in profile?
SANDRO: What is it? Is something wrong with me?
SANDRO: But your friend is waiting for you downstairs.
ANNA: She'll wait.

Image:

Sandro's apartment: a small room with white stucco walls, crowded with books and draftsman's materials. He moves across the room quickly, straightening his things.

He puts a towel in the bathroom. Anna runs up the stairs leading to the room and they embrace as she reaches the top. They part, and she stares at him intently. Walking to the center of the room, she turns around to stare at him again; then she turns away, drops her bag on a table, and goes to the balcony window. Sandro advances uncertainly to the center of the room and Anna stares again, appraising him with her eyes, judging.

Sandro faces her, somewhat baffled by her silence and the intensity of her regard.

He puts his suitcase down and strikes a pose of mock nobility, turning sideways.

Anna circles him slowly and silently, then begins to unbutton her dress, looking back at him to see his reaction.

She walks toward the bedroom; he follows.

Anna enters the bedroom, and through the, grillwork of the bedstead, we see her remove her dress. Sandro walks in and, finding her in her slip, takes her in his arms and kisses her.

Anna presses herself up against him with such a violent passion that Sandro is somewhat dismayed. But only for an instant. Soon they are feverishly kissing each other, and it is almost with a sense of sheer animal pleasure that Sandro abandons himself.[8]

Commentary: What actually goes on between the two characters takes place on the image track. Detached from the image track, the text would not make sense. It does not consist of ordinary, "natural" speech, but a highly stylized form of language. This is even more evident at other points in the script. The difference between the inner movement of the filmic image and the movement of the dialogue paradoxically makes us aware of the sound of language. This device can also be found in films by Roman Polanski and Louis Malle.

(2) Alain Resnais, Marguerite Duras, *Hiroshima mon amour* (1959)

Image and Text:

(*The streets of Hiroshima, more streets. Bridges. covered lanes. Streets. Suburbs. Railroad tracks. Suburbs. Universal banality.*)

SHE: ... I meet you.
     I remember you.
     Who are you?
     You kill me.

You feel good to me.
How could I have known that this city was made to the size of
    love?
How could I have known that you were made to the size of my
    body?
I like you. How great. I like you.
What slowness all of a sudden.
What softness.
More than you can know. You kill me.
You feel good to me.
You kill me.
You feel good to me.
I've got the time.
Devour me.
Deform me, make me ugly.
Why not you?
Why not you in this city and in this night so much like the
    others you can't tell the difference?
Please ...

(*Very abruptly the woman's face appears, filled with tenderness.
turned toward the man's.*)

SHE: It's extraordinary how beautiful your skin is.

(*He sighs.*)
    You ...

(*His face appears after the woman's. He bursts out into an ecstatic
laughter that has nothing to do with their words.*)[9]

Commentary: Here we have a pure instance of parallelism
between image and literary text. The image track does not settle on any
particular scene; Instead, moving shots of bridges and streets dissolve
into each other and form a kind of impressionist tableau. This tableau
effect also emanates from the sound track. The visual texture colors the
language; the spoken text modifies the meaning of the image track.
Both resonate with associations of Hiroshima/Nevers—love, death, and
so on. The method of composition is basically the same as in music by
Richard Wagner or Richard Strauss. The film here taps emotional connotations which exist in the social imaginary, in the spectator's head,
rather than in the film itself. Without this point of reference, images
and words would disintegrate, as would the Duras text, with its abrupt
changes of mood. The immersion of language in image, the emergence
of language from image, the mutual pursuit of verbal and visual texts,
figures of parallelism and collision, polyphony—all these word/image
constellations can be found in this work and in Resnais's other films as

well. Even if one resents the pathos of the texts, one has to acknowledge Resnais's originality.

(3) Ferdinand Khittl, *The Parallel Street* (1961)

Image Track:

A title card with the number 305. Documentary footage of Tahiti, an island in the Pacific: shots of a fishing expedition, of a girl named Roarai, of whaling, of a seaplane starting and landing in the laguna between a coral reef and the beach. Then a series of shots from the burial site "at the big rock" near the capital of Madagaskar, Tananarive: the ceremony of Famadhina, the so-called turning of the dead. A body that has been dead for three years is disinterred and given a new shroud, a "lamba." The corpse remains laid out for twenty-four hours, surrounded by dancing and celebrations; then it is returned to the burial chamber.

Sound Track:

"The plane is due at eight. If you have ever been in love, you know that the plane can come at any time. That it always comes at eight. The farewell without meaning recalls the spot behind the ear. The arc below the knee. To arrive only to say good-bye. Having never before thought of the warmth of this hair.

"Everyone listens to the dying odor of the old fish. The airplane comes at eight. Try not to think of it: the heart has already given up. A forgotten caress—your skin. A boat without wings, its sails smelling of hibiscus flowers. *la ora na*—welcome."[10]

Commentary: The text in this case confronts a rather stark, naive image track. The author of the images and the writer are two different individuals who evidently did not succeed in integrating their respective intentions. The image track diverts attention to some degree from the bombastic quality of the text; but as a result, image and text move along in a rather disconnected manner. The effect at first is one of surprise, owing to the juxtaposition of unrelated elements; also, the fixed speed of the film tends to impair our literary judgment in a way that does not hold in the case of reading a written text. Such surprise tactics, however, will not produce a cinematic integration of word and image. The words spill over the margins of the image. A film does not acquire a poetic quality through words alone. Nonetheless, *The Parallel Street* enjoyed a considerable success at various festivals, in particular with the leading French reviewers at Cannes in 1964. This once again confirms the impression that if one arbitrarily accumulates interesting ingredients and adds some sort of text, one ends up with an arbitrary product that may still reap success, since "he who gives generously, offers something to everyone."

(4) Orson Welles, *Citizen Kane* (1941): a sequence from the "News on the March" section

Text and Image:

Its humble beginnings, in this ramshackle building, a dying daily.	Street. Truck passing to left exits, showing old Inquirer Building in background— three colored men standing at left by window—one skates across to right ...
Kane's empire, in its glory, held dominion over thirty-seven newspapers, two syndicates, a radio network, an empire upon an empire.	Picture of map of U.S. Circles widening out on map.
The first of grocery stores ...	Building. Camera shooting across street to Kane grocery store—convertible car passing in foreground.
... paper mills ...	Mill. Huge roll of paper moving up to foreground.
... apartment buildings ...	Street. Camera shooting up over trees to row of apartments at right background.
... factories ...	Factory. Camera shooting over smokestacks of a factory, steam pouring out of them.
... forests ...	Lake. Man in foreground— tree crashing into lake below in background.
... ocean liners.	Ocean. Camera shooting down to liner moving to foreground below.[11]

Commentary: This is an example of voice-over used in a fictional context. Of course, *Citizen Kane* also uses dialogue that differs little from conventional dramatic dialogue and obviously is not crucial to the textual and stylistic principles of the film. The voice-over commentary in this sequence more or less describes what we see on the image track. One could say that the image illustrates the text just as the text illustrates the image. When the voice-over speaks of "forests," the image track uses the rhetorical device of *pars pro toto* and shows a tree. When the text concerns the perspective of a whole continent through a long shot so extreme as to suggest that the continent could not be captured in a single image, the voice-over implies this extensity by way of enumeration. When connotations of "humble" and "ramshackle" dominate the commentary, three black people can be seen in one of the lower windows of the building. The mutual energizing of text and image is rather schematic, but at the same time incredibly robust. *Citizen Kane* is the kind of film in which neither sound nor image track, in itself, has much artistic distinction, although together they constitute a work of art.

It would be interesting to explore further examples of the interaction of word and film, especially in the large realm of commercial film. The current use of language in film is likely to come across as highly dilettante. Often an especially badly written text serves to underscore the common remark, "the camera work was excellent." On the map of the arts, film has always been placed next to photography. As a thorough inquiry into the history of cinematic forms would probably show, film has a much greater affinity with literature than with photography.

VI

Cinema depends upon language not only within each film but also through all the stages of preparation and planning. Without highly differentiated skills of articulation, no filmmaker can approach the realization of his ideas. Author, cinematographer, and producer need to communicate with each other, a task for which the prevailing jargon of the industry is crudely inadequate. The unnecessary hierarchy that determines the production process of special features is just one aspect of this lack of verbal differentiation; another is the "speechlessness" which characterizes the studio sound of the ordinary commercial film. The organizational structure of film production in Germany only aggravates these problems; but these problems are not intrinsic to filmmaking, nor is the prevailing organization of production unalterable. According to a well-known nineteenth-century German thinker and political economist, all thought is mediated by language. Unlike the classical arts (and even television, which actually employs a considerable number of intellectuals), cinema has to compensate for a lack of tradition. Therefore, cinema is in a situation different from that of the classical arts, whose very purpose is to escape tradition. German cinema would benefit greatly from intellectual centers, which would have to be established independently from the commercial centers of production so as to exert influence upon the latter. Such intellectual centers, however, should above all foster an awareness of the immense lead that literary language still has over the expressive means of the mass media.

Cinema today stands at the crossroads of an important development. On the one hand, we can already envision a complexity of expression that film could achieve and the kind of intellectual institution that would encourage such complexity; on the other hand, we can just as well imagine an institutionalization of filmmaking that would merely canonize the inferior products of the status quo and make film into a specialized branch of the mass media, thus perpetuating the current ratio of ten percent specials to ninety percent regular commercial features. Such films cheat not only the loyal patrons in whose name they pretend to be made, but also those who produce them, not to mention those who expect to see a work of art. It would be better if academies designed to teach that kind of filmmaking did not exist at all. The worst that could happen to film would be to be banished to its own domain.

Notes

1. Authors quoted in the original German version of this text are Walter Hagemann, *Der Film, Wesen und Gestalt*, Heidelberg, 1952; Curt Hanno Gutbrod, *Von der Filmidee zum Drehbuch: Handbach für Autoren*, Wilhelmshaven, 1954; Béla Balázs, *Der Film: Werden und Wesen einer neuen Kunst*, Vienna, 1961; N. A. Lebedew, *Literatur und Film*, Leipzig, 1954; Fedor Stepun, *Theater und Film*, Munich, 1953; Feldmann, Goergen, Keilhacker, Peters, *Beiträge zur Filmforschung*, Emsdetten, 1961; and Rudolf Arnheim, *Film als Kunst*, Berlin, 1932.—TRANS.

2. Hagemann, *Der Film, Wesen und Gestalt*, pp. 46ff.

3. In addition to its conventional meaning, the term *epic* here invokes the particular connotations of Brecht's concept of epic theater.—TRANS.

4. Max Horkheimer and Theodor W. Adorno, *Dialectic of Enlightenment*, Amsterdam, Querido, 1947, p. 169; translated from the German original.

5. Jules Amédée Barbey d'Aurevilly, "A un dîner d'athées," in *Les diaboliques: les six premières*, Paris, Editions Garnier Frères, 1963, p. 288; translated from both the original and the German version cited in the text.

6. Implied here is a critique of the *Gesamtkunstwerk* as developed in the context of the Frankfurt School. This critique focuses on the ideological trajectory linking Wagner's aesthetics with the total mobilization of effect in both the capitalist culture industry and fascist mass spectacles; cf. Walter Benjamin's epilogue to "The Work of Art in the Age of Mechanical Reproduction" in *Illuminations*, New York. Shocken, 1969, Theodor W. Adorno, *In Search of Wagner* (1937–38), London, New Left Books, 1981, and the chapter on the culture industry in *Dialectic of Enlightenment*, New York, Seabury, 1972.—TRANS.

7. These examples are taken at random from a medical and an industrial documentary. They may sound idiotic, but they highlight the interaction between commentary and images which go beyond mere illustration.

8. Michelangelo Antonioni, *L'Avventura*, New York; Grove; 1969, pp. 15–16; and *Screenplays of Michelangelo Antonioni*, New York, Orion Press, 1963, pp. 99–100.

9. Marguerite Duras and Alain Resnais, *Hiroshima mon amour*, New York, Grove, 1961, pp. 24–25. Translation slightly emended.—Ed.

10. Ferdinand Khittl, *Parallelstrasse*, script in *Spectaculum: Texte moderner Filme*, Frankfurt, Suhrkamp, 1961, pp. 346–47.

11. Pauline Kael et al., *The Citizen Kane Book*, New York, Bantam, 1974, pp. 317–18.

Questions and Projects

- Choose a single film or sequence from a film (perhaps Jane Campion's *Portrait of a Lady* [1996]) that employs one or more literary uses of language (voice-over, dialogue, poetic background descriptions) and analyze how the images and those languages interact to communicate meanings that may be different from what language or images could achieve on their own.

- Are there modern or contemporary films—by, for instance, Jean-Luc Godard, Peter Greenaway, Sally Potter, or by Kluge himself—that answer Kluge's challenge to create a dynamic interaction between its literary components and its filmic ones? What are the specific complications in interpreting these films as they set literary language and structures against cinematic forms? And do they inevitably move in the social and political directions that Kluge urges?

10

CURRENT PERSPECTIVES
AND METHODS

The readings in this chapter, as in the previous chapter, introduce arguments that are sometimes aimed at individual movies and sometimes move to more general points about the interaction between film and literature. Besides the insights they may offer or the polemics they may provoke, these selections represent some of the prominent contemporary approaches to films and to film and literature.

The different styles and strategies of acting have always been a major ingredient in adaptations and distinctions between film and literature. The following excerpt from Braudy's 1976 book introduces that often overlooked dimension in the differences between film and literature: namely, what distinguishes the portrayal of characters in drama and film. Braudy's analysis has a useful historical overview, which places the question in the context of theatrical acting from Aristotle and Shakespeare through the increasingly naturalistic acting of the nineteenth century. The heart of this piece traces the dominant acting styles in theater and film through the twentieth century, making crucial distinctions about how the two forms make available different meanings for characters.

"Acting: Stage vs. Screen"
from *The World in a Frame*
Leo Braudy

Acting in Europe and America has been historically defined by the varying interplay of the heightened and the normal, the theatrical and the nonchalant, in the conception of the role. Until the Renaissance, there was little attempt to place any special value on the absorption of the rhythm, themes, and gestures of everyday life into drama or acting style. Aristotle had taught that the most intense feelings possible in drama were those in tragedy, when the characters and the acting style were on a much higher plane than the normal life of the audience. Everyday life, where the characters and the way they behave tend to be on the same or lower social levels than the audience, was primarily a source of stylized comedy. The stage was raised above the audience in part because the characters and their impersonators were not to be considered as individually as the audience might assess each other. In Greek, Roman, and medieval society, actors therefore tended to portray beings purer than the audience, the somber figures of myth and the caricatures of comedy—a division of acting labor not unlike that of the silent screen.

Shakespeare helped make an enormous change in this rotation between the audience and the actors by elaborating the analogies possible between the world and the stage. He began the European theater's effort to absorb and reflect the life of the audience as much as to bring the audience out of itself into another world. Comedy could therefore become more serious because it was no longer necessary to involve emotions lower than the grand style of tragedy. More intimate theaters and better lighting permitted a more nuanced acting style. By the mid-eighteenth century David Garrick had become the first to attempt historical authenticity in costuming, once again asserting the need to ground the play and the style of acting in some possible and plausible setting rather than a special world of theater. The "fourth wall" theories of the latter nineteenth century further defined theatrical space and dramatic acting as an extension of the world of the audience. Stylized acting did not disappear, of course. The broader styles remained in opera, ballet, and popular comedy, as well as revivals of classics, symbolic and proletarian drama, and the experiments with ritual theater from the end of World War Two to the present.

Acting on stage had necessarily developed a tradition of naturalness as well. In the eighteenth century Diderot had argued that the paradox of acting is that an actor must be cold and tranquil in order to project emotion. Actors who play from the soul, he said, are mediocre and uneven. We are not moved by the man of violence, but by the man who possesses himself. In the early twentieth century, Konstantin Stanislavsky turned Diderot's view of the actor self-possessed in passion into a whole style. He rejected theories of acting based on imitation and emphasized instead an actor's inner life as the source of energy and authenticity for his characterizations. More "mechanical" and expressionist styles of stage acting implicitly attacked Stanislavsky's methods by their emphasis on the intensity of emotion and the visual coherence of the stage ensemble. Minglings of the two traditions produced such hybrids as the Group

Theater, in which the interplay between ensemble and individual produced a thematic tension often missing from Eisenstein's productions, whether on stage or in film. Elia Kazan's film style, for example, with its mixture of expressionistic, closed directorial style and open, naturalistic acting, is a direct descendant of this tradition.*

Our ability to learn what films can tell us about human character has suffered not only from preconceptions derived from the novel of psychological realism, but also from assumptions about acting that are drawn from the stage. We know much better what our attitude should be toward characters in fiction and drama. Unlike those forms, films emphasize acting and character, often at the expense of forms and language. Films add what is impossible in the group situation of the stage or the omniscient world of the novel: a sense of the mystery inside character, the strange core of connection with the face and body the audience comes to know so well, the sense of an individuality that can never be totally expressed in words or action. The stage cannot have this effect because the audience is constantly aware of the actor's impersonation. Character in film generally is more like character as we perceive it everyday than it is in any other representational art. The heightened style of silent film acting could be considered an extension of stage acting, but the more personal style allowed by sound film paradoxically both increased the appeal of films and lowered their intellectual status. The artistic was the timeless, Garbo not Dietrich, Valentino not Gable.

But character in sound film especially was not so much deficient as it was elusive. Films can be less didactic about character because the film frame is less confining than the fictional narrative or the theatrical proscenium. Sound films especially can explore the tension between the "real person" playing the role and the image projected on the screen. The line between film actor and part is much more difficult to draw than that between stage actor and role, and the social dimension of "role" contrasts appropriately with the personal dimension of "part." Film acting is less impersonation than personation, part of personality but not identifiable with it. "Can Ingrid Bergman commit murder?" ask the advertisements for *Murder on the Orient Express* (Sidney Lumet, 1975); the casual substitution of actress for character crudely makes an assertion that better films explore more subtly. Unlike the stage actor, the film actor cannot get over the footlights. Although this technical necessity may seem to make him less "real" than the stage actor, it makes his relation to the character he plays much more real. Audiences demand to hear more about the private life of the film actor than the stage actor because film

---

*Diderot's *Paradoxe sur le comédien* was not published until 1830, although it was written in the late 1760s. A later printing in 1902 may have had an influence on Stanislavsky's theories.

creates character by tantalizing the audience with the promise of the secret self, always just out of the grasp of final articulation and meaning. The other life of a stage character is the real life of the person who plays him. But the other life of a film character is the continuity in other films of the career of the actor who plays him. In plays the unrevealed self tends to be a reduced, meaner version of the displayed self; in films it is almost always a complex enhancement. Within the film a character may have a limited meaning. But the actor who plays him can potentially be a presence larger than that one part, at once more intimate and more distant than is ever possible on stage.*

Film preserves a performance that is superior to the script, whereas stage performances and plays are separate realities, with the performance often considered second best. The stage actor is performing a role: he may be the best, one of the best, the only, or one of many to play that role. But the role and its potentials will exist long after he has ceased to play it, to be interested in it, to be alive. The film actor does not so much perform a role as he creates a kind of life, playing between his characterization in a particular film and his potential escape from that character, outside the film and perhaps into other films. The stage actor memorizes an entire role in proper order, putting it on like a costume, while the film actor learns his part in pieces, often out of chronological order, using his personality as a kind of armature, or as painters will let canvas show through to become part of the total effect. If the movie is remade and another actor plays the part, there is little sense of the competition between actors that characterizes revivals on stage. "Revival" is a stage word and "remake" is a film word. Hamlet remains beyond Booth's or Olivier's or Gielgud's performance, but Alan Ladd as Gatsby and Robert Redford as Gatsby exist in different worlds.

Filmmaking is a discontinuous process, in which the order of filming is influenced more by economics than by aesthetics. Film actors must therefore either have stronger personalities than stage actors or draw upon the resources of personality much more than stage actors do. Strong film actors can never do anything out of character. Their presence defines their character and the audience is always ready for them to reveal more. Even though studio heads like Louis Mayer forced actors and actresses to appear "in character" offscreen as well, we sense and accept potential and variety from the greatest movie actors, while we may reject less flamboyant fictional characters as "unreal" or refer to the woodenness of stage characterization. Continuity in stage acting is thematic continuity:

---

*In these remarks and in most of the section to follow, I am obviously talking not so much about the craft of acting as about the effects of acting on the audience. I would hope, however, that what I say has implications for craft and method as well, at least in terms of a test of effectiveness beyond the pleasures of theory.

"Watch in happiness someone whom you will soon see in sorrow" is one of the fatalistic possibilities. But the discontinuities of film acting allow the actor to concentrate on every moment as if it were the only reality that existed. No matter how conventionalized the plot, the film actor can disregard its clichés and trust instead to the force and continuity of his projected personality to satisfy beyond the more obvious forms of theme and incident. Because he must present his play in straightforward time, a stage director will work with the actor to get a "line" or a "concept" of the character that will permeate every scene. But movie acting, bound in time to the shooting schedule and the editing table, must use what is left out as well as what is expressed. The greatest difference between a film and a stage version of the same work is less in the "opening" of space that films usually emphasize than in the different sense of the inner life of the characters we get.

Going to the theater is a social occasion in a way that going to films is not. Stage characters always exist in a society, and the great plays are almost all plays about the problems of living within a social context. Any bad film brings the audience more directly in touch with human presence than the actually present human beings of the stage because on stage there is so much emphasis on the correct filling of the role, parallel to the correct filling of the social role. The Shakespearean metaphor of the world as a stage expresses the new Renaissance awareness of self-presentation as a process of social interaction in which one defined oneself by social roles, the ones rejected as much as the ones accepted. On the stage we appreciate character generally as part of an ensemble of actors or in brief individual moments, and our understanding of those characters comes from our understanding of the relations between characters— how the stage looks—much more than from the revelations of an inner life. Olivier's *Hamlet* (1948), for example, with its Oedipal interpretation, is less forceful than the play because Hamlet's secrets are not the problems of interpretation—what's really stopping him?—but problems of decision *in front of other people*. Plays, and therefore theatrical acting, emphasize acting out, being seen, being overheard, or being spied upon. A common theme of all drama from the Renaissance on is the problem of honor, fame, and reputation—in short, all the ways in which the individual is known socially. But this theme appears only rarely in films. In its place is the problem of personal identity: who is Charles Foster Kane? who is Charlie Kohler? When a film is set in the context of a mannered society (like *The Awful Truth*, Leo McCarey, 1937, or *Blume in Love*, Paul Mazursky, 1972), the question of the film involves the benevolent discovery of the "real" nature of the characters, not the satiric exposure of that real nature, which would be the theatrical way of organizing the action. The faults of hypocrisy and insincerity—two other traditional themes of drama—also appear very rarely in films. The hypocrite on stage, or the audience's awareness of a character who says one thing and does another, becomes in films the character who deceives himself as well. In films, the theatrical emphasis on the importance of the role is replaced by the authenticity of feelings, the preserved human being with whom we have come into contact. Film acting expands the ability of art to explore the varieties of the intimate self, apart from social awareness, outside of ceremonial or semi-ceremonial occasions, with a few others or even alone.

Movies therefore stand between the strongly social emphasis of theater and the strongly individual emphasis of novels, incorporating elements of both. At a play we are always outside the group, at the footlights. But at a film we move between inside and outside, individual and social perspectives. Movie acting can therefore include stage acting better than stage acting can include movie acting. George C. Scott, for example, is essentially a stage actor who also can come across very well in films. When he was making *Patton* (Franklin Schaffner, 1970), he insisted that he repeat his entire first speech eight times to allow for the different camera angles; he refused to repeat only the sections that corresponded to the rephotographing. His sense of the character was therefore what I have been describing as a stage sense of character, in which the continuity is linear and spelled out. The performance is excellent and effective, but Scott's way of doing it tells us nothing of the differences in stage and film acting. It may have a touch of the New York stage actor's almost traditional hostility to films. At best, it is only another example of the way a newer art can more comfortably embrace the methods of an older art than the other way around. In fact, virtuosity in films tends to be a characteristic of second leads or medium minor characters, not stars, and the Academy Awards perpetuate the stage-derived standards by giving so many awards to actors and actresses cast against type, that is, for stage-style "virtuosity."

The film actor emphasizes display, while the stage actor explores disguise. But stage acting is still popularly considered to be superior to film acting. An actor who does a good job disappears into his role, while the bad (read "film") actor is only playing himself. The true actor, the professional craftsman, may use his own experience to strengthen his interpretation. But the audience should always feel that he has properly distanced and understood that experience; it is another tool in his professional workchest. The false actor, the amateur actor, the film actor, on the other hand, works on his self-image, carries it from part to part, constantly projecting the same thing—"himself." Such a belief is rooted in an accurate perception; but it is a false interpretation of that perception. The stage actor does project a sense of holding back, of discipline and understanding, the influence of head over feelings, while the film actor projects effortlessness, nonchalance, immediacy, the seemingly unpremeditated response. Thus, when stage actors attack film actors, they attack in some puritanical way the lack of perceptible hard work, obvious professional craft, in the film actor's performance. Like many nonprofessionals in their audience, such stage actors assume that naïveté, spontaneity, "being yourself," are self-images that anyone in front of a camera can achieve. A frequent Actors Studio exercise, for example, is "Private Moment," in which the student is asked to act out before the group something he or she ordinarily does alone that would be very embarrassing if someone happened to see. Private self-indulgences and private games are thereby mined for their exposable, group potential. But the concentration of film, its ability to isolate the individual, makes every moment that way, and so the problem of the film actor may be to scale down intimacy rather than discover and exaggerate it.

How do we know the "themselves" film actors play except through the residue of their playing? How much do film actors, as opposed to stage actors, model their offscreen selves to continue or contrast with their screen images? To accuse an actor of "playing himself" implies that we have seen and compared the "real" and "false" selves of the actor and reached a conclusion. Film acting deposits a residual self that snowballs from film to film, creating an image with which the actor, the scriptwriter, and the director can play as they wish. Donald Richie has recorded that the Japanese director Yasujiro Ozu said: "I could no more write, not knowing who the actor was to be, than an artist could paint, not knowing what color he was using." Ozu's remark indicates how a director takes advantage of a previously developed image in order to create a better film. But the stage actor in a sense ceases to exist from play to play; we experience only the accumulation of his talent, his versatility. In our minds the stage actor stays within the architectures he has inhabited, while the film actor exists in between as well, forever immediate to our minds and eyes, escaping the momentary enclosures that the individual films have placed around him.

"Playing yourself" involves one's interpretation of what is most successful and appealing in one's own nature and then heightening it. Film actors play their roles the way we play ourselves in the world. Audiences may now get sustenance from films and from film acting because they no longer are so interested in the social possibilities of the self that has been the metaphysic of stage acting since Shakespeare and the Renaissance, the place of role-playing in the life of the audience. The Shakespearean films of Laurence Olivier and Orson Welles clearly express the contrast. The tendency in stage acting is to subordinate oneself to the character, while the great film actor is generally more important than the character he plays. Our sense of Olivier in his Shakespearean roles is one of distance and disguise: the purified patriotism of Henry V, in which all the play's negative hints about his character have been removed; the blond wig he uses to play Hamlet, so that, as he has said, no one will associate him with the part; the bent back, twisted fingers, and long black hair of Richard III. But Welles assimilates the roles to himself. Costume for Welles is less a disguise than a generation from within and so he presented it in various television appearances of the 1950s, gradually making up for his part while he explained the play to the audience, until he turned full face into the camera and spoke the lines. In theater we experience the gap between actor and role as expertise; in film it may be described as a kind of self-irony. The great stage actor combats the superiority of the text, its preexistence, by choosing his roles: Olivier will play Hamlet; Olivier will play a music-hall comic. The great film actor, assured that his image absorbs and makes real the script, may allow himself to be cast in unpromising roles, if only for visibility. In the audience we feel Welles's character to be part of his role, whereas we perceive not Olivier's character but his intelligence and his ability to immerse himself in a role. Olivier is putting on a great performance, but Welles feels superior enough to the Shakespearean text to cut, reorganize, and invent. Olivier is a great interpreter; Welles is an equal combatant. For both, Shakespeare is like a genre, similar to the western, that offers materials for a contemporary statement. But Olivier sticks closely to the language and form of the play itself. We judge Olivier finally by Shakespeare, but we judge Welles by other films. Both choose those Shakespearean plays that emphasize a central character. But Olivier's willingness to allow Shakespeare the last word frees him for the more assertive political roles, whereas Welles stays with the more domestic or even isolated figures of Macbeth and Othello. Olivier began his Shakespearean film career with the heroic self-confidence of Henry V, while Welles, at least for the moment, has ended his with Falstaff—the choice of the ironic imagination of film over the theatrical assertion of social power.

These distinctions between stage acting and film acting are, of course, not absolute but points on a slippery continuum. Marlon Brando's career, for example, is a constant conflict between his desire to be versatile—to do different kinds of films, use different accents, wear different costumes—and the demand of his audience that he elaborate his residual cinematic personality. Brando tries to get into his roles, and often sinks them in the process, while Cary Grant pumps them up like a balloon and watches them float off into the sky. The main trouble that Chaplin has in *A Countess from Hong Kong* (1967) is taking two actors (Brando and Sophia Loren), whose own sense of their craft emphasizes naturalistic, historically defined character, and placing them within a film world where they would best exist as masks and stereotypes. Their efforts to ground their characters destroys the film. It may be funny if Chaplin or Cary Grant vomited out a porthole, but it's not funny when Brando does it. Brando can be funny in films only as a counterpoint to our sense of "Brando," for example in *Bedtime Story* (Ralph Levy, 1964). When he is acting someone else, the ironic sense of self-image that is natural to a film actor does not exist. We share Cary Grant's sense of distance from his roles, whether they are comic, melodramatic, or whatever, because it corresponds to our sense of personal distance from our daily roles in life. The sense of "putting it on" that we get from Brando's greatest roles—*A Streetcar Named Desire*, *Viva Zapata!*, *The Wild One*, *On the Waterfront*—stands in paradoxical relation to Method theories of submergence in the role. Brando's willingness to cooperate with Bernardo Bertolucci in the commentary on and mockery of his screen image that forms so much of the interest of *Last Tango in Paris* may indicate that he no longer holds to the theatrical definition of great acting. His progenitor role in *The Godfather* seems to have released him to create the paradox of the self-revealed inner life of a screen image elaborated by *Last Tango*. In the films of the 1970s, character, and therefore acting as well, has taken on the central importance in film. And the stage actor in film finds that his virtuosity is more a parlor trick than a technique of emotional and artistic power. Films make us fall in love with, admire, even hate human beings who may actually in the moment we watch them be dead and dust. But that is the grandeur of films as well: the preservation of human transience, the significance not so much of social roles as of fragile, fleeting feelings.

Questions and Projects

- Analyze how Marlon Brando interprets the role of Stanley in *A Streetcar Named Desire*. What, in his acting, is a product of its presentation on film and how might he portray that character differently on stage?

- To what extent does an actor's interpretation of a character change with the time and place. Examine the history of a character, say Jo in Louisa May Alcott's *Little Women* (1994) and analyze the specifics changes and transformations that take place in several film embodiments of that character from George Cukor's 1933 version with Katherine Hepburn to Gillian Armstrong's 1994 adaptation featuring Winona Ryder.

One of the more productive directions in recent film criticism has attended to the precise historical details that shape films and film culture. This perspective holds that careful historical and cultural discriminations need to be made when investigating film forms— where they originate, and how they change. In this excerpt from The Classical Hollywood Cinema *(1985), Kristin Thompson examines the social and industrial pressures that promoted the development of movies not only from drama and novels but also from short stories and magazine culture. Detailed historical groundings such as this lead to more precise evaluations of how certain forms and patterns in the movies (like those derived from literary subjects and structures) were employed and understood at the time and how they should be understood now by the viewer attuned to history.*

"Novel, Short Story, Drama: The Conditions for Influence" from *The Classical Hollywood Cinema*

Kristin Thompson

As films grew longer, the status of the individual film on a program changed. Initially, eight or so short films might fill a twenty-minute slot in a vaudeville program of several hours. The overall emphasis was on variety, and the disparate films formed an act. As a consequence, no individual film was expected to stand by itself. But with the advent of the nickelodeon and the standardized 1,000-foot reel, a program would typically consist of only three or four films; each occupied a distinct place within the complete show, separated by song-slide presentations and possibly other live acts. Internal coherence became a more central issue. And when the feature film came to occupy virtually an entire evening's program (with overture and other entertainment often tailored to the film), it had to carry the burden of sustaining audience interest. Expanded length and the change in viewing circumstances undoubtedly played a large part in turning filmmakers away from a vaudeville model of narrative toward fiction and the drama.

In the early years, films had competed only with other vaudeville acts for a place on a program in an art form that had an established audience. But with the phenomenal growth of the film industry, its product began to vie with other entertainment commodities for customers. By the first half of the teens, films were competing with inexpensive popular fiction—short-story magazines and novels, *The Saturday Evening Post* and *Collier's*, for instance, offered 'one or two nights' enjoyment of the best serials and short stories for five cents.'[18] To lure those readers in at a similar price for a shorter period, film producers felt they had to raise the quality of their offerings. Thus, for the short film at least, the popular short story offered an existing model to be emulated.

The feature film, on the other hand, offered a more expensive, often lengthier evening's entertainment, one directly comparable to that offered by a play, and entrepreneurs showed early features in legitimate theaters with prices based upon live-drama admissions. The situation in the theater industry of the early teens gave film a competitive advantage and probably fostered the industry's move into features during that period. That advantage derived from the organization of the theatrical business around the turn of the century.

The legitimate theater in the early years of this century operated as a cluster of touring troupes, controlled by a small number of entrepreneurs centralized in New York. This centralized touring system had replaced the country's earlier theatrical organization, the individual local professional repertory company, around 1870. Theater historian Jack Poggi sums up the changes in the theater industry:[19]

> What to the American theater after 1870 was not very different from what happened to many other industries. First, a centralized production system replaced many local, isolated units. Second, there was a division of labor, as theater managing became separate from play producing. Third, there was a standardization of product, as each play was represented by only one company or by a number of duplicate companies. Fourth, there was a growth of control by big business.

The characteristics which Poggi lists have obvious parallels to the development of the film industry as described in Part Two. Film was able to compete successfully with legitimate drama because it provided a more efficient, more centralized system for staging a performance only once, recording it, and reproducing it for the mass audience with minimal transportation costs.[20] Because of its success in competing with the drama, the film industry was able to standardize the multiple-reel feature, which in turn encouraged the move to a classical continuity system. But again, in order to compete with the drama for its audience, filmmakers realized the necessity of raising the quality of their offerings.

To a considerable extent, raising the quality of films to attract consumers of short fiction, novels, and plays required drawing directly or indirectly upon these other arts. Chapter 12 has shown that the film companies did this by adapting plays, stories, and novels. So for sources of subject matter, films turned definitively away from vaudeville skits. Producers also wanted to lure personnel, particularly established stars, away from the theater; adaptations of drama and literature, plus a general elevation of film's status among the arts, helped accomplish this.

But film drew upon these other arts in ways other than the direct appropriation of stories and personnel The original scenarios used by the companies, whether done by their own staff writers or by freelancers, already felt the indirect impact of existing literary models. The film industry was fortunate in being able to tap a huge marketplace for popular fiction and drama. The writers working in this marketplace were often trained in popularized versions of traditional rules, and they could apply these rules to film scenarios as well.

✳ The large freelance market for novels and short fiction had arisen only a few years before the invention of film. The development of a wide-spread native fiction had been discouraged by the lack of an international copyright law. Publishers tended to bring out editions of European novels and stories, which they could obtain without payment, rather than to pay American authors to write for them. Before 1891, when an international copyright law took effect, there had been only a very limited output of American short stories.[21] From about 1824 into the 1840s, literary annuals, ladies' magazines, and later gentlemen's magazines, fostered a brief flowering of the tale or sketch; these were generally considered hack work, although at their best such periodicals brought out the works of Hawthorne, Irving, and Poe. The 1850s were a fallow period for short fiction, but the tremendous commercial successes in America of Dickens's novels and of Stowe's *Uncle Tom's Cabin* (1852) marked the rise of the popular novel in America. With the founding during the 1860s of *The Atlantic Monthly* and *The Nation*, short fiction became increasingly respectable, and by the mid-1880s, the writing of short stories was becoming lucrative. The number of writers increased steadily.[22]

After the new international copyright law of 1891, popular fiction underwent a huge growth. Brander Matthews, a leading critic of the period, commented in 1898: 'This is perhaps the most striking fact in the history of the literature of the nineteenth century—this immense vogue of the novel and of the short story. Fiction fills our monthly magazines, and it is piled high on the counters of our bookstores.'[23] Novels were relatively easy to sell but took more time to write. Also, short stories were so popular at the time that a payment for a single story often was as great as the total royalties on a novel. For the vast number of part-time or casual writers, the short story proved attractive. By the late 1890s, there were so many weekly magazines and newspaper supplements that the writing of short stories could be considered an industry. And by 1900, syndicates existed to write, buy, and sell stories.[24]

There were also freelance playwrights, although this market was much smaller. A writer could not sell a play nearly so easily as a piece of fiction; the financial rewards, however, were potentially greater:[25]

> Although there is far more pecuniary profit to the author from a successful play than from the average successful novel, and although in some countries, notably in France, the authorship of a play brings more instant personal recognition, playwriting demands a long and arduous period of apprenticeship. Even after years of familiarity with technical stagecraft, it is far more difficult to get a manuscript play accepted than it is to secure publication for a manuscript novel. Most authors choose, or are forced to follow, the easier path.

Authors could mail plays directly to managers or to stars, but many worked through agents. Chances of a sale were relatively slim. One 1915 playwriting manual described how an author could expect to wait while his or her manuscript languished for months on a manager's shelf.[26] Once a playwright succeeded in getting one play produced, however, she or he usually would be considered a professional, receiving reasonably high, regular royalties. There was also a small market for freelance writers of vaudeville playlets.[27] Again, the procedure involved royalties rather than outright sales.

The film industry entered the literary market in part by hiring established writers and in part by inviting submissions of synopses and scenarios. Staff writers and scenario editors came to the studios from a variety of backgrounds, but the most common previous occupations were journalism and popular-fiction writing. Journalists were presumably well-suited to the task because they had professional experience in writing and editing synoptic narratives. A trade journal noted in 1916: 'The best school for the would-be photoplay writer is the newspaper office. Many who were formerly newspaper men are now successful as writers for the silent drama. They know life, a good story, and the value of a gripping situation.'[28] Edward Azlant's examination of screenwriting before 1920 discusses several dozen prominent scenarists at the studios.[29] The largest number of this group came from journalism, followed by magazine-fiction writing, novel writing, and playwriting. These divisions are not hard and fast, however. Many writers worked in several or all of these fields. Given the huge, lucrative freelance story market, few writers of any type failed to submit something to the magazines. Reporters, copy readers and editors working for magazines and newspapers wrote short stories. (Stephen Crane, Edna Ferber, Willa Cather, James Cabell, Irwin Cobb, and Sinclair Lewis were among those who got their starts this way.)[30] Writers who worked at the studios or sent in their freelance efforts would usually have some experience with the popular fiction forms of the period.

Historians have dealt extensively with the impact of the drama and the novel on film form and style.[31] The concomitant influence of the short story, however, has been largely overlooked. An examination of the close relations between the freelance short story and scenario markets will demonstrate some of the conditions which encouraged narrative principles from all of these arts to enter the cinema.

In order to make narrative films on a regular, efficient basis, producers began to use the detailed division of labor described in Part Two. Narrative filmmaking necessitated a steady source of stories, a need which eventually resulted in the scenario staff. These workers performed specialized tasks: among other things, they wrote many of the original stories used and read the freelance synopses or scenario-scripts submitted to the studio. Chapter 12 has suggested that the heyday of the amateur scenarist was actually brief (from about 1907 to 1914), but these were important years in the transition from primitive to classical filmmaking. Vast changes took place in ideas about how a narrative film should be constructed. The backgrounds of both studio and freelance writers, as well as the normative advice they received, helped shape those ideas.

By 1910, the methods of obtaining stories for purposes resembled those of the popular fiction magazines, which, as we have seen, had become popular in the 1890s. The prominent *Black Cat* magazine, for instance, started a trend toward using contests to encourage submissions of short stories. Motion-picture companies followed this strategy, and there were scenario contests conducted through the trade journals in the early teens.

Whether encouraged by prizes or by flat-fee purchases, amateur and professional freelance writers flooded the studios with scenarios. Usual estimates in the trade journals and scenario guides suggest that only about one in a hundred scripts was actually accepted, and scenario editors frequently complained about the poor quality of the material they had to plow through. Very quickly, the studios' dependence on such submissions declined. By 1912, copyright problems and the expanding production of multiple-reel films made unsolicited stories less attractive; contract writers in scenario departments proved a more reliable, efficient source, and the most promising freelancers could be hired. Amateur scenarios were used almost exclusively for one- or two-reel films, the production of which declined as the feature became the standard basis for production in the mid-teens.

Little direct evidence indicates what proportion of the freelance material came from writers who had also tried their hand at short stories. Few films of this period credited their scenarists. But some indirect evidence suggests the importance of popular short fiction as a model for film narrative. For one thing, some of the books on how to write scenarios of the period came from authors who also provided advice on short-story writing.[32] In addition, a few major scenarists of the time have recalled their beginnings as short-story freelancers. Frances Marion wrote fiction until requests for the screen rights to her stories led her to try doing scenarios; she eventually became a staff writer for several West Coast companies. Clifford Howard, who later became scenario editor for the Balboa and the American companies, wrote of having turned his outlines for short-story plots into scenarios when he heard how easy they were to sell. Others who had written short stories (usually in addition to work in other prose or dramatic forms) include: Roy L. McCardell, Lloyd Lonergan, Emmett Campbell Hall, Epes Winthrop Sargent, James Oliver Curwood, Eustace Hale Ball, Mary H. O'Connor, Beulah Marie Dix, and Clare Beranger.[33] There were undoubtedly others, but most freelancers remained anonymous, and their backgrounds are now untraceable. At least some, however, had learned their craft from magazine freelancing, rather than from the stage.

Most explicitly, trade journals recognized a parallel between the scenario and popular short story markets. These comparisons tend to come a little later in the period, during the middle and late teens, but they indicate an awareness that writers were often working for both markets. By about 1915 the industry began to realize that it was competing with the popular fiction magazines for good stories. *Motography* noted in early 1915: 'An able and recognized short story writer can command from five to ten cents a word for his manuscript. To such a writer an average short story of three thousand words brings a check for one hundred to three hundred dollars.' The article contrasted this with the average payment for a scenario, which ranged well below $100, and pointed out that 'at present the short story writer is only tempted to submit something made over from an oft-rejected story manuscript.' The author concluded: 'The film producers can afford to pay better prices than the magazines. Encourage the writer to try his ideas in scenario form first; he can make over his rejected scenarios into magazine articles as easily as he can do the opposite.'[34] A *Motion Picture News* editorial pointed out that fiction magazines attracted a large middle-class audience and educated it to appreciate good stories:[35]

> They are sharp critics, these readers. They want pictures up to their established fiction standards.
> It is regrettable, but it is a fact, that up to a few years ago, the large percentage of pictures released were of the same ordinary adventurous or sentimental or funny character of the fiction in our popular publications of *thirty years* ago.
> What is to be done then to get good stories?
> Simply this: Pay the price....
> Go directly to the best magazine writers and get their work by *paying at least what the magazine will pay*.

Throughout 1915 and into 1916, similar articles in the trade press called for the producers to raise their fee for scenarios, to attract something beyond the leavings of the fiction magazines.[36]

The possibility for influence from the short story, then, came in part from the contact with writers who sold stories in both the magazine and film markets. In addition, many of the writers who were employed as permanent staff members came from a similar background. Along with the novel and the drama, the short story provided classical models upon which the early film could draw.

Notes

18. 'The Weakness of the strong,' *MPN*, 11, no. 1 (9 January 1915): 29.

19. Jack Poggi, *Theater in America: The Impact of Economic Forces 1870–1967* (New York: Cornell University Press, 1968), p. 26.

20. The touring theater company, the touring vaudeville act, and the film can all be seen as ways of distributing a theatrical entertainment to a farflung mass audience.... See *ibid.*, pp. 6, 78, 36.

21. C. Alphonso Smith, *The American Short Story* (Boston: Ginn & Co., 1912), p. 39; Fred Lewis Pattee, *The Development of the American Short Story* (New York: Harper & Bros, 1923), pp. 81, 130.

22. Pattee, *The Development of the American Short Story*, pp. 31, 70–5, 145, 150, 167, 191, 310.

23. Brander Matthews, 'The study of fiction,' [1898], in his *The Historical Novel and Other Essays* (New York: Charles Scribner's Sons, 1901), p. 81....

24. Bliss Perry, *A Study of Prose Fiction* (Boston/New York: Houghton, Mifflin & Co., 1902), p. 330; Pattee, *The Development of the American Short Story*, p. 337.

25. Perry, *A Study of Prose Fiction*, p. 65.

26. Charlton Andrews, *The Technique of Play Writing* (Springfield, Mass.: Home Correspondence School, 1915), p. 230.

27. At least one book-length guide appeared to dispense advice on writing playlets and other vaudeville forms: Page's *Writing for Vaudeville*.

28. Gilson Willets [Selig staff writer], 'Photoplay writing not an easy art,' *Motography*, 16, no. 14 (30 September 1916): 763.

29. Edward Azlant, 'The theory, history, and practice of screenwriting, 1897–1920' (PhD dissertation, University of Wisconsin, 1980).

30. Pattee, *The Development of the American Short Story*, p. 337.

31. ... Concentration on film and the nineteenth-century novel ... stemm[ed] primarily from Colin MacCabe's 'Realism and the cinema: notes on some Brechtian theses,' *Screen*, 15, no. 2 (Summer 1974): 7–27. In *Film and the Narrative Tradition* (Norman: University of Oklahoma Press, 1974), John L. Fell relates early film to a variety of nineteenth-century narrative arts.

32. Besides his manuals on *The Photodrama* ... and *The Feature Photoplay...*, Henry Albert Phillips also authored *The Plot of the Short Story* and *Art in Short Story Narration*.... J. Berg Esenwein was editor of the Home Correspondence School's 'Writer's Library.' In addition to coauthoring *Writing the Photoplay...*, he contributed many works on short fiction to the series.

33. 'Film stories change rapidly,' *Motography*, 18, no. 16 (20 December 1917): 813; Clifford Howard, 'The cinema in retrospect,' *Close Up*, 3, no. 5 (November 1928): 18; Azlant, *The Theory, History, and Practice of Screenwriting*.

34. 'The need for more originality,' *Motography*, 13, no. 5 (30 January 1915): 167.

35. William A. Johnston, 'About stories,' *MPN*, 11, no. 21 (29 May 1915): 35. Emphases in original.

36. See also, 'The story writers' opportunity,' *Motography*, 14, no. 20 (13 November 1915): 1025; 'The weakness of the strong,' *MPN*, 11, no. 1 (9 January, 1915): 29, 48.

Questions and Projects

- Investigate the social or economic "conditions of influence" at a specific point in history between the film industry and the world of literary publications or theatrical productions.

- Compare a work of literature from one period to its adaptation in another period to show how different historical conditions for the production and reception of those works can alter or determine their meanings.

*C*oncentrating on the single issue of adaptation, Dudley Andrew's *1981 study uses contemporary semiotics, theories of representation and interpretation, and finally sociological and historical determinants to situate the exchanges between film and literature. Within these frameworks, Andrew provides two directions in thinking about adaptation. First, adaptation becomes part of larger philosophical and epistemological projects in interpretation and thus connects adaptation with other questions linking the human and social sciences today. Second, unlike past tendencies to generalize about fundamental theoretical relations between film and literature, this framework allows a person to discriminate and distinguish between different tactics in individual acts of adaptation, placing each interpretive strategy in a specific social context. In that sense, this essay has a clear pragmatic direction, as Andrew's three modes of adaptation provide a starting point for differentiating individual acts of adaptation and for examining how a single film may attempt to convert a literary work.*

"Adaptation"
from *Concepts in Film Theory*
Dudley Andrew

The Sources of Films

Frequently the most narrow and provincial area of film theory, discourse about adaptation is potentially as far-reaching as you like. Its distinctive feature, the matching of the cinematic sign system to prior achievement in some other system, can be shown to be distinctive of all representational cinema.

Let us begin with an example, *A Day in the Country*. Jean Renoir set himself the task of putting his knowledge, his troupe, and his artistry at the service of a tale by Guy de Maupassant. No matter how we judge the process or success of the film, its "being" owes something to the tale that was its inspiration and potentially its measure. That tale, "A Country Excursion," bears a transcendent relation to any and all films that adapt it, for it is itself an artistic sign with a given shape and value, if not a finished meaning. A new artistic sign will then feature this original sign as either its signified or its referent. Adaptations claiming fidelity bear the original as a signified, whereas those inspired by or derived from an earlier text stand in a relation of referring to the original.

The notion of a transcendent order to which the system of the cinema is beholden in its practice goes well beyond this limited case of adaptation.[1] What is a city symphony, for example, if not an adaptation of a concept by the cinema?[2] A definite notion of Berlin pre-existed Walter Ruttman's 1927 treatment of that city. What is any documentary for that matter except the signification by the cinema of some prior whole, some concept of person, place, event, or situation. If we take seriously the arguments of Marxist and other social theorists that our consciousness is not open to the world but filters the world according to the shape of its ideology, then every cinematic rendering will exist in relation to some prior whole lodged unquestioned in the personal or public system of experience. In other words, no filmmaker and no film (at least in the representational mode) responds immediately to reality itself, or to its own inner vision. Every representational film *adapts* a prior conception. Indeed the very term "representation" suggests the existence of a model. Adaptation delimits representation by insisting on the cultural status of the model, on its existence in the mode of the text or the already textualized. In the case of those texts explicitly termed "adaptations," the cultural model which the cinema represents is already treasured as a representation in another sign system.

The broader notion of the process of adaptation has much in common with interpretation theory, for in a strong sense adaptation is the appropriation of a meaning from a prior text. The hermeneutic circle, central to interpretation theory, preaches that an explication of a text occurs only after a prior understanding of it, yet that prior understanding is justified by the careful explication it allows.[3] In other words, before we can go about discussing and analyzing a text we must have a global conception of its meaning. Adaptation is similarly both a leap and a process. It can put into play the intricate mechanism of its signifiers only in response to a general understanding of the signified it aspires to have constructed at the end of its process. While all representational films function this way (as interpretations of a person, place, situation, event, and so forth), we reserve a special place for those films which foreground this relation by announcing themselves as versions of some standard whole. A standard whole can only be a text. A version of it is an adaptation in the narrow sense.

Although these speculations may encourage a hopelessly broad view of adaptation, there is no question that the restricted view of adaptation from known texts in other art forms offers a privileged locus for analysis. I do not say that such texts are themselves privileged. Indeed, the thrust of my earlier remarks suggests quite the opposite. Nevertheless, the explicit, foregrounded relation of a cinematic text to a well-constructed original text from which it derives and in some sense strives to reconstruct provides the analyst with a clear and useful "laboratory" condition which should not be neglected.

The making of film out of an earlier text is virtually as old as the machinery of cinema itself. Well over half of all commercial films have come from literary originals—though by no means all of these originals are revered or respected. If we confine ourselves to those cases where the adaptation process is foregrounded, that is, where the original is held up as a worthy source or goal, there are still several possible modes of relation between the film and the text. These modes can, for convenience, be reduced to three: borrowing, intersection, and fidelity of transformation.

Borrowing, Intersecting, and Transforming Sources

In the history of the arts, surely "borrowing" is the most frequent mode of adaptation. Here the artist employs, more or less extensively, the material, idea, or form of an earlier, generally successful text. Medieval paintings featuring biblical iconography and miracle plays based on Bible stories drew on an exceptional text whose power they borrowed. In a later, secular age the artworks of an earlier generation might be used as sacred in their own right. The many types of adaptations from Shakespeare come readily to mind. Doubtless in these cases, the adaptation hopes to win an audience by the prestige of its borrowed title or subject. But at the same time it seeks to gain a certain respectability, if not aesthetic value, as a dividend in the transaction. Adaptations from literature to music, opera, or paintings are of this nature. There is no question of the replication of the original in Strauss's *Don Quixote*. Instead the audience is expected to enjoy basking in a certain pre-established presence and to call up new or especially powerful aspects of a cherished work.

To study this mode of adaptation, the analyst needs to probe the source of power in the original by examining the use made of it in adaptation. Here the main concern is the generality of the original, its potential for wide and varied appeal; in short, its existence as a continuing form or archetype in culture. This is especially true of that adapted material which, because of its frequent reappearance, claims the status of myth: *Tristan and Isolde* for certain, and *A Midsummer Night's Dream* possibly. The success of adaptations of this sort rests on the issue of their fertility not their fidelity. Frank McConnell's ingenious *Storytelling and Mythmaking* catalogues the garden of culture by examining borrowing as the history of grafting and transplantation in the fashion of Northrop Frye or even Carl Jung.[4] This direction of study will always elevate film by demonstrating its participation in a cultural enterprise whose value is outside film and, for Jung and others, outside texts altogether. Adaptation is the name of this cultural venture at its most explicit, though McConnell, Frye, and Jung would all immediately want to extend their theories of artistic fertility to "original" texts which upon inspection show their dependence on the great fructifying symbols and mythic patterns of civilization.

This vast and airy mode of borrowing finds its opposite in that attitude toward adaptation I choose to call "intersecting." Here the uniqueness of the original text is preserved to such an extent that it is intentionally left unassimilated in adaptation. The cinema, as a separate mechanism, records its confrontation with an ultimately intransigent text. Undoubtedly the key film exhibiting this relation is Robert Bresson's *Diary of a Country Priest*. André Bazin, championing this film and this mode,[5] claimed that in this instance we are presented not with an adaptation so much as a refraction of the original. Because Bresson featured the writing of the diary and because he went out of his way to avoid "opening up" or in any other way cinematizing the original, Bazin claims that the film *is* the novel as seen by cinema. To extend one of his most elaborate metaphors,[6] the original artwork can be likened to a crystal chandelier whose formal beauty is a product of its intricate but fully artificial arrangement of parts while the cinema would be a crude flashlight interesting not for its own shape or the quality of its light but for what it makes appear in this or that dark corner. The intersection of Bresson's flashlight and the chandelier of Bernanos's novel produces an experience of the original modulated by the peculiar beam of the cinema. Naturally a great deal of Bernanos fails to be lit up, but what is lit up is only Bernanos, Bernanos however as seen by the cinema.

The modern cinema is increasingly interested in just this sort of intersecting. Bresson, naturally, has given us his Joan of Arc from court records and his *Mouchette* once again from Bernanos. Straub has filmed Corneille's *Othon* and *The Chronicle of Anna Magdalena Bach*. Pasolini audaciously confronted Matthew's gospel with many later texts (musical, pictorial, and cinematic) which it inspired. His later *Medea*, *Canturbury Tales*, and *Decameron* are also adaptational events in the intersecting mode. All such works fear or refuse to adapt. Instead they present the otherness and distinctiveness of the original text, initiating a dialectical interplay between the aesthetic forms of one period with the cinematic forms of our own period. In direct contrast to the manner scholars have treated the mode of "borrowing," such intersecting insists that the analyst attend to the *specificity* of the original within the *specificity* of the cinema. An original is allowed its life, its own life, in the cinema. The consequences of this method; despite its apparent forthrightness, are neither innocent nor simple. The disjunct experience such intersecting promotes is consonant with the aesthetics of modernism in all the arts. This mode refutes the commonplace that adaptations support only a conservative film aesthetics.

Unquestionably the most frequent and most tiresome discussion of adaptation (and of film and literature relations as well) concerns fidelity and transformation. Here it is assumed that the task of adaptation is the reproduction in cinema of something essential about an original text. Here we have a clear-cut case of film trying to measure up to a literary work, or of an audience expecting to make such a comparison. Fidelity of adaptation is conventionally treated in relation to the "letter" and to the "spirit" of the text, as though adaptation were the rendering of an interpretation of a legal precedent. The letter would appear to be within the reach of cinema for it can be emulated in mechanical fashion. It includes aspects of fiction generally elaborated in any film script: the characters and their inter-relation, the geographical, sociological, and cultural information providing the fiction's context, and the basic narrational aspects that determine the point of view of the narrator (tense, degree of participation and knowledge of the storyteller, and so on). Ultimately, and this was Bazin's complaint about faithful transformations, the literary work can readily become a scenario written in typical scenario form. The skeleton of the original can, more or less thoroughly, become the skeleton of a film.

More difficult is fidelity to the spirit, to the original's tone, values, imagery, and rhythm, since finding stylistic equivalents in film for these intangible aspects is the opposite of a mechanical process. The cinéaste presumably must intuit and reproduce the feeling of the original. It has been argued variously that this is frankly impossible, or that it involves the systematic replacement of verbal signifiers by cinematic signifiers, or that it is the product of artistic intuition, as when Bazin found the pervasive snowy decor in *Symphonie Pastorale* (1946) to reproduce adequately the simple past tense which Gide's verbs all bear in that tale.[7]

It is at this point that the specificity of these two signifying systems is at stake. Generally film is found to work from perception toward signification, from external facts to interior motivations and consequences, from the givenness of a world to the meaning of a story cut out of that world. Literary fiction works oppositely. It begins with signs (graphemes and words) building to propositions which attempt to develop perception. As a product of human language it naturally treats human motivation and values, seeking to throw them out onto the external world, elaborating a world out of a story.

George Bluestone, Jean Mitry, and a host of others find this opposition to be most graphic in adaptations.[8] Therefore they take pleasure in scrutinizing this practice even while ultimately condemning it to the realm of the impossible. Since signs name the inviolate relation of signifier to signified, how is translation of poetic texts conceivable from one language to another (where signifiers belong to different systems); much less how is it possible to transform the signifiers of one material (verbal) to signifiers of another material (images and sounds)? It would appear that one must presume the global signified of the original to be separable from its text if one believes it can be approximated by other sign clusters. Can we attempt to reproduce the meaning of the *Mona Lisa* in a poem, or of a poem in a musical phrase, or even of a musical phrase in an aroma? If one accepts this possibility, at the very least one is forced to discount the primary articulations of the relevant language systems. One would have to hold that while the material of literature (graphemes, words, and sentences) may be of a different nature from the materials of cinema (projected light and shadows, identifiable sounds and forms, and represented actions), both systems may construct in their own way, and at higher levels, scenes and narratives that are indeed commensurable.

The strident and often futile arguments over these issues can be made sharper and more consequential in the language of E. H. Gombrich or the even more systematic language of semiotics. Gombrich finds that all discussion of adaptation introduces the category of "matching."[9] First of all, like Bazin he feels one cannot dismiss adaptation since it is a fact of human practice. We can and do correctly match items from different systems all the time: a tuba sound is more like a rock than like a piece of string; it is more like a bear than like a bird; more like a romanesque church than a baroque one. We are able to make these distinctions and insist on their public character because we are matching equivalents. In the system of musical instruments the tuba occupies an equivalent position to that enjoyed by the romanesque in its system of architectural styles. Nelson Goodman has treated this issue at length in *The Language of Art* pointing to the equivalence not of elements but of the position elements occupy vis-à-vis their different domains.[10] Names of properties of colors may thus metaphorically, but correctly, describe aspects of the world of sound (a blue note, a somber or bright tone). Adaptation would then become a matter of searching two systems of communication for elements of equivalent position in the systems capable of eliciting a signified at a given level of pertinence, for example, the description of a narrative action. For Gombrich adaptation is possible, though never perfect, because every artwork is a construct of elements built out of a traditional use of a system. Since humans have the general capacity to adapt to new systems with different traditions in achieving a like goal or construct, artistic adaptation poses no insurmountable obstacles. Nevertheless attention to such "proportional consistencies" demands that the study of adaptation include the study of both art forms in their proper *historic* context.

Gombrich and Goodman anticipated the more fashionable vocabulary of semiotics in their clarification of these issues. In *Film and Fiction, The Dynamics of Exchange*, Keith Cohen tries to justify this new, nearly scientific approach to questions of relations between these arts; he writes, citing Metz:

> A basic assumption I make is that both words and images are sets of signs that belong to systems and that, at a certain level of abstraction, these systems bear resemblances to one another. More specifically, within each such system there are many different codes (perceptual, referential, symbolic). What makes possible, then, a study of the relation between two separate sign systems, like novel and film, is the fact that the same codes may reappear in more than one system.... The very mechanisms of language systems can thus be seen to carry on diverse and complex interrelations: "one function, among others, of language is to name the units segmented by vision (but also to help segment them), and ... one function, among others, of vision is to inspire semantic configurations (but also to be inspired by them)."[11]

Cohen, like Metz before him, suggests that despite their very different material character, despite even the different ways we process them at the primary level, verbal and cinematic signs share a common fate: that of being condemned to connotation. This is especially true in their fictional use where every signifier identifies a signified but also elicits a chain reaction of other relations which permits the elaboration of the fictional world. Thus, for example, imagery functions equivalently in films and novels. This mechanism of implication among signs leads Cohen to conclude that "narrativity is the most solid median link between novel and cinema, the most pervasive tendency of both verbal and visual languages. In both novel and cinema, groups of signs, be they literary or visual signs, are apprehended consecutively through time; and this consecutiveness gives rise to an unfolding structure, the diegetic whole that is never fully *present* in any one group yet always *implied* in each such group."[12]

Narrative codes, then, always function at the level of implication or connotation. Hence they are potentially comparable in a novel and a film. The story can be the same if the narrative units (characters, events, motivations, consequences, context, viewpoint, imagery, and so on) are produced equally in two works. Now this production is, by definition, a process of connotation and implication. The analysis of adaptation then must point to the achievement of equivalent narrative units in the absolutely different semiotic systems of film and language. Narrative itself is a semiotic system available to both and derivable from both. If a novel's story is judged in some way comparable to its filmic adaptation, then the strictly separate but equivalent processes of implication which produced the narrative units of that story through words and audio-visual signs, respectively, must be studied. Here semiotics coincides with Gombrich's intuition: such a study is not comparative between the arts but is instead intensive within each art. And since the implicative power of literary language and of cinematic signs is a function of its use as well as of its system, adaptation analysis ultimately leads to an investigation of film styles and periods in relation to literary styles of different periods.

We have come round the other side of the argument now to find once more that the study of adaptation is logically tantamount to the study of the cinema as a whole. The system by which film involves us in fictions and the history of that system are ultimately the questions we face even when starting with the simple observation of an equivalent tale told by novel and film. This is not to my mind a discouraging arrival for it drops adaptation and all studies of film and literation out of the realm of eternal principle and airy generalization, and onto the uneven but solid ground of artistic history, practice, and discourse.

The Sociology and Aesthetics of Adaptation

It is time for adaptation studies to take a sociological turn. How does adaptation serve the cinema? What conditions exist in film style and film culture to warrant or demand the use of literary prototypes? Although adaptation may be calculated as a relatively constant volume in the history of cinema, its particular function in any moment is far from constant. The choices of the mode of adaptation and of prototypes suggest a great deal about the cinema's sense of its role and aspirations from decade to decade. Moreover, the stylistic strategies developed to achieve the proportional equivalences necessary to construct matching stories not only are symptomatic of a period's style but may crucially alter that style.

Bazin pointed to an important instance of this in the immediate postwar era when adaptations from the stage by Cocteau, Welles, Olivier, Wyler, and others not only developed new ways for the cinema to be adequate to serious theater, but also developed a kind of discipline in *mise-en-scène* whose consequences go far beyond the production of *Macbeth*, *Les Parents terribles*, *The Little Foxes*, and *Henry V*.[13] Cocteau's film, to take one example, derives its style from Welles's use of interior shooting in *Kane* and *Ambersons*, thus responding to a new conception of dramatic space, but at the same time his film helped solidify a shooting style that would leave its mark on Alexandre Astruc and André Michel among others. Furthermore his particular cinematic *écriture* would allow Truffaut to set him against the cinema of quality in the famous 1954 diatribe.[14] It is instructive to note that while Truffaut railed against the status quo for its literariness and especially for its method of adaptation, the directors he praised were also working with literary originals: Bresson adapting Bernanos, Ophuls adapting Maupassant and Schnitzler, and Cocteau adapting his own theater pieces. Like Bazin, Truffaut looked upon adaptation not as a monolithic practice to be avoided but as an instructive barometer for the age.

The cinema *d'auteur* which he advocated was not to be pitted against a cinema of adaptation; rather one method of adaptation would be pitted against another. In this instance adaptation was the battleground even while it prepared the way for a stylistic revolution, the New Wave, which would for the most part avoid famous literary sources.

To take another sort of example, particular literary fashions have at times exercised enormous power over the cinema and, consequently, over the general direction of its stylistic evolution. The Romantic fiction of Hugo, Dickens, Dumas, and countless lesser figures originally set the stylistic requirements of American and mainstream French cinema at the end of the silent era. Similarly Zola and Maupassant, always of interest to French cinéastes, helped Jean Renoir muscularly reorient the style of world cinema in the 1930s. Not only that, through Luchino Visconti this naturalist impulse directly developed one strain of neorealism in his adaptations of Giovanni Verga (*La Terra Trema*) and James M. Cain (*Ossessione*).

This latter case forces us to recall that the "dynamics of exchange," as Cohen calls it, go both ways between film and fiction. Naturalist fiction helped cinema develop its interest in squalid subjects and a hard-hitting style. This in turn affected American hard-boiled novelists like Cain and Hammett, eventually returning to Europe in the film style of Visconti, Carné, Clouzot, and others. This general trading between film and literature in the currency of naturalism had some remarkable individual incidents associated with it. Renoir's adaptation of *The Lower Depths* can serve as an example. In 1881 Zola had cried out for a naturalist theater[15] and had described twenty years before the time precisely the sort of drama Gorki would write in *The Lower Depths*: a collection of real types thrown together without a domineering plot, the drama driven by the natural rhythms of little incidents and facts exposing the general quality of life in an era. Naturalism here coincided with a political need, with Gorki's play preceding the great uprisings in Russia by only a few years.

In another era and in response to a different political need, Renoir leapt at the chance to adapt the Gorki work. This was 1935, the year of the ascendancy of the Popular Front, and Renoir's treatment of the original is clearly marked by the pressures and aspirations of that moment. The film negotiates the mixture of classes which the play only hints at. Louis Jouvet as the Baron dominates the film, descending into the social depths and helping organize a collective undoing of Kastylylov, the capitalist landlord. Despite the gloomy theme, the murder, jailing, deaths by sickness and suicide, Renoir's version overflows with a general warmth evident in the airy setting by the Marne and the relaxed direction of actors who breathe languidly between their lines.

Did Gorki mind such an interpretation? We can never know, since he died a few months before its premier. But he did give Renoir his imprimatur and looked forward to seeing the completed version, this despite the fact that in 1932 he declared that the play was useless, out of date, and unperformable in socialist Russia. Perhaps these statements were the insincere self-criticism which that important year elicited from many Russian artists. I prefer, however, to take Gorki at his word. More farsighted than most theorists, let alone most authors, he realized that *The Lower Depths* in 1932 Russia was by no means the same artwork as *The Lower Depths* in the France of the Popular Front. This is why he put no strictures on Renoir assuming that the cinéaste would deal with his play as he felt necessary. Necessity is, among other things, a product of the specific place and epoch of the adaptation, both historically and stylistically. The naturalist attitude of 1902, fleshing out the original plans of Zola, gave way to a new historic and stylistic moment, and fed that style that Renoir had begun elaborating ever since *La Chienne* in 1931, and that despite its alleged looseness and airiness in comparison to the Gorki, would help lead European cinema onto the naturalist path.

This sketch of a few examples from the sociology of adaptation has rapidly taken us into the complex interchange between eras, styles, nations, and subjects. This is as it should be, for adaptation, while a tantalizing keyhole for theorists, nevertheless partakes of the universal situation of film practice, dependent as it is on the aesthetic system of the cinema in a particular era and on that era's cultural needs and pressures. Filmmaking, in other words, is always an event in which a system is used and altered in discourse. Adaptation is a peculiar form of discourse but not an unthinkable one. Let us use it not to fight battles over the essence of the media or the inviolability of individual art works. Let us use it as we use all cultural practices, to understand the world from which it comes and the one toward which it points. The elaboration of these worlds will demand, therefore, historical labor and critical acumen. The job of theory in all this is to keep the questions clear and in order. It will no longer do to let theorists settle things with a priori arguments. We need to study the films themselves as acts of discourse. We need to be sensitive to that discourse and to the forces that motivate it.

Notes

1. For this idea I am indebted to a paper written by Dana Benelli in a class at the University of Iowa, autumn term 1979.

2. The "city symphony" is a genre of the 1920s which includes up to fifteen films all built on formal or abstract principles, yet dedicated to the presentation of a single city, be it Berlin, Paris, Nice, Moscow, or the like.

3. In the theory of interpretation this is generally attributed to Wilhelm Dilthey, although Martin Heidegger has made much of it in our century.

4. Frank McConnell, *Storytelling and Mythmaking* (New York: Oxford University Press, 1979).

5. André Bazin, *What Is Cinema?* (Berkeley: University of California Press, 1968), p. 142.

6. *Ibid.*, p. 107.

7. *Ibid.*, p. 67.

8. George Bluestone, *Novels into Film* (Berkeley: University of California Press, 1957), and Jean Mitry, "Remarks on the Problem of Cinematic Adaptation," *Bulletin of the Midwest Modern Language Association* 4, no. 1 (Spring 1971): 1–9.

9. Gombrich, *Art and Illusion*, p. 370.

10. Goodman, *Languages*, esp. pp. 143–48.

11. Keith Cohen, *Film and Literature: The Dynamics of Exchange* (New Haven: Yale University Press, 1979), p. 4. Cohen's citation from Metz comes from Metz, *Langage et cinéma*, pp. 20–21.

12. Ibid., p. 92.

13. Bazin, *What Is Cinema?* p. 76.

14. François Truffaut, "A Certain Tendency in French Cinema," in Nichols, *Movies*, pp. 224–36.

15. Émile Zola, "Naturalism and the Theater," in *The Experimental Novel and Other Essays*, tr. by Belle Sherman (New York: Haskell House, 1964).

Questions and Projects

- Must a single film operate in only one of Andrew's three modes of adaptation or might a film move between all three? Select either a single film (such as the provided example of Jean Renoir's *A Day in the Country* [1946] and Guy de Maupassant's "A Country Excursion") or a different filmed version of the same literary source (such as the Oz story in Victor Fleming's *Wizard of Oz*, David Lynch's version of *Wild at Heart* [1990], and perhaps Martin Scorsese's *After Hours* [1985]) to illustrate or test, concretely and precisely, one or more of Andrew's three adaptation strategies.

- Using these or other films, argue how a particular style and tactic of adaptation is "symptomatic" of the movie styles and forms of the period in which it was made. Do, for instance, silent adaptations use tactics specific to the period to interpret literature? Is there a postmodern style of interpretation that influences how literature is adapted for the movies?

The following section from Judith Mayne's 1985 book addresses the differences between readership and spectatorship as ways of bridging experiences of novels and films. For Mayne the most influential models for reading have been established by the nineteenth-century novel. Under the sway of a growing consumer culture late in that century, those ways of reading merge with new ways of seeing that would shape the movie experience through much of the twentieth century. While responding carefully to historical changes, her wide-ranging argument moves from nineteenth-century novels through film history of the 1940s. In the process she raises central issues in current film scholarship: about gender and women as readers and viewers; about consumerism, immigrant culture, and literacy; about the ways film and literature negotiate the boundaries between public and private life.

"Readership and Spectatorship"
from *Private Novels, Public Films*
Judith Mayne

Central to the classical American cinema is a myth of authorship, and the importance of adaptations of nineteenth-century novels has to do largely with the sustenance of that myth. Parallel to the function of authorship in the relationship between the novel and film is that of readership. Consider, for example, the Robert Stevenson-directed adaptation of *Jane Eyre* (1944). There are many omissions and condensations in this film, some of which are examined by Asheim.[34] And following Bluestone, we might consider how successfully the Brontë novel is used as a point of departure to create an "autonomous" work of art. But there is another kind of work in this film, irreducible to either a celebration or a denial of authorship. The film begins with a close-up of a leather-bound volume of *Jane Eyre*, and closes with a symmetrical close-up of a page marked "The End." Such a "framing" of a film with reference to its literary source is common to many Hollywood adaptations of the period. *Jane Eyre* suggests some of the implications of this parallel between book cover and screen, between page and frame.

Throughout this film, pages from the book appear on the screen as structuring devices, with specific passages illuminated. The adult voice of Jane (Joan Fontaine) reads these passages aloud in voice-over. Occasionally these pages correspond to actual passages from *Jane Eyre*, but by and large they do not. "Chapter one," for example, on screen, begins: "My name is Jane Eyre. I was born in 1830, a hard time." This is a far cry from the actual opening of Charlotte Brontë's novel: "There was no possibility of taking a walk that day. We had been wandering, indeed, in the leafless shrubbery an hour in the morning."[35] These imaginary passages in the film form one of the many strategies by which the novel is condensed for the screen version. They recall producer David O. Selznick's description of "bridging scenes":

> I have discovered that the public will forgive you for any number of omissions—particularly of subordinate material which is not directly connected with the main plot—but it won't forgive you for deliberate changes. For that reason I have found it best to make the bridging scenes which span the omissions as suggestive as possible. That is, by picking up dialogue and even phrases from other parts of the book and using such to construct the bridging scenes, the audience is given the illusion of seeing and hearing that with which they are already familiar.[36]

The "illusion of seeing and hearing": such a description of those "well-beloved" works brought to the screen suggests an interesting parallel between the itineraries of reading and viewing. The pages are selectively illuminated, light separated from dark, and thus the arrangement of words on a page is not unlike the arrangement of figures in a landscape. The female voice narrates, while we read what she has ostensibly "written." The female character is thus simultaneously a reader and a narrator within the film.

The reading process represented in the film is of a special type. One might certainly criticize the substitutions that occur in the film and dismiss them in the terms used by Asheim: "The assumed level of audience comprehension is generally lower for the film than for the novel."[37] But Charlotte Brontë's novel has a rather unique status, for, like Emily Brontë's *Wuthering Heights*, it is a nineteenth-century classic frequently read by adolescent girls. The distortions of Brontë's novel in the illuminated pages on screen are as much the reflection of an adult's memory of the adolescent experience of reading this novel, as they are the result of a film industry determined to simplify for its mass audience at all costs. *Jane Eyre* is adapted to the screen in such a way, then, that film viewing becomes, through the book, through the novel, a form of memory of a certain kind of reading.

Memory is essential to the way in which the itineraries of reading and viewing are intertwined in this film. The film is structured so as to constantly refer to associations of the reading process, and to integrate those associations into the act of film viewing and comprehension. And thus the film version of *Jane Eyre* presents itself as a fantasy of how we remember the novel. I am reminded here of how Sergei Eisenstein spoke of Charles Dickens: "All of us read him in childhood, gulped him down greedily, without realizing that much of his irresistibility lay ... in that spontaneous, childlike skill for storytelling."[38] At the heart of D. W. Griffith's narrative skill was, according to Eisenstein, an understanding of the importance of that "childlike skill." Similarly, many of the cinematic adaptations of classical novels evolve from an understanding of the special function of reading in childhood and adolescent fantasies of the self in relation to the world. An essential component of classical film narrative is the memory recaptured by the experience of film viewing, and recaptured twice over: there is the memory of childhood, and the memory of reading. Cinematic adaptations evoke childhood memories of reading, and the transaction between viewer and screen is shaped by the contours of family identities, with the figure of the author as lover and father, as narrative authority.

Orson Welles' *Citizen Kane* (1941) brings together in a particularly striking way the implications, for classical film narrative, of the myths of authorship and readership inherited from the middle-class novel. *Citizen Kane* is less about one man's life than it is about the very possibility of telling that story in the first place. The film begins with the death of Charles Kane, and moves to a newsreel obituary. We then witness a series of interviews with Kane's acquaintances, conducted by the journalist Thompson whose assignment is to discover the significance of Kane's last word, "rosebud." That enigma has become one of the most classic in film history. Rosebud may represent lost innocence and mother-love, but it represents equally forcefully the impossibility of a facile understanding of one individual's life.

Yet it is not just any individual life which is impenetrable, but the life of an individual who has become a public figure. In the scene where the sled called Rosebud appears, when Mr. Thatcher comes to fetch the child Kane and take him away to the city and to wealth, it is as if Kane crosses an absolute threshold separating private and public spheres. Indeed, there is virtually no other private sphere in Kane's world after he leaves his home. First wife Emily seems to be as important as the President's niece as she is as Kane's wife, and second wife Susan Alexander is quickly transformed by Kane into a failed public figure herself.[39] The very structure of the film is informed by the potential negotiation of private and public spheres—from the newsreel, a collection of documents about the public man that is narrated by an authoritative voice-over, to the quest, a collection of different perspectives which make up a mosaic of glimpses into the private life concealed beneath the public façade. *Citizen Kane* does not correspond uniquely to what I have called the fantasy of reconciliation, nor to the nightmare of reification. Private and public selves never are totally integrated, but neither can it be said that *Citizen Kane* puts forth a private sphere invaded by the forces of the public sphere. For the private sphere in

Citizen Kane remains, quite simply, separate and unknowable. And even if one accepts a dime-store Freudian explanation of Rosebud, the knowledge that Kane suffered all his life from separation anxiety is, to say the least, somewhat anti-climactic.[40]

More important than the figure of Kane himself is the attention given, in *Citizen Kane*, to the particular position of the film spectator vis-à-vis the complicated journey from public to private existence. As a reflection on spectatorship, *Citizen Kane* is a turning point of sorts in the history of the relation between classical film narrative and the novelistic tradition. Of central importance in *Citizen Kane* is the particular way in which the film spectator is implicated in the process of discovery of the enigma. To be sure, we are given privileged access to the meaning of Rosebud, but it would be a mistake to ignore the irony with which such privileged access is given. For the spectator within the film, that character who mirrors our own relation to the screen, is Thompson, and not his boss Rawlston, who is convinced that Rosebud will unlock a hidden meaning in Kane's life.[41] Thompson concludes his failed search with the remark that there is no single word or sign which could explain a man's life. And the "No Trespassing" sign appears at the end of the film as it did at the beginning, reminding us that Rosebud solves everything, and nothing at all.[42]

Yet Rosebud may not really be the object of Thompson's search. Robert Carringer argues persuasively that the little glass globe with its snow scene is endowed with much more narrative significance, and it is towards this object that Rosebud always leads us. Carringer writes: "The little glass globe (not Rosebud) is the film's central symbol. A mediating symbol of inner and outer, of subjective and objective, it stands at once for what we have seen and seek to recover, the psychic wholeness of Kane, and for the totality of Kane as a force, the man whose life and works are empires and private worlds. The shattering of the globe (not the appearance of Rosebud) is the film's main symbolic 'event.'"[43] That globe is, we recall, the object we see at the moment of Kane's death at the beginning of the film. It seems to occasion the utterance of 'Rosebud,' and once smashed on the floor, it is a lens through which we see Kane's room and an arriving nurse. We see another such globe on a bureau in Susan Alexander's apartment at the moment that Kane speaks of his mother and his childhood. The snow scene in the globe recalls, of course, the scene in the film of Kane's youth when Thatcher comes to take him away. And it recalls as well the estate of Xanadu, constructed by Kane as if to possess the glass globe on a large scale.

The glass globe links present and past, private and public selves. Xanadu has a similar function, but now in nearly hysterical proportions. Carringer says that the glass globe "condenses the whole experience of Xanadu, his last and most ambitious monument to himself."[44]

For Xanadu is a private sphere erected as a public monument, within which there is nothing but space, never private but not quite public either. The narrative function of the glass globe in *Citizen Kane* is reminiscent, on several levels, of what writer Christa Wolf calls "miniatures," bits and pieces of the past, the results of a "furtive process hard to avoid, a hardening, petrifying, habituating, that attacks the memory in particular." Wolf writes: "We all carry with us a collection of miniatures with captions, some quaint, some gruesome. These we occasionally bring out and show round, because we need confirmation of our own reassuringly clear feelings: beautiful or ugly, good or evil. These miniatures are for the memory what the calcified cavities are for people with tuberculosis, what prejudices are for morals: patches of once active life now shut off. At one time one was afraid to touch them, afraid of burning ones fingers on them; now they are cool and smooth."[45] For Kane the globe is a miniature of lost innocence, and for the viewer, an equally forceful miniature of the very possibility of recapturing that past. How appropriate that Wolf should describe these miniatures as the province of cinema, and should then go on to insist that "prose should try to be unfilmable."[46] Indeed, *Citizen Kane* is informed by a resistance to that very process which, following Wolf's metaphor, is particularly characteristic of the cinema.

Citizen Kane puts forth a vision of private and public existence riddled with ambiguities. The ambiguity of the *quest* for the private man, and not the private man himself, is foregrounded in the film. Thus in *Citizen Kane* the transaction between viewer and screen in the public sphere of the movie theatre has become problematized. And perhaps the most striking ambiguity of all in *Citizen Kane* is that the film tells a story which, it insists, somewhat in the spirit of Christa Wolf, is "unfilmable."

That the evolution of spectatorship is tied to the function of readership is suggested in a different way by the presence of characters who function primarily as "spectators within the film," like the journalist Thompson in *Citizen Kane*. Whether major characters or not, the primary function of these figures is to establish narrative perspective. As is the case with many of the devices of film narrative, equivalences could be established between the use of the spectator within the film, and the forms of narration and point-of-view that occur in the novel. The intertextual links between novel and cinema are more strongly suggested, however, by the fact that frequently spectators within the film are identified as *readers*. Readership thus becomes a form of narrative participation incorporated into cinematic narrative.

In George Cukor's *Gaslight* (1944), there is a rather comic, elderly woman character who is constantly in the vicinity of the central action of the film, but never directly involved in it. She lives in the same neighborhood where the murder of opera singer Alicia took place, and is thus a bystander to the crime which determines the narrative development of the film. Throughout the film this woman functions as an observer, sometimes as a busybody who tries to glean information from servants, sometimes as a gossip who thoroughly enjoys discussing the past and present affairs of her neighbors. This character is first introduced to us in a train compartment she happens to share with Paula (Ingrid Bergman), the central female character of the film. The elderly woman is reading a suspense novel, which she describes for Paula: a man, who has murdered six wives and buried them all his basement, has just taken a new wife. This novel parodies the film we are watching. The elderly woman has, she tells Paula, only reached page one hundred, and so she is certain that there is still more to come. Indeed there is, for the woman becomes a kind of reader of the equally suspenseful plot that thickens in her own neighborhood.

Gaslight's incorporation of a reader into its narrative reminds us of how, in the development of the middle-class novel, the conditions of readership were gradually and persistently incorporated and embedded into the narrative. We recall the significant resonances of Elizabeth's development as a reader in *Pride and Prejudice*, for instance. We have already seen this process at work in the early years of motion picture history: films would cease to bear titles like *Grandpa's Reading Class*, but those figures of vision would still be apparent, here and there and across the narrative structures of later films. So too within the classical Hollywood cinema there is the development of the novelistic in such an "embedded" way. The example of *Gaslight* is particularly striking, for the conditions of (cinematic) observation are precisely those of readership.

Spectatorship in the cinema evokes parallels between watching a film and reading a novel, and in this sense incorporates readership into the classical cinema. In a more general way, spectatorship in the cinema is structured by the relationship between private and public existence. The separation of private and public spheres to which the middle-class novel responds has, in the era of cinema, changed dimensions. Narratives of private and public life have been appropriated from one set of historical circumstances to another. The development of consumerism in the early twentieth century is an essential aspect of the changing relation between private and public spheres. With consumerism, the reification of the private sphere appears to be complete. In his study of the evolution of consumerism, for instance, Stuart Ewen describes how the home became increasingly perceived as a kind of factory in its own right: "As the housewife assumed more of a factory-operative status, the home became a place where the values of factory production, and the conditions if not the pay of the wage worker, were replicated and reinforced on a day-to-day basis."[47] The class dimensions of consumerism were essential to the reification of the private sphere. An imaginary ideal of homogeneity was put forth, whereby working-class and middle-class aspirations could be united around the pursuit of leisure and goods.[48]

We have seen how the early motion pictures offered glimpses of consumerist ideals; and how the audience for moving pictures developed, like the very phenomenon of consumerism, in cross-class terms. An important aspect of the classical cinema is the way in which the movie theatre seems to provide a space in which class differences temporarily dissolve. I do not mean that working-class and middle-class audiences would respond to films in identical ways; rather, film narrative would work on multiple levels, so that different class-defined responses would be condensed within a single film.

The relationship between private and public spheres, as a narrative theme and structure, would become an essential means to cut symbolically across class lines. Consider the film *My Sister Eileen* (1942), for example, in which two sisters, Ruth and Eileen, leave their Columbus, Ohio, home to look for work (Ruth as a writer, Eileen as an actress) in New York City. The Greenwich Village apartment they share—their private space—is constantly invaded by external forces, usually male figures, representing professional, sexual, or proprietal authority. The two sisters make uneasy accommodations by adopting a variety of family roles in relationship to each other. Eileen acts as housewife when her older sister goes out to look for work; Ruth comforts and gently disciplines her younger sister as a mother would a child; and when the sisters are frightened by the street activity that keeps them from sleep, they share a not-quite conjugal bed. The women's world is more gently invaded by another male figure, Ruth's professional mentor, who accepts her first story for publication and conveniently falls in love with her at the same time. The romantic resolution of the film marks a restoration of order, as the union of male and female coincides with the readjustment of private and public space to complementary rather than conflicting spheres.

Central to that resolution is the question of class. Ruth and Eileen leave a middle-class existence in a town which symbolizes a middle-class way of life, to live in an ethnic, working-class neighborhood. The middle-class life they leave represents security and boredom; the working class environment they enter may represent danger, but it is also full of color and excitement. The editor whose entrance into Ruth's life allows a balance of personal and public selves is also a mediator of class differences. He promises *both* middle-class security and the vivacity of an urban environment. Viewers of this film encounter the potential mediation of class differences, but in order to arrive at that conclusion they can follow quite different paths. To a middle-class audience, the

Greenwich village characters correspond to comic ethnic stereotypes, while to a working-class urban audience, the trials and tribulations of two middle-class provincials must have been laughable and amusing.

Given the historical parallels between cinema and the emergence of a consumerist culture, it is perhaps tempting to define American cinema as an agent of consumerist culture. Such a definition has been put forth persuasively by Charles Eckert who, in describing how cinema actively contributed to the cause of consumerist culture, says that in the first decades of the twentieth century, "the conditions were right for Hollywood to assume a role in the phase of the capitalism's life-history that the emerging philosophy of consumerism was about to give birth to."[49]

Eckert's explorations into the "almost incestuous hegemony" which characterized Hollywood's connections with big business provide some of the most illuminating evidence for the very special role of cinema within consumerist culture. Inscribed within film from the very beginning, says Eckert, are "innumerable opportunities for product and brand-name tie-ins. But more than this, [motion pictures] functioned as living display windows for all that they contained; windows that were occupied by marvelous mannequins and swathed in a fetish-inducing ambiance of music and emotion."[50] Throughout the decade of the 1930s, films would function as "living display windows." Extensive tie-ins with a variety of manufacturers assured the visibility of specific products and brand-names on the screen. In addition, entire industries would be built around the kinds of clothing and furnishings shown on screen. The female viewer was central throughout. If, in the novels of two centuries before, she occupied a strategic central position in the private sphere, in Hollywood narrative woman was central as consumer, as the strategic center of yet another stage in the relationship between private and public existence.[51]

Central, then, to Eckert's view of Hollywood is the decisive contribution of American cinema to the shaping of consumerist culture. "Hollywood ... did as much or more than any other force in capitalist culture to smooth the operation of the production-consumption cycle by fetishizing products and putting the libido in libidinally invested advertising."[52] Yet at the same time that consumerism was developing as a major phenomenon of twentieth-century capitalist societies, there persisted the nineteenth-century ideal of family life as a separate, isolated realm. Zaretsky writes that in the twentieth century, the "proletariat itself came to share the bourgeois ideal of the family as a 'utopian retreat.'"[53] If consumerism is built upon the reification of the private sphere, that ideal of a haven, of a "utopian retreat" persisted. And with a contradictory twist, that ideal was often actively foregrounded as a central image in advertising.

While it is true that moving pictures became, in Eckert's words, "living display windows" for the products of consumer society, the movies had an equally important function in the maintenance of the ideal of the private sphere as a privileged, separate realm. Cinema is a form of spectacle, governed by consumerist principles. Cinema is also a narrative form, governed by principles not so quickly nor so easily assimilable to the phenomenon of consumer society. Thus as spectacle and narrative, cinema emerges both from the new consumerist culture and from the eighteenth- and nineteenth-century novelistic tradition. The classical American cinema is spectacle and narrative; a vehicle for consumerism and a link to a narrative tradition. Put another way, the classical American cinema is an arena where the contradictions of the changing dimensions of private and public life are enacted.

Within the public space of the movie theatre, private fantasies are indulged: this has been a relative constant in the history of narrative cinema. But the contours of that public space, and of the transaction between viewer and screen, are always determined by specific historical conditions. In the 1940s those conditions led directly or indirectly to World War II. If the space of the movie theatre allowed a temporary dissolution of class differences, and if films were constructed to allow different forms of class identification, then moving pictures would serve an important function in the war effort. And if cinema of the 1940s explored in depth the relation of private and public spheres, it was in part because private and public existence had become problematized in American social life. The symbolic mediation of private and public life thus spoke to a kind of historical urgency.

The demands of war economy meant a heightened awareness of private and public life, the most striking symptom of which was the participation of women in the war industries. Indeed, the ways in which women were encouraged to take on work outside the home during the war is a fascinating case study of how consumerist culture would be grounded in a curious contradiction whereby the private sphere was at once a refuge from, *and* an extension of, the public sphere. One thinks of the various wartime images of women created by advertising, and Rosie the Riveter in particular stands out, dressed in overalls and carrying a lunchpail to the factory. However emancipated Rosie the Riveter might have appeared, the image of the working woman still focused on woman's traditional place in the private sphere. The popular image of woman which evolved during the war years suggested that American women had never worked outside the home before (even though women had in fact been entering the job market steadily for decades), and that women had never performed factory work before (even though they had been working in factories for years).[54] In particular, it was assumed that if women worked to support the war effort, they were *really* working for their men. One newspaperwoman spoke, typically, of the "deep satisfaction which a woman of today knows who has made a rubber boat which may save the life of her aviator husband, or helped to fashion a bullet which may avenge her son."[55] In short, then, the image of Rosie the Riveter and her compatriots corresponded to a pre-war ideal. Thus historian Leila Rupp writes that "the appeals used to recruit women for war work strengthened the impression that the public Rosie was, inside her overalls, the same prewar woman who cooked, cleaned, and cared for her family."[56]

One could of course criticize these images of woman as blatant distortions of the real situations of women workers, but the goal of advertising, after all, is to create myths, not to reproduce reality. Yet the myth thus created is anything but simple. Rupp points out that Rosie the Riveter is an "exotic creature" who seems somehow out of place in the public sphere of men's work, and so the potentially jarring quality of the image is softened by the appeal to women's traditional roles as wives and mothers.[57] Perhaps during any war, the relation between private and public spheres is bound to be problematic. But particular to 1940s America is that the institutions of consumerism, advertising in particular, were firmly in place. Never before had there been such fastidious orchestrations of the possible harmonious interchanges between the two spheres—the battlefront and the home-front, the world of men and the world of women. The home would be regarded, simultaneously, as a recuperative refuge *and* as a battlefront. If American films of the 1940s, whether specifically devoted to war themes or not, revealed a profound ambivalence towards private and public life, it is because the culture was straining under the tension of different ideals of private and public existence. Emblematic of that strain was the wartime woman worker. Her participation in war industries suggests an integration of the private and the public, but she was constantly addressed (through advertising in particular) as if she were a pure creature of domesticity.

We know that film attendance peaked during the war, and given the number of men overseas, women viewers were more visible than usual. Some theatre managers commented on the increasing number of unescorted females who were attending moving pictures.[58] Given the strategic importance of women's roles vis-à-vis the private and the public, we might look at how, in the 1940s, women were addressed as film viewers.[59] Newsreels were shown with virtually all feature films, and a strategy first developed in Detroit to attract women to the newsreels is an interesting example of how cinema's narrative capacities were adapted to wartime conditions. Noting that women were less inclined than men to be interested in newsreels, exhibitors put together a one-hour program, focusing when possible on footage of areas where

Michigan soldiers had been sent. Advertisements were put in the newspapers offering free admission to mothers and wives of soldiers, who were asked to send in the names of their relatives in service. The program proved to be a smashing success, leading to an extended run and similar programs in other cities. The drawing card, of course, was the possibility of identifying loved ones. On opening day in Detroit, one woman saw a newsreel of a plane landing in Egypt, and recognized the plane as her son's from its number and nickname. And when she returned home that day, there was a letter from him confirming what she had just seen at the movie theatre.[60] One can hardly imagine a more striking mediation of the personal and the social: newsreel journalism becomes a narrative of family life. And it comes, perhaps, as no surprise that, as *Variety* reported, "it is believed numerous identifications are erroneous and it does not detract from the mounting interest. Houses have reported that different families have asked for film snips of the same soldier, both insisting he is their son."[61]

Not all film viewing in the 1940s would be so explicitly conditioned by the war, or by the possible connections between private and public life evidenced in this particular marketing strategy. But all commercial films of the period would connect to the war in one way or another. For the problematic relationship between private and public existence was not a simple result of the war, but rather was a fundamental aspect of that society which had undergone the transformation of consumerism.

David O. Selznick and the glass globe in *Citizen Kane*, cinematic versions of authors in *Madame Bovary* and *The Life of Émile Zola*, are suggestive of the changing dimensions of classical film narrative in the 1940s. The influence of the novel is in evidence from the earliest years of cinema. But in the 1940s, something changes. The confluence of increased production costs, a growing consciousness of the institutional quality of the medium, and an increasingly close relationship—with varying shades of mercantilism—between film and the novel, created a cinematic narrative institution of new depth and maturity. Kane, Selznick, and James Mason as Gustave Flaubert: these are the figurative sons of D. W. Griffith, and Kane's glass globe and Selznick's well-worn copy of *David Copperfield* are 1940s analogues to the sword that inspired *His Trust/His Faithful Trust*, the object which in Griffith's memory of childhood and then on the screen, represented the scope of narrative.

And casting an eye toward the film audience, the woman wartime worker is heir to another tradition. She may not be appropriately designated as Griffith's daughter, but the woman spectator in the 1940s, whether seeking imaginary narrative reconciliations of the two spheres or looking for loved ones in newsreels, is the descendant of two other traditions: that of the woman reader, and that of the immigrant spectator. Like them, American women viewers of the 1940s exemplify the changes in private and public existence which would be enacted in a variety of ways in the movie theatre.

Notes

34. Asheim, "Summary," p. 268.

35. Charlotte Brontë, *Jane Eyre* (1847; reprint, New York: Penguin, 1966), p. 39.

36. Cited in Margaret Farrand Thorp, *America at the Movies* (New Haven: Yale University Press, 1939), pp. 242–43.

37. Asheim, "Summary," pp. 263.

38. Sergei Eisenstein, "Dickens, Griffith and the Film Today," *Film Form*, ed. and trans. Jay Leyda (1949; reprint, Cleveland: World Publishing Co., 1957), p. 201.

39. David Bordwell, "*Citizen Kane*," in Ronald Gottsman, ed., *Focus on Citizen Kane* (Englewood Cliffs, N.J.: Prentice Hall, 1976), says that Kane sees "love solely in terms of power," p. 118.

40. Welles said of Rosebud: "It's a gimmick, really, and rather dollar-book Freud." See Joseph McBride, *Orson Welles* (New York: Viking Press, 1972), p. 44.

41. Joseph McBride says of Thompson: "The reporter, who stands for the audience, also stands for the artist approaching the contradictions of his subject-matter" (Ibid., p. 38).

42. Joseph McBride says: "We see the 'solution' for which we and Thompson have been searching, and we realize that it does in fact solve nothing" (Ibid., p. 42).

43. Robert Carringer, "Rosebud, Dead or Alive: Narrative and Symbolic Structure in *Citizen Kane*," *PMLA* 91, no. 2 (1976): 187.

44. Ibid., p. 191.

45. Christa Wolf, "The Reader and the Writer," in *The Reader and the Writer*, trans. Joan Becker (New York: International Publishers, 1977), p. 190.

46. lbid., p. 193.

47. Stewart Ewen, *Captains of Consciousness* (1976; reprint, New York: McGraw Hill, 1977), p. 164.

48. See Eli Zaretsky, *Capitalism, the Family, and Personal Life* (New York: Harper and Row, 1976), p. 67.

49. Charles Eckert, "The Carole Lombard in Macy's Window," *Quarterly Review of Film Studies* 3, no. 1 (1978): 2.

50. Ibid., p. 4.

51. Ibid., pp. 6, 19–20.

52. Ibid., p. 21.

53. Zaretsky, *Capitalism, the Family, and Personal Life*, p. 61.

54. See Leila J. Rupp, *Mobilizing Women for War: German and American Propaganda, 1939–1945* (Princeton: Princeton University Press, 1978), p. 177.

55. Ibid., p. 157.

56. Ibid., p. 153.

57. Ibid., p. 151.

58. *Variety* reported on a Pittsburgh theatre manager who said, "Gals have to get their romantic kicks vicariously since Uncle Sams been pulling so many eligibles out of circulation" (March 11, 1942, p. 1).

59. Yet it should be kept in mind that women have virtually always been regarded as key audiences for Hollywood films. *Variety* (August 4, 1942, p. 3) published the results of a new Gallup poll which claimed that as many men as women went to the movies. The following week a film critic responded: "It is not the percentage of men as against women that counts. It's *how* did *most* of them get there?" (August 12, 1942, p. 12). Whether men go to the movies or not, the critic claims, it is women who do the choosing.

60. The event is described in *Variety*, March 31, 1943, p. 23.

61. Ibid.

Questions and Projects

- How is the activity of reading (or writing) foregrounded in a film—such as Francois Truffaut's *400 Blows* (1959), Stephen Frears's *Dangerous Liaisons* (1988), or Quentin Tarantino's *Pulp Fiction* (1996)—and what significance does reading in these movies have in the public and private lives of the characters? How are reading and writing related to the activity of seeing or viewing in the film?

- Choose an adaptation in which the gender or sexual preferences of the characters play a prominent role (for example, one of the *Jane Eyre* adaptations [from 1934 to the 1990s] or Sally Potter's *Orlando* [1993]). Fashion an argument that discusses how gender influences the choices, changes, and omissions in moving from the literary work to the film.

*M*illicent Marcus's piece is a recent and detailed example of the importance of cultural and national perspectives in discussing the relationship between film and literature. Her reading is not only a detailed analysis of a Pasolini adaptation of Boccaccio's original Decameron, but also an accessible coordination of some of the most influential perspectives in cinema studies over the last two decades—including auteurism, semiotics, ideological analysis, the figuration of the body, and the contextualization of specific historical moments. Indeed, with these perspectives as guides, this essay demonstrates the numerous currents and crosscurrents that can inform an adaptation project when a literary text and a film contest each other for cultural authority.

"Pasolini's *Decameron*: Writing with Bodies" from *Filmmaking by the Book*

Millicent Marcus

Where *The Gospel According to St. Matthew* precipitated a stylistic crisis in Pasolini's filmmaking and forced him to revolutionize the technique that had served him so well in *Accattone*, *Mamma Roma*, and *La ricotta*, *The Decameron* signaled a radical thematic and ideological shift in his approach to his art.[1] As the first film of the *Trilogy of Life*—a triptych that was to include *The Canterbury Tales* (1972) and *The Arabian Nights* (1973)—*The Decameron* marked a move away from overt ideological filmmaking, with its cultivation of elite audiences, its renunciation of mainstream representational codes, and its fixation on the difficulty of communication, toward a more easily consumable cinema that reveled in its popular appeal.[2] It is no accident that *The Decameron* became one of the highest grossing films of 1971, and that it inspired an entire subgenre of sequels: *Decameroticus*, *Decameron proibitissimo*, *Le calde notti di Giovanni Boccaccio*, *Decameron nero*, *Quando le donne si chiamavano Madonne*, *Il meglio del Decameron e degli scrittori erotici del '500*, *Boccameron: una cavalla tutta nuda*, and the ingeniously entitled *Racconti proibiti di niente vestiti*.[3] Thus the film industry as well as the viewing public joined Pasolini in the celebration of the physical world, in the gaiety and "the sheer joy of telling and recounting" that freedom from overt ideological imperatives conferred on his art.[4] "Up to the time of the *Trilogy* my filmmaking motivations were ideological," Pasolini told Oswald Stack and Rosamund Lomax. "Now they're ontological. When you're young, you have a greater need of ideology in order to live. But when you grow older, life becomes more restricted and sufficient unto itself. This *Trilogy* constitutes a declaration of love to life."[5] But elsewhere, Pasolini attributes his withdrawal from ideological filmmaking to darker causes. The gaiety of the *Trilogy*, "the great desire to laugh is born from the definitive setting aside of 'hope.' I'm devoid, practically and ideologically, of every hope," he told Sergio Arecco. History has not fulfilled the Marxist-Hegelian promise that thesis and antithesis will eventuate in the longed-for synthesis of social justice. "My dialectic is no longer ternary, but binary. There are only oppositions, irreconcilable: *no sole del futuro*, no better world."[6]

This withdrawal into a mythic past and the loss of faith in historical progress do not by any means imply a rejection of the contestatory role of art, however. If there are only irreconcilable oppositions, then the artist must bear witness to them, occupying the firing line of public debate, playing the dissident role of Matthew's Jesus or the Old Testament prophet who constantly reminds us of unpleasant truths. Pasolini chooses to represent the past not to escape social relevance but to engage the present in polemical comparison. "I prefer to move in the past now because I believe the past to be the only force that can contest the present," Pasolini told Gideon Bachmann.[7] Here, as elsewhere in his art, sexuality provides the weapon for Pasolini's frontal attack on the contemporary status quo. Far from an entertaining romp in the medieval hay, the eroticism of the *Trilogy* is strategic—it stands as an alternative to the compromised and fallen expressivity of the technological world. With the "unreality of the subculture of the mass media and therefore of mass communication, the last bulwark of reality appeared to be 'innocent' bodies in the archaic, dark, vital violence of their sex organs," Pasolini wrote in the "Abiura dalla *Trilogia della vita*."[8] The untrammeled physicality of the *Trilogy*, its insistent creatural realism, means that each character "communicates with his own body, his own sanguine humors, his own material made color, mud, shattered teeth, sex, sweat," as Sandro Petraglia so aptly put it.[9]

Pasolini's recourse to the past and to the great erotic storytelling tradition from England to the Middle East is thus recourse to the naked human body as an irreducible medium of communication, to a semiosis of corporeality unobstructed by the civilizing veils of clothing and libidinal repression that culture has imposed upon it. Free to indulge their appetites, exposed in all their imperfections and innocence, the nude bodies of men and women in the *Trilogy* constitute a primal language, a prelapsarian physiological expressivity. But there is another side to Pasolini's vitalism. *The Decameron* is pervaded by a sense of death—for every naked reveler there is a corpse swathed in burial shrouds being carted along in a casket or carried aloft on a plank."[10] Tingoccio's exuberant fornication with his *comare* (mother of his godchild) is seen to be terminal—the jump cut from his postcoital return home to his postmortem funerary journey suggests a cause-and-effect linkage, John Donne's candle burning at both ends.

The dark side of Pasolini's vitalism and the insistence that this past contest the present make his film anything but the easily consumable product that its commercial success and its numerous cinematic offspring would suggest. Pasolini's corporeal semiotics, his technique of "writing with bodies," has the effect of defamiliarizing the Middle Ages, just as his antispectacular approach to the Christ story defamiliarized *The Gospel According to St. Matthew*. By removing the gowns and doublets and armor that clothe the nudity of medieval characters and by omitting the tapestries and the warm blazing hearths that mask the physical discomfort of their domestic life, Pasolini denies us the cozy complacency of conventional representations in storybooks and film.[11] Living in dark, mold-encrusted rooms, fighting dental problems unsuccessfully, coping with outdoor plumbing, Pasolini's characters in their corporeal expressivity convince us of the physical hardship of medieval life and increase the experiential distance between our reality and theirs.

But Pasolini's most consequential defamiliarizing operation is cultural, for the filmmaker is reacting not just to his textual source but to what Italian civilization has made of it in the intervening six centuries: a mainstay of the canon, a *Galateo* of polite behavior, a model of linguistic decorum. It is to this last that Pasolini directs his most obvious criticism, for the *questione della lingua* so importantly arbitrated by the Tuscan *trecentisti* receives a very un-Tuscan solution in Pasolini's film. By translating Boccaccio's normative latinizing prose into Neapolitan street talk, Pasolini is challenging the Tuscan-centricity of the Italian language and thereby criticizing Tuscany's dominance over the entire culture since the time of Boccaccio. In his essay "Nuove questioni linguistiche," Pasolini credits this linguistic autocracy with the imposition of a pseudonational language on the whole country in defiance of its plurilinguistic, regional, dialectal nature.[12] By replacing Boccaccio's exemplary Tuscan prose with Neapolitan dialect, the filmmaker is figuratively restoring to the common folk control of linguistic usage—a gesture whose political implications accord with Pasolini's overall popularizing intent. Accordingly, early in the film he makes explicit this linguistic strategy in the interval between the tales of Andreuccio and Masetto, when an old man gives a public reading of *The Decameron*, specifically the second story of the ninth day. The teller quotes Boccaccio's first sentence directly from the text, then interjects one phrase of some interest to our argument. Quoting Boccaccio he reads, "Super dunque dovete in Lombardia" ("You must know, therefore, in Lombardy"); then he improvises, "Dove ce stanno quelli che parlano toscano" ("Where those who speak Tuscan live"); and then he finishes Boccaccio's sentence. Impatient with the reading, the teller tosses the book aside and continues, "Signori miei, mo' ve spiego alla napoletana" (Gentlemen, now I'll explain it Nepolitan style).[13] The telling in dialect is clearly more successful than the reading in Tuscan, but here Pasolini carries his linguistic critique a step further. As the speaker develops the lively tale of the abbess who mistakes her lover's britches for a wimple, the attentive audience becomes prey to a pick-pocket whom we later recognize as Ser Ciappelletto. The story telling has put the listeners off guard, making them as inattentive as the poorly dressed abbess in the tale. Pasolini here seems to be attacking verbal narration as itself distracting, at variance with empirical experience and therefore to be replaced with the semiotics of bodies, the "corporeal writing" that will lead our attention back to the only reality that can be authentically lived.

This episode exemplifies what I would call an "allegory of adaptation" or an "umbilical scene" in which the film reveals the traces of its derivation from the parent text and discloses its interpretive strategy. The street-corner storyteller is a figure for Pasolini himself who transforms the elitist, literary source into an accessible item of popular entertainment. "Mo' ve spiego alla napoletana" could serve as the film's epigraph in its revelation of Pasolini's intent to restore the popular origins of Boccaccio's own storytelling art by reversing the medieval writer's refinement and elevation of his narrative raw materials. Thus where Boccaccio homogenized and gentrified his culturally disparate sources, which ranged from gossip, practical jokes, proverbs, folk legend, fabliaux, chronicle, exempla, and romance to hagiography, Pasolini returns to the popular roots of Decameronian inspiration and restores that legacy to the mass culture from which it derived.[14]

The filmmaker is at his most antiliterary in his very first complete episode—the tale of Andreuccio (2.5)—where the only character in the entire film to speak Boccaccio's language, full of grammatical inversions, hypotaxis, gerunds, and so forth, is the Sicilian prostitute, Fiodaliso. It is the very style of her telling that convinces Andreuccio of its unassailable truth. Pasolini accentuates the treacherous elegance of her tale within a tale by implicitly comparing it to a parallel, though differently styled, internal narration—that of Andreuccio as he recounts his adventures to the two robbers who have found him by olfactory clues. The protagonist's style is the diametrical opposite of Fiodaliso's, for his is paratactic, devoid of causal links, ordered by no device more complex than chronology. Andreuccio's naive discourse proves nearly as fatal to him as Fiodaliso's had been, for he thereby inadvertently reveals to the thieves how easily he can be duped, Not a whit too soon, Andreuccio learns his lesson and discovers how to read other speakers' verbal cues, as his had been read by his predators. When the thieving sacristan assures his accomplices that "i morti non mangiano gli uomini" ("the dead don't eat men") (26), Andreuccio correctly decodes this verbal message to his own belated advantage. In fact, many of the stories that Pasolini chooses to include in his film are about the instability and duplicity of language. Thus Caterina is able to invoke the nightingale to escape her overprotective parents and enjoy the embraces of her beloved (5.4), and through the language of incantation Don Gianni succeeds in making a cuckold of Pietro while not quite succeeding in making a horse of Gemmata (9.10). Most importantly, Ser Ciappelletto's false confession reveals the extremes to which linguistic falsification, and listener gullibility, can lead.

In this attack on verbal discourse as unstable and deceptive, Pasolini rejects Boccaccio and at the same time endorses his innermost significance. As author of the literary text, Boccaccio is indeed a self-conscious manipulator of dangerous and misleading verbal discourse. But he is also his own harshest critic, continually exposing the verbal ruses and deceptions of his characters, and hence of himself as the supreme manipulator of words. By introducing the volume with the tale of Ser Ciappelletto, the arch-storyteller who creates a fictional self and is canonized for it, Boccaccio issues a warning to his readers about the untrustworthiness of literary discourse, his own in particular. Thus, Pasolini's critique of Boccaccio's literariness coincides with the medieval writer's own frank appraisal of his poetic vocation. Where Boccaccio challenges literary discourse *from within*, using language in playful and self-sabotaging ways that call its truthfulness into question, Pasolini replaces literary discourse with corporeal writing, denuding the book of its refined integument, de-euphemizing its sexuality, reducing its obscene metaphors to the literal level of brute bodily referents. Thus Masetto's elaborate conceit of working the garden (3.1) is given concrete literal embodiment throughout the episode, and Pasolini explicitly weds tenor and vehicle in an imagistic juxtaposition that suggests the nuns' willing participation in the forthcoming sexual harvest. "Well, I have heard from all the women who have come here that nothing in the world is sweeter than what a woman does with a man" (29), says one nun to her companion. As she speaks, Pasolini photographs this nun in medium close-up with a huge cluster of grapes festooning the vine to her left. A cut to a subjective, low-angle shot of Masetto on a ladder gives visual prominence to his genitals and makes explicit their metaphoric link to the fruit of the vine. Pasolini literalizes an obscene metaphor by similar imagistic juxtaposition in the tale of Peronella (72). When the enterprising wife has her husband enter the jar to clean it from within, she has cleared the way for her lover Giannello to complete his exertions from without. With the words "Scrape, my husband, scrape, let's do things as we should! Uhm, higher, uhm, lower. That's right.... Come on, come on, scrape well. That's how I like it!" (36) Peronella engages in such successful double-talk that two mutually exclusive tasks are completed in obedience to one set of commands. The film enables us to see both the literal and figurative referents of her utterance and invites us to compare Peronella explicitly to the jar as a vessel to be entered by men and to be sold as a commodity. When Giannello promises to give Peronella's husband seven *denari*, the price includes an item that the seller had not bargained for: the sexual favors of his wife, enjoyed with impunity.

Because it is the profit motive that blinds Peronella's husband to his cuckoldry, the story well supports Pasolini's antibourgeois polemic. Much of Pasolini's adaptational strategy is dictated by this ideological requirement, such as the decision to juxtapose the tale of the nightingale (5.4) with that of the pot of basil (4.5), where the difference between comic and tragic outcomes in otherwise similar stories of forbidden young love hinges on the social status of the suitor.[15] Lisabetta's class-conscious brothers murder Lorenzo because his plebeian origins preclude marriage into the bourgeoisie, while Caterina's parents smile upon the union of their daughter with the well-born Ricciardo Manardi. To heighten the asperity of his social criticism, Pasolini relegates Boccaccio's Lorenzo from the Pisan working class to the Sicilian proletariat, adding regional bias to the victim's socioeconomic disadvantage.[16] The film's most scathing indictment of the bourgeoisie occurs in this episode, where Pasolini gives considerable dramatic development to the highly perfunctory textual murder. Boccaccio dispatches Lorenzo in two extremely compressed periods.

> The three brothers jested and chatted with Lorenzo in their usual manner, until one day they pretended they were all going off on a pleasure-trip to the country, and took Lorenzo with them. They bided their time, and on reaching a very remote and lonely spot, they took Lorenzo off his guard, murdered him, and buried his corpse.[17]

Pasolini's sequence, instead, is an agonizing exercise in homicidal foreplay, where the brothers amuse themselves with their victim and extract every possible ounce of psychological balm for their wounded middle-class male egos. The first grievance to redress is Lorenzo's slight to their masculine pride in his secret consorting with Lisabetta. In their fatherless family, the three unnamed and undifferentiated brothers serve as a collective paternal stand-in whose honor resides in their ability to protect Lisabetta's maidenhead and eventually to deliver her, intact, to the spouse of their choice. By violating their prerogative, Lorenzo has challenged their paternal authority and their very identity as males—an identity predicated on their exclusive control over Lisabetta's sexuality. Pasolini's fraternal threesome redresses this wound to its collective masculine pride in a ritual of communal urination. "Lorenzo, piss with us, it doesn't cost a thing. Come on, let's go," says the first brother with locker-room camaraderie. "But you, Lorenzo, don't think that we aren't men....

You thought wrong, you understand! We're men. We're men! Don't you see that we're men?" (53–54). This ominous flaunting of genitals foreshadows the climactic opportunity to vindicate their manhood which Lorenzo's murder affords them.

But Lorenzo's affront to the brothers is also socioeconomic, and they avenge their honor in a way that symbolically reasserts their class superiority. The entire sequence begins with a long shot of the hill that dominates the landscape and figures their proprietary hold on it, as well as furnishing Lisabetta with a topographical clue to Lorenzo's eventual burial site. What masquerades as a playful run through the woods has a twofold seriousness: it serves as a tour of the brothers' territorial wealth, and it anticipates the real predatory chase that is to follow. Pasolini's camera becomes an accomplice in this strategy, revealing the vastness of the property through long dolly shots that track the men as they race through the landscape at such speed that the horizontal lines of the terracing tend to break up this space into an abstract expanse of pure line, color, and movement. The effect is to denaturalize this nature as it becomes the arena for the enactment of man's most antisocial instincts. When the runners finally come to rest, the didacticism of their plot is made clear. This is "nostra compagna," one of the brothers observes. "Sit down, Lorenzo, because today there are no servants and masters" (54). This mock egalitarianism only heightens our awareness of the class gap and of the role it plays in motivating the conspiracy. To prove that this is indeed a day of fun and games, brother number two slathers the face of brother number one with grapes to the accompaniment of forced fraternal hilarity. Lorenzo plays along with what he takes to be innocent clowning, and reaction shots show him eating the proffered fruit, smiling, unaware that his will be the next face to be slathered—not with grape juice, but with the soil that Lisabetta will eventually clean off his features to ascertain the identity of the newly unearthed corpse. A cut to a low-angle shot reveals the brothers again in motion, now jumping over a pit that seems to mark the transition from benign foreplay to homicidal chase. Lorenzo hesitates on the brink of the pit, realizing that this leap will be irreversible.[18] A series of shots and reaction shots photographically recapitulates this war of wills, whose concentration of numbers and power on the predators' side makes its outcome a foregone conclusion. In a medium close-up of the three brothers, Pasolini matches their cajoling facial expressions with their choral encouragements to jump: "*Forza*, let's go, come on. What's he doing? *Forza*. Join the race. Let's go, Lorenzo" (54).

A cut to Lorenzo shows the sudden seriousness of one who has belatedly caught on, who has seen the murderous underside of this jesting. After the camera singles out brothers number two and three in their enticements, Lorenzo's reaction shot is his most consequential, for it marks the delivery of his only word of dialogue in the entire sequence:

"Why?" (55). This is a truly subversive question in that it challenges the social hierarchy of servants and the masters whose motivations are above employee scrutiny, and it disrupts the literal level of the brothers' murder plot by subjecting it to interpretation. When the third brother asks "What's wrong?" Lorenzo's seriousness gives way to a new kind of smile—no longer the smile of the innocent dupe, but the stoic acceptance of the victim who knows what awaits him on the other side. The tracking shots of the earlier part of the sequence resume, but the camera's movement is no longer horizontal as it follows Lorenzo up a slope, cutting back and forth from predators to prey until the sound of three rapiers being unsheathed confirms all our tragic presentiments. A jump cut to Lisabetta's window spares us the spectacle of the slaughter but intensifies its imaginative impact by forcing the viewers to complete the sequence with a murder of his or her own devising. Thus where Boccaccio's text dwells on Lisabetta's pathology of grief in decapitating her lover, planting the head in a basil pot, and worshipping its vegetal luxuriance until the brothers deprive her of even that consolation, Pasolini's emphasis is on the revenge itself and the way that the fraternal plot symbolically restores the proprietary and sexual power that Lorenzo had unwittingly usurped.

A similar antibourgeois stance dictates Pasolini's adaptive strategy in the Andreuccio tale (2.5). As the horse dealer who has come to Naples to buy wholesale in order to then sell the animals retail in Perugia, Andreuccio is the quintessential capitalist, the middleman who profits not by producing anything or performing a vital service, but by investing in a commodity and turning a profit by increasing its price without increasing its value. In making Andreuccio the pretext for antimercantile satire, Pasolini is following Boccaccio's lead where the tale's conclusion compresses into one period the intricate saga of capitalist trial and error. Advised to leave Naples immediately, Andreuccio "returned to Perugia, having invested, in a ring, the money with which he had set out to purchase horses" (McWilliam, 155). Part of the joke of this story is that Andreuccio thinks that he has come to Naples as a consumer—of horses, of wine, of women, and of food—and instead it is he who is consumed by a variety of con artists, from *la bella siciliana* to the two thieves who use him to rob the archbishop's tomb.

Pasolini takes Boccaccio's joke one step further. If Andreuccio is consumed by the city, he is also excreted from it in an analogy that explains an important omission from the text and a series of spatial and chromatic choices on Pasolini's part. In the *Decameron* story, Andreuccio experiences three infernal descents and three resurrections, a number whose theological ramifications are obvious and strategically used.[19] After the fall into the cesspool, Andreuccio is lowered into a well to be cleansed and is finally dropped into the tomb. Though Pasolini would hardly be averse to using trinitarian symbolism in a satiric way, he chooses to leave out the second descent, preferring to keep Andreuccio in his fecal state throughout the remainder of the episode.[20] Accordingly, the entire sequence is suffused with darkness and a chromatic predominance of browns and grays, and Naples is photographed as a series of dim, winding streets with distinctly intestinal overtones. Though it is never named in the film, Boccaccio explicitly labels the ill-famed neighborhood of Andreuccio's nocturnal wanderings "Malpertugio" or "evil opening" in an infernal allusion to the Dantesque Malebolge and in a revelation of the protagonist's obliviousness to the dangers of his setting. "The maid conveyed him to the lady's house, which was situated in a quarter called The Fleshpots [Evil Opening], the mere name of which shows how honest a district it was. But Andreuccio neither knew nor suspected anything of all this, being of the opinion that he was on his way to see a gentlewoman in a perfectly respectable part of the city" (McWilliam, 143). The long shot of Andreuccio's escape from the cesspool as he climbs out of a tiny opening in a sewage shaft, himself covered with feces, suggests that he is indeed the waste product of Malpertugio, of the intestinal system of the Neapolitan *mala vita* that consumes and excretes its victims when it has no more use for them. But the fact that Andreuccio succeeds in his business venture, recouping his original capital investment and actually turning a profit (the ruby ring was worth more than the 500 florins of his initial cash outlay), makes his fecal status at the end of the film's episode a telling retrospective commentary on the mercantile economy that underwrites his actions.

Other Pasolinian departures from Boccaccio's text have anticlerical logic. In the book, Masetto attributes his sudden restoration of speech to divine intervention—a fiction that the gullible abbess is only too happy to accept—while the film's Masetto confesses that his disability was a hoax, so that it befalls the mother superior to invent the fiction of the miracle. While Boccaccio's abbess is merely lecherous and gullible, Pasolini's is a deceiver—a conscious and self-interested abuser of her church's power to command belief. Similarly, in Pasolini's version of the Gemmata story (9.10), Don Gianni emerges as more villainous than Boccaccio's priest in his exploitation of the couple's abject poverty. Though Boccaccio describes Compar Pietro as "poverissimo" in the exposition to the tale, Pasolini makes explicit the causal link between poverty and the couple's sexual victimization by the priest in the dialogue preceding his consent to work his magic. "I beg you, for the love of God, Don Gianni, you see how poor we are. Perform this act of charity for us!" (60). The squalid domestic setting of the tale gives visual reinforcement to Pietro's plea for poverty relief through the priest's supernatural offices.

In the tale of Tingoccio and Meuccio, however, Boccaccio's own anticlericalism is put to other ideological uses. The *Decameron* story is a spoof on theological quibbling, on the scholastic mania for distinctions and degrees—a mania that finds legalistic expression in Dante's contrivance of the appropriate *contrappassi* for every possible subdivision of sin. Thus when Meuccio asks Tingoccio's ghost what punishment he suffers for sleeping with his *comare*, the sinner dismisses any theological hierarchy of "better" or "worse" adulteries. "Be off with you, you fool! There's nothing special down here about the mother of a godchild" (McWilliam, 582), Tingoccio had been told by a companion in the afterlife who was well versed in the nuances of divine justice. Though the film's Tingoccio makes the same profession of purgatorial indifference to *comari*, Pasolini's intent is less to spoof theological distinctions than to promote a generalized creed of free love.[21] When Meuccio races through the predawn streets of Naples to his own *comare*'s house and exuberantly mounts her, exclaiming "It's not a sin," the lasting message has nothing to do with godparentage and everything to do with generic sexual permissiveness. The referent of "It's not a sin" is what we see on the screen—two bodies copulating—not the pseudoscholastic quibble of Boccaccio's fabliau. It is appropriate that Pasolini's final episode gives retrospective justification to the film's corporeal semiotics, where naked bodies are seen as the only remaining vehicles of untainted expressivity in a technologically tainted world, "the last bulwark of reality," as he concluded in the "Abiura." Rereading the film in the light of Meuccio's proclamation, a series of episodes lines up behind the banner of guilt-free sexuality, beginning with the nun's insistence that copulation with Masetto "è un paradiso," where the metaphor retains its literal affiliation with the prelapsarian garden state. No story is more redolent of wholesome sexuality than that of Ricciardo and Caterina (5.4) whose lovemaking is neither prurient nor sentimentalized in the film. The predawn nuptials performed on the near-naked couple by Caterina's accommodating parents are an exercise in Edenic innocence, where for once the institutionalized powers of family and church see fit to sanction the course of natural passion.

Pasolini's politics of adaptation require him to make drastic changes in Boccaccio's figure of the artist as he is represented within the text. Though the medieval author internalizes himself within *The Decameron* as the isolated defender of the humanities against his philistine attackers in the introduction to the fourth day and again in the conclusion, it is in the ten frame-story youths that he most importantly incarnates the figure of the artist. Pasolini, instead, dispenses with the *brigata* of socially privileged storytellers who exemplify the courtly ideals of language and decorum so dear to the Italian elite and replaces these artist figures with the character of the fresco painter—Giotto's disciple—whose working-class affinities would make him more amenable to Pasolini's political strategy. The painter constitutes a rejection of all the middle-class behavioral ideals embodied in Boccaccio's *brigata*. The young people's attention to propriety in dress, meals, and diversion is utterly disregarded by the painter, who is at home in peasant's mantle, wolfs down his food, and obviously cares nothing for appearances. Though Pasolini's figure of the artist is clearly modeled on Giotto himself as he emerges from Boccaccio's fifth tale of the sixth day, the filmmaker has carefully edited out the opening lines of the *Decameron* story which reveal in Giotto a landowner returning from his property in the Mugello. In fact, Pasolini's Giotto has little in common either with Boccaccio's or with the somewhat business-minded Giotto we get from medieval archives.[22] Instead, Pasolini's painter is an anachronistic construct of a post-Romantic age: the genius rapt with inspiration who takes his models from life but must be motivated by some transcendent creative impulse. This new Giotto is thus not only a convenient vehicle for Pasolini's politics of art, he is a personal analogue to the filmmaker's idealized mode of creation.[23]

Nor is the Giotto figure alone in realizing his art. Pasolini goes to great lengths to document the teamwork on which his fresco painting depends, from the pigment grinding and chromatic mixing to the placement of scaffolding and the offering of brushes. Four of the fragments that intervene between tales in the film's second half involve Giotto's co-workers, whose interactions range from pranks and banter to serious, even inspired, cooperation. Though Giotto eats in the refectory with the friars while his apprentices dine less ceremoniously among themselves, the maestro shares sleeping quarters with them and seems to prefer their company. The workshop is a prime example of the Pasolinian utopias already explored in *Accattone* and *The Gospel According to St. Matthew* where a male community bonds in the service of a superhuman ideal, be it a spiritual or an aesthetic one. That this is a collective, working-class ethos, untainted by notions of property, family prestige, or personal honor, is proved by its opposition to the dystopia of Lisabetta's brothers, whose feigned egalitarianism and pseudocamaraderie had led to Lorenzo's fatal entrapment. Bound by their commitment to ownership and sexual control, the brothers formed a Pasolinian anticommunity whose governing assumptions revealed, by contrast, the positive values of the workshop's corporate identity.

The filmmaker's disposal of Boccaccio's frame story has momentous formal as well as political implications. True, Pasolini replaces Boccaccio's *cornice* with a bipartite frame of his own when fragments of the Ser Ciappelletto story intervene between successive tales to glue together the first half of the film, while the Giotto figure gives rise to a framing figure for the second half.[24] But such a technique is fraught with ambiguities. When characters emerge from tales to become protagonists in a frame story that contains other tales, we are approaching the Chinese box structure that Pasolini will use to such advantage in *The Arabian Nights*. There, however, the ambiguity is authorized by the textual source, while here it is used to subvert the original by challenging its cherished assumptions about form. When a frame no longer serves to distinguish the work of art from that which is without, when container and contained coextend like the two edges of a Möbius strip, our deepest held convictions about aesthetic form are called into question. In the very narrations of his tales, Pasolini issues the same kind of formal challenge to his viewers. Because the transitions between episodes are so abrupt and unexpected that we often find ourselves well into the next story before we realize that the previous one is over, we miss any sense of narrative closure that would retrospectively order the tales.[25] Thus Pasolini denies us the formal satisfactions of complete stories with beginnings, middles, and ends just as he fails to give his film an expository introduction or a conclusion that would retroactively explain and organize the whole. In fact, the concluding frame-story fragment shows Giotto before the three panels of his fresco, but only two of them have been completed. The third panel remains empty, making the fresco cycle as imperfect (in the etymological sense of the term) as the film itself.[26]

By dispensing with Boccaccio's elegant and elaborate frame story, by playing havoc with the original sequence and thematic progression of the tales, by making personal and arbitrary the principle of order that had been so public and necessary in Boccaccio, Pasolini issues his most serious statement about the cultural and historical distance separating the medieval text from its cinematic imitation. Boccaccio's work, bearing witness to the decline in the scholastic worldview, nonetheless nostalgically holds onto its rigorous sense of structure, wherein the principles of order had to be explicit enough for the viewer "to re-experience the very processes of architectural composition," according to Erwin Panofsky.[27] By rejecting The Decameron's meticulous structure, Pasolini is perhaps scolding Boccaccio for clinging to a vestige of scholastic order that was already obsolete—a hollow fiction at great variance with the realities of trecento Italian culture. But the criticism goes both ways, for Boccaccio's ordered cosmos points to the very impossibility of such ordering in the contemporary world. Pasolini thus endorses Frederic Jameson's argument that literary genres are predicated on the ideological possibilities offered by a culture at a given point in its development.[28] Boccaccio's culture offered (if somewhat nostalgically) the raw material for complete, coherent narrative forms, whereas Pasolini's obviously does not.

In the fresco painter, Pasolini combines a politically acceptable equivalent to the figure of the artist with a perfect medieval analogy to the filmmaker. Both the fresco cycle and the film require team efforts for their realization, both narrate through visual images, thus potentially reaching a much broader, more democratic audience than literature can, and both juxtapose a series of still frames to tell a story that unfolds in time and space. To further the analogy between the two media, Pasolini casts himself in the role of Giotto, and when the painter wanders in the marketplace outside the church to find models for his art, he literally constructs a frame with the fingers of both hands, placing two fingers vertically and crossing them with two fingers horizontally to form a square.[29] Thus, Giotto the painter sights his models the way Pasolini the filmmaker sets up his next shot. And not surprisingly, the figures that Giotto sights in the crowd are the protagonists in Pasolini's next episode.

This analogy between fresco painting and filmmaking lies at the heart of Pasolini's metafilm, for it is here that he can make explicit the mechanics of his medium and define the language appropriate to the cinema in opposition to the language of his literary source. In Boccaccio's *Decameron*, he has chosen a paragon of literariness against which to posit his own semiotics of corporeality. Again and again in his theoretical writings, Pasolini insists that the film lexicon, unlike the symbolic systems of verbal languages, has its source in reality. "If the cinema is thus no more than the written language of reality ... it means that it is neither arbitrary nor symbolic, and therefore it represents reality through reality."[30] Though this source in reality does not deny film language the double articulation accorded all linguistic systems, it does give cinema a concreteness and an immediacy that distinguish it from purely symbolic codes. In the figure of Giotto, Pasolini is able to dramatize the genesis of film language in reality as the painter sights models from the "real-life" crowd in the marketplace outside the church. Indeed in these sequences Pasolini analyzes the constituents of his cinematic code, providing a visual gloss for his remarks in the essay "La lingua scritta della realtà."[31] As Giotto selects out the single elements to be included in his fresco panel, Pasolini implies the *cinémi*, or indivisible formal units that he equates to the phonemes of verbal languages. The completed fresco panel is the *inquadratura*, the smallest complete unit of meaning, or the cinematic equivalent of the linguists' moneme. In the juxtaposition of adjacent panels in the fresco cycle, Pasolini suggests the celluloid strip itself with its succession of still photographic compositions. Contiguity in the fresco cycle provides the linkage that montage accords cinematic stills. Pasolini's insistence on foregrounding the editing process is part of his anti-Hollywood polemic, his rejection of mainstream conventions that govern the "seamless" flow of images and render natural their succession, even while constantly shifting camera angles and shot distances. The Italian filmmaker instead employs a disjunctive editing style that flaunts the opacity of technique by being intrusive, by making us aware at every moment that our perspective is being manipulated. As Geoffrey Nowell-Smith so aptly observes, Pasolini displays "a wilful disregard of the constructive nature of the editing process ... [and] a firm positive insistence on the single shot as the unit of reality."[32] Indeed, the format of the episode film makes more explicit than ever the disjunctions of montage, because the abrupt transitions between various tales are like so many jump cuts—seemingly arbitrary and unmotivated juxtapositions of discontinuous *inquadrature*. In a sustained fiction film, the logic of the narration may distract us from the crude fact of montage, whereas the episode film constantly reminds us of the mechanics of linkage.

Though his tendency to break up the surface of reality into fragments, along with his use of pastiche, suggest a postmodernist Pasolini, there are powerful counterarguments for such an alignment. Pasolini revels in the thickness and unity of meaning, in the proliferation of semantic levels, that deny postmodernist disjunction and superficiality, for all his art ultimately tells the same Ur-story of humanity's fall from a state of primal innocence and grace into the anti-Eden of contemporary urban industrial existence. This makes his *Decameron* a serious critical reading whose moments of surface jollity hardly suffice to conceal its pervasive inner tension. Thus Pasolini polemically engages Boccaccio whenever the text departs from the filmmaker's ideological agenda, whenever Boccaccio's Middle Ages resist Pasolini's need to idealize this archaic, subproletarian alternative to the contemporary status quo. Perhaps the most serious polemic revision of *The Decameron* can be found in Pasolini's treatment of the tale of Ser Ciappelletto, whose structural position at the beginning of Boccaccio's text signals its supreme importance for the medieval writer's own literary program.

The first contrast to note is one of tone or atmosphere, an almost ineffable difference in the aura of the two canonization scenes. Boccaccio, through the narrator Panfilo, describes the friar-confessor's sermon and its public consequences as follows:

> And in brief, with a torrent of words that the people of the town believed implicitly, [alle quali era dalla gente della contrada data intera *fede*], he fixed Ser Ciappelletto so firmly in the minds and affections of all those present that when the service was over, everyone thronged around the body, to kiss his feet and his hands, all the clothes were torn from his back, and those who succeeded in grabbing so much as a tiny fragment felt they were in Paradise itself. (McWilliam, 80)

Immediately the term *fede* should put us on guard, for it is a vestige of the con game that Ser Ciappelletto has been playing all along—as a notary he has been selling his *fede* expensively, and the Burgundians have been described as especially gullible, especially prone to believing any and all sworn oaths. Moving in a herd toward this body, ready to tear off its shroud in their eagerness for physical tokens of transcendence, Boccaccio's Burgundians are little more than medieval groupies, brainless materialists incapable even of conceptualizing the beatitude to which they aspire through saintly contact. Panfilo's narrative voice speaks from the superior perspective of class and demystified reason, and he has nothing but contempt for Ciappelletto worship.

Pasolini's canonization scene is devoid of such condescension. His camera participates in the reverence of the suppliants who replace the violence and bestiality of Boccaccio's Burgundians with dignity, grace, and reserve. Shot in the Gothic vaulted crypt whose geometric center is occupied by the shrouded body on a tall black catafalque, the entire scene has a balanced, classical beauty heightened by the strains of Gregorian chant. The sequence ends with the poignant mise-en-scène of hands reaching from all sides to touch the corpse. Though the camera's perspective is that of a detached and physically elevated observer, it has none of the patronizing, demystified superiority of Panfilo's narrative voice, choosing instead to enter into the worshippers' own sense of awe at the spectacle of sanctity.

The reverential atmosphere of this canonization scene and several Pasolinian interpolations suggest that Ser Ciappelletto's confession may not have been mere showmanship after all. In the film's final tale, Pasolini has Tingoccio give Meuccio an apt reminder. "Oh, they say that at the moment of death whoever repents is saved!" (62). Significantly, the narrative of Tingoccio's death is interrupted by a dream vision that awakens the Giotto character—it is a vision of the Scrovegni Chapel Last judgment in which the Christus Pantocrator is replaced by the Madonna and Child. By substituting the mother intercessor for the Judging Christ, Pasolini's film gives clemency priority over punishment, mercy over divine retribution. This takes us back to Ser Ciappelletto's deathbed confession and to the question of his soul's fate in the afterlife. Despite some metaphysical hedging, Boccaccio finally damns Ciappelletto in Panfilo's epilogue to the tale:

> Nor would I wish to deny that perhaps God has blessed and admitted him to His presence. For albeit he led a wicked, sinful life, it is possible that at the eleventh hour he was so sincerely repentant that God had mercy upon him and received him into His kingdom. But since this is hidden from us, I speak only with regard to the outward appearance, and I say that this fellow should rather be in Hell, in the hands of the devil, than in Paradise. (McWilliam, 81)

It is here that Pasolini's adaptation moves in the direction of ambiguity, for his oft-professed irrationalism, his mistrust for bourgeois positivist thought, leads him to entertain the possibility of what Panfilo dismisses as "occulto" ("hidden").[33] Thus Pasolini engages in a double adaptive strategy—theologically elevating and stylistically reductive—in characterizing Ser Ciappelletto. The text's protagonist is a subtle and ingenious con artist who runs rhetorical circles around the somewhat simpleminded friar confessor. He bamboozles the holy man through a variety of confessional tactics, including (1) telling half-truths that leave out the damning second half—for example, that he is a virgin (because his sexual preference is for men); (2) the confession of trivial sins, such as his craving for lettuce while fasting; and (3) the reversal of roles, such as his reprimand of the friar for spitting in church and his insistence on the general need for greater spiritual stringency. Pasolini's Ser Ciappelletto lacks such rhetorical inventiveness and, in fact, appears as simple as the friar in his verbal self-presentation. The film's dialogue descends to the level of a vaudeville routine in its comic tug-of-war when Ciappelletto offers to confess his worst sin and then backs down out of feigned cowardice. "Tell it, and we'll pray to God together," begs the friar confessor. "I can't," cries Ciappelletto. "Come on, son, speak." "I can't, father." "But, son, make this effort." "Nooo!" "In the name of God!" "No." "Yes." "No." "Yes." "No." "Yes." "O.K. If you promise to pray for me, I'll tell you" (42–43). The comic silliness of this exchange is only heightened by the sobbing intensity of both men's delivery and the repetitive camera-work of cross-cuts to close-ups of each speaker as he utters his respective monosyllabic plea. At this point, the camera cuts to the two eavesdropping brothers who serve as the demystified public to the confession and confirm our sense that this is a virtuoso performance indeed. "The man is dying, but he's doing all this for us? Well, then, he really is a saint!" (43).

Clerical reassurances prompt Ser Ciappelletto's final outcry: "Oh what are you saying, father? My sweet mother, who carried me in her womb, day and night. For nine months she carried me in her womb" (43). It is crucial that, unlike Boccaccio's Ciappelletto, Pasolini's expires in the course of confessing and that his final sentence invokes his pregnant mother. Photographed in extreme close-up as he utters these last words, "For nine months she carried me in her womb," the protagonist dies with in utero thoughts. A cynical reader of this scene would ascribe Ciappelletto's new infancy to his final self-forgery, the delivery of a new baby fiction ready to start its life as the sanctified object of Burgundian gullibility. But recourse to medieval iconography would suggest other-wise. With Pasolini's training in art history and his love of figurative quo-tation, I cannot imagine that the Pisan "Triumph of Death" fresco, where the souls are imaged as newborns issuing from the mouths of corpses, was far from his mind when he conceived the dialogue and the mise-en-scène of Ciappelletto's last rites. Pasolini's focus on the dying man's mouth as he speaks of his prenatal past suggests that these final words have double reference—semantically to his first birth, iconographically to his second.

Death of old forms and rebirth into new ones is, of course, a way of talking about adaptations, especially transgressive adaptations that destroy as they create, challenging and subverting the authority of their textual models. If Ciappelletto's spirit leaves his flesh to find new life in the hereafter, Pasolini's resurrected *Decameron* does the opposite, giving flesh back to words, literalizing sexual euphemisms, replacing nightingales with genitals—in short, writing with bodies. Unfortunately, Pasolini's newfound corporeal expressivity was to be short-lived, as the "Abiura della *Trilogia dalla Vita*" so bitterly announces. "The 'reality' of innocent bodies has been violated, manipulated, tainted by consumer power: indeed, such violence on bodies has become the most macroscopic datum of the new human era."[34] In *Salò* (1975), Pasolini will continue to write with bodies, but these will no longer serve as the site for prefallen physiological expressivity. Now the naked flesh can express only allegorically—as the tablet on which Fascist history will write its most violent and obscene inscriptions on the Italian body politic.

Notes

1. This is a revised and expanded version of an earlier article entitled "*The Decameron*: Pasolini as a Reader of Boccaccio," *Italian Quarterly* 21 (Fall 1980–Winter 1981), 175–80. For an outline of Pasolini's narrative sequence, synopses of the individual tales, and the film's credits, see the Appendix.

2. On the new phase in Pasolini's production, see Peter Bondanella, *Italian Cinema from Neorealism to the Present* (New York: Continuum, 1991), p. 287; and Adelio Ferrero, *Il Cinema di Pier Paolo Pasolini* (Padua: Marsilio, 1977), p. 118.

3. On this "sequel mania," see Bondanella, *Italian Cinema*, p. 291; and Mario Quaragnolo, *Dove va il cinema italiano?* (Milan: Pan, 1972), p. 165.

4. Gideon Bachmann, "Pasolini Today," *Take One* 4 (1973), 21.

5. Interview published in *Pier Paolo Pasolini*, ed. Paul Willemen (London: British Film Institute, 1977), p. 71.

6. Sergio Arecco, *Pier Paolo Pasolini* (Rome: Partisan, 1972), pp. 74–75. See also Fabien Gérard, *Pasolini, ou le Mythe de la Barbarie* (Brussels: Éditions de l'Université de Bruxelles, 1981), p. 84.

7. Bachmann, "Pasolini Today," p. 21

8. "Abiura dalla *Trilogia della vita*" is included in the volume of screenplays by Pasolini, *Trilogia della vita: Il Decameron, I racconti di Canterbury, Il fiore delle mille e una notte*, ed. Giorgio Gattei (Milan: Mondadori, 1987), p. 7. See also Fulvio Panzeri, *Guida alla lettura di Pasolini* (Milan: Mondadori, 1988), pp. 140–41.

9. Sandro Petraglia, *Pier Paolo Pasolini* (Florence: La Nuova Italia, 1974), p. 108.

10. On the *eros-thanatos* connection, see Vito Attolini, *Dal romanzo al set: Cinema italiano dalle origini ad oggi* (Bari: Dedalo, 1988), p. 176; and Ferrero, *Il cinema di Pasolini*, p. 121. *Vitalism* is Ferrero's term.

11. On the deglamorizing of the medieval image in the media, see the review by Colin Westerbeck, Jr., in *Commonweal* 95 (November 12, 1971), 158.

12. The essay is published in *Empirismo eretico* (Milan: Garzanti, 1981), pp.

5–24. For the English translation, see Louise K. Barnett, ed., *Heretical Empiricism*, trans. Louise K. Barnett and Ben Lawton (Bloomington: Indiana University Press, 1988), pp. 3–20.

13. Pasolini, *Trilogia della vita*, p. 26. All quotes from the film's dialogue come from this edition of the screenplay. The translations are mine, and subsequent page references are included in the text.

14. On Pasolini's reversal of Boccaccio's gentrifying operation, see David Bevan's superb insights in "Pasolini and Boccaccio," *Literature/Film Quarterly* 5 (1977), 26ff.; and Ferrero's elegant commentary in *Il cinema di Pasolini*, p. 119. Several critics have read this scene as an explicit formulation of Pasolini's adaptive mode. See Bondanella, *Italian Cinema*, p. 287; Bevan, "Pasolini and Boccaccio," 27; and Ben Lawton, "Theory and Praxis in Pasolini's *Trilogy della vita*," *Quarterly Review of Film Studies* 2 (November 1977), 400. The reader is referred to Lawton's learned and thorough study, whose explication of Pasolini's thematic patterns and art historical allusions, especially to the work of Giotto and Breughel, are invaluable interpretive contributions, and ones to which my own reading is deeply indebted.

15. Several critics have seen this juxtaposition as ideologically motivated. See Bondanella, *Italian Cinema*, p. 288; and Lawton, "Theory and Praxis," p. 404.

16. Bondanella, *Italian Cinema*, p. 288.

17. Giovanni Boccaccio, *The Decameron*, trans. G. H. McWilliam (Middlesex, Penguin, 1981), p. 367. Henceforth, page references will be included in the body of the text with the notation "McWilliam."

18. In "Pasolini and Boccaccio," p. 28, Bevan aptly observes: "The brothers ... feel the need to play with their victim until the moment when he finally understands that he is about to be killed."

19. For a fine study of Boccaccio's satire of the sacraments in this tale, see Greg Lucente, "The Fortunate Fall of Andreuccio da Perugia," *Forum Italicum* 10 (1976), 323–44.

20. Angelo Moscariello has another explanation for Pasolini's omission of the well episode, suggesting that the filmmaker wanted to avoid the "aspetto avventuroso" of the original. See *Cinema e/o letteratura* (Bologna: Pitagora, 1981), p. 148.

21. On the film's categorical endorsement of guilt-free sexuality, see Bondanella, *Italian Cinema*, p. 289.

22. John Larner, *Culture and Society in Italy, 1290–1420* (New York: Scribner, 1971), p. 274.

23. Naomi Greene sees an analogy between the fresco painter's delight in the physical aspects of his art (pigments, cartoons, etc.) and Pasolini's lifelong impulse to "'seize' reality in a tangible way." See *Pier Paolo Pasolini: Cinema as Heresy* (Princeton, N.J.: Princeton University Press, 1990), p. 186. In contrast, several critics read this figure of the artist as self-satire, as a putdown of artistic pretensions. See, for example, Westerbeck's review in *Commonweal* 95, p. 158.

24. On this twofold frame, see Greene, *Pier Paolo Pasolini*, p. 188.

25. According to Philip Strick in his review for *Sight and Sound* 41 (Spring 1972), 110, this technique is detrimental to the humorous effect of the punchline.

26. For his extremely thought-provoking speculations on this third panel, see Lawton, "Theory and Praxis," p. 409.

27. Erwin Panofsky, *Gothic Architecture and Scholasticism* (New York: Meridian Books, 1968), p. 59.

28. Frederic Jameson, "Metacommentary," *PMLA* 86 (1971), 9–18.

29. On fresco painting as a form of medieval didactic filmmaking, see Lawton, "Theory and Praxis," pp. 406–7. On the collaborative nature of fresco painting and filmmaking, see Roger T. Witcomb, *The New Italian Cinema* (New York: Oxford University Press, 1982), p. 128. On the epistemological implications of Pasolini's inclusion of himself as *subject* in *The Trilogy*, see Gian Piero Brunetta, "La visione di Pasolini," *Italian Quarterly* 82–83 (Fall 1980–Winter, 1981), 152ff. For Pasolini's comments on his performance of the Giotto role, see Petraglia, *Pasolini*, p. 107.

30. Pasolini, "Battute sul cinema," in *Empirismo eretico*, p. 229. For the English translation, see Barnett, *Heretical Empiricism*, p. 225.

31. This essay is published in *Empirismo eretico*, pp. 198–226. For the English translation, see Barnett, *Heretical Empiricism*, pp. 197-222.

32. Geoffrey Nowell-Smith, "Pasolini's Originality," in Willemen, *Pier Paolo Pasolini*, p. 10. On Pasolini's tendency to "decompose to the maximum the narrative unity," see Gian Piero Brunetta, *Storia del cinema italiano dal 1945 agli anni ottanta* (Rome: Editori Riuniti, 1982), p. 662.

33. On Pasolini's irrationalism, see his comments in *Pier Paolo Pasolini nel dibattito culturale contemporaneo* (Pavia: Amministrazione provinciale di Pavia, 1977), pp. 92ff.

34. Pasolini, "Abiura," p. 8. On Pasolini's progressive disenchantment with liberated sexuality, see Ben Lawton, "The Evolving Rejection of Homosexuality, Sub-Proletariat, and the Third World in Pasolini's Films," *Italian Quarterly* 82–83 (Fall 1980–Winter 1981), 170.

Questions and Projects

- Choose another adaptation that highlights cultural or cross-cultural issues—such as John Huston's 1956 *Moby Dick*, Akira Kurosawa's *Ran* (adapted from *King Lear*), Grigori Kozintsev's 1964 Russian *Hamlet*, or Marleen Gorris's *Mrs. Dalloway* (1997). Are there features of the adaptation that reflect the culture of the film rather than the culture of the literary work?
- For his 1971 adaptation of *The Decameron*, Pasolini chooses a literary work composed between 1349 and 1353. Choose an adaptation in which the literary source is from a different historical period, and analyze what that period offers the filmmaker in adapting the work to his or her present day.

*Q*uestions of race and related ideological concerns can often figure in adaptations or other movements between film and literature. While the 1950s were a turbulent and creative period for many
writers connected to the movies, Mark A. Reid's examination of the
predicament of African-American writers opens a rich dimension
within it. He makes clear that writing itself, and especially writing
for the movies, is fraught with politics and other visible or hidden
concerns. For black writers and other groups marginalized by the
film industry (then and now) such social and professional politics
can create thorny and frustrating contexts in which opportunities are
the product of many historical forces, such as the growing box-office
power of those groups. For Reid, strong writers and filmmakers find
a way to challenge the dominant forces on their own terms and produce a "textual dialogue" within the finished work that reveals a
vision that, in the best cases, still retains its racial origin.

"Literary Forces Encouraging the Use of Black Writers" from *Redefining Black Film*

Mark A. Reid

Hollywood did not produce black family films written by African-
American writers until the late 1950s. The new opportunities for black
film writers in Hollywood resulted in part from studio interest in film
adaptations and partly from Hollywood's recognition of the popularity
of African-American literature. The industry's preference for screen
adaptations of popular works is evidenced by the Academy of Motion
Picture Arts and Sciences 1956 creation of the Best Writing Award for
the Best Adapted Screenplay. This move affected the subject matter and
themes that studio films would choose to dramatize.[2]

Between 1940 and 1960 one short story and a few novels by
African-Americans had received such acclaim that film studios decided
to adapt them for the screen. Frank Yerby's best seller, *The Foxes of
Harrow* (1946), was produced by Twentieth Century-Fox in 1947.
Willard Motley's two novels *Knock on Any Door* (1947) and *Let No Man
Write My Epitaph* (1958) were produced by Columbia in 1949 and 1960,
respectively. MGM produced *Bright Road* (1953), a screen adaptation of
Mary E. Vroman's short story "See How They Run" (1951).

Moreover, black-oriented dramas written by African-Americans
were increasingly accepted by mainstream American theaters and professional critics during the 1950s. In 1953, Louis Peterson's *Take a Giant*

Step appeared on Broadway. *Take a Giant Step* was revived off-Broadway in 1956 and received critical acclaim. The off-Broadway Greenwich Mews Theatre produced William Branch's historical dramatization of John Brown and Frederick Douglass, *In Splendid Error* (1954). Alice Childress's satire on black stereotypes, *Trouble in Mind* (1957), and Loften Mitchell's dramatic treatment of school desegregation in *A Land Beyond the River* (1957) were also produced for the stage. In 1959, the most significant event of the decade for black theater occurred when Hansberry received the Critics Circle Award for *A Raisin in the Sun*.[3]

By the end of the fifties, major studios were hiring African-Americans to write scenarios for studio-produced black-oriented films. With the integration of black writers came more pressure for studios to broaden their depiction of African-American life and experiences. The development of a third subtype of African-American family film is the result of the hiring of black scenarists, the increasing popularity of black-oriented film fare, and the impact of the civil rights movement.

The literary exchange between studio executives and black writers during this period resembles the relationship that newly independent African nations enjoyed with their former colonial administrators. The black writer, like the newly independent African nation, was still beholden to the system of production, distribution, and consumption. Individual writers or nations could not disrupt the flow and if they tried, other blacks would eagerly replace them. In fact, the film industry now engaged in a sort of neocolonial relationship between black artists, their audience, and mass-produced black art. Only through the processes of negotiation and resistance could African-American writers and white studio executives generate a filmic portrait of the African-American family. On the one hand, this neocolonial relationship usually ensured that formal conventions were respected. On the other hand, black scenarists used subversive rhetorical strategies that obscured the over-determined nature of the American film industry, which demanded adherence to the generic form. For example, in accordance with the requirements of the film industry, most early black-authored family films, such as *Take a Giant Step*, *The Learning Tree*, and *Black Girl* (1972), focus on the qualities of one family member.

During this period, there were a few short-lived rebels who penned scenarios that broke with the genre's insistent focus on one member of the family. *A Raisin in the Sun* and *The River Niger* brought attention to the dreams of individual family members and thereby revealed the genre's ability to speak to a multitude of black others whose voices were not confined to one black hero(ine). The neocolonial partnership between studio and black writer requires one to study how the industry packages a black-authored film for consumption by an audience. This requirement is as important as a close reading of the film text. Film analysis must include descriptions of the industry, the product, and consumer-related issues as well as aesthetic concerns that involve the relationship between film and spectator.

Regardless of the film industry's assumption of an "average" African-American moviegoer and attempts to market films to such, black audiences employ different reading strategies based on their class, ethnicity, gender, and sexual orientation. Even within the limited confines of neo-colonial black film production, the reactions of black *or* white audiences are far from predetermined. Finally, the reception of this subtype is equally indeterminate if one views these films as examples of the disjointed nature of products issued from a relationship between the colonizer (the master or patriarchal discourse) and the colonized (those bound to masters or confined within a patriarchal system).

...

A Raisin in the Sun

One of the earliest major examples of a black family film that was written by a black scenarist and independently produced for a major studio is the David Susskind and Philip Rose Production of *A Raisin in the Sun*. The film was directed by Daniel Petrie, and Hansberry adapted her original play for the screen.

Susskind was interested in producing *Raisin* because he recognized that it would be a financially and critically successful Broadway play. *Variety*'s coverage of the play's pre-Broadway tryouts was one way in which Susskind may have developed an interest in *Raisin*. On 28 January 1959, *Variety* reported,

> Whatever the theatre shortage in Gotham may be, there must be room for "A Raisin in the Sun." Already of solid substance in tryout form, the Lorraine Hansberry drama is loaded with smash potentials that should ripen into substantial Broadway tenancy.

Variety also heralded the fact that the play was "written, directed and acted by Negroes, (with only one white role in the cast)." This mode of production, which entailed black control over three major aspects of dramatic art, was adopted by a mainstream American entertainment institution—Broadway. Later, Hollywood would institute a similar mode of production and thereby rejuvenate the black commercial film movement within the dominant structure of Hollywood studios.

The content of *Raisin* seemed to be far different from the content of plays made by whites about blacks, and *Variety* hinted at this: "*Raisin* stands out as a shining example of talent potential if given the opportunity. The play should draw comment not only for the quality of its presentation but also for the depth of its message."

On March 11, 1959, *Raisin* opened on Broadway and received rave reviews. Two days later, Susskind wrote to Sam Briskin, Columbia Pictures vice-president in charge of production, and expressed his interest in a screen adaptation of *Raisin*. Susskind wrote:

> I have an inside track on this property as a consequence of my relationship with the author and her attorney. I think if you were to manifest real interest I could be granted a pre-empt right on the play for motion pictures at the best price offered by any competitor. At this writing, United Artists, Harry Belafonte, Metro-Goldwyn-Mayer, Paramount, Fox, Hall-Bartlett and the Mirisch Brothers have expressed strong interest in purchasing the play.[14]

At this early date, at least six major film producers were interested in a screen adaptation of the play. Susskind, writing in the same letter, recognized that the play presented "a warm, frequently amusing and profoundly moving story of [N]egro life in which *for once*, the race issue is not paramount." He reassured Briskin that a film version featuring Poitier would attract an audience: "after *The Defiant Ones* and the upcoming *Porgy and Bess*, Sidney Poitier would be an important box office element."

By the 16th of March, Briskin wrote "we [Columbia] have had this interest ... since we first learned of the play and its pre-New York openings ... we have been approached by others both in and out of the studio."[15] Before a month had passed, *Variety* reported on 1 April 1959 that Columbia Pictures in association with Susskind and Rose had acquired the film rights to *Raisin* for $300,000. Susskind formulated the preproduction package that had been accepted by the studio. The package included himself and Rose as co-producers, Hansberry as scenarist, Poitier as featured star, and costars Claudia McNeil, Ruby Dee, and Diana Sands.

Martin Baum, the agent for Poitier and *Raisin*'s black stage-director Lloyd Richards, initially suggested that Richards direct the film version. Columbia's vice-president of publicity and advertising Paul Lazarus discussed this possibility with Briskin, who inquired about Richards's CBS-TV videotape production of *Raisin*. In a letter to Lazarus, Briskin reported that "when it got down to the last couple of days of rehearsal and the cameras were placed on the act he [Richards] seemed lost and CBS had to throw in a TV director to help him."[16]

Thus, Columbia refused to give Richards an opportunity to direct the film adaptation of the Broadway play that he directed. Columbia studio executives were both cautious and backward. They wanted to produce *Raisin* because of its financial and critical success, yet they did not want to make the same gamble that Broadway had made with Richards, one of the first blacks to direct a Broadway play. When

Columbia executives approved Susskind's three-picture contract with director Daniel Petrie, *Raisin* had its director.[17] Petrie had made one film, *The Bramble Bush* (Warner, 1960), and was safe according to Columbia's standards.

Even though Columbia executives rejected Richards as the director, they accepted Hansberry as the scenarist. The primary reason that Columbia accepted Hansberry was *Raisin*'s status as a very hot property which gave its writer some leverage in deals with the studio. However, Briskin would not allow Hansberry any changes or additions to the screenplay which might threaten a mass audience. For example, Hansberry's first draft of the screenplay included Travis Younger having to bring fifty cents to school for special books about African-Americans. Columbia production executives Briskin and Arthur Kramer and the story editors William Fadiman and James Crow "agreed that this should be deleted from the screenplay," because it was not in the play. In addition, the Columbia production team "agreed that the addition of race issue material ... should be avoided." because "the introduction of further race issues may lessen the sympathy of the audience, give the effect of propagandistic writing, and so weaken the story, not only as dramatic entertainment, but as propaganda too."[18]

The production team also sought to eliminate Beneatha's comment that "all Africans are revolutionaries today," calling it an example of "surplus in the race issue category and potentially troublesome to no purpose." In addition, executives argued that "Beneatha's dialogue about Africans needing salvation 'from the British and French' could give the picture needless trouble abroad."[19]

These suggested deletions are examples of the sort of censorship that occurs in Hollywood-produced and -distributed black commercial films. Since Hollywood films are produced for international markets and most black commercial films include social criticisms, studios usually tone down criticism of their potential audiences.

In *Raisin*'s case, Columbia story editors and executives were quick to reject Beneatha Younger's pan-African consciousness because their audience was not going to be limited to black pan-Africanists and white liberals like Susskind and Rose. Columbia's intended audience for *Raisin* included British and French colonialist sympathizers, and Columbia's recommended deletions acknowledged their presence. The audience for whom a black-oriented film is made determines film content and form and thus affects the filmic representation of black culture. Critics must identify the studio's estimation of an "intended audience" and describe and interpret the underlying ideology.

In the above instance, Columbia's executives suggested three deletions in *Raisin*'s sociopolitical and cultural elements. The power to delete certain ideological expressions of black culture highlights the limitations that Hollywood places on black scenarists and black directors involved in black commercial cinema. Film theoretician Gladstone Yearwood writes, "if the practice of black cinema is derived from that of Hollywood, then it will serve to reproduce the unequal relations characteristic of blacks in society."[20]

When black artists are involved in the mode of production as writers and directors, however, then these films become something other than mere Hollywood films. The presence of blacks in positions of power forces the critic to reformulate terms and elaborate new definitions. This critical process involves defining variables of image control (as in Beneatha's pan-African remarks, which were not cut) and determining the studio's actual exercised power. I use the term "colonized" to describe major studio productions, such as King Vidor's *Hallelujah* (MGM, 1929), which are written or solely directed by whites. In addition, I use the term "neocolonized" to refer to major studio productions. such as *Raisin*, which are written or directed by black people. These two categories distinguish the two forms of black-oriented major studio productions.

The critical success of the film adaptation of *Raisin* is demonstrated by the letters that Susskind received from people in the film and television industries. NBC special projects producer-director Robert K. Sharpe wrote,

> Perhaps more in this industry than any other we are judged by what we do when we have the opportunity to do it. In "Raisin in the Sun" I feel not only have you been loyal to a property which could have been changed in so many ways for expediency, but you and your associates have produced an even more immediate and compelling piece than the play itself. It is indeed a credit to the movie industry and certainly will be to this country overseas.[21]

This congratulatory letter conveys the prestige value *Raisin* had for its studio and the United States. However, the owner of William Goldman Theatres expressed an important reservation when he thanked Susskind: "We are presently in consultation with Columbia as to the best approach ad-wise in order to garner the greatest possible return at the box office. I am sure you realize that the picture does present a problem from a selling standpoint due to its subject matter. It is imperative that we reach a mass rather than just a class audience."[22] One way in which Columbia attempted to solve this problem, as well as exploit what Sharpe had discerned as "a credit to the movie industry," involved promoting *Raisin* as a prestige picture. Columbia made *Raisin* a United States entry in the 1961 Cannes Film Festival. The film thereby acquired an international prestige that grew when the festival gave *Raisin* a special award. The Screenwriters Guild also nominated it for the Best Screenplay of the Year award that same year. This award and nomination helped increase Hollywood's acceptance of black writers and the black family film genre.

On 10 January 1962, *Variety* reported that *Raisin's* domestic rentals amounted to $1,100,000.[23] *Variety's* estimated domestic rentals for *Raisin* nearly equaled Columbia Picture's $1,500,000 production costs reported in *Ebony* magazine.[24] Thus, *Raisin* was neither a financial disaster nor a box-office success. *Raisin* offered the studios proof that a low-budget, skillfully written black scenario about a black family which features well-known black performers can accrue prestige as well as return a moderate amount of money to its distributor. The film's effect on audiences and film critics, however, did not equal the play's critical acclaim and popularity among both black and white theater audiences. This imbalance may have resulted from the different expectations of theater and film audiences. Major film productions like *Raisin* require mainstream audience approval, but theater productions like *Raisin* can attract an interracial audience and still focus on topics that would offend a mainstream film audience. It is understandable that the film had little effect on mainstream film audiences, and that most film critics ignored the importance of this film.

It is an unquestionable fact that the first priority of the film industry is to avoid products that threaten its major markets. Nonetheless, if one performs a close reading of the black family films adapted from African-American literary sources, one discovers the resiliency of the ongoing struggle that black writers have waged against dehumanized images of black family life.

Textual Dialogue in *A Raisin in the Sun*

Like most committed black artists, Hansberry developed the story of the Younger family by experiencing its sociological equivalent. Hansberry attended Englewood High School on Chicago's southside, where she made friends with the black working-class youth who attended her school. James Baldwin wrote that "much of the strain under which Lorraine worked was produced by her knowledge of this reality, and her determined refusal not to be destroyed by it." Baldwin observed that he "had never in (his) life seen so many black people in the theatre. And the reason was that never before, in the entire history of the American theater, had so much of the truth of black people's lives been seen on [the Broadway] stage. Black people had ignored the theater because the theater had always ignored them."[25]

Granted, it is problematic to assert that an imaginative work like *Raisin* reflects the collective voices of working-class black America. But Hansberry's working film script generates a dialogic language that empowers a black working-class family in a particular region and at a particular time—post-World War II Chicago. The following discussion of the Youngers will serve as a case study of the filmic dramatization of political diversity within a black working-class family.

In *Raisin*, textual dialogism results from the family members who express different aspirations and political and religious beliefs. Lena's religious beliefs are an area of conflict between herself and her children. Walter Lee, her thirty-five-year-old son, wants to purchase a liquor store while Ruth, the wife of Walter Lee, considers abortion. Beneatha, Lena's daughter at college, freely questions the existence of God and the value of marriage.

Raisin attempts verbally and visually to affirm Afro-American working-class interests, especially through the two white male characters who interact with Walter Lee and the Younger family. Mr. Arnold is the representative *sign* of white corporate America. His relationship to Walter is determined by the socioeconomic relationship between unskilled, black America and a postindustrialized America. Walter represents black men who live in northern, industrialized cities. Karl Lindner portrays the intra-class racial hostility of working-class American ethnics. Lindner's relationship to the Younger family signifies the white working-class that practices racially restrictive housing covenants that forbid blacks from purchasing homes in white neighborhoods. Thus, Lindner is the representative *sign* of this white collectivity. The interaction between Lindner and the Youngers occasions a dialogic discourse that wealthy Mr. Arnold and corporate America resist. Raisin explores linear mobility along class lines *the integration of predominantly white working-class neighborhoods* but neglects or is unable to suggest an integration of the unskilled black into white corporate America.

The Younger family articulates desirous dream discourses that generate an inter-familial dialogue. Lena's dreams encompass three different actions: placing $3000 in a savings account for her daughter's (Beneatha) medical school education, placing a $3500 down payment on a home for the Younger family, and giving her son $3500 to open a checking account. It is Lena Younger's three-fold dream that includes the dreams of Beneatha, Ruth, and her deceased husband Big Walter. The promise of a medical school education for her college-trained daughter represents the advancement of black women. The purchase of a home for the Younger family shows a desire for better housing and permits the family melodrama to critically discuss the issue of racially segregated housing.

Raisin begins with Ruth Younger leaving the bedroom and entering the living room where her son, Travis, is asleep on the couch. Travis must sleep in the living room because there is not enough room in the two-bedroom apartment in which five family members live. Ruth awakens Travis and rushes him into the hallway bathroom that the Youngers share with their neighbors. Returning to the bedroom, she proceeds to do the same to her husband. He responds with two questions that reveal their marriage is "festering like a sore." Walter's first response questions the logic behind waking him up to go to a bathroom already occupied by his son. His second response illustrates his growing obsession with the $10,000 insurance money. He asks Ruth about the money and then asks her to persuade Lena to give him the insurance money so he can purchase a liquor store with his two friends Willie and Bobo. Ruth rejects Walter's request because she believes that the money belongs to Lena.

The opening dialogue and action establish that Walter Lee has displaced the collective Younger voice for that of an individual desire. Walter has assimilated the rhetoric of small business without its necessary requirement—experience and training. When Ruth rejects Walter's request, he counters with "I'm trying to talk to you about me!" Here, the reference "me" does not include the promise of a medical education for his sister Beneatha, nor does it include placing a down payment on a new home for the Younger family. Walter's desire does not encompass a group consciousness, and his entrepreneurial desire ignores the collective dreams that sustain the Younger family.

It is a bit obtuse to characterize Lena as a matriarch who dominates the members of her household. Throughout the play, Lena refers to her deceased husband Big Walter as an agent of her actions. Her son Walter Lee, on the other hand, repudiates Lena's dreams and the mythic qualities of Big Walter. In the assimilative mode, he constantly compares himself to wealthy Mr. Arnold and similar white men. Walter develops an entrepreneurial interest in a liquor store as a means to escape poverty and says that he must have the $10,000 insurance money that Lena will receive for the death of her husband.

The scene that presents Big Walter as the imaginary signifier of the black working-class and Lena as its poet takes place when Walter has left the apartment. Lena is "paying witness" to the memory of her deceased husband. She says, "You know Big Walter always hated the idea of being a servant. Always says man's hands wasn't meant to carry nobody's slop jars and make their beds. Always used to say they was meant to turn the earth with, make things. That husband of yours, Walter Lee, he's just like him." Lena's statement precedes a scene that presents Walter in his chauffeur uniform busily polishing Mr. Arnold's black limousine. The off-camera voice of Mr. Arnold is heard over a loud speaker: "Walter, bring the car around. Please." The camera follows Walter as he drives the car around the expanse of Mr. Arnold's mansion. Then the camera fades in on Walter rushing to open Mr. Arnold's car door. Arnold exits from the car, hands Walter a newspaper, leaves the camera frame, and enters a downtown office building. Walter, like many who aspire to enter corporate America through unskilled beginnings, is exposed to the world of Mr. Arnold and wants to be like him. But Mr. Arnold only offers Walter a newspaper. Walter lacks the education and the opportunities that would admit him into the office building that towers over him. Walter stands outside the building. He does not participate in corporate deals, he observes them with a sense of frustration.

Walter's position as a passive onlooker with frustrated dreams results in an oppositional language that explores the dynamics of the frustrated, black, male ego. His ego, having disregarded the myth of Big Walter, tells us about Mr. Arnold's myth. In Walter's attempt to measure up to Arnold, he totally neglects the survival strategies of Big Walter and the memories of Lena his mother.

Lena encourages aspiration through education and racio-familial memory; these are elements that transcend the individualistic aspirations of Walter. Unlike her son, Lena wants to devote the $10,000 insurance payment to three different purposes: education, housing, and savings. The purchase of a two-flat house represents the failed dream of Big Walter and Lena. The dream is secured but it remains the responsibility of the family to pay the mortgage. Lena says that she will use "part of the insurance money for a down payment and everybody kind of pitch in." The house is a collective sign that signifies the possibility of achieving a group aspiration. The two-flat is no mere signifier of middle-class desires for home ownership nor does it represent a desire to live in an integrated neighborhood. The new home carries forth Big Walter's dream since it connects his past struggle with the present state of the family's crowded living quarters. The house also becomes the collective sign of the Youngers' ability to resist the white Clybourne Park Improvement Association's bribe to forego their civil rights.

When Walter is entrusted with the responsibility to open the savings account for Beneatha and the checking account for himself, he gives the $6500 to Willie Harris, who absconds with the money. Walter's entrepreneurial dreams are crushed but they resurface when Mr. Lindner appears. Lindner is the representative of the Clybourne Park Improvement Association, a group of white homeowners who want to buy the two-flat from the Youngers at an inflated price. Earlier in the story, Walter had refused Lindner's offer but he now reconsiders it. After being swindled by Willie Harris, Walter asks Lindner to return to the Younger apartment because he now will accept the bribe. Lindner returns and Ruth tries to send Travis downstairs to prevent him from witnessing Walter accept the bribe. But Lena insists that Travis witness his father's actions. Lena says, "No. Travis, you stay right here. And you [Walter] make him [Travis] understand what you're doing.... You teach him good. Like Willie Harris taught you. You show where our five generations done come to. Go ahead son." Walter takes on the mantle of his deceased father and the five generations of Youngers. He affirms the collective memory and thereby educates the sixth generation in the resistance struggle. Walter says,

> I have worked as a chauffeur most of my life—and my wife she does domestic work in people's kitchens. So does my mother. My father ... was a laborer most of his life. And that's my sister over there, and she's going to be a doctor. This is my son, who makes the sixth generation of our family in this country. We have thought of your offer and have decided to move into our home because my father ... my father, he earned it.

Walter Lee's monologue articulates a collective working-class voice, a racial consciousness, and a vision of black womanhood as mothers, laborers, and soon-to-be professionals.

Raisin explores, then, three major issues: race, class, and gender. The film shows the constant friction between the laboring class of white Mr. Lindners and the equally laboring class of black Youngers. It portrays the racial and class differences between the wealthy, white Mr. Arnold, and the dreams and vision of an unskilled, black Walter Lee. It mirrors the black woman's growing awareness of her right to reject motherhood and plan parenthood around her professional career. The film celebrates the African-American vision of a collective consciousness in which polyphony reigns.

Raisin simultaneously portrays a black matriarchal family structure that is rooted in several value systems—capitalism, black feminism, religious fundamentalism, and pan-Africanism. In *Raisin*, family members discuss residential segregation, abortion, atheism, and the liberation of African nations. The presence of conflicting desires between family members and those outside the family circle permits interfamilial and extrafamilial dialogue and, simultaneously, avoids the erasure of black generative discourses.

The film industry's increasing need to attract African-American audiences requires it to create black-oriented products. But to understand this industrial necessity, one must also discern the ways in which blacks participated in the artistic construction of black-oriented films. Film industry executives, even during the period of independently-produced, studio-distributed films, such as *Take a Giant Step* and *A Raisin in the Sun*, reaffirmed the dominant visual representation of the black family. However, black screenwriters such as Peterson and Hansberry used dialogue to undermine a film's apparent middle-class values. This indeterminacy of meaning is only one of the levels at which tension occurs. Similarly, certain forms of reception can assimilate, appropriate, and resist any visual representation of black family life.

The illusory nature of dominant racial-gender discourses generated by most films helps to circumvent the threatening nature of a popularized "black" form and its reception. Consequently a subversive black character, such as Beneatha in *A Raisin in the Sun*, is unthreatening in her affirmation of black socialism. Beneatha's indeterminate reception permits the production of subversive works. Her pan-African and black feminist subjectivity refuses assimilation by a mass audience. Her dialogue on Africa, planned parenthood, and feminism invites a resistant spectatorial positioning. The indeterminate receptive quality of black family films, then, permits dominant and subversive readings.

By the seventies, the independently-produced, studio-distributed African-American family film permitted a broader vision of black American life. Black middle-class family melodramas, such as *Take a Giant Step* and *A Raisin in the Sun*, spoke to the era of integration and polite militancy.

During this period the black film market required films that spoke to despairing urban youths, rather than to parents who remained hopeful that social programs would return. Black and white youths demanded and regularly paid the price of admission. Urban black youths frequented inner city movie theaters while white youths went to those in the suburbs. Many inner city theaters showed films that attracted a black youth audience. Consequently, black family films no longer hid the single-parent welfare family behind smiles of hope. They revealed the grim reality of urban uprisings, abandoned buildings, gang violence, and a new generation locked into economic dependency and psychological poverty. Some of the films that document this period are J. E. Franklin's screen adaptation *Black Girl*, Eric Monte's screenplay *Cooley High* (AIP, 1975), and Joseph A. Walker's screen adaptation *The River Niger*.

The hybrid black family narrative, like the hybrid minstrelsy humor of Eddie Murphy, can conceal its racist, sexist, and homophobic elements. Such an ability to conceal becomes equal to the hybrid's ability to reveal itself as one with the majority of its *imagined* audience at a particular time in history....

Notes

2. Andrew Dowdy, *The Films of the Fifties* (New York: William Morrow and Company, 1973), 90. Dowdy writes, "The decline of original scripts in favor of films based on popular novels [and plays] inextricably tied the larger studios to the increasing permissiveness of American fiction."

3. Genevieve Fabre, *Drumbeats, Masks, and Metaphor: Contemporary Afro-American Theatre* (Cambridge, Mass.: Harvard University Press, 1983), 13.

...

14. David Susskind to Sam Briskin, 13 March 1959. This and all other Susskind letters cited are in the David Susskind Papers, Wisconsin State Historical Society, Madison, Wisconsin.

15. Sam Briskin to David Susskind, 16 March 1959.

16. Sam Briskin to Paul Lazarus, 5 November 1959.

17. Harold Stern to Bernard Birnbaum, 1 June 1960. This letter is from Petrie's attorney to Columbia Pictures assistant treasurer-secretary Birnbaum. Also see Jack Pittman, "Real Things vs. Studio Mockups," *Variety*, 20 July 1960, 23.

18. Arthur Kramer to David Susskind, 30 December 1959.

19. It should be noted that during the late 1950s and well into 1960 Africa was witnessing the Mau Mau liberation movement against British colonialists in Kenya, the Algerian liberation movement against its French colonialist government, and civil unrest in the Belgium Congo.

20. Gladstone L. Yearwood, "Toward a Theory of a Black Cinema Aesthetic," in *Black Cinema Aesthetics*, ed. Gladstone L. Yearwood (Athens, Ohio: Ohio University Center for Afro-American Studies, 1982), 71.

21. Robert K. Sharpe to David Susskind, 21 March 1961.

22. William Goldman to David Susskind, 3 April 1961.

23. "1961: Rentals and Potentials," *Variety*, 10 Jan. 1962, 58.

24. In "A Raisin in the Sun," *Ebony* (April 1961): 53, the author states: "with all obstacles overcome and the movie an accomplished fact, Columbia is eagerly awaiting the day when it can recoup its $1½ million investment."

25. James Baldwin, introduction to *To Be Young, Gifted and Black*, by Lorraine Hansberry (New York: New American Library, 1970), xii.

Questions and Projects

- Look closely at the 1961 *A Raisin in the Sun* and analyze in as much detail as possible the elements in it that reveal both the presence of mainstream cinema and the counterforces of an African-American literary voice.

- The exchanges between literature and film can dramatize a politics of race in many ways. Select another racially charged work—such as Spike Lee's *Malcolm X*, David Lean's 1984 *A Passage to India*, or the 1998 big-budget adaptation of Tony Morrison's *Beloved*—and discuss how race informs many of the questions or problems that surround these scripts and movies.

*M*ichael Renov's analysis of a film by filmmaker Jonas Mekas is
an important addition to the film/literature discussions as it
continues to bring more experimental and documentary or nonfiction
film into the debates. Arguing Mekas's connection with the literary
essay, Renov draws on a tradition that extends back through the sixteenth century and the writings of Michel de Montaigne. Although the
essay has changed a great deal over the centuries—appearing as
didactic editorials, self-portraits, and photo-journalism—it has
remained on the edges of conventional literature where its unpre-
dictability and protean forms have made it difficult to categorize while
allowing it special access to the changes in private and public life. To
make this point, Renov introduces a variety of recent critics and theoreticians who focus sometimes difficult arguments about subjectivity,
public experience, or the fragmentations of memory. One of the implicit points here (and in much modern discussion of the essay) is that the
essay may respond better than any other literary or film form to the
disjointed realities and experience in the twentieth century.

"*Lost, Lost, Lost*: Mekas as Essayist" from *To Free the Cinema*

Michael Renov

And so the opinion I give is to declare the measure of my sight, not
the measure of things.
—Montaigne, *Essays*

Of course, what I faced was the old problem of all artists: to merge
Reality and Self, to come up with the third thing.
—Mekas, "The Diary Film"

In the conclusion of a remarkably perceptive review of Jonas Mekas's
Lost, Lost, Lost appearing soon after the film's 1976 release, Alan
Williams suggests a relationship between the autobiographical project of
this, the first volume of *Diaries, Notes, and Sketches*, and "the spirit of
Montaigne and self-examination."[1] In so doing, Williams situates the
work within an essayistic tradition whose roots, though traceable to
Montaigne's three-volume *Essays* of the late sixteenth century, might be
said to include certain writings of Nietzsche, Adorno, and, most recently,
Roland Barthes. Indeed, the essay form, notable for its tendency toward
complication (digression, fragmentation, repetition, and dispersion)
rather than composition, has, in its four-hundred-year history, continued
to resist the efforts of literary taxonomists, confounding the laws of genre

and classification, challenging the very notion of text and of textual economy. In its heterogeneity and inexhaustibility ("with an 'amoeba-like' versatility often held together by little more than the author's voice" [Bensmaia 1987, ix]), the essayistic work bears with it a logic that denies the verities of rhetorical composition and of system, indeed of mastery itself.[2] Knowledge produced through the essay is provisional rather than systematic; self and object organize each other, but only in a temporary way—"Nothing can be built on this configuration, no rules or methods deduced from it" (Good 1988, 4).

The Montaignean essay derives in part from disparate precursor forms—the confessional or autobiography as well as the chronicle—insofar as its codetermining axes, its concern for self and other ("the measure of sight" as well as the "measure of things" [Montaigne 1948, 298]), enact what Gerard Defaux has called the *Essays'* "two-fold project." Descriptive and reflexive modalities are coupled; the representation of the historical real is consciously filtered through the flux of subjectivity. Neither the outward gaze nor the counter-reflex of self-interrogation alone can account for the essay. Attention is drawn to the level of the signifier ("let attention be paid not to the matter, but to the shape I give it" [Montaigne 1948, 296]); a self is produced through a plurality of voices, "mediated through writing, forever inscribed in the very tissue of the text" (Defaux 1983, 77).

This plurality of voices provides a clue to a fundamental if implicit presumption of the essayistic mode, namely that of indeterminacy. Neither locus of meaning—neither subject nor historical object—anchors discourse so much as it problematizes or interrogates it. This foundation of epistemological uncertainty has been widely theorized, initially by Montaigne himself, as in his essay "On Repentance": "The world is but a perennial movement. All things in it are in constant motion.... I cannot keep my subject still.... I do not portray being, I portray passing.... If my mind could gain a firm footing, I would not make essays, I would make decisions, but it is always in apprenticeship and on trial" (Montaigne 1948, 3.2.610–11). That more contemporary essayist, Roland Barthes, claimed that the fragmentary or discontinuous writing of his latter works enacted a counter-ideology of form inasmuch as "the fragment breaks up what I would call the smooth finish, the composition, discourse constructed to give a final meaning to what one says, which is rule of all past rhetoric.... [T]he fragment is a spoilsport, discontinuous, establishing a kind of pulverization of sentences, images, thoughts, none of which 'takes' definitively" (Barthes 1985, 209–10).

Despite the epistemic distance separating Montaigne and Barthes, their respective writing practices enforce a shared refusal. If neither being-as-essence nor final determinations (neither first nor last causes) arise in the essays of Montaigne or Barthes, this reticence can be attributed in part to the protocols of (essayistic) writing they share. Essayistic practices achieve a degree of commonality not through thematic consistency (as is the case with genre) but through formal and ideological resemblances.

For the young Georg Lukács, the essay was an "intellectual poem" whose first exemplar was not a literary trace but the life of Socrates. Unlike tragedy, whose end informs the whole of the drama, the life of Socrates and the essay form alike render the end an arbitrary and ironic moment. "The essay," declared Lukács, "is a judgment, but the essential, the value-determining thing about it is not the verdict ... but the process of judging" (Lukács 1974, 18). Socrates as essayistic phenotype comes to stand for a method that is active, fragmentary, and self-absorbing—ever in pursuit of a question "extended so far in depth that it becomes the question of all questions" (14). In Reda Bensmaia's phrase, the essay is an "open-ended, interminable writing machine," for just as the real resists the strictures of representation (how to frame or carve out a historical personage or event without the loss of authenticity), so too are the fixity of the source and the 'subject of enunciation called into question. The interminability of the essay follows from the process-orientation of its activity, the mediation of the real through a cascade of language, memory, and imagination. Montaigne's "book of the self," the essay as autobiography, refuses any notion of simple or self-evident origins in a manner consistent with the Barthesian pronouncement: "I am elsewhere than where I am when I write" (Barthes 1977, 169).

In classical poetics, the coherence and the synthetic power of a work are the aesthetic manifestations of a rather different epistemological assumption, that of the unity and stability of the subject. Montaigne's refusal of being-as-stasis is one precursor of the more radical contemporary theoretical position that wishes to suggest otherwise: "In the field of the subject," writes Barthes, "there is no referent" (ibid., 56). As formulated in the latter works of that writer, the essay form is the textual manifestation of indeterminacy par excellence; heterogeneous and resistant to precise boundaries, it is metaphorizable as a Japanese stew, a broken television screen, a layered pastry. Consequently, the essay eschews grand design; Bensmaia (1987) characterizes its formal procedure as a "tactics without strategy" (51).

Little wonder that films such as *Lost, Lost, Lost* and the remainder of Mekas's *Diaries, Notes, and Sketches*, Raul Ruiz's *Of Great Events and Ordinary People* (1979), Chris Marker's *Sans soleil* (1982), Trinh T. Minh-ha's *Naked Spaces: Living Is Round* (1985), or the pair of television series produced by Jean-Luc Godard and Ann-Marie Mieville, "Six fois deux" (1976) and "France/Tour/Detour/Deux/Enfants" (1978)—all of which could be termed essayistic—have alternately intrigued and puzzled audiences and critics alike with their failure to conform to generic expectation or classical structuration.[3] In all cases, the works would appear to straddle certain of the antinomies that have defined the boundaries of film scholarship: fiction/nonfiction, documentary/avant-garde, even cinema/video. Frequently, the critical appraisal of the taxonomically unstable film or video work returns to the name of the author: the television efforts of the seventies are an extension or revision of earlier Godard obsessions; *Naked Spaces* grapples with issues of Third World feminism and the limits of language as Trinh has done in previous film and literary efforts; *Sans soleil* is the summum of Marker's career as itinerant gatherer of images and sounds. And *Lost, Lost, Lost* is the work of the chief polemicist and celebrant of the New American Cinema. The diary films of Mekas thus can be said to spring from (the) underground; the autobiographical renderings of an artist can only be art.

Yet it is my purpose to speak of Mekas as essayist, to claim for *Lost, Lost, Lost* and the other volumes of *Diaries, Notes, and Sketches* a discursive position shared by the aforementioned as well as by other essayistic works, a position mobile in its resistance to generic encirclement, one that traces a trajectory within and across the historical fields of the documentary as well as of the avant-garde. Far from being a mere quibble over scholarly classification, the discussion of Mekas's work within a documentary context yields several dividends: on the one hand, the relatively moribund critical discourse surrounding nonfiction is enlivened, its aesthetic horizons broadened; on the other, *Lost, Lost, Lost* is more easily delivered of its status as a key work of contemporary film historiography, a work that teaches us about history and about the limits within which the filmic inscription of history is possible. Finally, the placement of *Lost* within a documentary context is essential for the present enterprise in another way. There can be little doubt that Mekas's diary-film project offers one of the most exhaustive instances of self-examination in the history of the cinema. And yet, as has been established, the essayistic is notable for its enmeshing of two registers of interrogation—of subjectivity and of the world. It is my contention that *Lost, Lost, Lost* shares with Montaigne's *Essays* an unyielding attentiveness both to the measure of sight and to the measure of things. My greatest concern in what follows will therefore be for the shape and tactical dynamics of a *documenting* gaze and a desire—to retrace the visible and the historical—that impels the film.

The placement of *Lost* within the documentary tradition remains consistent with the genesis of Mekas's project. According to the filmmaker, the documentary intent of the earliest diary efforts constitutes *Lost*'s prehistory: "The very first script that we [Jonas and his brother Adolfas] wrote when we arrived in late 1949, and which was called *Lost, Lost, Lost, Lost*, was for a documentary on the life of displaced persons here" (MacDonald 1984, 84). Significantly, the kinship between the founding intention and the project's eventual outcome has remained generally unremarked. Indeed, virtually every critic who has written about *Lost, Lost, Lost* has focused on the emergence of an authorial voice that develops over the thirteen-year period covered by the three-hour film (1949–1963), a voice instantiated by a series of visible stylistic shifts.[4] Perhaps inevitably, this pattern is rendered teleological, an ascension toward a full-blown gestural style familiar from the work of Brakhage and others. The steadfastly observational camera of the first two reels devoted to the activities of the Lithuanian exile community becomes the sign of the artist as yet unaware of his true vocation. "When you were first starting to shoot here," asks MacDonald, "did you feel that you were primarily a recorder of displaced persons and their struggle, or were you already thinking about becoming *a filmmaker of another sort?*" (MacDonald 1984, 84 emphasis mine).

The Documentary Detour

In fact, this assumed pilgrimage toward artistic progress deserves further examination, as does the essayistic character of the film's textual mapping, but not before a brief consideration of the nonfiction realm to which *Lost, Lost, Lost* is here being consigned. What is necessary in this instance is a kind of critical disengagement from the received limits of the nonfiction film in order to comprehend its historical as well as its discursive parameters. Mekas himself talks about his early literary efforts undertaken in Lithuania in the mid-forties, his pursuit of a kind of "documentary poetry" that employed poetic means—pace and prosody—to achieve largely descriptive ends. This hybridization of literary modes in itself echoes the essential dialogism of the essayistic enterprise. But, we are told in an interview with Scott MacDonald, this merger of the poetic and the nonfictional did not survive the move into cinema a few years later:

> When I began filming, that interest [documentary poetry] did not leave me, but it was pushed aside as I got caught up in the documentary film traditions. I was reading Grierson and Rotha and looking at the British and American documentary films of the '30s and '40s. I feel now that their influence detoured me from my own inclination. Later, I had to shake this influence in order return to the approach with which I began. (MacDonald 1984, 93–94)

The notion of a return to origins is intrinsic to Mekas's filmic oeuvre. But the return is always itself a reworking, a movement of recuperation and renewal, in this case to a documentary poetics from which Mekas never entirely retreated. It is worth noting, for example, that the traditional documentary approach to which Mekas unfavorably refers, discernible in the fervent recording of expatriate activities in *Lost*'s early reels, is circumscribed and absorbed by the complex weave of the film's sound/image orchestration. We can only imagine the Griersonian intent of the raw footage, now dialogized by auditory elements (narration and music) and the film's rhythmic self-presentation; for the spectator of *Lost, Lost, Lost*, Mekas' departure is already contained within his return.

The reference to Grierson and Rotha in the interview quoted above is significant inasmuch as they were the chief polemicists for a vision of the documentary film as a tool for propaganda and social education during the embattled decades of depression and war. For Grierson, son of a Calvinist minister, the screen was a pulpit, the film a hammer to be used in shaping the destiny of nations. When Mekas's attachment to the Lithuanian exile community gave way to broader as well as more personal concerns and the engagement with formal questions, when the fixation on national identity subsided, it was historically as well as aesthetically apt that the Griersonian model should cease to hold sway. But a wholesale disavowal of the documentary tradition threatens to obscure the tangency between Mekas's literary and filmic practices of many decades' standing, embroiled as they have been in the materiality of everyday life, and certain currents of work in nonfiction. The diary-film project deserves its place in that filmic domain.

The documentary film has, since its beginning, displayed four fundamental, often overlapping tendencies or aesthetic functions; at some moments and in the work of certain cinéastes, one or another of these characteristics has frequently been over- or underfavored. They are stated here in the active voice appropriate to their discursive agency.

1. *To record, reveal, or preserve.* This is perhaps the most elemental of documentary functions, familiar since the Lumières, traceable to the photographic antecedent. In one of several of Mekas's efforts to parse the filmic firmament (this one circa 1961), the "Realist Cinema"—a category that bridges the fiction/nonfiction divide—is named as one of three general approaches to cinema, the one that most prizes the revelational potential of the medium:

> The third approach [the others being "Pure Cinema" and "Impure Cinema"] could be called Realist Cinema, and could be summed up as the tradition of Lumière. The film-maker here is interested primarily in recording life as it is. His personality, instead of creating a new reality, goes mainly into revealing the most essential qualities of the already existing reality, as it is seen at the moment of happening. Flaherty attempted it in *Nanook*, Dziga Vertov ("The Camera-Eye") devoted his life to it. (Mekas 1961, 12)

This emphasis on the replication of the historical real links anthropology and home movie since both seek what Barthes in his *Camera Lucida* has termed "that rather terrible thing which is there in every photograph: the return of the dead" (Barthes 1981, 9). The preservational instinct—resisting the erosion of memory, the inevitability of passage—is the motor force behind this, the first of documentary's aesthetic functions.

Mekas remains the visual chronicler throughout *Lost*. The stark black and white of certain images early on evokes the best of thirties documentary photography in its combination of precise compositional values and compelling subject matter: the arrival of displaced persons at the Twenty-Third Street Pier, the spare ramshackle of a Williamsburg front stoop or the round faces of the exiled young framed in tenement windows. But the specter of Méliès hovers nearby. Even in the midst of the most faithfully atmospheric renderings of place or person, one recalls the images with which the film commences: the brothers mugging playfully before the camera and Adolfas's magic tricks. Conjury and *actualité* are made to coexist.

Documentary has most often been motivated by the wish to exploit the camera's powers of revelation, an impulse rarely coupled with an acknowledgment of the mediational processes through which the real is transformed.[5] At times, as with Flaherty, the desire to retain the trace of an already absent phenomenon has led the nonfiction artist to supplement behavior or event-in-history with its imagined counterpart. The wish to preserve images of the traditional walrus hunt of the Inuit led Robert Flaherty to suggest the anachronistic substitution of harpoons for rifles in his *Nanook of the North*. In *Lost*, Mekas's voice-over narration speaks his desire for a recovery of the past (his obsessive witnessing of events is frequently accompanied by the spoken refrain "I was there"), even while the efficacy of such a return is repeatedly contested by the film's conflictual voices.[6] The spectator is constantly reminded of the distance that separates the profilmic event and the voiced narration written years afterward. Mekas's vocal inflections themselves enforce the separation, the words delivered with a hesitancy, a weary delight in their sonorous possibilities. Thus a discomfiting retrospection on an irretrievable past is mixed with a pleasurable if provisional control over its filmic reproduction.

Moreover, the sense of indeterminancy that has been suggested as a crucial ingredient of the essayistic comes to the fore in the choice of sound elements, particularly for several of the early sequences. Rather than reinforcing the pathos of loss and displacement evoked in the scenes that document the activities of the Lithuanian expatriate community, Mekas frequently chooses to play against or at oblique angles to the anticipated emotional response. Early scenes of Jonas walking the streets of New York, alone and dispossessed, gather great force from the plaintive Kol Nidre chant that accompanies them. The reference to the holiest of Hebrew prayers and its call to atonement on Yom Kippur Eve sounds the right liturgical note even while crossing cultural bound-

aries (and a particularly charged cultural boundary it is, given the troubled history of the Jewish Lithuanian population in this century). The
resonances—and frequent dissonances—between sound and image consistently challenge the retrieval of untroubled or available historical
meaning from documentary images.

"And I was there, and I was the camera eye, I was the witness, and
I recorded it all, and I don't know, am I singing or am I crying?" These
words accompany images from the early fifties—of placard-bearing
Lithuanians, traditionally clad, marching along Fifth Avenue, protesting
the Soviet occupation of their land, or of the impassioned oration of exiled
leaders speaking to packed halls. The private and idiosyncratic character
of the images enforces Mekas as the first reader of the text; his own
uncertainty about the impact or affect engendered by his project
demands that we too suspend our own certain judgments. On more than
one occasion, *Lost* renders itself as undecidable—at the level of emotional response as well as of historical-interpretive activity.

Mekas's diary images document a variety of historical moments; in
fact, *Lost* provides access to a *series* of histories that can be traced across
the film. In the first instance, there is the discourse on the displaced person and the Lithuanian community that shares his or her exile in
Brooklyn. But if the pictures of life—of work, recreation, family rituals—
strain toward faithful evocation, the filmmaker's spoken refrain dis-
suades us from our apparent comprehension: "Everything is normal,
everything is normal," Mekas assures us over the images of everyday life.
"The only thing is, you'll never know what they think. You'll never know
what a displaced person thinks in the evening and in New York."
Occurring in the opening minutes of the film, this is the first lesson to be
drawn from the *Diaries*, applicable to all forays into historiography
through film. Historical meanings are never simply legible or immanent.
Understanding arises from the thoughtful interrogation of documents
(the real in representation) and the contradictions that are produced
through their overlay. Mekas here reminds us of the irreparable breach
between experience and its externalized representation, a notion implied
by the film's very title. We are all of us lost in the chasm between our
desire to recapture the past and the impossibility of a pristine return—
no one more so than Mekas himself.

The Lithuanian émigré experience, equivocal though our understanding of it may be, thus emerges as the first strand of *Lost*'s historio-
graphic braid. It is, however, possible to trace a second preservational
trajectory through the film's elaboration of a kind of postwar urban geo-
history. Mekas's odyssey from Williamsburg to Manhattan crisscrosses
virtually every sector of New York—Orchard Street, East Thirteenth
Street, Avenue B, Times Square, City Hall, Madison Avenue, Fifth
Avenue, Park Avenue South, Washington Square, and the obsessive

return to Central Park. There and elsewhere, Mekas finds himself inexorably drawn to the energy and tenacity of the picketers and the poets who agitate for their personal visions. The leaflet women of Forty-Second Street (appearing near the end of the fourth reel) who face public indifference on the coldest day of the year inspire Mekas's lyric testimonial, evinced at the level of word and image. "I was with you. I had to be. You were, you were … the blood of my city, the heartbeat. I wanted to feel its pulse, to feel its excitement. Yes, this was my city."

The cropped and canted composition of the leafleting trio celebrates at a historical—and a stylized—remove; it also recalls the Three Graces on the Stony Brook beach near the close of reel 2, the trio of émigrés preserved in a moment of unselfconscious revelry. The leafleteers likewise anticipate the final instance of this figure at film's end—Barbara and Debby wading fully clothed, awash in the same sea as the original celebrant trio, two decades later. Each of the film's three sections thus contains near its close a strikingly composed female figure group. Far from performing a merely decorative function, these imaged women are drawn from milieux particular to each stage of Mekas's life chronicle—from the Lithuanian nationalist period to the years of social activism to the consolidation of artistic identity. These dreamily eroticized avatars—part comrade, part goddess—are apt figures for a sensibility that obsessively couples the historical with the aesthetic. Endowed with a kind of grandeur, even monumentality (evoked through their framing and musical accompaniment), they bestow benediction on memory.

It is worth considering further the figural tableaux that conclude each of *Lost*'s three sections. Thick with classical and romantic allusions, their repetition is a marker of the autobiographical in the sense established by Jacques Derrida. In his analysis of Nietzsche's *Ecce Homo*, Derrida approaches the question of signature—and hence the attribution of the autobiographical—for literary and philosophical texts, particularly those that problematize self-presentation. He posits a dynamic borderline between the "work" and the "life," the system and the subject of the system, a "divisible borderline [that] traverses two 'bodies,' the corpus and the body, in accordance with laws that, we are only beginning to catch sight of" (Derrida 1985, 5–6). This borderline—mobile, divisible—is a site of contestation, the place where the proper name or signature is staged. Thus the recurrence of the invested iconographic figure in *Lost, Lost, Lost* can be said to speak the artist's subjectivity even as it reproduces the concreteness of historical detail. As Mekas himself has remarked, "Therefore if one knows how to 'read' them [the details of the actual], even if one doesn't see me speaking or walking, one can tell everything about me" (Mekas 1978, 193).

In his own writing, Mekas has tended to reduce the dynamism of the work/life borderline through his claim for the primacy of the subjective in the *Diaries*. "As far as the city goes, of course, you could say something also about the city, from my *Diaries*—but only indirectly" (ibid., 193). Indeed, New York is more than a passive wrapping for Mekas's personal odyssey. The fourteen-year period encompassed by the film coincides with a crucial period of thaw for America's cultural crossroads; New York, fast becoming the lodestone of art movements and accelerating social protest, is shown to experience a maturation in tune with the filmmaker's own.

But the surest focus of Mekas's witnessing throughout much of *Lost, Lost, Lost* is the constellation of creative pressures that produces the New American Cinema. The growth and development of that movement is the subject of a third history charted from the moment of this title card's appearance in the third reel: "Film culture is rolling on Lafayette Street." From the East Thirteenth Street apartment that doubles as *Film Culture*'s headquarters to the New Yorker Theater and its gathering of cinephiles to the Park Avenue South offices of the Film-Makers' Co-op, these are the urban spaces that frame the actions of the New Cinema's protagonists. What they do there is much the subject of the film. But the altered aims and methods of Mekas's creative drive testify to the historical development of the new aesthetic with equal cogency; a heightened spontaneity of camera movement, flickering shot duration, and a series of high-compression vignettes, the Rabbit Shit Haikus, are the chief markers of this shift.

Lost thus documents a succession of events significant in the formation of a cultural moment that hold an equally crucial place in the "discovery" of the artist's vocation. Exemplary instances include the collective efforts around the publication of *Film Culture* from 1955 onward, the shooting of Mekas's first feature, *Guns of the Trees* (1961), and the assault on the self-annointed arbiters of documentary purism at the Flaherty Seminar. The footage from the set of *Guns of the Trees* was, in fact, shot by Charles Levine; the exploration of the artist's subjectivity, increasingly foregrounded in the latter portions of *Lost*, is here suborned to the demands for a physical witnessing, to cinema's preservational function. "It's my nature now to record," says Mekas at the close of reel 4, "to try to keep everything I am passing through ... to keep at least bits of it.... I've lost too much.... So now I have these bits that I've passed through."

Mekas's preservational instincts serve to salvage the past for others as well. In this regard, Mekas may, in his later years, have come full circle, from an attention to the needs of the extended family of displaced persons to those of the nuclear family. His sense of the historical or popular memory function of the diary films is expressed with appropriate tenderness in his "Film Notes" to *Paradise Not Yet Lost, a/k/a Oona's*

Third Year (1979): "It is a letter to Oona [Mekas's daughter], to serve her, some day, as a distant reminder of how the world around her looked during the third year of her life—a period of which there will be only tiny fragments left in her memory—and to provide her with a romantic's guide to the essential values of life—in a world of artificiality, commercialism, and bodily and spiritual poison" (Mekas 1980).

As we shall see, there is no contradiction between the elemental documentary impulse, the will to preservation, and the exploration of subjectivity; indeed, it is their obsessive convergence that marks the essayistic work. It is, however, the irreconcilable difference between retention in representation and experiential loss that lends urgency to the diary project, driving the filmmaker toward an unobtainable, ever-deferred resolution.

2. *To persuade or promote.* This is the dominant trope for many of the films of the Grierson group during the Empire Marketing Board period (*Night Mail* [1936], *Housing Problems* [1937]), and for a majority of state-supported works ranging from Dziga Vertov's *Three Songs for Lenin* (1934) to Santiago Alvarez's *Now!* (1965) or *Hasta la Victoria siempre* (1967).[7] While Mekas remained for decades the most visible polemicist for the "new" or personal cinema through *Film Culture* and the "Movie Journal" column in the *Village Voice*, his filmmaking practice exhibits little of the rhetorical intent of a Vertov or an Alvarez. In his "Call for a New Generation of Film-Makers," appearing in *Film Culture* in 1959, Mekas issued a surrealist-inspired manifesto for an American avant-garde: "Our hope for a free American cinema is entirely in the hands of the new generation of film-makers. And there is no other way of breaking the frozen cinematic ground than through a *complete* derangement of the official cinematic senses" (Mekas 1959, 3). This directive is visibly executed in the last third of the film through the gestural style that received Mekas's critical endorsement. But the. film exceeds the programmatic; its plurality outstrips polemics. As is the case with essayistic discourse generally, *Lost* is at odds with the kind of epistemological or affective certainty necessary for overt persuasion. Recall herewith the emotional ambivalence ("Am I singing or am I crying?) and the unhinging of interpretive stability ("You'll never know what they think"), both conditions ill-suited to the goal-orientation of propaganda. The gap of history and feeling that separates the images of 1949 from the voice that reassesses their meaning a quarter of a century later produces resonant or ironic effects rather than discursive streamlining. If there is a promotional impetus to be found in *Lost* it is for a life defined through a perpetual act of self-creation rather than for a articular political or aesthetic position.

3. *To express.* This is the rhetorical/aesthetic function that has consistently been undervalued within the nonfiction domain; it is, neverthe-

less, amply represented in the history of the documentary enterprise. While the Lumières' *actualités* may have set the stage for nonfictional film's emphasis on the signified, a historically conditioned taste for dynamic if not pictorialist photographic composition accounts for the diagonal verve of the train station at La Ciotat. Most sources agree that Robert Flaherty was the documentary film's first poet as well as itinerant ethnographer. Flaherty's expressivity was verbal as well as imagistic in origin; to the in-depth compositions of trackless snowscapes in *Nanook of the North*, one must consider as well the flair for poetic language ("the brass ball of sun a mockery in the sky"). The cycle of "city symphony" films of the twenties (*Man with a Movie Camera, Berlin: Symphony of a Great City, A propos de Nice*) declared their allegiance in varying degrees to the powers of expressivity in the service of historical representation. The artfulness of the work as a function of its purely photographic properties was now allied with the possibilities of editing to create explosive effects—cerebral as well as visceral. The early films of the documentary polemicist Joris Ivens (*The Bridge* [1928], *Rain* [1929]) evidence the attraction felt for the cinema's aesthetic potential, even for those artists motivated by strong political beliefs.

In his earliest attempt to categorize film types, Mekas had suggested that the "document film" encompassed both the "interest film" (newsreels, instructionals, films on art) and the "documentary film—realist, impressionist or poetical, the primary purpose of which is non-instructional (though teaching)" (Mekas 1955, 15–16).[8] Parker Tyler, a frequent contributor to *Film Culture*, suggested his own rather cumbersome category of poetic film, "the naturalistic poetry document," a grouping that included *The River* and *The Blood of the Beasts* (Tyler 1970, 173). Difficulties arise in such efforts to distinguish among film forms as ideal types, a problem reduced through attention to discursive function rather than to the erection of discrete categories.

It is important to note in the context of taxonomic confusion that certain works of the avant-garde canon (Brakhage's "Pittsburgh Trilogy" or Peter Kubelka's *Unsere Afrikareise*) share with mainstream nonfiction a commitment to the representation of the historical real. However, the focus of these pieces typically remains the impression of the world on the artist's sensorium and his or her interpretation of that datum (Brakhage's tremulous hand-held camera as he witnesses open-heart surgery in *Deus Ex*) or the radical reworking of the documentary material to create sound-image relationships unavailable in nature (Kubelka's "synch event"). Critical differences of emphasis such as these notwithstanding, the realm of filmic nonfiction must be seen as a continuum within which the Mekas diary films constitute a significant contribution. That a work undertaking some manner of historical documentation renders that representation in an innovative manner (in silence or soft focus, for example) should in no way disqualify it as nonfiction since the question of expressivity is, in all events, a question of degree. All such renderings require a series of authorial choices, none neutral, some of which may appear more "artful" or purely expressive than others. There can be little doubt that such determinations ("artful documentary" or "documentary art") depend on various protocols of reading that are historically conditioned.

One expressive vehicle common to Mekas's diary films deserves special mention: the use of the filmmaker's voice. Rich in performance values, Mekas's voice functions as an instrument of great lyric power—measured, musical in its variation, hesitation, and repetition. The incantatory tone reinforces *Lost*'s bardic quality, inaugurated by the epic invocation that is the filmmaker's first utterance: "O sing, Ulysses, sing your travels...." The poetic use of language is strategically counterweighted, however, by the alternation of first and third person in the narration, never more effectively than at the film's conclusion: "He remembered another day. Ten years ago he sat on this beach, ten years ago, with other friends. The memories, the memories, the memories.... Again I have memories.... I have a memory of this place. I have been here before. I have really been here before. I have seen these waters before, yes, I've walked upon this beach, these pebbles—" Spectators are brought to their own recollections from a shared experience of some three hours' viewing; the young Lithuanian women on the beach at Stony Brook, captured in blissful dance, who recur as the leaflet women halfway through the film, are brilliantly recapitulated by the paired female figures at the film's end. We too have been here before. As with the poetic figure anaphora, so frequently invoked in the triplets of the Rabbit Shit Haikus and elsewhere ("the memories, the memories, the memories"), repetition proves to be not simple duplication, but a play of revision and erasure.

4. *To analyze or interrogate*. If the question of expressivity has plagued discussions of documentary, the analytical function has been virtually ignored.[9] The imperative toward analysis (of the enunciated and of the enunciative act) offers an intensification of and challenge to the record/reveal/preserve modality insofar as it actively questions nonfictional discourse—its claims to truth, its status as second-order reality. On what basis does the spectator invest belief in the representation? What are the codes that ensure that belief? What material processes are involved in the production of this "spectacle of the real," and to what extent are these processes rendered visible or knowable to the spectator? While many of these questions are familiar from the debates on reflexivity and the Brechtian cinema, applicable to fiction and nonfiction alike (the films of Vertov, Godard, and Straub and Huillet—essayists all—have most frequently inspired these discussions), their urgency is particularly

great for documentary works, which can be said to bear a direct, ontological tie to the real.

As noted in the discussion of expressivity, nonfiction film is the
result of determinate mediations or authorial interventions, some of
which may be perceived as "style." The analytical documentary is likely
to acknowledge that mediational structures are formative rather than
mere embellishments. In *Man with a Movie Camera*, the flow of images
is repeatedly arrested or reframed as the filmic fact is revealed to be a
labor-intensive social process that engages camera operators, editors,
projectionists, musicians, and audience members. Motion pictures are
represented as photographic images in motion, variable as to their projected speed, duration, or screen direction: galloping horses are capable
of being halted midstride, water can run upstream, smiling children can
be transformed into bits of celluloid to be inspected at editor Svilova's
workbench.

In the sound era, the breach between image and its audio counterpart has rarely been acknowledged; synchronized sound, narration, or music is meant to reinforce or fuse with the image rather than
question its status. Such is not the case in Alain Resnais's *Nuit et
brouillard* (1955) with its airy pizzicati accompanying the most
oppressive imagery of Holocaust atrocities. Chris Marker's *Letter
from Siberia* (1958) is another departure from the norm. The conno-
tative power of nonlinguistic auditory elements (music, vocal inflection) is confirmed by the repetition of an otherwise banal sequence;
the sequencing of images and the narration remain unchanged while
the accompanying music and tonal values of the narrating voice create differing semantic effects. Every viewer is forced to confront the
malleability of meaning and the ideological impact of authorial or
stylistic choices that typically go unnoticed. In Straub and Huillet's
Introduction to *"An Accompaniment for a Cinematographic Scene,"* a
musical composition, Schoenberg's Opus 34, is "illustrated" by the
recitation of Schoenberg's correspondence as well as by his drawings,
photographs (of the composer and of the slain Paris Communards),
archival footage of American bombing runs over Vietnam, and a newspaper clipping about the release of accused Nazi concentration camp
architects. A process of interrogation is thus undertaken through the
layering and resonance of heterogeneous elements. Schoenberg's
music, the work of a self-professed apolitical artist, becomes the
expressive vehicle for an outrage whose moral and intellectual dimensions exceed the parochial bounds of politics proper. Yet the collective
coherence of the filmic elements remains to be constructed by a thinking audience. The analytical impulse is not so much enacted by the
filmmakers as encouraged in the viewer.

The analytical impulse so rarely activated in mainstream nonfiction is strong in *Lost, Lost, Lost*, primarily due to the distance that separates the images, spanning more than a decade of the filmmaker's life, and the auditory elements, chosen years later, that engage them in dialogue. The relations between sound and image maintain a palpable tension throughout the film's duration, aided by the poignancy of silence. It is largely through the orchestration of acoustic effects (not least among them silence) that the film establishes its tonality. Despite the alterity of word and image, which occupy quite disparate planes of signification, conventional nonsync narrational techniques frequently attempt to sustain the impression of illustration, the visible enacting the spoken. In *Lost*, however, the breach between the seen and the heard remains irreparable; indeed, the sound elements themselves seem rarely to resolve into a "mixed" track—words, music, and effects remain discrete, virtually autonomous. From the clattering of subway trains to the plucking of stringed folk instruments to the subtle voicing of narration, each element retains its sovereign (that is, nonnaturalized) status.

Particularly through his spoken commentary, Mekas seized on the nonfiction film's ability to reassess human action even while revisiting it. Williams concluded his review of the film with a discussion of this aspect of its structure: "*Lost* is a particularly moving film because of the distance between the Jonas Mekas who shot—who wrote—the footage used in the work and the Jonas Mekas who assembled it in the 1970s. In this distance lies the material for powerful interactions between levels of experience" (Williams 1976, 62).

"When I Am Filming, I Am Also Reflecting"

The reflexive character of the film, its will to analysis of self and events, returns us to the domain of the essayistic. While all documentary films retain an interest in some portion of the world *out there*—recording, and less frequently interrogating, at times with the intent to persuade and with varying degrees of attention to formal issues—the essayist's gaze is drawn inward with equal intensity. That inward gaze accounts for the digressive and fragmentary character of the essayistic, as André Tournon's assessment of Montaigne's *Essays* suggests: "Thought can abandon its theme at any time to examine its own workings, question its acquired knowledge or exploit its incidental potentialities" (Tournon 1983, 61).

Long before the appearance of his diary films, Mekas wrote admiringly of Alexandre Astruc's "camera stylo." Indeed, the work of Mekas, like that of Godard, Marker, and other prose writers turned filmmakers, offers important insight into the essayistic as a modality of filmic inscription. In a lecture on *Reminiscences of a Journey to Lithuania*, Mekas addressed the relationship between the diaristic in film and its literary counterpart; his reflections inform our consideration of filmic autobiography and of the defining conditions of historiographical pursuits more generally.

> At first I thought that there was a basic difference between the written diary which one writes in the evening, and which is a reflective process, and the filmed diary. In my film diary, I thought, I was doing something different: I was capturing life, bits of it, as it happens. But I realized very soon that it wasn't that different at all. When I am filming, I am also reflecting. I was thinking that I was only reacting to the actual reality. I do not have much control over reality at all, and everything is determined by my memory, my past. So that this "direct" filming becomes also a mode of reflection. Same way, I came to realize, that writing a diary is not merely reflecting, looking back. Your day, as it comes back to you during the moment of writing, is measured, sorted out, accepted, refused, and reevaluated by what and how one is at the moment when one writes it all down. It's all happening again, and what one writes down is more true to what one is when one writes than to the events and emotions of the day that are past and gone. Therefore, I no longer see such big differences between a written diary and the filmed diary, as far as the processes go. (Mekas 1978, 191–92)

Mekas's diaristic project is writerly at every turn, both because the process of inscription is foregrounded throughout and because, consistent with Barthes's description of the writerly in *S/Z*, *Lost* as text approaches the status of the "triumphant plural, unimpoverished by any constraint of representation.... We gain access to it by several entrances, none of which can be authoritatively declared to be the main one; the codes it mobilizes extend *as far as the eye can reach*" (Barthes 1974, 5–6). It is writing of a certain sort that suffuses the film; the sense of sketch or palimpsest is retained throughout, in contrast with, for example, the florid, unwavering signature of Straub's Bach, whose piety engenders artistic as well as moral certitude in *Chronicle of Anna Magdalena Bach* (1967). The intermittently imaged snatches of written diary in *Lost* conjure for us a process of self-inscription that is painfully, materially etched. "October 3d, 1950," intones Mekas, from the distance of decades. "I have been trying to write with a pencil. But my fingers do not really grasp the pencil properly, not like they used to grasp it a year, two years ago. From working in the factory my fingers became stiff. They don't bend, they lost their subtlety of movement. There are muscles in them I haven't seen before. They look fatter. Anyway, I can't hold the pencil. So I go to the typewriter and I begin to type, with one finger." Apocryphal or not, this account of graphological vicissitudes is corroborated at every turn of the text. Typographic emendations are foregrounded in Mekas's imaging of the diary pages. Significantly, it is

I tried to sleep,

sed a⁀round in my

exhausted, deep s

The Process of Self-Inscription—Painfully, Materially Etched

the overstroke rather than the erasure that prevails; the trace of each failed gesture remains legible beneath each correction. As so many theorists of the essay have noted, it is the process of judgment far more than the verdict that counts. Mekas is at pains to restore to his filmed diaries the physicality and sheer effort of their provenance.

The diary inserts thus reinforce our sense of the text as a handcrafted and provisional one, always subject to reconsideration. The provisional character of all filmed material in *Lost* is dramatically borne out by its occasional transfiguration in other volumes of *Diaries, Notes, and Sketches*. In addition, then, to the potential reassessment of each image by a narrating agency at great historical remove, these same images can be reinvested and reframed—in a manner consistent with Freud's notion of *nachtraglichkeit*, or deferred action.[10]

The triumphant plurality of which Barthes speaks results from the film text's temporal fluidity, the multiple styles and perspectives it mobilizes (mingling color with black-and-white film stock as well as footage shot by others) and its several historical foci. *Lost* mimes the richness of lived experience through its modulation of a range of filmic elements. It is the sheer extent and heterogeneity of Mekas's *Diaries, Notes, and Sketches* that is most responsible for producing the sense of Barthes's inexhaustible text.

But the heterogeneity of Mekas's oeuvre is distinguishable from Godard's unceasing referentiality, Straub's geologic stratification, and Marker's Borgesian labyrinths. While it is likely that, among these film practitioners, Mekas's diary format most approximates Montaigne's flight from final judgments, the writing practices of the two emerge from very different philosophical contexts. Montaigne's refusal of the preexisting limits of thought and literary protocol was vested in an intellectual skepticism that valorized reflection and the ceaseless revisionism it dictated. Mekas, on the other hand, responds to a tradition that embraces spontaneity over thought. The expansiveness of the diaries arises from the conviction that art and life are indissoluble.

> The spontaneity of the new American artist is not a conscious or an intellectual process: it is rather his way of life, his whole being; he comes to it rather intuitively, directly.
>
> The new artist neither chooses this spontaneous route himself nor does he do so consciously: it is imposed upon him by his time, as the only possible route. (Mekas 1960, 19)

That pronouncement, made in 1960, was slightly revised two years later, the emphasis having shifted from the involuntary (and apparently unknowable) source of art making to the art *process* and its institutional reception. This reassessment, responsive to the politicized environment of the New York art scene of the early 1960s, shares something of the rhetoric if not the material circumstances of the new Latin American cinema emergent at that moment. Mekas, however, spoke his refusal from the very nerve center of dominant culture rather than from its periphery; he wrote against the art establishment, not against the mass-culture colonizers. "I don't want any part of the Big Art game. The new cinema, like the new man, is nothing definitive, nothing final. It is a living thing. It is imperfect; it errs" (Mekas 1970, 88).

Diaries, Notes, and Sketches owes a great deal to the raw power of the improvisatory art Mekas championed at the time of those writings. Several sequences in *Lost* offer documentation of the people and activities of the Living Theater. In 1959, Mekas awarded the first independent Film Award to John Cassavetes' *Shadows*; Drew Associates' *Primary*, which was said to reveal "new cinematic techniques of recording life on film," was the recipient of the third award. The 1962 essay "Notes on the New American Cinema" shares the spirit of the Willem de Kooning epigram it quotes in apparent admiration: "Painting—any kind of painting, any style of painting—to be painting at all, in fact—is a way of living today, a style of living, so to speak." (Mekas 1970, 88). Indeed, *Lost, Lost, Lost* shares something of the edgy immediacy of the art that prevailed in the moment of its shooting.

But *Lost* exceeds its roots in improvisation, in the capture of an uncontrolled reality, in a wished-for fusion of art and life. At last, it is through its character as essayistic work that the film yields its surplus. Vast in its purview, elliptical in its self-presentation, complex in its interpolation of historical substrata and textual voices, the film struggles with "the old problem"—"to merge Reality and Self, to come up with the third thing." But *Lost* resists the snares of resolution or completion, even in the dialectical beyond. Moreover, a belief in the revivification or recapture of experience in the crucible of art is actively disavowed, even if, as in Marker's *Sans soleil*, loss itself becomes ritual celebration.

In assessing the film four decades after its inception, the Lukácsian prescription might well apply. *Lost, Lost, Lost* will survive as a triumph of judgment independent of the world or psyche that it reveals. And "the value-determining thing about it is not the verdict ... but the process of judging" (Lukács 1974, 18).

Notes

1. Williams 1976, 62. Although Williams reviewed *Lost, Lost, Lost* soon after its release, he was already familiar with the third volume of the autobiographical project *Walden* (1968), filmed between 1964 and 1968.

2. In an appendix to *The Barthes Effect: The Essay as Reflective Text*, Reda Bensmaia offers the historical and theoretical grounds for his claims for the essay as an "impossible" genre: "Among all the terms that relate to literary genres, the word Essay is certainly the one that has given rise to the most confusion in the history of literature.... A unique case in the annals of literature, the Essay is the only literary genre to have resisted integration, until quite recently, in the taxonomy of genres. No other genre ever raised so many theoretical problems concerning the origin and the definition of its Form: an atopic genre or, more precisely, an *eccentric* one insofar as it seems to flirt with all the genres without ever letting itself be pinned down, the literary essay such as Montaigne bequeathed it to posterity has always had a special status.... [T]he Essay appears historically as one of the rare literary texts whose apparent principal task was to provoke a 'generalized collapse' of the economics of the rhetorically coded text" (Bensmaia 1987, 95, 96, 99). In my writing on the essayistic in film and video, I have chosen to resist the lure of genre, preferring instead to consider the essayistic as a modality of filmic inscription. The invocation of mode rather than genre sidesteps the difficulties raised by the latter's far greater historical stake in taxonomic certainty, as well as the presumption of thematic consistency attached to it. Conversely, the determining principle of resemblance for the mode is a formal or functional one. As Jacques Derrida notes, quoting a distinction framed by Gerard Genette: "Genres are, properly speaking, literary or aesthetic categories; modes are categories that pertain to linguistics or, more precisely, to an anthropology of verbal expression" (Derrida 1980, 210). In the instance of the essayistic for film and video, formal, functional, and ideological commonalities converge as defining characteristics.

3. There is considerable elasticity inherent in my formulation of the essayistic, with the result that no enumeration of exemplary texts will suffice to name its borders. of course, laws of membership and exclusion always pose a problem for aesthetic taxonomies, which must remain open and therefore "impure" sets. Certain principles of composition do, however, remain useful indicators of the essayistic enterprise for film and video as they have for literature. The "twofold project," descriptive and reflexive, enfolding self and other, the outward (documentary) glance coupled with the interrogation of subjectivity—these are the signs of a discursive practice termed essayistic. For further discussion of the essayistic for film and video, see Renov 1989.

4. See in particular MacDonald 1986, as well as his *October* interview with Mekas (1984). A more conceptually ambitious account of Mekas's career and

achievements, contained in James 1989, continues to treat the development of an increasingly personal style through the *Diaries* as a kind of spiritual elevation, producing a filmic mode that "entirely fulfills [underground film's] aesthetic and ethical program" (100). This tendency to describe a progressive stylistic shift as a heightening or purification of form is a romantic notion traceable in the first instance to the filmmaker's own writings over several decades. To be sure, some notion of historical development is inescapable in the discussion of *Lost*, inasmuch as the film's image track appears to be structured chronologically. That irreversibility is, however, consistently undone by the voice-over, which ranges across time and memory speaking from a place of knowledge: "Paulius, Paulius— I see you. Remember, that day, that evening, that evening we all danced around a young birch tree outside of the barracks. We thought it will all be so temporary, we'll be all home soon." MacDonald (1986) suggests that the six reels of the film can be grouped as three couplets: the first pair focusing on the Lithuanian community in Brooklyn, the second on the formation of a new life in Manhattan and the beginnings of a new community around *Film Culture*, the last on the development of a cinematic aesthetic of spontaneity and personalism. Any critical engagement with the film must, in the first instance, comprehend this play of the progressive and the reversible.

5. For a further discussion of the necessity and variability of mediation for the documentary film, see Renov 1986.

6. The notion of a preservational obsession held in tension with its opposite, the need to release the past or deny its efficacy in the present through representation, provides a crucial underpinning for *Lost, Lost, Lost*. Another film to be situated within the realm of the essayistic, Chris Marker's *Sans soleil*, explores similar terrain through an equally variegated textual mapping of temporality and experience. Even while fragments from the filmmaker's past return obsessively—from his own films such as *La jetee* (1962) or *Le mystere Koumiko* (1964) or from Hitchcock's *Vertigo* (1958)—Marker celebrated their annihilation through a ritual destruction that in turn memorializes their loss; representation becomes that system through which retention and dissolution clan be fused. "Memories must make do with their delirium, with their drift," says Marker in *Sans soleil*. "A moment stopped would burn like a frame of film blocked before the furnace of the projector." *Lost* and *Sans soleil* share a fascination for cinema's special admixture of presence and absence, a chemistry examined by generations of film theorists.

7. Convents (1988) argues that the documentary film was recruited for the purposes of propagandizing colonialist efforts in Africa as early as 1897.

8. Besides the "document film," Mekas's categorization of cinematic forms includes the film drama, the film poem, and the cinema of abstraction or "cineplastics."

9. The many studies of reflexivity in cinema have focused on fictional works almost exclusively (e.g., the *Screen* debates on Brecht from the 1970s or Walsh 1981). Among the writings that do address this problem in the documentary context, the best may be Allen 1977, Kuhn 1978, and Ruby 1988.

10. As discussed in Laplanche and Pontalis 1973, Freud's use of the term *nachtraglichkeit* is intended to convey the manner by which experiences, impressions, or memory traces are altered after the fact as a function of new

experiences and are thus rendered capable of reinvestment, producing new, even unexpected effects of meaning. As Freud wrote to his confidant, Wilhelm Fliess: "I am working on the assumption that our psychical mechanism has come about by a process of stratification: the material present in the shape of memory-traces is from time to time subjected to a *rearrangement* in accordance with fresh circumstances—is, as it were, *transcribed*" (Laplanche and Pontalis 1973, 182–83).

Bibliography

Allen, Jeanne. 1977. "Reflexivity in Documentary." *Cine-tracts*, 1, no. 2 (Summer): 37–43.

Barthes, Roland. 1974. *S/Z*. Trans. Richard Miller. New York: Hill and Wang.

———. 1977. *Roland Barthes*. Trans. Richard Howard. New York: Hill and Wang.

———. 1981. *Camera Lucida*. Trans. Richard Howard. New York: Hill and Wang.

———. 1985. *The Grain of the Voice: Interview, 1962–1980*. Trans. Linda Coverdale. New York: Hill and Wang.

Bensmaia, Reda. 1987. *The Barthes Effect: The Essay as Reflective Text*. Trans. Pat Fedkiew. Minneapolis: University of Minnesota Press.

Convents, Guido. 1988. "Documentaries and Propaganda before 1914: A View on Early Cinema and Colonial History." *Framework* 35: 104–13.

Defaux, Gerard. 1983. "Readings of Montaigne." Trans. John A. Gallucci. In *Montaigne: Essays in Reading*. Yale French Studies 64: 73–92.

Derrida, Jacques. 1980. "The Law of Genre." *Glyph* 7: 202–32.

———. 1985. "Octobiographies." Trans. Avital Ronell. In *The Ear of the Other*, 1–38. New York: Schocken Books.

Good, Graham. 1988. *The Observing Self: Rediscovering the Essay*. London: Routledge.

James, David. 1989. *Allegories of Cinema: American Film in the Sixties*. Princeton: Princeton University Press.

Kuhn, Annette. 1978. "The Camera I—Observations on Documentary." *Screen* 1, no. 2 (Summer): 71–83.

Laplanche, Jean, and Jean-Bertrand Pontalis. 1973. *The Language of Psychoanalysis*. Trans. Donald Nicholson-Smith. New York: W. W. Norton.

Lukács, Georg. 1974. "On the Nature and Form of the Essay." In *Soul and Forms*, trans. Anna Bostock, 1–18. Cambridge: MIT Press.

MacDonald, Scott. 1984. "Interview with Jonas Mekas." *October* 29 (Summer): 82–116.

———. 1986. "Lost Lost Lost Over *Lost, Lost, Lost*." *Cinema Journal* 25, no. 2 (Winter): 20–34.

Mekas, Jonas. 1955. "The Experimental Film in America." *Film Culture* 19: 1–4.

———. 1959. "A Call for a New Generation of Film-Makers." *Film Culture* 19: 1–4.

———. 1960. "Cinema of the New Generation." *Film Culture* 21: 1–20.

———. 1961. Introduction to "The Frontiers of Realist Cinema: The Work of

Ricky Leacock (from an interview conducted by Gideon Bachmann)." *Film Culture* 22–23: 12.

———. 1970. "Notes on the New American Cinema." In *Film Culture Reader*, ed. P. Adams Sitney, 87–107. New York: Praeger Publishers.

———. 1978. "The Diary Film (A Lecture on *Reminiscences of a Journey to Lithuania*)." In *Avant-Garde Film: A Reader Theory and Criticism*, ed. P. Adams Sitney, 190–98. New York: New York University Press.

———. 1980. "Film Notes." In *Jonas Mekas*, ed. Judith E. Briggs. Minneapolis: Film in the Cities/Walker Art Center.

Montaigne, Michel de. 1948. *The Complete Works of Montaigne*. Trans. Donald M. Frame. Stanford: Stanford University Press.

Renov, Michael. 1986. "Re-Thinking Documentary: Toward a Taxonomy of Mediation." *Wide Angle* 8, no. 3–4: 71–77.

———. 1989. "History and/as Autobiography: The Essayistic in Film and Video." *Frame/Work* 2, no. 3: 5–13.

Ruby, Jay. 1988. "The Image Mirrored: Reflexivity and the Documentary Film." In *New Challenges for Documentary*, ed. Alan Rosenthal, 64–77. Berkeley and Los Angeles: University of California Press.

Tournon, André. 1983. "Self-Interpretation in Montaigne's Essays." *Montaigne: Essays in Reading*. Yale French Studies 64: 51–72.

Tyler, Parker. 1970. "Poetry and the Film: A Symposium, with Maya Deren, Arthur Miller, Dylan Thomas, Parker Tyler." In *Film Culture Reader*, ed. P. Adams Sitney, 171–86. New York: Praeger.

Walsh, Martin. 1981. *The Brechtian Aspect of Radical Cinema*. London: BFI Publishing.

Williams, Alan. 1976. "*Diaries, Notes and Sketches*—Volume I ('Lost, Lost, Lost')." *Film Quarterly* 30, no. 1: 60–62.

Questions and Projects

- Renov suggests four documentary strategies in his discussion of the essay and Mekas's film. Select another film that might be described as an essay film (for example Trinh T. Minha's *Naked Spaces: Living Is Round* [1985] or Chris Marker's *Sans soleil* [1982]) and show how they employ these four (or other) essayistic strategies.

- Analyze a specific literary essay and a specific essay film that may have similar topics (such as self-portrait or travel or criticism). One might choose essays with clear connections: for instance, compare a critical essay written about Werner Herzog's 1982 *Fitzcarraldo* and Les Blank and Maureen Gosling's film account of the making of that movie, *Burden of Dreams* (1982). How do their methods differ? How does the comparison reveal certain limitations or possibilities in each practice?

*T*his 1997 survey of Shakespearean adaptations in the last decade
    spotlights how the popularization of Shakespeare (especially in
the United States) raises a variety of questions about contemporary
exchanges between film and literature. To address this complex relationship between popularization and classic literature, the essay presents some old and new themes in the film / literature debates: What
do we mean by originality and authenticity? What does it mean to
distinguish high-brow, middle-brow, and low-brow culture as a hierarchy? How does the image and name of Shakespeare (perhaps like
other classic literatures today) become for many as much a part in
the adaptations as the texts of the plays themselves. In addressing
much of the recent television and film work on Shakespeare, this
piece also indicates how gender, age, commercialism, and the tension
between nationalism and globalization can shape the contemporary
meaning of a century-old encounter between film and literature.

"Totally Clueless? Shakespeare Goes Hollywood in the 1990s" from *Shakespeare, The Movie*

Lynda E. Boose and Richard Burt

A short sequence in the 1995 summer film comedy *Clueless* (dir. Amy
Heckerling) offers what might be considered a mini-allegory of
Shakespeare's circulation within the popular culture of the 1990s.
Based on Jane Austen's *Emma*, the film narrates the coming of age of
"Cher," a Beverly Hills high school ingenue and media-savvy teen
queen who reformulates the pleasures of discourse into side-by-side
telephone conversations conducted on mobile telephones. In the manip-
ulation of cultural capital as a means for asserting status, Cher (Alicia
Silverstone) clinches her superiority inside of a contest that defines
itself through Shakespeare. When her stepbrother's excessively
Harvard girlfriend attributes "to thine own self he true" to Hamlet and
Cher corrects her, the girlfriend then rejects Cher's substitution of
"that Polonius guy" and slams home her apparent victory with the
smugly dismissive line, "I think I remember *Hamlet* accurately." But
Cher beats her, point, set, and match, with the rejoinder that while she,
by comparison, may not know her *Hamlet*, she most certainly does
know her Mel Gibson!

We begin with *Clueless* because it complicates present moves in
cultural studies about Shakespeare. With its Los Angeles location and
youth market for Shakespeare, *Clueless* offers an opportunity for certain kinds of questions. For openers, just who is its Shakespeare joke

on—the girlfriend, Cher, or just whom? Just what is the high-status cultural currency here, and how does "Shakespeare" function as a sign? Does the fact that Cher knows *Hamlet* not via the presupposed Shakespearean original but only via Mel Gibson's role in Zeffirelli's movie signify her cultural illiteracy—or her literacy? Or does this exchange perhaps point us away from any presumptive original, be it Jane Austen's or Shakespeare's, and direct us instead toward a focus on just its mediating package, what might be called the Hollywoodization of Shakespeare in the 1990s? In a postmodern way that effectively mocks all the presumed distinctions between high and low culture, *Clueless* does not merely relocate high culture to a low site (Los Angeles): after all, this is Beverly Hills, not the Valley, and no one is more vigilant than Cher and her friends about maintaining standards and eschewing tastelessness. Instead, *Clueless* elaborates on films like *L.A. Story* (dir. Steve Martin, 1991) in which Steve Martin begins by reciting a speech in praise of L.A. that parodies John of Gaunt's deathbed speech to Richard II, substituting "this Los Angeles" for the concluding words, "this England"; and on Jean-Luc Godard's *Lear* (1987), in which William Shakespeare Junior the Fifth goes to Hollywood to produce his ancestor's plays, which end up being edited by Woody Allen. Like these two films, *Clueless*'s repeated reference to technologies such as movies, televisions, mobile phones, head sets, car radios, CDs, computerized wardrobes, intercoms, and other devices that record, transmit, amplify, and likewise reshape meaning formulate the mediating power of Los Angeles as the contemporary site where high/low distinctions are engaged in endlessly resignifying themselves.

Cher's recoding of *Hamlet* could be located in a wider range of 1990s *Hamlet*(s). The *Hamlet* created by the 1990s wasn't big just among the literati—he was so big that he was making guest appearances in all sorts of unexpected places, with different implications of its gendered reception. In 1991, Oliver Stone cast the Kennedy assassination through the lens of *Hamlet* in *JFK*. In 1994, Danny DeVito and the US Army found *Hamlet* to be the perfect force for transforming wimps and misfit soldiers into the STRAK army company that concludes *Renaissance Man* (dir. Penny Marshall) reaffirming the male bond in "Sound Off" lyrics that inventively substitute "Hamlet's mother, she's the Queen" for the usual female object of cadenced derision. Similarly, Disney's 1994 *The Lion King* (dir. Roger Allers and Ron Minkoff), reworked *Hamlet* for a younger generation. In 1995, Kenneth Branagh released his *A Midwinter's Tale*, a film about a provincial English production of *Hamlet*, and then in 1996 and 1997 his own full-length and abridged versions of *Hamlet*.

Ultimately, however, it was Arnold Schwarzenegger's 1992 film, *The Last Action Hero* (dir. John McTiernan), that most clearly allegorized the transformation of Hamlet from melancholy man into an image that could be valued by the young male consumers to whom the newly technologized violence of the 1990s was being played. In a displacement explicitly fictionalized as the direct product of a young male viewer's contemporary fantasies of masculinity, on screen the image of Olivier hesitating to kill the praying Claudius literally dissolves into a Schwarzenegger Hamlet who is actively engaged in "taking out the trash" of the something-rotten Denmark into which he is thrust. And in a clever bit of metatheatricality, the substitution of Schwarzenegger, America's highest paid actor of the early 1990s, is situated as the ultimate insurance that movie houses will stay open and movies will keep on playing. Kids like the film's ardent young filmviewer will keep right on getting sucked into the action-packed worlds of heroically imagined male violence that is both promulgated by American film and simultaneously guarantees the industry its seemingly unassailable hegemony. Though ironic, it is nonetheless true that the *Hamlet*(s) of the 1990s construct a world even more obsessively masculine than did the *Hamlet*(s) that preexisted any articulated feminist critique of popular culture. Mel Gibson as Hamlet means *Hamlet* as *Lethal Weapon Four*. But Mel also means Hamlet as Hollywood Hunk, an object of desire who, like Glenn Close's Gertrude, projects an image implicitly accessible to female and male viewers alike.[1] Zeffirelli's film may well be *Lethal Weapon Four* but Hamlet-as-Mel suggests Shakespeare's prince as 1990s model of unrestrictedly appropriatable desire, and it was through an appropriation of Mel-as-Hamlet that Cher triumphs over her truly clueless adversary, eventually winning a college guy (read: Harvard Law) boyfriend at the film's close.

Rather than assessing the various new *Hamlet*-sites in terms of possibilities for contradictory readings or as evidence anew of an American cultural imperialism, we are more interested in the critical developments that such a proliferation may signal. In the wake of the present displacements of book and literary culture by film and video culture and the age of mechanical reproduction by the age of electronic reproduction, the traditional literary field itself has already, to some extent, been displaced as an object of inquiry by cultural studies. And the Shakespeare moment in *Clueless* perhaps interests us for the very way it enacts this displacement, invoking the high status literary text only to dismiss it in favor of the actor's performance. For Shakespeare studies, what the transition from a literary to an electronic culture logically presages is exactly what, in fact, seems to be happening: an increased interest in the strategies of performance accompanied by a decreased focus on the poetic and rhetorical, the arena where New Criticism once so powerfully staked its claim.[2] If Michael Berube (1995) is right in assessing that the move to cultural studies primarily involves taking a less serious relation to criticism and its subjects, then Shakespeare (and Renaissance) Studies appears to be following suit, its dialogue lightening up a bit. New ways of reading the transvestism of the Renaissance stage, for example, are being discovered by contextualizing the cross-dressed Shakespeare heroine alongside pop culture figures like Michael Jackson and Madonna (see Garber 1992, 1995) and films like *The Crying Game* (dir. Jordan, 1992; see Crewe 1995).

It could be said that this shift to a cultural studies approach opens new possibilities for a kind of Shakespeare criticism with wider appeal to a non-academic public (which presumes, of course, that the Shakespearean academic necessarily wants such a popular audience.) It must also be said, however, that the shift raises a number of new questions, many of which relate to the new influence that Hollywood, Los Angeles, and American capitalism are already exerting on the popularization of Shakespeare. The media in 1990s America—film, video, television, and advertising—seemed suddenly prepared to embrace the Bard with all the enthusiasm (and potentially crushing effect) that such wholehearted American embraces have come to harbinger for much of the world. Thus the question of potential diminishment that has always been raised about putting Shakespeare on film reappears, reinvigorated by the very technologies that make Shakespeare more accessible. We have yet to imagine how Shakespeare will be staged on the Internet, but for many of those who, unlike Cher, do know their Shakespeare, the transfer from "live" theater to the absent presence of the technologically produced filmic (or digitized) image invites a distinct ambivalence much like that which betrays the voice of *New York Times* writer Frank Rich, here writing in 1996 about Fredericke Warde, the star of the recently rediscovered silent 1912 *Richard III*. Noting that Warde blamed what he perceived as a "fall off" of Shakespeare theatrical productions on schools and literary societies for turning acting texts into objects of intellectual veneration, Rich, for whom the discovery of this venerable old Shakespeare film seems to have acted as catalyst for his own lament for a lost golden age, characterizes Warde as a thoroughly clueless innocent, someone who "didn't have a clue that movies were harbingers of a complete cultural transformation that would gradually lead to the desensitized pop media environment of today."[3]

In the larger sense, however, Shakespeare's disappearance, his status as ghostwriter, precedes the 1990s. In some ways, the present historical moment only clarifies the way Shakespeare has always already disappeared when transferred onto film. Taken on their own terms, films like Greenaway's *Prospero's Books*, Derek Jarman's *Tempest*, and Godard's *Lear* involve not merely the deconstruction of Shakespeare as author but his radical displacement by the film director; and the interest in any of these films could legitimately be said to lie less in its relation to Shakespeare's play than in its relation to the director's own previous *oeuvre*. Even films which adapt the Shakespeare script as faithfully as does Branagh's *Much Ado About Nothing* speak within a metacinematic discourse of self-reference in which, through film quotation, they situate themselves in reference as much to other films as to a Shakespeare tradition.[4]

Yet judging from the commentary and the advertising matrix surrounding the release of the most recent Shakespeare adaptations, the fact that Shakespeare is the author seems to be becoming not only increasingly beside the point but even a marketing liability—an inference that *Los Angeles Times* movie critic David Gritten quite clearly picks up from the voices of both the director and producer of Ian McKellen's 1995 *Richard III*:

> Here on the set of *Richard III*, a film adaptation of one of the world's best known plays starring a bunch of distinguished classical actors, it comes as a surprise that everyone is trying to play down the S-word. The S-word? That stands for "Shakespeare." He's the guy who wrote *Richard III* some four hundred years ago, in case you weren't quite sure. In truth, the people behind this *Richard III* ... are hoping to attract those very people who aren't quite sure of the film's provenance. "I'm encouraging everyone working on this film not to think of it as Shakespeare," says director Richard Loncraine. "It's a terrific story, and who wrote it is irrelevant. "We're trying to make the most accessible Shakespeare film ever made," says producer Lisa Katselas Pare. (Gritten 1995: 39, 41)

The similar trend that Don Hedrick points out in an essay in [*Shakespeare, The Movie*]—that any mention of Shakespeare is exactly what was under avoidance in the marketing of Branagh's *Henry V*—is a truism equally applicable to Zeffirelli's *Hamlet*. Likewise, Gus Van Sant (1993: xxxviii) notes about the making of *My Own Private Idaho* that while the foreign producers wanted to put in as much Shakespeare as possible the American producers wanted to cut out as much possible.[5] Yet just when we might assume that the Bard's name was truly a marketing liability or that veneration of Shakespeare had come to be regarded in popular contexts as uncool,[6] the notably cool film director Baz Luhrmann put out a new *Romeo and Juliet* that is unquestionably situated in the pop culture, made-for-teens film market and is called *William Shakespeare's Romeo and Juliet*.[7]

The popularization of Shakespeare on film, video, and television—which began inside the stalwartly liberal tradition of noblesse oblige attempting to bring culture to the masses—now finds itself, in America at least, in a strictly market-responsive milieu in which literary knowledge is in general a decidedly low capital, frequently mockable commodity, caught within the peculiarly American ambivalence about intellectualism, and therefore to be eschewed at all costs. When Gus Van Sant imports the various Hal and Falstaff scenes from the *Henry IV* and *Henry V* plays and sticks them into *My Own Private Idaho*'s world of contemporary Portland gay hustlers and street dwellers, neither the film nor the characters speaking the lines register any acknowledgment that they are drawing upon Shakespeare. If this film is a Shakespeare spin-off, no one has to admit knowing it. But as a market screening device, the omission must have worked, since only those people who had read the Henriad or read commentary on the film in specifically "intellectual" magazine and review venues seemed conscious of any Shakespeare connection. The same might be said of *L.A. Story*. While many members of the audience may have picked up the allusions to *Hamlet* and other Shakespeare plays, only a Shakespearean would have read the movie as a rewriting of the play. Likewise, the connection between *Clueless* and Jane Austen's *Emma* got intentionally excluded from the film's promotional packet and was left to become known via strategically leaked news items designed to be circulated by word of mouth to intrigue the elite without turning off the intended teen market.

But while pride in anti-intellectualism has long roots as an American tradition and is a force which the 1980s and 1990s have seen assume a renewed political ascendancy, quite the opposite has historically been true of British cultural life, where Shakespeare and the English literary tradition have long been a rallying point of national superiority. The quotation of Shakespeare lines seems, in fact, to be used in Britain as a special, high-status kind of sub-language, a signalling code of sorts that regularly shows up in the language of even British detective novels. It is thus frankly impossible to imagine the making of a British film like *Clueless* in which success would be correlated with a pride in *not* knowing one's Shakespeare. Nonetheless, the apparent dominance of Hollywood capitalism so thoroughly determines the market that Britain's famous Shakespearean actors now find even themselves playing roles within plays which require that they "not think of [the play] as Shakespeare."

But Hollywood's relationship to Shakespeare is marked by more than just the avoidance of the S-word. When Gus Van Sant turned to the Shakespeare narrative that he then consciously veiled in *My Own Private Idaho*, he even approached it through a layered mediation, essentially rewriting not Shakespeare's second tetralogy but Orson Welles's version of the second tetralogy, *Chimes at Midnight*. Van Sant's film thus participates in a peculiarly American norm by which Hollywood, up until Branagh's box office successes of the early 1990s, chose to maintain a significant distance from the direct—or "straight

Shakespeare"—adaptational model that made both Olivier and Welles famously associated with all that was once included in the meaning of "a Shakespeare film." And while American television has shown some "straight" American versions of Shakespeare that do not modernize the verbal idiom or rewrite the story (most notably, televised versions of filmed theatrical productions, such as the American Conservatory Theater's famous 1971 *The Taming of the Shrew*), apparently the last instance in which a definably Hollywood film seriously tried to produce Shakespeare straight was Stuart Burge's 1970 *Julius Caesar*—itself an attempt to remake Joseph Mankiewicz's far more successful 1953 *Julius Caesar*. And although Japanese, German, Russian, Swedish (and etc.) straight Shakespeare films apparently feel perfectly comfortable doing Shakespeare with casts made up from their own national back lots, when Hollywood has made that same commitment, the casting list betrays a special American insecurity in its inevitable compulsion to import a large number of Royal Shakespeare Company actors to surround the American star.

Perhaps because Shakespeare is such a signifier for British cultural superiority, America's relationship to the Bard has frequently been marked by all the signs of a colonized consciousness. All in all, the preferred American approach to Shakespeare has been decidedly oblique; up until the sudden, Branagh-inspired boom in straight Shakespeare of the mid-nineties, Hollywood has distinctly felt more comfortable reworking Shakespeare into new, specifically American narratives such as Woody Allen's *A Midsummer Night's Sex Comedy* (1982) or Paul Mazursky's *Tempest* (1982), for example. America's best made for film Shakespeare productions may, in fact, be the musicals *Kiss Me, Kate* (dir. George Sidney, 1953) and *West Side Story* (dirs. Robert Wise and Jerome Robbins, 1961), where the Bard is recreated within a particular theatrical idiom that is thoroughly home-grown.

Even on the English side of the Atlantic, where Shakespeare has been apotheosized into the primary signifier for patriotism, nationhood, and national culture, the end of a tradition of turning Shakespeare plays into big fuss, high culture, capital-letter films has already been allegorized in the film *The Playboys* (dir. Gillies MacKinnon, 1992). An Irish acting troupe touring Ireland in the 1940s witnesses its Americanized production, part *Othello*, part adaptation of *Gone With the Wind*, be displaced and their troupe broken up by the arrival of the real thing, the Hollywood movie and a newly opened movie house in the town they have just played. To be sure, the late 1980s saw the English tradition of Shakespeare film refurbished by Kenneth Branagh into an enterprise comparable in energy to that of the 1940s when Sir Laurence Olivier was making *Richard III*, *Henry V*, *Hamlet*, and, in 1955, starring in Stuart Burges's *Othello*. But what Branagh has done is infuse the filming of Shakespeare with a marketeer's sense of popular culture. In his productions, high and low culture meet in moments where Shakespeare's scripts get subtly reframed inside of references to Hollywood pop culture: Branagh's adaptation actually rewrites *Henry V* as Clint Eastwood's "dirty Harry."[8] and his *Much Ado about Nothing* opens with a with visual evocation of *The Magnificent Seven*.

The sudden contemporary renaissance in filmed Shakespeare is British-led, but by 1995 even British casting practices had changed to reflect the exigencies of market capitalism. Following in the direction that Zeffirelli had been the first to seize upon, the new British productions were now promoting their global commerciality through a mixture of what has been derisively referred to as a cast made up of "British actors" and "American stars."[9] Branagh's 1989 *Henry V* had been filmed with a British cast. But by the time of *Much Ado About Nothing*, the British principals were surrounded by American pop film stars that made brothers out of America's most popular black actor (Denzel Washington) and America's most popular teen heart-throb (Keanu Reeves). There were, admittedly, some problems with casting Americans: in Branagh's *Much Ado*, Don John's line about Hero, "She's a very forward March chick," was cut for fear that Keanu Reeves would appear to be reverting to American slang rather than reciting Shakespeare.[10] And as Alan Bennett, who, when making a film of his play *The Madness of George III*, had to retitle it as *The Madness of King George* because American backers feared their audiences would think they had missed the first two parts, ruefully comments: apparently ... there were many moviegoers who came away from Branagh's film of *Henry V* wishing they had seen its four predecessors" (1995: xix). Yet the trend of using American stars continues, sometimes with particularly fortuitous implications that suggested new levels of narrative. In a production released in 1995, the presence of American actors Annette Bening and Robert Downey, Jr. in Richard Loncraine's World War II-era rewrite of *Richard III* provided a fitting way for the film to mark Edward IV's queen, Elizabeth, and her brother, Lord Rivers, as distinctive outsiders to the royal family, and, through dress and hair-style, encourage visual allusions that suggested Bening-cum-Elizabeth, outsider wife to Edward IV, as that famous American divorcee and outsider wife to another King Edward, Wallis Simpson. By 1995 Branagh, too, had gone American: Hollywood's Lawrence Fishburne played the Noble Moor to Branagh's Iago, and in 1996 Branagh's *Hamlet* included such box office draws as Billy Crystal (first gravedigger), Robin Williams (Osric), Charlton Heston (the Player King), and Jack Lemmon (Marcellus). Yielding to the implicit logic of such casting, Baz Luhrmann simply invited the stars of his *Romeo and Juliet* "to speak the famous lines in their own American accent."[11]

In what seems relatively new to British filmed Shakespeare (albeit certainly not to staged productions), the plays were also being cut loose from the tradition of the pseudo-"Elizabethan" setting and relocated in the viewer's own milieu: a 1991 British film of *As You Like It* featured Rosalind in levis, and 1995 saw Britain rehistoricizing its own history by taking *Richard III* into the modernized territory that 1980s stage productions of the histories (especially the English Shakespeare Company's "Wars of the Roses' extravaganza) had shown to be highly viable. Thus, shortly after Great Britain solemnly celebrated the fifty-year anniversary of the end of World War II, *Richard III* replayed that history by reinscribing it into the cycle of dark days that had eventually led to the Tudor triumph, British mythology now promising an Elizabeth (II) for an Elizabeth (I). By the end of 1995, it was increasingly clear that the trademarks of pop culture were determining the productions of not only such well-known popularizers as Zeffirelli, but had caught up with the Shakespeare industry at large and were putting it into the fast lane. According to the *L.A. Weekly's* review of the 1995 *Othello*:

> Writer-director Oliver Parker has opted for a spin on *Othello* that would make Shakespeare himself dizzy. With more pop than poetry, more snap than savvy, this variation of the tragedy finds the ever-appealing Lawrence Fishburne center court.... The production may be trashy and too fast by half—it makes Mel Gibson's galloping *Hamlet* seem sleepy—but the tenderness in Fishburne's eyes is startling.... While there's nothing wrong in mucking around with the classics when it comes to adaptations, the selectiveness of Parker's approach puzzles. Why, for instance, is there something so creepy and so very O.J. in the initial love scene between Othello and Desdemona...? (Dargie 1995: 67)

Similarly, Margo Jefferson noted that Shakespeare's "metaphors and cadence ... passions, convictions, and conflicts must meet up with ours in a world of rock, rap, gospel, and schlock pop, all just a radio station away from Prokofiev and Mozart. Shakespeare must adjust to city street and suburban mall English" (1996: C11). All in all, the message from the mid-nineties would seem to be that Shakespeare was busting out all over: Branagh having shown Hollywood that there was a market, production money seemed suddenly to be flowing; Branagh released his complete, uncut *Hamlet* (1996); Trevor Nunn—having demonstrated his entitlement on stage by directing big bucks productions of *Les Miserables* and *Cats*—directed a new *Twelfth Night* that debuted at Telluride (1996); another *Romeo and Juliet* in addition to Baz Luhrmann's 1996 production was on its way out; the Loncraine/McKellen *Richard III* (1994) had broken new ground in terms of reframing Shakespeare inside of pop-culture strategies; and, using an inventive new format for producing a Shakespeare film, Al Pacino had allegorized his own experience of playing *Richard III* in a documentary called *Looking for Richard* (1996).

Just how Hollywood's new interventions in a territory hitherto tacitly conceded to the Brits must look to the newly colonized former colonizer forms the potential subtext for Ian McKellen's remark about the difficulty he had in finding producers in Hollywood to fund the kind of *Richard III* film he wanted to make: "Of course, if Ken or Mel, or best of all Arnie or Sly were cast as Richard, it would have been easier" (McKellen 1996: 25–6). Baz Luhrmann (an Australian) put "William Shakespeare" in the title of his *William Shakespeare's Romeo and Juliet*, almost as if to insist on its authenticity. And as if to emphasize some kind of essential difference between the English kind of Shakespeare and the kind implicitly associated with American models, the Telluride announcement for Trevor Nunn's *Twelfth Night* (1995) asserts, with a barely concealed sneer: "the film succeeds in part due to Nunn's decision to ignore the box office lure of Hollywood stars, and to cast all the parts with outstanding British actors who can actually speak Shakespeare's lines with proper cadence and clarity."[12] Perhaps because he rightly sensed that strategies such as the above would fail, Kenneth Branagh made a more canny compromise, casting American stars not as leads but in multiple cameo parts for his 1996 *Hamlet*.[13] In these terms, the film promo that was most risky of all is that for Adrian Noble's *A Midsummer Night's Dream* (1996), the cast was made up not of Hollywood stars but a core of the same actors who played in the (1995) Royal Shakespeare Production. Perhaps for this reason the film's U.S. release was delayed.

However much a British director might wish to preserve a British Shakespeare, American production money is the hidden engine that drives Britain's Shakespeare films. The disappointing overall outcome of the 1980s televised BBC Shakespeare series was due, at least in part, to Time-Life Corporation's determination to produce televised "classics" that would exhibit a uniform fidelity to imagined assumptions about Shakespeare's text and times.[14] Doing "culture" for an educational enterprise apparently provoked one extreme of the American colonial response. But Hollywood hegemony over the global market combined with the new, bottom-line-only mentality of the 1990s may now threaten Shakespeare from quite another direction. In light of Hollywood's 1995 decision to revise the heavy puritanism and somber morality of *The Scarlet Letter* (dir. Roland Joffe, 1995) into a film that would be more fun for an audience and would get rid of that "downer" of a Hawthorne ending, can a film of Nathum Tate's *King Lear*, in which Demi/Cordelia lives and marries Bruce/Edgar be far behind?

Of all the films of the 1990s, some of the most innovative come from an avant-garde tradition whose energies are infused both by popular culture and an international mode of film production. Through avant-garde filmmaker Peter Greenaway's very attempt to unpack the place that intellectual and aesthetic elitism has played in Western culture, *Prospero's Books* (1990), forms in many ways an important investigation of the idea of "the popular." A meditation on *The Tempest*, the film reproduces Shakespeare's play as caviar to the general and grants few if any concessions to the popular; Greenaway's revision of *The Tempest* relocates Prospero in the image of the elite filmmaker bidding farewell to a tradition that he himself, as technological magus, participates in destroying. In a science fiction bound together by a technologically produced iconography of western culture stretching from the pages of Renaissance humanism to computer-generated models of virtual reality, the revels seen as ending in this latest rendition of Shakespeare's final play are played out as a kind of intellectualized, nostalgic farewell to even the existence of a culture that might be called learned or elite. The book disintegrates, and before us we see a virtual meltdown of all that symbolizes the learned tradition, even the word itself. Yet in a kind of acknowledgment—indeed, almost an allegory—of the end of the twentieth century's new culture and its new possessors, it is Caliban, its implied inheritor, who reaches into the flood and saves the First Folio from the literary armageddon on screen before us. Meanwhile, at the margin, orchestrating the deluge, stands the figure of the maker—the Gielgud who is Prospero who is Shakespeare who is Peter Greenaway—mournfully bidding culture—at least as he and we have hitherto imagined it—into oblivion. Elite reproductions, whether avant-garde or devoted to the "classics," as well as popular productions, then, meet in the disappearing of Shakespeare.

Dealing with specifically filmic reproductions or appropriations of Shakespeare means that "the popular" must be thought through not only the media and institutions in which Shakespeare is now reproduced—mass culture, Hollywood, celebrity, tabloid—but above all, youth culture. For as Shakespeare becomes part of pop culture and Shakespearean criticism (especially film criticism) follows suit, both move into an arena increasingly driven by a specifically youth culture, and Hollywood has clearly picked up on that fact. The animated versions already released for more than a dozen of the plays and scheduled for additional releases are only the most literal version of this development. Clearly playing to the potent consumerism of what is recognized as a notoriously visual subculture, all four of the so-called "big" tragedies have recently been reproduced in sophisticated comic-book form, appropriate for college students; major Shakespeare critics are turning their talents to readings of MTV videos; and teen idols like

Keanu Reeves are being lifted out of movies like *Bill and Ted's Excellent Adventure* (dir. Stephen Herek, 1989) to play Van Sant's modern-day Prince Hal in America's contemporary Shakespearorama.[15] But the production that went the furthest in enunciating itself as a teen film was the 1996 production of *William Shakespeare's Romeo and Juliet*, orchestrated by a director whose claim to fame rested in his previous direction of *Strictly Ballroom* (1992) and starring Leonardo DiCaprio as Romeo (star of the sit-com "Growing Pains," co-star of *What's Eating Gilbert Grape* [dir. Lasse Hallstroem, 1994] and star of *Basketball Diaries* [dir. Scott Kalvert, 1995]) plus Clare Danes (star of MTV's "My So-Called Life") as Juliet. Two journalists (Maslin 1996: C12; Corliss 1996: 89–90) compared the film to an MTV rock video; MTV News did a segment on it; MTV itself aired a half-hour special on the film three times the week before its United States release; and, also the week before release, the film sponsored the TV show "My So-Called Life," ads blaring forth clips from the soundtrack CD with music by bands such as Garbage, Radiohead, Everclear, and Butthole Surfers. As has become standard for all films, even a website was announced.[16] Perhaps the ultimate statement of just how thoroughly *William Shakespeare's Romeo and Juliet* had constructed itself as a youth culture film lay in the way it was market-tested. At the screened tests done at U.C. Berkeley the summer before its opening, studio moguls handed out market surveys that specifically asked that those who filled them out be only those viewers who were thirty-nine or younger.[17] The marketing campaign proved successful: *Romeo and Juliet* came in first at the box office the week of its release in the United States.[18]

Yet the strategies of casting teen idols and the co-construction of youth culture as popular culture were themselves part of the box office stroke mastered some time ago by Zeffirelli in both *Romeo and Juliet* and *The Taming of the Shrew*. Indeed, as Robert Hapgood aptly suggests in an essay [in *Shakespeare, The Movie*], if Zeffirelli's *Hamlet* was less of a success than were his earlier Shakespeare films, it was because his *Hamlet* was far less oriented to a young audience. In all American-made film versions of *Romeo and Juliet*, the culture has inscribed itself into forms of racial tension replayed within an ethnically marked youth culture, as in *West Side Story*, *Valley Girl* (dir. Martha Coolidge 1988), *Love Is All There Is* (dir. Joseph Bologna and Renée Taylor 1996) and the Luhrmann production, which was set in a Cuban-American community, Verona Beach. The trend toward making films directed almost exclusively at youth culture is a global one, and the 1987 Finnish-made film, *Hamlet Goes Business* (dir. Aki Kaurismaki), confirms its relevance through the film's staging of Ophelia's suicide: after gazing at a photo of Hamlet, Ophelia drowns herself in a bathtub while listening to a teen pop lyric in which the boyfriend wishes only to make up with his girlfriend so that all his dreams will be fulfilled. Yet while the inventiveness of some of these popularizations should rightly be applauded, at some point the devolution of Shakespeare to pop culture/youth culture (for which we may also read masculine culture) must give some critics, particularly feminists, pause: if we may read the increasing portrayal of regressively stupid white males (*Forest Gump* [dir. Robert Zemekis, 1994] and *Dumb and Dumber* [dir. Peter Farallay, 1994]) as a kind of Hollywood pandering to the anti-intellectual machismo of its adolescent buyer, just what kind of an American *Hamlet* is destined to succeed Mel Gibson's action hero is indeed a topic to puzzle the will.

Given that popularization is linked to youth culture, the crucial question for cultural critics rests, finally, with the pedagogical implications of Shakespeare's popularization on film, TV, and video. Popularization has meant the proliferation of representations, on the one hand, and thus an enlargement of what can be legitimately studied as part of the Shakespeare canon. But it has also meant the disappearance of (what was always the illusion of) a single, unified Shakespeare whose works could be covered. Students in today's average, college-level Shakespeare course are now more often shown select scenes from two or more versions of a given play than they are a single production in its entirety (productions like the 1980s BBC Shakespeare renditions, initially aired on a PBS series, that were ultimately designed and marketed specifically for classroom purpose). CD-Rom editions of the plays necessarily further this fragmentation.[19] With film and/or digital image as the version through which Shakespeare is primarily known, Shakespeare's accessibility is guaranteed, but along with this move to film comes a perhaps inevitable new sense of Shakespeare's reproduction, one which offers certain challenges to cultural criticism of Shakespeare as it is now practiced.

Consider, once again, the scene of Shakespeare pedagogy as narrated in *The Last Action Hero*. In this film, the kid who plays hookey in order to see action films starring Schwarzenegger grudgingly returns to class in time to hear his teacher regaling the students with the pleasures of *Hamlet*. The scene offers a bit of caviar to the theater-going elite in the private knowledge that the teacher is being played by Joan Plowright, Olivier's wife of many years and herself a renowned Shakespearean actress. The in-joke is included, but it is at the same time made purely extraneous to the pleasures of *The Last Action Hero*, where pleasure is distinctly located in the smash-bang thrills of pop culture. As the truant takes his seat and the teacher informs the students that they may recognize the actor, Sir Laurence Olivier, from his work in a television commercial or from playing Zeus in *Clash of the Titans* (dir. Desmond Davis, 1981), the relevance of Shakespeare seems most vividly represented by the comically outmoded 16mm projector through which the old Olivier film is being shown. The old-fashioned, dated feel of Olivier's film may be accounted for, at least in part, by the way the scene in *The Last Action Hero* marks a new relation between the plays and their audience, one in which the aura that pervaded the filmed Shakespeare "classics" is gone, and, with it, the sense of embodied intimacy between the audience and Shakespeare himself. The displacement of Olivier by Arnold Schwarzenegger marks the disappearance of an older sense of the actor as someone who actually knew Shakespeare, who communed with him, understood his mind, and perhaps at times even thought that he himself was Shakespeare.

Nonetheless, this film marks neither the unequivocal triumph of a new American cultural imperialism nor the displacement of a Shakespeare understood to be English by one who has become brashly American. As much as the film would seem to dismiss Shakespeare, it may also be understood as playing out one more version of the way that America, through the aesthetic medium that is as peculiarly American as the stage is English, tries to come to terms with its own, unregenerate fascination with the Bard of Avon. As apparently irrelevant as *The Last Action Hero* would seem to make Shakespeare, in this and all such recent filmic moments in which the Bard is suddenly invoked, William Shakespeare is still somehow a necessary signifier. He is that which must be posited and the debt that must be acknowledged before—and in order for—popular culture to declare itself so unindebted to the S-guy that it may get on with the production of itself and its own narratives.

Notes

1. The issue of just whose sexual fantasies Gibson's image plays to is itself an example of the contradictory impulses that the culture's new sophistication about media now allows. On the one hand, in vehement defense of the hunky hero's body as an object for female fantasies only, Mel's spokesMEN have gone so far as to literally to deny the right of any fanzines (the new, technologized fan magazine produced by fans and circulated on Internet) to produce gay narratives about Gibson—the narratives that are, of course, encouraged by the distinctly homoerotic overtones of the male partnered relationship in the *Lethal Weapon* film series—overtones that have indeed become progressively more blatant as the rejection of them has become simultaneously more vocal. For more on Mel, see Hodgdon (1994). If there is any gender equality to be offered at all, it is probably to be found only in the newly explicit bisexuality of pop culture's film star images that sexualize us all into universal consumers. In particular, see Marjorie Garber's chapter on "Bi-sexuality and Celebrities" (1995).

2. It appears that Shakespeare's legitimacy, at least in the United States, depends on his status as screen writer rather than playwright. In a program on Shakespeare in the weekly television series *Biography This Week*, with interviews of British scholars like Andrew Gurr and Stanley Wells, the narrator con-

cluded by remarking that "Shakespeare is now Hollywood's hottest screenplay writer" (broadcast November 9, 1996, on A&E). And Al Pacino's *Looking for Richard*, which includes footage of Pacino at the reconstructed Globe and interviews of Branagh and Gielgud, nevertheless focuses on the American film stars acting in the play.

3. See Rich (1996): Rich goes on to say, "But if audiences inevitably giggle a bit at the 1912 *Richard III*, they should also look at it as a window on an even more distant past when Americans didn't have to be spoon fed a great dramatist but were united in their passion for one who gave them characters who mirrored their own complex humanity, not to mention sublime poetry, along with the requisite dose of sex and violence. Exciting as this extraordinary find is [i.e., the movies], we will see in its frames the ghosts of something far larger that we have lost."

We would add as well that the use of American film stars in Shakespeare film productions is nothing new. Witness the Max Reinhardt *A Midsummer Night's Dream* with James Cagney and Mickey Rooney or the Joseph Mankiewicz *Julius Caesar* with Marlon Brando; and of course, there is a long tradition of Shakespeare burlesques in America and elsewhere. See Levin (1988). What has changed, in our view, is the reception of American stars in Shakespeare, both among the viewing public and academia. Moreover, the present moment of Shakespeare reproduction includes new spin-off products from films in addition to videos, many of which are regularly cross-referenced: CD-Roms; laserdiscs; soundtrack CDs; MTV specials; Internet websites.

4. The opening sequence with its quotation from *The Magnificent Seven* of the four riders galloping abreast, for example.

5. Hollywood's skepticism about Shakespeare is of course nothing new. Shortly before his death in 1984, Richard Burton commented "Generally if you mention the word Shakespeare in Hollywood, everybody leaves the room, because they think he's box office poison" (Levine 1988: 53). As we make clear, the Brits' responses to this skepticism differ in the 1990s.

6. That it is uncool is clearly the message in John Power's (1996) review of Al Pacino's *Looking for Richard*: "Through it all, the movie spotlights Pacino's dewy eyed reverence for Shakespeare, which is touching in its unadorned dweebiness.... Most stars would sooner die than look this uncool."

7. Several months prior to opening, the Luhrmann film had apparently been market tested on the summer Shakespeare classes at U.C. Berkeley. According to one of the teachers, the questionnaire the viewers were asked to respond to actually included a query that asked "whether the Shakespeare language in the film had bothered you or not." Our thanks to Grace Ioppulo for telling us about the market survey.

8. See Don Hedrick's essay in this collection.

9. Consider that as recently as the mid-1980s the notion of casting Hollywood rather than British actors in Shakespeare film was still a joke. In *Dead Poets Society*, a teacher played by Robin Williams mimics Marlon Brando playing Antony in *Julius Caesar* (which Brando had done) and John Wayne as Macbeth (a conjunction apparently only imagined, to our knowledge).

10. Our thanks to Lance Duerfahrd for bringing this change to our attention.

11. See "Production Notes," http://web.idirect.com/-claire/rjintor.html, 2.

12. John Storey, Telluride publicist.

13. The Nunn strategy distancing his film from American efforts went wholly lost on the American journalists/publicists. The *New York Times* ran a full-page ad with a blurb from a critic comparing it favorably to "To Wong Foo" and "The Birdcage," a comparison that was, in fact, echoed by *Time* Magazine's David Ansen (Ansen 1996) and in the film's own website.

14. Even the BBC felt the pressure of contemporary popular English culture. Roger Daltrey, lead singer of The Who, played Dromio in *The Comedy of Errors*, and John Cleese of *Monty Python* played Petruchio in *The Taming of the Shrew*.

15. The choice for defining pop film's Shakespearean daughter is another face familiar from L.A. teen films, Molly Ringwald, who played both Miranda in Mazursky's *Tempest* and Cordelia in Godard's *Lear*.

16. An ad for a website appears on the video of the Parker *Othello*, and a website address appeared at the end of movie theater trailers of Branagh's *Hamlet*.

17. According to one teacher, the questionnaire included a query that asked "whether the Shakespeare language in the film bothered you or not." For other adolescent responses, see Smith 1996. Of course, age may take its revenge on youth through the use of Shakespeare. Consider the rehabilitation and recovery of George III and with him the institution of the monarchy through the use of *King Lear* and *Henry IV, Part 2* in the 1994 film of *The Madness of King George* (dir. Nicholas Hytner).

18. E! Television, November 4, 1996.

19. From MLA and Shakespeare Association conventions of the past few years, many academics are familiar with the brilliant scholarly tool into which Pete Donaldson has turned the multimedia, multi-production model. See also Al Braunmuller's excellent CE-edition of *Macbeth*. Further electronic Shakespeare can be found in the CD-Roms released by Fox International of *William Shakespeare's Romeo and Juliet* and Castle Rock Entertainment of Oliver Parker's *Othello*. In 1997, Stephen Greenblatt's Norton edition of Shakespeare was published both as a book alone and as a book with a CD-Rom (one CD-Rom for students and another for professors).

References

Ansen, David (1996) "It's the 90s, So the Bard Is Back," *Time*, November 4, vol. 128, no. 19, 73–4.

Bennet, Alan (1995) *The Madness of King George*, New York: Random House.

Berube, Michael (1995) *Public Access*, New York and London: Routledge.

Burr, Ty (1996) "The Bardcage," *Entertainment*, November 15, 353: 49.

Corliss, Richard (1996) "Suddenly Shakespeare," *Time*, November 4, vol. 148, no. 21, 88–90.

Crewe, Jonathan (1995) "In the Field of Dreams: Transvestism in *Twelfth Night* and *The Crying Game*," *Representations*, 50: 101–23.

Dargie, John (1996) "*Othello*," *L.A. Weekly*, December 27.

Garber, Marjorie (1992) *Vested Interests: Cross-Dressing and Cultural Anxiety*, New York and London: Routledge.
—— (1995) "Some Like It Haute," *World Art*, 1, 30–3.
Gritten, D. (1995) "Shakespeare Is One Happening Dude," *Los Angeles Times*, December 27: 39, 41.
Hodgdon, Barbara (1994) "The Critic, the Poor Player, Prince Hamlet, and the Lady in the Dark," in *Shakespeare Reread: the Text and New Contexts*, ed. Russ McDonald, London and Ithaca: Connell University Press.
Jefferson, Margot (1996) "Welcoming Shakespeare into the Caliban Family," *New York Times*, November 12: C11, C16.
Levine, Lawrence (1988) "Shakespeare in America," in *Highbrow / Lowbrow: The Emergence of Cultural Hierarchy in America*, Cambridge, MA: Harvard University Press.
Maslin, Janet (1996) "Soft, What Light? It's Flash, Romeo," *New York Times*, November 1: C1, C12.
McKellen, Ian (1996) *William Shakespeare's Richard III*, Woodstock, New York: The Overlook Press, 25–6.
Powers, John (1996) "People Are Talking About Movies," *Vogue*, vol. 186, no. 10, October, 210.
Rich, Frank (1996) "A Banished Kingdom," *New York Times*, September 21, 19.
Smith, Lynn (1996) "Language Barrier Can't Keep Apart Lovers of 'Romeo and Juliet,'" *Los Angeles Times*, November 7, F15.
Van Sant, Gus (1993) *Even Cowgirls Get the Blues and My Own Private Idaho*, New York: Faber & Faber.

Questions and Projects

- Compare two or more recent filmed versions of Shakespeare's plays, such as Baz Luhrmann's *William Shakespeare's Romeo and Juliet*, Derek Jarman's *Tempest* (1979) and Kenneth Branagh's *Much Ado About Nothing* (1993). How are specific forms of popular culture used in each? How do they add to or distract from the meanings of the original?
- With one Shakespeare film or one other literary classic as an example, argue as to why this work seems especially suited (or not) to two or three central issues in contemporary life (such as debates about gender, race, technology, family, nationhood, or others).

BIBLIOGRAPHY

A bibliography should, I believe, point to the major documents without overwhelming the reader with the sheer weight of the field. That has been my goal in creating a list of works that is comprehensive without being too intimidating or exhausting. I have not included many of the innumerable articles and essays on film and literature, unless they were exceptional cases. Also missing are many of the broadly based studies that may have some discussion appropriate to the study of film and literature. A separate bibliography could be assembled of remarks by novelists, poets, and playrights on their experiences with or perspectives on film, but I trust these can be tracked down through the sources below (such as Geduld's *Authors on Film*) or by investigating the bibliography of the individual author (to locate, for instance, James Baldwin's or Gertrude Stein's essays and comments on the movies). Students of film and literature should consult *Literature / Film Quarterly* and other journals that may devote special issues to adaptation or other dimensions of the relationship between film and literature. There are also many texts in foreign languages addressing this topic that have not been included.

Abel, Richard. *French Cinema: The First Wave, 1915–1929*. Princeton, NJ: Princeton University Press, 1984.

Altick, Richard. *The Shows of London*. Cambridge, MA: Harvard University Press, 1978.

Andrew, Dudley. *Concepts in Film Theory*. New York: Oxford University Press, 1984.

Appel, Alfred, Jr. *Nabokov's Dark Cinema*. New York: Oxford University Press, 1974.

Arheim, Rudolf. *Film as Art*. Berkeley, CA: University of California Press, 1957.

Ayock, Wendell, and Michael Schoenecke, eds. *Film and Literature: A*

Comparative Approach to Adaptation. Lubbock, TX: Texas Tech University Press, 1988.

Balázs, Béla. *Theory of Film: Character and Growth of a New Art*. New York: Dover, 1970.

Ball, Roger Hamilton. *Shakespeare on Silent Film*. London: George Allen and Unwin Ltd., 1968.

Barthes, Roland. *Image-Music-Text*. Trans. Stephen Heath. New York: Hill & Wang, 1977.

———. *Camera Lucida: Reflections on Photography*. Trans. Richard Howard. New York: Hill & Wang, 1981.

Baudelaire, Charles. "The Salon of 1859." Trans. Judith Mayne. In *Modern Art and Modernism: A Critical Anthology*. Ed. F. Frascina and C. Harrisop. New York: Harper Collins, 1983, pp. 19–21.

Bazin, André. *What Is Cinema?* 2 vols. Berkeley, CA: University of California Press, 1971.

Beja, Morris. *Film and Literature*. New York: Longman, 1979.

Benjamin, Walter. *Illuminations*. Ed. Hannah Arrendt and trans. Harry Zohn. New York: Schocken, 1969.

Bloom, Harold. "The Visonary Cinema of the Romantics." In *William Blake: Essays for S. Foster Damon*. Ed. Alvin Rosenfeld. Providence, RI: Brown University Press, 1969.

Bluestone, George. *Novels into Films*. Baltimore, MD: Johns Hopkins University Press, 1957.

Boose, Lynda E., and Richard Burt, eds. *Shakespeare, The Movie: Popularizing the Plays on Film, TV, and Video*. London and New York: Routledge, 1997.

Bordwell, David. *Narration in the Fiction Film*. Madison, WI: University of Wisconsin Press, 1985.

Bordwell, David, Janet Staiger, and Kristin Thompson. *The Classical Hollywood Cinema: Film Style and Mode of Production to 1960*. New York: Columbia University Press, 1985.

Boyum, Joy Gould. *Double Exposure: Fiction into Film*. New York: Universe Books, 1985.

Brakhage, Stan. *Metaphors on Vision*. Ed. P. Adams Sitney. Film Culture, Inc., 1963.

Braudy, Leo. *The World in a Frame*. 2nd ed. Chicago, IL: University of Chicago Press, 1984.

Brecht, Bertolt. "The Film, the Novel, and Epic Theatre." In *Brecht on Theatre*. Ed. John Willett. New York: Hill & Wang, 1964, pp. 47–51.

Brookeer-Bowers, Nancy. *The Hollywood Novel and Other Novels about Film: An Annotated Bibliography*. New York: Garland, 1985.

Brunetta, Gian Piero, ed. *Letteratura e cinema*. Bologna: Zanichelli, 1976.

Bulman, J. C., and Coursen, H. R., eds. *Shakespeare on Television: An*

Anthology of Essays and Reviews. Hanover, NH: University Press of New England, 1988.

Burch, Nöel. *Theory of Film Practice*. Trans. Helen Lane. Princeton, NJ: Princeton University Press, 1981.

Cartmell, Deborah, et al., eds. *Pulping Fictions: Consuming Culture across the Literature/Media Divide*. London: Pluto Press, 1996.

Caughie, John, ed. *Theories of Authorship: A Reader*. London: Routledge, 1981.

Cavell, Stanley. *The World Viewed: Reflections on the Ontology of Film*. 2nd ed. New York: Viking, 1979.

Chatman, Seymour. *Story and Discourse: Narrative Structure in Fiction and Film*. Ithaca, NY: Cornell University Press, 1978.

———. *Coming to Terms: The Rhetoric of Narrative in Fiction and Film*. Ithaca, NY: Cornell University Press, 1990.

Cocteau, Jean. *Cocteau on the Film: Conversations with Jean Cocteau Recorded by Andre Fraigneau*. Trans. Vera Traill. New York: Dover, 1972.

Cohen, Keith. *Film and Fiction: The Dynamics of Exchange*. New Haven, CT: Yale University Press, 1979.

———. *Writing in the Film Age*. Niwot, CO: University Press of Colorado, 1991.

Colie, Rosalie L. *Shakespeare's "Living Art."* Princeton, NJ: Princeton University Press, 1974.

Conger, Syndy M., and Janice Welsch, eds. *Narrative Strategies: Original Essays in Film and Prose Fiction*. Macomb, IL: Western Illinois University Press, 1980.

Corkin, Stanley. *Realism and the Birth of the Modern United States: Literature, Cinema, and Culture*. Athens, GA: University of Georgia Press, 1996.

Corrigan, Timothy. *A Cinema without Walls: Movies and Culture after Vietnam*. New Brunswick, NJ: Rutgers University Press, 1991.

Davies, Anthony. *Filming Shakespeare's Plays*. Cambridge, MA: Cambridge University Press, 1988.

Durgnat, Raymond. *Films and Feeling*. Cambridge, MA: MIT Press, 1967.

Eckert, Charles W. *Focus on Shakespearean Films*. Englewood Cliffs, NJ: Prentice Hall, 1972.

Edel, Leon. "Novel and Camera." In *The Theory of the Novel: New Essays*. Ed. John Halperin. New York: Oxford University Press, 1974.

Egerton, Gary R., ed. *Film and the Arts in Symbiosis: A Research Guide*. New York: Greenwood Press, 1988.

Eidsvik, Charles. *Cineliteracy: Film among the Arts*. New York: Random House, 1978.

Eisenstein, Sergei. *The Film Sense*. Ed. and trans. Jay Leyda. New York: Harcourt, 1947.

————. *The Film Form*. Ed. and trans. Jay Leyda. New York: Harcourt, 1947.

Ellis, John. "The Literary Adaptation: An Introduction." *Screen* 23, 1 (1982): 3–4.

————. *Visible Fictions*. London: Routledge, 1982.

Fell, John L. *Film and the Narrative Tradition*. Berkeley, CA: University of California Press, 1974.

Fleishman, Avrom. *Narrated Films: Storytelling Situations in Cinema History*. Baltimore, MD: Johns Hopkins University Press, 1992.

French, Philip, and Ken Wlaschin. *The Faber Book of Movie Verse*. London: Faber and Faber, 1993.

Geduld, Harry M., ed. *Authors on Film*. Bloomington, IN: Indiana University Press, 1972.

Giddings, Robert, et al. *Screening the Novel: The Theory and Practice of Literary Adaptation*. London: Macmillan, 1990.

Goldstein, Laurence. *The American Poet at the Movies: A Critical History*. Ann Arbor, MI: University of Michigan Press, 1994.

Goodwin, James. "Literature and Film: A Review of Criticism." *Quarterly Review of Film Studies* 4, 2 (1979): 227–246.

Gould, Evlyn. *The Fate of Carmen*. Baltimore, MD: Johns Hopkins University Press, 1996.

Hamilton, Ian. *Writers in Hollywood, 1915–1951*. New York: Carroll & Graf, 1991.

Hansen, Miriam. *Babel and Babylon: Spectatorship in American Silent Film*. Cambridge, MA: Harvard University Press, 1991.

Harrington, John, ed. *Film and/as Literature*. Englewood Cliffs, NJ: Prentice Hall, 1977.

Heath, Stephen. *Questions of Cinema*. Bloomington, IN: Indiana University Press, 1981.

Heath, Stephen, and Patricia Melencamp, eds. *Cinema and Language*. Frederick, MD: University Publication, 1984.

Hedges, Inez. *Languages of Revolt: Dada and Surrealist Literature and Film*. Durham, NC: Duke University Press, 1983.

Higgins, Lynn A. *New Novel, New Wave, New Politics: Fiction and the Representation of History in Postwar France*. Lincoln, NE: University of Nebraska Press, 1996.

Horton, Andrew, and Joan Magretta. *Modern European Filmmakers and the Art of Adaptation*. New York: Ungar, 1981.

James, David. *Allegories of Cinema: American Film in the Sixties*. Princeton, NJ: Princeton University Press, 1989.

Jenkins, Henry. *Textual Poachers: Television Fans and Participatory Culture*. London and New York: Routledge, 1992.

Jinks, William. *The Celluloid Literature*. Beverly Hills, CA: Glencoe Press, 1971.

Jorgens, Jack. *Shakespeare on Film.* Bloomington, IN: Indiana University Press, 1977.

Jost, Francois. *L'Oeil / Camera: entre film et roman.* Lyon: Presses Universitaires de Lyon, 1987.

Kawin, Bruce. *Mindscreen: Bergman, Godard, and First-Person Cinema.* Princeton, NJ: Princeton University Press, 1978.

———. *Faulkner and Film.* New York: Ungar, 1977.

———. *Telling It Again and Again: Repetition in Literature and Film.* Ithaca, NY: Cornell University Press, 1972.

Kittredge, William, and Steven M. Krauzner, eds. *Stories into Film.* New York: Harper Colophon Books, 1979.

Klein, Michael, and Gillian Parker, eds. *The English Novel and the Movies.* New York: Ungar, 1981.

Kliman, Bernice. *Hamlet: Film, Television, and Audio Performance.* Cranbury, NJ: Fairleigh Dickinson Press, 1988.

Kline, T. Jefferson. *Screening the Text: Intertextuality in New Wave French Cinema.* Baltimore, MD: Johns Hopkins University Press, 1992.

Kozloff, Sarah. *Invisible Storytellers: Voice-Over Narration in American Fiction Film.* Berkeley, CA: University of California Press, 1988.

Krutnik, Frank. "Desire, Transgression, and James M. Cain." *Screen* 23 (1982): 31–42.

Langer, Susanne. *Feeling and Form.* New York: Scribners, 1953.

Laurence, Frank M. *Hemingway and the Movies.* Jackson, MS: University of Mississippi Press, 1981.

Lawder, Standish. *The Cubist Cinema.* New York: New York University Press, 1975.

Lindsay, Vachel. *The Art of the Moving Picture.* New York: Liveright, 1970.

Luhr, William. *Raymond Chandler and Film.* New York: Ungar, 1982.

Luhr, William, and Peter Lehman. *Authorship and Narrative in the Cinema.* New York: Oxford University Press, 1977.

McCabe, Colin. *Tracking the Signifier: Theoretical Essays.* Minneapolis, MN: University of Minnesota Press, 1985.

MacCann, Richard Dyer, ed. *Film: A Montage of Theories.* New York: Dutton, 1966.

McConnell, Frank. *The Spoken Seen.* Baltimore, MD: Johns Hopkins University Press, 1976.

———. *Storytelling and Mythmaking: Images from Film and Literature.* New York: Oxford University Press, 1970.

McDougal, Stuart Y. *Made into Movies: From Literature to Film.* Niles, IL: Holt, Rinehart, & Winston, 1985.

Magny, Claude-Edmunde. *The Age of the American Novel: The Film Aesthetic of Fiction between the Two Wars.* New York: Ungar, 1972.

Manvell, Roger. *Shakespeare and the Film.* New York: Praeger, 1972.

Marcus, Fred. *Short Story / Short Film*. Englewood Cliffs, NJ: Prentice Hall, 1977.

———. *Film and Literature: Contrasts in Media*. Scranton, PA: Chandler, 1971.

Marcus, Millicent. *Filmmaking by the Book: Italian Cinema and Literary Adaptation*. Baltimore, MD: Johns Hopkins University Press, 1993.

Mast, Gerald, et al., eds. *Film Theory and Criticism*. 3rd ed. New York: Oxford University Press, 1992.

Mayne, Judith. *Private Novels, Public Films*. Athens, GA: University of Georgia Press, 1988.

Metz, Christian. *Film Language*. Trans. Michael Taylor. New York: Oxford University Press, 1974.

Miles, Peter, and Malcolm Smith. *Cinema, Literature, and Society: Elite and Mass Culture in Interwar Britain*. London: Croom Helm, 1987.

Miller, Gabriel. *Screening the Novel: Rediscovered American Fiction in Film*. New York: Ungar, 1980.

Mistral, Gabriela. "The Poet's Attitude toward the Movies." In *The Movies on Trial*. Ed. William J. Perelman. New York: Macmillan, 1936.

Mitry, Jean. "Remarks on the Problem of Cinematic Adaptation." Trans. Richard Dyer. *Bulletin of Midwest Modern Language Association* (1971): 1.

Monaco, James. *American Film Now: The People, the Power, the Money, the Movies*. New York: New American Library, 1984.

Morrissette, Bruce. *Novels and Film: Essays in Two Genres*. Chicago, IL: University of Chicago Press, 1985.

Morse, Margaret. "Paradoxes of Realism: The Rise of Film in the Train of the Novel." In *Explorations in Film Theory: Selected Essays from Cine-Tracts*. Ed. Ron Burnett. Bloomington, IN: Indiana University Press, 1991.

Moses, Gavriel. *The Nickel Was for the Movie: Film in the Novel from Pirandello to Puig*. Berkeley, CA: University of California Press, 1995.

Munsterberg, Hugo. *The Film: A Psychological Study: The Silent Photoplay in 1916*. New York: Dover, 1970.

Murray, Edward. *The Cinematic Imagination: Writers and the Motion Pictures*. New York: Ungar, 1972.

Murray, Timothy. *Like a Film: Ideological Fantasy on Screen, Camera, and Canvas*. London and New York: Routledge, 1993.

———. *Drama Trauma: Specters of Race and Sexuality in Performance, Video, and Art*. London and New York: Routledge, 1997.

Nicoll, Allardyce. *Film and Theatre*. New York: Crowell, 1936.

Orr, Christopher. "The Discourse of Adaptation." *Wide Angle* 2 (1984): 72–84.

Orvell, Miles. *The Real Thing: Imitation and Authenticity in American*

Culture, 1880–1940. Chapel Hill, NC: University of North Carolina Press, 1989.

Peary, Gerald, and Roger Shatzkin, eds. *The Classic American Novel and the Movies*. New York: Ungar, 1977.

———. *The Modern American Novel and the Movies*. New York: Ungar, 1980.

Pellow, Kenneth. *Films as Critiques of Novels: Transformational Criticism*. Lewiston, NY: Mellen Press, 1995.

Pendo, Stephen. *Raymond Chandler on Screen: His Novels into Film*. Metuchen, NJ: Scarecrow Press, 1976.

Peucker, Brigitte. *Incorporating Images: Film and the Rival Arts*. Princeton, NJ: Princeton University Press, 1995.

Phillips, Gene. *Conrad and Cinema*. New York: Lang, 1995.

———. *Hemingway and Film*. New York: Ungar, 1980.

Potamkin, Harry Alan. *The Compound Cinema: The Film Writings of Harry Alan Potamkin*. Ed. Lewis Jacobs. New York: The Teachers College Press, 1977.

Read, Herbert. "The Poet and the Film." In *A Coat of Many Colours*. London: Routledge, 1945.

Richards, Jeffrey. *Films and British National Identity*. Manchester: Manchester University Press, 1997.

Rosen, Philip, ed. *Narrative, Apparatus, Ideology*. New York: Columbia University Press, 1986.

Ross, Harris. *Film as Literature: Literature as Film*. New York: Greenwood, 1987.

Richardson, Robert. *Literature and Film*. Bloomington, IN: Indiana University Press, 1969.

Ropars-Wuilleumier, Marie-Claire. *De la littérature au cinéma: genèse d'une écriture*. Paris: Armand Colin, 1970.

Rothman, William. "To Have and Have Not Adapted a Film from a Novel." In *The "I" of the Camera: Essays in Film Criticism, History, and Aesthetics*. New York: Cambridge University Press, 1988, pp. 108–116.

Ruchti, Unrich, and Sybil Taylor. *Story into Film*. New York: Dell, 1978.

Schickel, Richard. *D. W. Griffith: An American Life*. New York: Simon & Schuster, 1984.

Sillars, Stuart. *Visualization in Popular Fiction, 1860–1960*. London: Routledge, 1995.

Shattuck, Roger. "Fact in Film and Literature." *Partisan Review* 44 (1977): 539–550.

Sinyard, Neil. *Filming Literature: The Art of Screen Adaptation*. London: Croom Helm, 1986.

Sitney, P. Adams. *Visionary Film: The American Avant-Garde, 1943–1978*. New York: Oxford University Press, 1979.

Sontag, Susan. *Against Interpretation*. New York: Farrar, Strauss & Giroux, 1961.

Spiegel, Alan. *Fiction and the Camera Eye: Visual Consciousness in the Film and the Modern Novel*. Charlottesville, VA: University of Virginia Press, 1976.

Stam, Robert. *Reflexivity in Film and Literature: From Don Quixote to Jean-Luc Godard*. New York: Columbia University Press, 1992.

Talbot, Daniel, ed. *Film: An Anthology*. New York: Simon & Schuster, 1967.

Toles, George E., ed. *Film / Literature*. Winnipeg: University of Manitoba Press, 1983.

Van Wert, William. *The Theory and Practice of the Ciné-Roman*. New York: Arno, 1978.

Vardac, A. Nicholas. *Stage to Screen: Theatrical Method from Garrick to Griffith*. Cambridge, MA: Harvard University Press, 1949.

Wagner, Geoffrey. *The Novel and Cinema*. Rutherford, NJ: Fairleigh Dickinson University Press, 1975.

Waller, Gregory. *The Stage / Screen Debate: A Study in Popular Aesthetics*. New York: Garland, 1983.

Welch, Geoffrey Egan. *Literature and Film: An Annotated Bibliography, 1909–1977*. London: Garland, 1981.

Wicks, Ulrich. "A Researcher's Guide and Selected Checklist to Film as Literature and Language." *Journal of Modern Literature* 3, 2 (April 1973): 323–350.

Wilbur, Richard. "A Poet and the Movies." In *Man and the Movies*. Ed. W. R. Robinson. Baton Rouge, LA: Louisiana State University Press, 1967.

Williams, Linda. *Figures of Desire: A Theory and Analysis of Surrealist Film*. Urbana, IL: University of Illinois Press, 1981.

Williams, Raymond. *Culture and Society: 1780–1950*. New York: Columbia University Press, 1983.

Wilson, George. *Narration in Light: Studies in Cinematic Point of View*. Baltimore, MD: Johns Hopkins University Press, 1986.

Winston, Douglas Garrett. *The Screenplay as Literature*. Rutherford, NJ: Fairleigh Dickinson University Press, 1973.

Wollen, Peter. *Signs and Meaning in the Cinema*. Rev. ed. Bloomington, IN: Indiana University Press, 1972.

Wyatt, Justin. *High Concept: Movies and Marketing in Hollywood*. Austin, TX: University of Texas Press, 1985.

Yacowar, Maurice. *Tennessee Williams and Film*. New York: Ungar, 1977.

CREDITS

Vachel Lindsay, "Progress and Endowment," from *The Art of the Moving Picture* (New York: Liveright Publishing Corporation, 1970), pp. 253–271.

Hugo Munsterberg, "The Means of Photoplay," from *The Film: A Psychological Study* (New York: Dover Publications, 1970), pp. 74–81. Originally published as *The Photoplay* (1916).

Gabriela Mistral, "The Poet's Attitude toward the Movies," from *The Movies on Trial*, translated by Marion A. Zeitlin, edited by William J. Perelman, pp. 141–152. Reprinted with permission.

Walter Benjamin, "The Work of Art in the Age of Mechanical Reproduction," from *Illuminations*, translated by Harry Zohn, edited by Hannah Arendt, pp. 222–232 and 237–241. Copyright © 1955 by Suhrkamp Verlag A. M. English translation copyright © 1968 and renewed 1996 by Harcourt Brace and Company. Reprinted with the permission of the publishers.

Sergei Eisenstein, "Dickens, Griffith, and the Film Today," from *Film Form*, translated by Jay Leyda, pp. 195, 198–201, 204–213, and 232–233. Copyright 1949 by Harcourt Brace and Company, renewed © 1977 by Jay Leyda. Reprinted with the permission of Harcourt Brace and Company.

Béla Balázs, "The Script," from *Theory of Film: Character and Growth of a New Art* (New York: Dover Publications, 1970), pp. 246–257. Reprinted with the permission of the publisher.

Alexandre Astruc, "The Birth of a New Avant-Garde: La Caméra-Stylo," from *The New Wave*, edited by Peter Graham (New York: Doubleday, 1968), pp. 17–23. Reprinted with the permission of Martin Secker & Warburg, Ltd.

André Bazin, "Theater and Cinema," from *What Is Cinema?* Volume I, translated by Hugh Gray (Berkeley: University of California Press, 1971), pp. 76–124. Copyright © 1967 by The Regents of the University of California. Reprinted with the permission of University of California Press.

George Bluestone, "The Limits of the Novel and the Limits of the Film," from *Novels in Film* (Baltimore: The Johns Hopkins University Press, 1957), pp. 1–6 and 46–61. Reprinted with the permission of The Johns Hopkins University Press.

INDEX